SOCIAL CATHOLICISM
IN EUROPE

SOCIAL CATHOLICISM IN EUROPE

*From the Onset of Industrialization
to the First World War*

PAUL MISNER

CROSSROAD • NEW YORK

Uxori meae Barbarae

BX
1753
.M57
1991

1991

The Crossroad Publishing Company
370 Lexington Avenue, New York, NY 10017

Copyright © 1991 by Paul Misner

Printed in the United States of America
Typesetting output: TEXSource, Houston

Library of Congress Cataloging-in-Publication Data

Misner, Paul.
    Social Catholicism in Europe : from the onset of industrialization
to the first world war / Paul Misner.
        p.   cm.
    Includes bibliographical references and index.
    ISBN 0-8245-1097-6 (cloth)
    1. Sociology, Christian (Catholic)—Europe—History of
doctrines—19th century. 2. Sociology, Christian (Catholic)—
Europe—History of doctrines—20th century. 3. Church and social
problems—Europe—History—19th century. 4. Church and social
problems—Europe—History—20th century. 5. Catholic Church—
Doctrines—History—19th century. 6. Catholic Church—Doctrines—
History—20th century. 7. Church and social problems—Catholic
Church.   I. Title.
BX1753.M57 1991
261.8'08'822—dc20   90-25659
                                                              CIP

CONTENTS

ACKNOWLEDGMENTS

At the head of the acknowledgments belongs the bilateral West German/United States Fulbright Commission in gratitude for a research year in 1985–86. My hosts in Germany were the directors and staff of the Institut für Europäische Geschichte in Mainz. Their consideration for me and other foreign scholars went beyond the ordinary measure one might expect of such a center. The director and staff of the Katholische Sozialwissenschaftliche Zentralstelle in Mönchengladbach, West Germany, were another source of much encouragement and practical assistance, not only for German questions, but international ones as well.

The Bradley Institute for Democracy and Public Policy provided me with a complete semester in 1988 free for writing the chapters on Christian democracy in Catholic Europe before World War I. I am grateful to the Graduate School and the Religious Commitment Fund of Marquette University for other grants in aid of the project, as well as to the departmental Committee on Research for its recommendations. Marquette University also granted me a sabbatical leave in 1985–86; in tandem with the Fulbright award, this made it possible to get a good start on a protracted effort.

This book has been six years in the making. If I refrain from mentioning any names, it is from a reluctance to claim the approval of eminent scholars, even by implication, for my project, especially in its early, undeveloped stages. Most of the many scholars here and abroad who have encouraged and helped me are cited in the parenthetical references, along with many others on whom I was equally dependent, though exclusively by reading.

I presented parts of my work in progress before the College Theology Society in 1985 (on Adam Müller), and at meetings of the American Academy of Religion to the working groups on Nineteenth-Century Theology (on 1848 in Paris) and on Roman Catholic Modernism ("Social Modernism" in Italy). Such presentations proved valuable for the author, as did the Faculty Colloquium discussion on paternalism in my own Theology Department. Graduate students who read parts of the manuscript showed a critical appreciation that also calls for acknowledgment. I have enjoyed the help of capable research assistants over the years, especially James Patrick Callahan, who labored in the library and over the computer to bring text and bibliography into proper shape.

Crossroad Publishing Company (on the recommendation of Frank Oveis, I am sure) extended a contract to me early on, with the practical result of putting the project in a stronger position for research assistance from university sources. For this and for all the librarians, especially those in Mainz and Milwaukee, who have procured needed studies for me, I wish to express my debt of gratitude.

ABBREVIATIONS

AAS	*Acta Apostolicae Sedis.* Rome, 1909– .
AP	Action populaire.
ASS	*Acta Sanctae Sedis.* Rome, 1865–1908.
Catholicisme	*Catholicisme: Hier, aujourd'hui, demain. Encyclopédie.* Paris: Letouzey et Ané, 1948– .
DBMOF	*Dictionnaire biographique du mouvement ouvrier français* (1789–1864: 3 vols.; 1864–71: 6 vols.; 1871–1914: 6 vols.). Edited by Jean Maitron. Paris: Les Editions Ouvrières, 1964–82.
DC	Démocratie chrétienne *or* Democrazia cristiana.
DHGE	*Dictionnaire d'histoire et de géographie ecclésiastique.* Edited by Alfred Baudrillart. Paris: Letouzey et Ané, 1912– .
DMR	*Dictionnaire du monde religieux dans la France contemporaine.* Edited by Jean-Marie Mayeur and Yves-Marie Hilaire. Paris: Beauchesne, 1985– .
DS	Denzinger, Heinrich, and Adolf Schönmetzer, editors. *Enchiridion symbolorum, definitionum et declarationum de rebus fidei et morum.* 33d ed. Freiburg: Herder, 1965.
DSMCI	*Dizionario storico del movimento cattolico in Italia (1860–1980).* 3 vols. in 5. Edited by Francesco Traniello and Giorgio Campanini. Casale Monferrato: Marietti, 1981–84.
DTC	*Dictionnaire de théologie catholique.* Paris: Letouzey et Ané, 1923–72.
GcG	Gesamtverband der christlichen Gewerkschaften Deutschlands (League of Christian Trade Unions of Germany).
HDFSE	*Historical Dictionary of the French Second Empire, 1852–1870.* Edited by William E. Echard. Westport, CT: Greenwood Press, 1985.

HDTFR   *Historical Dictionary of the Third French Republic, 1870–
              1940.* Edited by Patrick H. Hutton. 2 vols. Westport, CT:
              Greenwood Press, 1986.

IESS   *International Encyclopedia of the Social Sciences.* New
              York: Macmillan, [1968]–1979.

JCSW   *Jahrbuch für christliche Sozialwissenschaften.* Münster: Re-
              gensberg, 1960– .

KSL   *Katholisches Soziallexikon.* Edited by Alfred Klose, W.
              Mantl and V. Zsifkovits. 2d ed. Vienna: Tyrolia/Styria,
              1980.

MEGA   *Karl Marx, Friedrich Engels Gesamtausgabe.* Berlin: Dietz,
              1972.

NDB   *Neue Deutsche Biographie.* Berlin: Duncker & Humbolt,
              1953.

NCR   *New Catholic Encyclopedia.* 17 vols. New York: McGraw-
              Hill, 1967–81.

OC   Opera dei Congressi.

OCCO   Oeuvre des cercles catholiques d'ouvriers.

RHE   *Revue d'histoire ecclésiastique.* Louvain, 1900– .

RN   *Rerum novarum* (in Carlen 1981, 2:241–61).

S. th.   Thomas Aquinas, *Summa theologiae.*

StL   *Staatslexikon: Recht, Wirtschaft, Gesellschaft.* 7th ed. Frei-
              burg: Herder, 1985– .

SWB   Wilhelm Emmanuel Freiherr von Ketteler, *Sämtliche
              Werke und Briefe.* Mainz: v. Hase and Koehler, 1977– .

ZgLb   *Zeitgeschichte in Lebensbildern.* Edited by Rudolf Morsey,
              with Jürgen Aretz and Anton Rauscher. 6 vols. Mainz:
              Grünewald, 1973–84.

INTRODUCTION

In the 1980s, Ronald Reagan and Margaret Thatcher presided over a resurgence of neo-liberal economic policy and practice in the Western world. At the same time, the liberation theology of the 1960s and 1970s came in for some severe criticism from both secular and ecclesiastical sources (Michael Novak may be named as a representative spokesman for both circles). And yet, swimming against the stream, other, more authoritative voices were raised in the churches, perhaps more clearly than ever before, against the "economistic" neglect of the ethical that neo-liberalism (also known as "neo-conservatism") seemed to espouse. In view of the failure of development schemes in the third world to alleviate poverty and marginalization, the largely Protestant constituency of the World Council of Churches developed an impressive body of modern social-ethical programs and propositions (see Duchrow 1987).[1] The Roman Catholic communion, just as heavily represented in the third world as the World Council of Churches, spoke out at many levels. Pope John Paul II took both the first and the second worlds to task in weighty encyclicals (most recently in *Rei socialis sollicitudo*). In 1986, after working quite publicly on the task for some years, the American Catholic bishops issued the widely noticed pastoral letter on Catholic social teaching and the U.S. economy, *Economic Justice for All*.

This part of the Catholic response disconcerts only those who either do not know, or underestimate the staying power, of a tradition of social teaching in the Roman Catholic Church that goes back to Pope Leo XIII in the last century and his famous social encyclical, *Rerum novarum* (1891).[2] In the flood of publications that has accompanied and resulted from the conflicts over human rights and economic or social injustice throughout the world, what has been missing is a history of the development of this distinctive modern Roman Catholic social consciousness. It is not that there have not

---

[1] Readers are referred to the comprehensive Reference List for full bibliographic data on works mentioned in the text (usually in parentheses).

[2] For papal documents without special source references, see the texts as edited by Claudia Carlen.

1

been successive treatments of the papal teaching (see, e.g., Hollen-bach 1979 and Dorr 1983 among more recent ones, or Jarlot 1964, 1973, and Calvez and Perrin 1961). But papal pronouncements do not take place in a vacuum. Catholic pioneers in social analysis have not only shaped the context needed to understand the papal teachings more adequately, but they have a value in themselves as a major part of the history of social Catholicism. They too have a claim on our historical awareness.

In one sense, it is not an option whether or not one forms a his-torical picture of the development of any present-day reality. Any thinking person necessarily forms such a history for himself or herself out of materials lying at hand. The basic justification for histori-ography is to construct a better-founded past than these often hazy but necessarily present constructions in the mind. This applies also, of course, to social ethics and in particular to the tradition of Roman Catholic social ethics that, since Vatican II, has become an ever more prominent conversation partner in national and world affairs. As it is, many otherwise keen observers of the current scene entertain mutu-ally contradictory scenarios of the historical relationship, for example, between Catholicism and capitalism: that the clergy have always been partisans of the bourgeoisie, for example, or that in their monkish dis-dain of monetary pursuits they have always been prejudiced against the making of money and the economic growth it stimulates. To re-place such inadequate views with a more judicious or critical account is the basic justification for presenting a new history of the social Catholic tradition.

The scope of the work is limited to "Europe in the nineteenth century" (a term that here designates the period from the onset of industrialization to the First World War). This work is conceived as the first of two volumes, the second of which will take up the story and bring it forward through the 1950s and into the Second Vatican Council.

The author is conscious that he cannot claim to present an ad-equate historical interpretation of the complex matter. He hopes to provide at least a roadmap of the terrain, indicating its main routes and junctions and most prominent features. The audience in view is the inquisitive observer of Catholicism in world affairs, but also researchers in a number of fields who have been handicapped by the lack of such a guide to the territory. The religio-political context of social Catholicism is what we call "Catholicism." "Catholicism" can be taken as designating not the Roman Catholic Church in all its manifestations, but more precisely the particular pattern of its public presence and activity that developed after the French Revolu-tion in the Catholic parts of Europe. It developed its new structures (new orders and congregations, along with lay associations of many types, including vocational groups, sometimes even political parties) over the course of the nineteenth century, in response to the changing conditions of modernization and secularization. The forms "Catholicism" had assumed in the early 1900s remained effective until after World War II, to be caught up then in the thorough transformation that is still going on (McLeod 1981, vi; see also Komonchak 1985, Kaufmann 1979, Poulat 1969b, 1977b).

The development of *social* Catholicism is here seen as one important aspect of the development of modern Catholicism as a whole. In a second crucial respect as well, it is a virtually unprecedented phenomenon in the history of the church. The term "social Catholicism" refers heuristically to Catholic responses to *economic modernization* in particular, hence to the industrialization process and its consequences in the social classes. This complex development, taken as a whole, constitutes a sharp turn in the history of humankind, a unique movement with no close analogies in prior history. It was in process even before the French Revolution and independently of it. The process commenced with the well-named industrial revolution in Great Britain. It reached Catholic countries first in Belgium and France in the 1820s and 1830s.

The book in hand represents the first attempt since Alec Vidler's lectures in 1964 to follow the story of social Catholicism from its beginnings in more than one country (Belgium, France, Germany — with Austria and Switzerland — and Italy). The only recent study with which to compare it is Martin Greschat's book of 1980. Greschat was even more ambitious in two respects: he deals with Catholics *and* Protestants in the Christian social movements of the period and takes in Great Britain as well. But Italy, a key location for the Catholic side of the story, was left out of account. With the new departure of liberation theologies before our eyes, it seems high time to approach the story of social Catholicism in greater depth than Vidler (or, for that matter, Greschat). And certainly it is time to take advantage of thirty-five more years of changing perspectives and scholarly studies that have accumulated since the appearance of the still standard work, that edited by Joseph N. Moody in 1953 under the title, *Church and Society: Catholic Social and Political Thought and Movements 1789–1950.*

The present work opens with a re-evocation of "the world we have lost" (to borrow a phrase from Peter Laslett). The traditional patterns of economic and social life must be set once more before the mind's eye, so as to understand the confusion or revulsion of many a Catholic spokesperson in the face of what many others could with reason call "progress." Social Catholicism took shape not in an ivory tower, but in the context of the successive waves of modernization that broke upon and wore these patterns away. The social thought of European Catholics of the Romantic period (Müller 1809) stands at the beginning of a continuing critical assessment of industrialism and capitalistic economic development in general on the part of small bands of concerned Catholics.

In the 1830s all Catholic roads led back to Lamennais, including the path of nascent social Catholicism. There was a more liberal and a more conservative variant of social Catholicism right from the beginning, with a Charles de Coux and an Edouard Ducpétiaux representing the former and an Alban de Villeneuve-Bargemont or an Armand de Melun giving voice to the latter. There was also already a more profound reflection, critical of both liberal and conservative pieties, represented by such thinkers as the Bavarian Franz von Baader and the young French Romantic philosopher and former disciple of Saint-Simon, Philippe Buchez.

The next section of the unfolding roadmap leads to 1848. In Paris, religious socialism showed its beneficent power in the first weeks of the February Revolution around a whole gallery of striking figures, only to suffer what seemed to be a resounding defeat, the divorce of religion and socialism. Henceforth religious people would ally themselves for the most part with the parties of civil order, while more or less revolutionary and anticlerical socialists wooed and won the proletariat.

If social Catholics, for their part, remained for the most part hostile to continental or classical liberalism (economic as well as cultural), in the second half of the nineteenth century they became increasingly opposed to the now "godless" or anti-religious socialism. In this period our story must concentrate on the forward-looking attempts of some pioneers, such as Kolping and Ketteler in Germany and (with less success) Maignen in France, to get beyond the paternalistic and sometimes even reactionary approach that prevailed in dealing with workers and their difficulties. But we must also note and account for the prevalent paternalism and acknowledge its merits, those of a Albert de Mun or a René de la Tour du Pin, for example. These few but dogged opponents of both the individualistic status quo and its collectivist, statist, socialist alternative strove to work out applications of traditional Catholic social ethics to modern economies in an international study group called the Union de Fribourg. They enjoyed the favor of Pope Leo XIII. When his social encyclical *Rerum novarum* came out in 1891, they felt their efforts had been vindicated.

The encyclical's origins and repercussions need to be looked into (chapter 11). It galvanized the *pusillus grex* of social Catholics just at the moment when industrialization was swinging into high gear for the sustained development of a second generation of industries (electrical, steel, chemical, automotive) in many parts of the continent. Coming out of the long slump that started around 1873, the industrial sector of the advanced European economies had to pay more attention to the care and treatment of its workers. The labor movement also went into a phase of rapid development from being virtually ineffectual to becoming a force to be reckoned with in its organized trade-union form. The encyclical's cautious endorsement of the right of workers to organize and its failure to declare strikes illicit, along with its denunciation of capitalist abuses and exploitation of labor, were a powerful inducement for a new generation of priests (like Pottier and Murri) and laity (such as Léon Harmel) to move from a paternalistic approach on the social question to a "Christian democratic" one with marked affinities to democratic socialism (chapters 12–15).

By the time World War I broke out, the Christian labor movement was established in its main forms. It would retain and develop its initiatives until the triumph of fascism in the different countries of continental Europe. It would reconstruct them with adaptations, but still as alternatives to socialism, after World War II. Before fascism, the labor movement fielded unions that played a tension-ridden part in the class struggle alongside socialist or communist labor unions. The Catholic unions were often allied with a Catholic political party comprising also middle-class electorships. This brought its own set of alliances and tensions. To what extent and in what sense were these "democratic" parties? To what extent were the labor unions autonomous in the economic measures they undertook for their membership? Or to what extent *ought* they to be autonomous in respect of the church hierarchy? These were the questions that were fought over repeatedly in sometimes bitter battles during the years of Leo XIII's successor, Pius X, down to the outbreak of the First World War.

In the second volume, the plan is to pursue this story through the ascendancy of the fascist regimes, their defeat in World War II, and the economic boom-cum-welfare-state that followed in the 1950s and 1960s (the "economic miracle"). The specifics of the American Catholic scene, and indeed of all specifically non-European developments, must be left to others to research and present. Thus this history should take the reader up to the threshold of liberation theology, but not directly into its origins or further history. The Second Vatican Council will bring the work to a close. It was the occasion on which European Catholicism discovered it was merely a part of the worldwide Roman Catholic communion, and not necessarily the determinative part. It was also a time when Christian Democratic parties were dominant in Europe, heirs jointly of a liberal Catholic tradition as well as of nineteenth-century social Catholicism.

Chapter 1

SOCIO-ECONOMIC LIFE
IN PREINDUSTRIAL
CATHOLIC EUROPE

Peasants and Farm Workers

Since the vast majority of people lived off the land, it is appropriate
to begin with the rural situation.

One often reads of the "feudal system" that prevailed in France
until the French Revolution abolished it in principle in 1789 (August
4; see Soboul 1976, 3/1:18). There, as in other European countries, the
process of emancipating rural laborers and rendering land subject to
free sale and purchase had started much earlier; in many places, it was
not finished until the middle of the nineteenth century. The obligation
to stay as a serf on the land where one was born had disappeared
centuries before in England and parts of Western Europe (Flanders
and the Rhineland, for example).

Feudalism had started in the early Middle Ages as a response to
the breakdown of public authority with general economic regression
to primitive agricultural conditions. Settlers and previous inhabitants
would be protected by the local lord in return for receiving the land
they worked from him "in fief," just as he received his local domain,
where he was lord and master, "in fief" from his liege lord and so on
up to the king, who received his overall authority (this was of course
a ticklish and never quite agreed-upon point) from the emperor or
the pope. As long as the vassal or subject was able to manage the
responsibility of the fief, it remained in his and his posterity's hands.

What was left of "feudalism" by the eighteenth century was the
part that affected land and the peasants who lived on it: various degrees of bondage or serfdom, traditional sets of rights and duties owed

7

by the landowner or "lord" to the peasant (unless the latter owned the land himself) and by the peasant to the lord. The full feudal authority of the lords, including political authority over such things as the administration of justice and private armies for defense and public order, had long since given way to the early modern monarchical or princely forms of a more or less centralized state authority.

In many areas, peasants had been released from the personal obligations of serfdom and could depart from the soil farmed by their family without the permission of the landowner. The landowner, reciprocally, was of course quit of all obligations to an emancipated serf who did in fact leave the land to which he had been bound.

In Austria, for instance, the enlightened Emperor Joseph II declared such serfdom at an end for large parts of Central Europe in 1781 (Rürup 1985, 26). Still, the duties that had gone with being a serf were merely transformed into those of a tenant farmer or "free" peasant. He no longer had to ask permission to get married or move away; nor could he be ejected from his living without cause. But as long as he farmed the land that his ancestors had farmed, he had to continue to work on the master's lands so many days a year and hand over so much of his own produce to him or his agents at harvesttime. This was called the "service" or "the duties" on the land and was referred to as the land's "burden" or "encumberment." It could be considered a form of rent.

A part of the land in and around a farming community was usually community pasture, stream, and woods. All inhabitants of the village and its surroundings were entitled to graze their yard animals there and gather wood for the fireplace, naturally with details governing these rights varying by custom from place to place.

There were often other obligations on the land, too, such as church tithes or road building and maintenance, all of which went with the land as a liability, even if it changed hands. Once a tenant farmer fell into arrears on the "duties" owed, of course, the landowner who extended credit could insist on a larger share of the production until accounts were settled. But it was not usually in the interests of the landowner to push his tenants over the brink into sheer destitution or into leaving the land, at least until alternative ways of getting it tilled became a real prospect.

Every plot of land had its own history and complicated bundle of claims and duties. In many areas, in the course of time, the plots had been subdivided and rearranged by inheritance and happenstance until each peasant in the village had only small fields scattered around the countryside at some distance from one another. There was no feasible mechanism for swapping or consolidating fields without the assertion of unrecognized claims to authority by the local lord or landowners (which the sovereign would not normally permit) or by the sovereign (who for a long time had no sufficient motivation or practical power to intervene).

Thus, before the French Revolution there was rarely any such thing as "clear title" to farm or woodland. The local country population had the right to remain there and to keep a certain proportion of what they could gather or produce for their own upkeep, thus limiting the owner's rights to change the use of the land. It was often illegal for the person or foundation whose property it was to put it up for sale. Church lands generally were withdrawn from commerce, subject, as the phrase went, to "mortmain." Common land, the village meadows, for instance, had their use fixed once and for all by the vested rights of the villagers. Even in the British colonies up until the American Revolution, heirs of estates or plantations often found their property "entailed," that is to say, not necessarily mortgaged or indebted, but inalienable. Such lands had to remain part of the estate and could not be sold in any straightforward manner.

In an idealized view of this state of things, the squire or lord of the manor was paternally diligent in looking after the arrangements that would assure the prosperity of the little community (or large family). He and his immediate family would plan and supervise the common projects, allow the peasant families enough time and provisions to cultivate their own plots, and settle any problems or quarrels that arose. The peasants in turn would see to it that the soil was properly worked, sown, and harvested with their labor.

Even apart from such an idealized view, this was a system that helped to put vast areas of Europe under cultivation and supported a slowly growing population and a large number of small cities with a more or less flourishing trade and culture. But of course, especially as time went on, a very large part of the system did not resemble the model in its more humane respects. Many domains were so large, and the lord so aloof in station if not remote in distance, that any personal bond of mutual loyalty between peasant and master was only a legalism; one could cite the great prince-bishops of Mainz, Cologne, or Salzburg, for instance, or the great abbeys in Catholic countries, not to mention secular princes or kings or great dynastic families such as the Schwarzenbergs in Bohemia or the Rohan in France, with their far-flung estates.

Then there were by no means unheard-of breaches of the system, where the strong would take advantage of the weak by simply confiscating their holdings or increasing their "duties," or the peasants would hold back on what amounted to rent in kind. Perhaps of more significance as to the survival of the system, however, were its built-in rigidities. Europe was a dynamic society without an overall central controlling instance; if a European nation did not make forward strides, it fell behind in relation to its neighbors. In such circumstances, the views of liberal economists such as Adam Smith as applied to agriculture fell on receptive ears. "Entails," he argued in *The Wealth of Nations*, "are founded upon the absurd...supposition that every successive generation of men have not an equal right to the earth...but that the property of the present generation should be restrained and regulated according to the fancy of those who died perhaps 500 years ago" ([1776] 1976, book III, ch. ii, 6, p. 384). Of course conservatives would reply that unrestrained buying and selling of farmland implied the absurd principle that the present generation may exploit the slowly built-up productivity of the land without giving any thought to future generations — yes, that was a conservative argument two centuries ago! In the circumstances, however, the liberal view was the more appropriate, in that it was more disposed to promote the rapid increase of foodstuffs that was necessary then and for generations to come.

When the social order of the *ancien régime* is seen as consisting of nobility, higher and lower clergy, bourgeois and peasants, one does not always remember as one should that a large part of the population lies below this horizon. There are not only the common workers in the towns to consider, but the large rural population who were less than peasants: who neither owned a farm of their own nor were settled permanently with the right to work on feudal property. These "servants" formed an underclass that picked up work when they could, sometimes attached themselves to a better-off peasant's or townsperson's family, but were most often not allowed to marry and were subject to the fate of the desperately poor.

Marrying, after all, was not among the expectations that everyone could entertain in this late feudal order. In principle, one had to show the economic basis that would permit one to start and raise a family. If a peasant inherited a farmstead, either as his own or in fief or as a tenant farmer, then marriage was in order, supposing the permission of the feudal lord or property-holder (parish, abbey, college, or other, as the case may be). Children born second or third were very often out of luck, where the inheritance was not divisible by reason of customary law or because it was already too small to support a family. Once new or newly available land was largely occupied (which had been the case long before eighteenth century except where war or famine or plague had carried off whole families), children of peasants who did not inherit or marry into an inheritance generally were not permitted to marry.

In these straitened circumstances, marriage became first and foremost a question of preserving or extending the family estate.

Romantic inclinations played no role. "One married the family," it has been said (Poulat 1977b, 256, citing P. Bourdieu); it could just as well be said that "one married the farm," the piece of land that was to be passed on in the family. Childbirths were numerous, but infant and child mortality was high — on average, one could count on only half of the children born to grow up and become a support for their parents in later years. For a good part of the eighteenth century in large areas of rural Europe, illegitimate children were relatively few. Social pressure as well as feudal customs (i.e., the need to receive permission to marry from the lord of the manor) evidently were successful in keeping premarital and extra-marital relations at a minimum. Those who married late or were not allowed to marry (such as the farm laborers, men and women) would not risk what must have been a very severe ostracism reserved for those who brought a child into the world unprovided for. Surplus marriageable children were, it is clear, a problem, even in a proper farmstead.

In fact, despite continuing high mortality, the population of Europe started to rise gradually around the middle of the eighteenth century for reasons that are not quite clear. The absence of plagues comparable to those of earlier times is one factor. The continuous slow overall improvement of transportation and trade helped in areas not too greatly affected by war. Improved medical care or knowledge does *not* seem to have been a factor until the last hundred years or so. A string of better than average harvests after about 1765 reduced the mortality by just enough, it seems, to give the population a decided upward momentum for a generation or so (Rürup 1985, 13–15, Fischer 1982, 52–56).

When this had happened in the past, a string of lean years or other catastrophes had always wiped out most of the gains. T. R. Malthus drew the famous conclusion in 1798 that such cycles of population growth, followed by shrinkage for sheer lack of nutrition, were embedded in the natural order of things and were hence inevitable. Many reluctantly agreed.

And yet, despite cholera epidemics and the potato famine of the 1840s and other hard times, there has been no such check on population growth since Malthus's time. With great regional variations, Europe's population doubled between 1750 and 1850 and rose 80 percent more by 1913 during the heyday of industrialization. Obviously the soil was capable, with improved cultivation, of feeding a much greater population than Malthus and his contemporaries could imagine. But a great part of this increased productivity could not have been achieved under feudal conditions — at least so it would seem (Vierhaus 1988, 20–28 and 48–50).

Prerevolutionary Industry and Commerce

An increasing part of this added population arose in or flocked to towns and cities. What was urban life like *before* this modern influx? What the town contributed to the economy was in the first place a marketplace, meaning both a center of trade and exchange for goods of all sorts as well as ready consumers of the produce of the land. In the second place, towns were the centers of manufacture, where the raw or half-worked materials from plant, animal, and mineral sources were turned into useful and marketable commodities (Adam Smith [1776] 1976, book III, chs. iii and iv). Towns and cities afforded, finally, the concentration of population that permitted and encouraged intellectual and cultural exchange, inquiry, learning, and art.

Italy was in the forefront of urban civilization in the Middle Ages. From their outset, as welcome as the development of cities had been for their services to religious, cultural, and economic-political society, they constituted a disturbing factor in medieval Christendom. Medieval urban "businessmen" could not be readily integrated into society in the harmonious and hierarchical scheme of things that most medievals seemed to wish to find. But in this overall scheme they still played a subordinate, if indispensable and increasingly important, role.

It is not for nothing that the seventeenth and eighteenth centuries are known as the age of absolutism. Enlightened monarchs and princes were often able to extend their control to areas that had formerly been beneath or beyond their attention. As to the economy, the rulers wished to exercise control over trade in such a way as to favor their own territories, taxing the export of food grains, for example, or encouraging the export of manufactures (Vierhaus 1988, 20). Their predecessors had tended to use tolls and customs duties simply to raise money. Now one began to encourage industry, roads, ports out of considerations of political economy. From this era, for example, date the royal porcelain factories that dot Europe: they were meant to bring in revenue by export, provide work, and not drain the territory of anything really useful such as food or precious minerals. Similar "manufactories" were encouraged for such luxury products as silk and crystal.

In such absolutist states, the court city required building projects and numerous officials and servants, the number depending on the degree of ostentation that the state could afford. The continuing subordination of businessmen in such baroque societies — including most of the Holy Roman Empire, with its ecclesiastical principalities — was hardly challenged by the thin bourgeois layer of educated townspeople (Vierhaus 1988, 50–57). If some could get rich serving the court, their position in the social pecking order remained humble unless and until they could get themselves ennobled. Even then they were the last and the least among their new "peers."

In the by then economically more dynamic northwest of Europe, the strains between the traditional order on the one hand and the well-to-do townspeople on the other were likely to be greater. Either of two groups could exercise dominance in the urban settings characteristic of preindustrial Europe, those engaged in commerce and banking or the ruling nobility with their country cousins. In France, the strong and absolute monarchy of the *ancien régime* and the dynamic new class of the bourgeois found themselves in an uneasy partnership, although courtly culture still dominated city life, almost as in Germany, but with more underlying ferment. In England, by contrast, and even more so in Holland, the leaders of banking, shipping, and trade, along with the businesslike great landed families, set the tone for urban society. As it happened, whether due to something inherent in Calvinism (Max Weber) or not, the conspicuously successful commercial or "bourgeois" (or even capitalist) societies were those of the Netherlands and England. Christian religion — Catholic, Lutheran, Calvinist, or Anglican — was prominent throughout, despite forebodings of secularity.

In any case, neither the French nor the British economists of the eighteenth century seriously questioned the predominance of agriculture as the most important and fundamental sector in a nation's economy. One modern, but prerevolutionary, development on the border between agriculture and industry is to be noticed, because it continued to play a significant role in providing work and products to the growing population of European countries well into the period of industrialization proper. This is the development of cottage industries in connection with the capitalist "putting-out system" of organizing the labor and the marketing of rural crafts, like weaving.

For centuries rural populations had produced cloth for their own clothing, linen out of flax and wool from sheep. Some areas had even become weaving centers for export, Flanders, for example. One speaks of a putting-out system when entrepreneurs organize this home industry for greater productivity and richer, more extended markets. On the one hand, the urban putters-out, or contractors, made contacts in more or less distant markets and tested these markets unscientifically to gauge the demand for possible products. On the other, they offered to pay the rural spinners and weavers for products meeting their specifications. Often it was necessary to advance payment, so that the sale price of the yarn or cloth came near to being a wage and the contractor was more or less equivalent to an employer. Often there was still some more finishing work to be done on the product, especially in the most widespread cottage industry, textiles; the putter-out ended up, perhaps, installing a central workshop for bleaching and dying. All that was required for the transition to industrialization after a while was to stop supplying the weavers with home looms and start installing mechanized power looms in a large central workshop, namely the "factory."

But this is getting ahead of the story. What is of importance at this juncture is to point out that the putting-out system enabled rural areas in several parts of Europe to support populations far in excess of those that could be gainfully employed in raising foodstuffs alone on the amount of land inhabited, and this before widespread mechanization or the use of coal for steam power. It was certainly in many cases only a subsistence-level prosperity for many workers, a necessary second occupation. This was the case where land had been divided into parcels inadequate to support a family — or where the number of landless laborers had created a veritable rural unemployment problem of worrisome dimensions.

Conversely, such rural industry seems to have contributed to a breakdown in the limitations on marriage that had been characteristic of rural European life, and perhaps even more so to a rise in the number of illegitimate children that appears in these regions at this juncture, well before the construction of factories and the poor housing clustered near them. By a process easy to imagine, the young couple starting to earn money from weaving or making clocks would feel that they had the wherewithal, between a plot of ground and their work for a putting-out contractor, to support themselves and a child or two. Instead of just being a seasonably employed farmhand and milkmaid, they would actually earn money during the winter. With or without the sanction of authority, they could have their baby and go on living. The pastoral reports of the country clergy were replete with complaints about such developments from this time on (Phayer 1977, 32). The social upheavals of an industrial age seemed to cast their shadows before them.

Church and Economic Society in the *Ancien Régime*

France was the country where the modern developments in social, political, and economic respects interacted most vigorously and directly with an articulate and traditionally dominant Catholicism. In France, the pastoral care of the church through the ministrations of more or less educated parish priests had finally reached and encompassed most of the peasant population. The ancient educational and charitable institutions of the church had also more or less kept pace with the times, often developing considerable growth and constituting models for the Western world, thus assuring Christian influence among the nobility and the educated. They, and the uneducated masses as well, imbibed a worldview communicated in its basic traits by Jesuit and Jansenist, higher and lower clergy alike. It was an as yet sacral, unsecularized worldview, and it lent divine significance to the lives of men and women in all, or nearly all, states of life. When a new "human type" (Groethuysen) arose, however, and constituted itself self-confidently as the bourgeois class, insuperable tensions arose between the baroque or early modern Christian view of social order and the new lifestyle of the bourgeois. It was this set of tensions and misunderstandings that would fuel both the setbacks and the successes of nineteenth-century Catholicism in the age of liberalism.

Knowing the course that the French Revolution took — into persecution of the church and attempts to set up a new, post-Christian philosophical religion at the service of the nation — one may suppose that Catholicism had lost all vital contact with the soul of the French nation by 1789. After all, the *philosophes*, with Voltaire at their head, had successfully spread a deistic or completely secular Enlightenment critique of Christianity among the educated elites, both nobles and commoners, against only feeble intellectual resistance. Perhaps the operative word here is "elites," suggesting that the mass of the population was not yet seriously affected by such thinking. John McManners (1969, 19) has reminded us, at any rate, that the Third Estate, as a matter or course, joined in the liturgical observances (procession, benediction) opening the Estates General in 1789. All indications are that they took for granted to the same extent as the clergy and nobility that the Catholicism of France would continue to form part of the French national identity.

The peasant population of France remained mostly illiterate. (Illustrative material for the major points of this section is to be found especially in Bernhard Groethuysen 1968 and in the fuller original of 1927, 1:1–64, and 1930, 2:9–42.) Their knowledge of Christian teachings, even in the many cases where they had once memorized catechism questions and answers, might not hold up under examination. Nevertheless they lived in a world of the miraculous, which was one way of picturing the supernatural — their way, for the most part. In any case, it could hardly escape them that the God of Christians held the poor, strange as it might seem, in a special regard. He was a demanding God, perhaps even, like the nature he controlled, uncanny, arbitrary and by turns angry and well-disposed. But for those who lived up to well-known minimum standards of conduct, the Ten Commandments, he held an eternal reward ready.

The fact that a poor person was of no account in society was no reflection of God's intentions in his or her regard. The whole Christian story, even imperfectly taken in, testified to God's love for the poor. Were not his Son, Mary and Joseph too, distinctly little ones as the world reckons? The ordinary person might treat his lessers with scorn, but did not God's saints on earth honor the poor in a special way? This message seems to have got through. It entered into the basic worldview of the country, even where one was not particularly pious and often preferred immediate gratifications to acting in the modest and self-sacrificing way that the church held up as the ideal.

According to Christian teaching, the fact was that God placed a few persons high and many low in social standing for gracious reasons of his own. There was even a certain advantage in *not* being placed high up, since leisure and wealth carried with them the potential for dissipation, vice, and abuse of power that the limited circumstances of common folk tended to rule out.

The great and noble, on the other hand, might seem to be almost disqualified as beneficiaries of God's grace. But they too had their honorable place in God's plan for society. They were to use their power and riches for the benefit of those whom God had, as it were, committed to their care: the poor and needy and victimized. A strand of Christian tradition going back to Paul (Romans 13) had seen the divinely appointed role of rulers to consist in repressing evil and violence, even if they must themselves use violent and worldly means to accomplish their task. It was certainly not an enviable role, but it was a necessary one in the here and now.

This line of thinking had been developed in the early modern period into the doctrine of the divine right of kings, with the concomitant duty of all Christians to obey royal authority. The church in France had come to embrace this doctrine, on the understanding that the king depended in turn on the church, the interpreter of God's will, for guidance. Otherwise France would not be France! Louis XIV or Louis XVI might be the absolute monarch, but his ideal had to remain at least in part the image of the saint and king and devoted servant of the church, Louis IX.

In the preaching of the church, the whole estate of the nobility had an analogous function: *noblesse oblige*. Their reason for being, in the Christian view, was to come to the aid of the much more numerous populations dependent upon them. Since the modern absolute monarchy had taken over and centralized defense and justice, the emphasis was naturally on the economic aspect: nobility as landowners and receivers of large revenues. In a word, the rich were established by God as rich so as to succor the poor. God made the poor so numerous precisely so that human beings, differentiated by lot and fortune, would come to be dependent on one another.

In the sermons directed to the wealthy, therefore, the clergy lost few opportunities to convince their listeners that, paradoxical as it may seem, the rich were also dependent upon the poor. This would become blindingly clear on the day of judgment; it had been long since revealed, however, in the parable of Lazarus and Dives. The foremost duty of the rich as an estate in Christendom, apart from the common duties of every Christian, was generous almsgiving. The rich could heap up for themselves riches in heaven by distributing alms now in this life. Given the dangers and temptations of life to the idle rich, or still more to the busy schemers and intriguers at court, almsgiving was practically the only way in which the rich could justify living in the station in which God had after all appointed them.

The simplicity of the paradoxical solution was appealing, even if putting it into practice was not. Being born in a palace had its Christian meaning and dignity, even if it was not a direct path of discipleship. One was not expected to impoverish oneself or one's family; one should maintain the style of life appropriate to one's station while, from the surplus or excess, as it was called, supporting the needy. In view of the fact that these needy were doing the wealthy a great favor just by calling forth their Christian works of mercy, one could say with conviction that God's plan for a society of unequals, with some rich and many poor, made both classes mutually dependent on each other and even caused each group to help the other forward on the way to heaven.

It was of course the First Estate, the clergy, that offered this world-view to both rich and poor. As its members necessarily were recruited either from nobility or from commoners, they were also expected to remain in the economic condition befitting their birth, and to live, as far as their church offices were concerned, from the estates (that is, the lands) attached as a sort of foundation to their pastoral cures. This was the Tridentine reform of the medieval benefice system. Although it creaked at the joints — there were always too many ill-paid working clergy alongside well-to-do or even enormously rich benefice-holders — it hardly impaired the conviction with which preachers high and low insisted that the existing order of society was ordained of God. People should remain in the station in which they were born, like "statues in the niches where their creator had placed them," as one priest put it (cited by Groethuysen 1930, 2:201).

The clergy was responsible for the education of France; clergymen not only encouraged almsgiving but also organized the charitable works by which they were applied to the benefit of the poor; they headed the administration of church and monastic property; they were responsible for the pastoral care of all classes and the confessional guidance of even the most powerful. Since their vision of

society supported order, subordination, and sharing of burdens between the unequally positioned members of society, it was not the
ideology of just one segment of society but the generally accepted underlying scheme of things, reflected by the dramatists and scientists
of the time as well as by the pious. Sensitive souls such as Pascal
may have been affected by a sense of cosmic dislocation already in
Galileo's time; independent-minded "libertines" may have scoffed at
church doctrine; but for a long time the order of society reflected in
the sermons of the clergy was taken for granted also by all significant
groups in society. But where did any of this indicate a role in society
for a practical-minded and upward-striving bourgeoisie?

For people of a middling sort, neither high and mighty nor low
and powerless, the preachers of seventeenth- and eighteenth-century
France also had some comforting if austere reflections to offer (Groethuysen 1930, 2:43–79 and 108–18). It was not as if the dramatic
baroque contrast between those born as lords over thousands of
acres, complete with the peasants to work them, and those born
in utter destitution or at least dependency and want, exhausted the
possibilities that the preachers considered. They also had well-to-do
peasant-owners of their own land and modestly prosperous artisans
and merchants in their congregations and on their minds. It was not
left solely to the Calvinists to preach the solid virtues of middle-class
life: thrift, sobriety, frugality, industriousness.

Hence it was a familiar theme that both great wealth and actual
poverty were dangerous states of life, more threatening to salvation
and morals than a modest but disciplined and unflamboyant existence in a workaday world. The Third Estate, the "civil" or bourgeois
members of society, who owned a bit of property and exercised a
profession or trade, were also part of France and of the church. The
way they fit into the cosmos of society was inconspicuous and resembled more closely the role of the small than that of the great. They
were not in positions of influence, the way churchly representatives
tended to see them — that was reserved to those who were born in
the appropriate station — and they were not to aspire for power or
influence.

Groethuysen points out repeatedly (e.g., 1930, 2:207–18) how such
an attitude could not be acceptable over time for a dynamic element
in the French nation whose power and influence was in fact increasing dramatically and whose self-image was that of benefactors and
active contributors to the prosperity and hence power of France. The
view of the bourgeoisie as an industrious but subservient middling
collection of people working at different trades, content to remain in
the social and economic status of their fathers, content also to take
their societal guidance from their "betters," might go down with the

petite bourgeoisie, but ran into increasing resistance from the new class in formation, the *grande* bourgeoisie.

The Usury Question

The issue that took center stage between representatives of Christianity and representatives of the bourgeoisie in the decades preceding the Revolution was ostensibly a question of purely economic ethics: usury, understood in the broad sense of the legitimacy of taking interest on loans. The church's answer had always been a negative one (Le Goff 1988). Taking interest on money that one lent out was wrong according to philosophical ethics (Aristotle) and, what is more important, according to the gospel (Lk 6:34).

Extending credit, however, was necessary in commerce and for purposes of state. Such transactions had been justified in Catholic economic ethics at least since the days of St. Antoninus of Florence in the fifteenth century, amid a great deal of controversy and disagreement, to be sure. In France, however, the old thought constructions of the scholastics again came under a drumroll of criticism. It is clear (DTC 15:2372–90) that not all defenders of the churchly tradition on usury were so inept as to overlook these developments and fall back on a broadbrush rejection of all forms of business credit and banking activities, but some certainly did (Groethuysen 1930, 2:167; Nelson 1949, 1969).

Pope Benedict XIV had had occasion in 1745 to issue an encyclical on the subject, called after its opening words *Vix pervenit* (Carlen 1981, 1:15–17). In it the pope confirmed one last time the traditional church semantics. No interest is legitimate in return "for a loan [of money] as such, simply by reason of the lending," as I might translate (*ipso mutuo, ipsius ratione mutui*). However, by reason of *other* sorts of considerations, any legitimate extension of credit, on terms of what the rest of the world called interest, might well be completely in order. Thus, for example, perhaps what the banker calls a loan is really the selling of rents for a certain period of time. Nothing stands in the way of insisting on receiving back not just the foregone rents but also a certain payment for financial inconveniences and disadvantages that the lender (no, the "seller," in the language of the then conventional moral theology) has to reckon with. One might well have avoided the term, "interest" and referred to a "finance charge," had the term existed then, and the theologians would have made no objection.

This was clearly understood by theologians outside of France and by Jesuits (Noonan 1957). But it does not seem to been understood or admitted by the parties to the public dispute in France in the 1770s and 1780s (after the Jesuits had been suppressed; they were expelled from France in 1762 and suppressed in all Catholic countries in 1773 by a decree of Pope Clement XIV; see Chadwick 1981a, 345–50).

Two French cities with an advanced economy figured prominently in the literature of this debate. Marseilles was a large port with much foreign and overseas trade. Lyon was even then, without steam-driven machinery, a center of silk processing and the garment trade. This was a capitalist "industry before industrialization." Estimates put the number of workers engaged in it (and hence dependent upon an economy possible only through credit) at between one hundred and two hundred thousand and 200,000 at the time when the controversy over usury was raging (Groethuysen 1930, 2:157–89, here 170–71, citing the *Lettre à Monseigneur l'archevêque de Lyon dans laquelle on traite du Prêt à Intérêt à Lyon*...[1763]). If the merchants and bankers of Lyon should cease borrowing and lending money at interest, one hundred thousand workers would be put out of work with no jobs to fill. Moreover, not to mention the entrepreneurs' ruin, "What would become of so many small investors, retired officers, single women and widows living on an inheritance, thrifty artisans who have saved up something for their declining years," if they could not put their modest capitals out at interest?

The exaggerations and misleading assumptions of such bourgeois polemics, one would think, would be speedily put right by citing *Vix pervenit*. But Gallicans that they were, the ecclesiastical response apparently left much to be desired — perhaps those writers who entered the lists on the side of tradition felt it was better simply to seize the high ground of principle. *Fiat justitia, ruat caelum.* Even the terms of *Vix pervenit*, of course, were hopelessly unreal and outmoded in bourgeois or enlightened eyes. Those who had knowledge of how trade was actually transacted or were developing theories of economics and trade, like Turgot, considered it a point of honor to despise scholastic intricacies and speculations in this as in other fields.[1]

The upshot was that increasingly, those who knew themselves to be honorable men of affairs and more than ordinarily productive citizens came more and more to the conviction that their aspirations and way of life were after all, as churchmen constantly insisted, incompatible with Christianity. The "Christian society" was already in place; it needed no far-reaching changes to be brought about. It was stable, one might say stationary, certainly in principle static. If disturbed or

---

[1]The church hierarchy finally came to terms with the question of interest and usury, not with a bang but a whimper. The bishop of Rennes inquired of Pope Pius VIII in 1830 whether the terms of *Vix pervenit* were to be insisted upon in the confession (DS 2722–24). The response was to let sleeping dogs lie ("*confessarios...non esse inquietandos*").

overthrown, one knew how it was to be restored and what it would look like. There would be the great and the small, the rich and the poor; in between there would be a middle estate, called for time out of mind the bourgeois. All would "be content with their lot" and know what role, basically unchangeable, they would be called upon to play. Sins there would be in every estate, but sins could be forgiven. If order were overturned, however, there was but one remedy: one must restore order, the only order that corresponded to God's will.

The upward-striving bourgeoisie of commerce, finance, and industry, however, could not settle for such a scheme of things as final and unchanging. They were not peasants or small townspeople, destined to spend their life in obscurity just because their ancestors were not already distinguished. They were not nobility, wed to a decrepit self-image that modern political and economic developments since the rise of the nation-state had undermined. They were not monks or clergy, clinging likewise to outmoded traditions of all sorts and making themselves the defenders of the indefensible in this world. They were certainly not the quiet, merely industrious and subservient lower middle class that the clergy would like them to be. They were a new human type, now developing a consciousness that they belonged to the class that must shape the future. This-worldly, pragmatic, rational, they could appreciate that the inequalities marking the old world would remain, but not necessarily at their expense; they came to realize, during the Revolution if not already beforehand (Groethuysen on Necker, 1930, 2:214), that the social teachings of the church that they themselves rejected were all the more necessary for the common people.

For themselves, it is clear that "the principle of a static order of society, laid down once for all," could never be reconciled with their class identity as bourgeois and as a force to be reckoned with in the highest echelons of secular life (Groethuysen 1930, 2:197). Nothing less than a complete emancipation from Christian attitudes seemed to them compatible with their self-respect as a major active partner in modern society. When they would in fact achieve a position of preeminence in nineteenth-century European society, another stage in the secularization of the Western world would commence. With it would commence, on the side of the church, the slow dissolution of the ahistorical notion of an unchanging, static societal order. More than a century later, all the same, Leo XIII (1878–1903) and Pius X (1903–14) would still presuppose a worldview in which the necessary inequality of social station was basic.

Chapter 2

INDUSTRIALIZATION IN CATHOLIC COUNTRIES: THE BEGINNINGS

In most Catholic areas (as in most Protestant ones on the continent), for a couple of generations, real industrialization was something one heard of from other parts of Europe. The first concrete experience of it often came with the railroads. Belgium and France had industrialized areas in the first half of the nineteenth century; the Rhineland and then other Catholic parts of Germany, Italy, and Switzerland followed by the end of the century (see Köhler in Jedin 1981, 9:226–27). The problems and opportunities that arose as a consequence were noted by at least a few of the lay and clerical leaders of the Catholic movement in these early stages. How they responded or failed to respond at the outset was to have great influence on the societal struggles that were to come and on the shape of the social Catholicism of the later nineteenth century, including the form it took in papal pronouncements from the time of Leo XIII on.

The British Head Start and the Continental Emulators

The first country to shift from a predominantly agricultural to a predominantly industrial economy, after Britain, was Belgium. Belgium was a Catholic country, having gained its independence from the Netherlands, dominated by Protestants, in 1830. The Belgian Catholic response to capitalist economic development therefore deserves continued notice all out of proportion to the size of the country.

Belgium — the southern Lowlands — was left to the Austrian Hapsburgs at the end of the Dutch wars of religion and independence

22

from Spain under William of Orange in the late sixteenth century. In the eighteenth century it was a somewhat backward country, despite its well-tilled farms in Flanders and a good deal of textile fabrication going on across the country in cottage industry and in one or two towns of the mostly French-speaking episcopal princedom, or "prince-bishopric," of Liège. It was a far cry from the late medieval and Renaissance times of urban prosperity and culture, when Bruges and Antwerp had been flourishing ports and Rubens put a finishing touch on the reputation of Flemish art. The Dutch cut off maritime access to Antwerp, thus putting it out of competition as a port. But Belgium had coal — some discovered as late as the present century — and iron. It had traditions of artisanry and banking that would stand it in good stead when the hour of industrialization struck.

The Belgians got their first chance to take advantage of the new conditions from revolutionary France, which annexed Liège and the "Austrian Provinces" in 1797. There was still not much sea trade to hope for, since France and England were in declared or undeclared war with one another until the fall of Napoleon in 1813/15; they blockaded each other's spheres of influence. But Belgians could now sell their products, starting with coal itself, in the vast French internal market, above all in and around Paris.

The same wars that made Belgium part of France, however, also delayed or made impossible an orderly development of commerce and industry, at precisely the same time that England, from behind its Channel shield, was becoming the first industrialized country. In that first phase of the industrial revolution, textiles, especially cotton, constituted the most dynamic and profitable sector of the economy. Iron products had their important place, too, especially in terms of the war matériel for which it was so easy to find customers. In both branches, British artisans and entrepreneurs had found ways to harness the power of coal, by way of the new steam engines, to multiply the productivity of its workers. In the aftermath of the Napoleonic upheavals, England dominated the continental and world markets in these manufactured goods with a head start that would be insuperable for most of the century.

It is a matter of some consequence for the development of Catholic responses to industrialization, therefore, that the earliest follower country, a "second-comer" rather than a latecomer to the way of economic development exhibited by Britain, was a Catholic country. The further course of industrialization in Europe could lead an incautious or prejudiced observer to the conclusion that there is something about Protestantism that gave Protestant countries an advantage in respect to modernization of all kinds and industrial development in particular. I am not thinking of the Weber-Tawney thesis here, but more

of a kind of nineteenth-century identification of progress with Protestantism. After all, in France, which was also a "Catholic country,"
but with a strong tradition of unbelief since the Revolution of 1789,
production of textiles and pig iron seemed to be mostly in the hands
of Protestant or unbelieving entrepreneurs, financed by banks in the
same hands or in the hands of Jews.

Was France's conversion to an industry-dominated economy
slower, stretching out into the twentieth century, because it was a
"Catholic country"? Recent students of European industrial and economic development hardly ever take that view. But in the 1880s and
1890s, when German industrial power was becoming evident, it went
without saying that Germany (Prussia) was a Protestant power. It
seemed to many, both Catholic and Protestant observers, that it was
somehow foreordained that one modernizing Protestant power should
take the lead from another, Great Britain, by the end of the century.
Then there were those other backward states, Austria-Hungary and
Italy, not to mention Spain. None of these Catholic countries could
hold a candle to Great Britain or the German Empire.

In actuality, one finds that the pattern is not quite so overwhelmingly in favor of Protestant leadership and that, in any case, factors
other than the confessional allegiance of the dominant classes in a
given country, factors more directly of economic relevance such as
the availability of coal or access to markets, are more important in
accounting for the timely success or lack of it in the industrialization
of a country. Certainly, if the difference between Protestant and Catholic culture were so significant in this question, Holland would have
capitalized on the relative advantages that it enjoyed over Belgium
in the preindustrial age and would have made the conversion to the
industrial form of society earlier, whereas in fact Belgium overtook
Holland in the course of the nineteenth century and still supported a
larger and slightly more prosperous national economy at the turn of
the century (Kossmann 1978, 418–19).

Rather than carrying over nineteenth-century mental schemas
formed in interconfessional polemic, it is more conducive to understanding to remember the ways in which the different Western Christian bodies resembled each other. They all had formed for themselves
by their pastoral ardor and discipline a more or less deeply rooted
peasant religio-cultural base. They had all made peace with and maintained a base in the aristocratic world of the nobility and even, with
major exceptions, that of the bourgeois magnates. There was in all
of them a greater or lesser tension between a traditional thought-
world, put into form by a scholastic theology, and the emancipatory
rationalism of a developing scientific worldview. If one is tempted
too readily to identify Calvinism as the confession of the bourgeoisie,

let one remember the immense role played by Jesuits and Jansenists in the education of French and Lowlands' Catholic laity and clergy. In other words, the various outlooks and sensibilities of the dynamic and decidedly Christian early modern Western European spirit had taken root variously in each of the principal Reformation and Counter-Reformation churches.

As regards Catholic areas, then, the first stage of industrialization was completed in Belgium already in the 1840s. Steam power was replacing manual and water power in the mines and weaving mills of the land (Ghent, Verviers). The death-knell of Flemish hand spinning and weaving would sound before 1850; linen was no longer competitive with cotton and cotton spinning could be done much more efficiently with the spinning jenny and the more recently introduced self-actor (Landes 1969, 166). Paris, Lyon, and the north of France (Lille) followed more slowly. Only in Belgium and the neighboring region of northwest France were the entrepreneurs as well as the workers Catholic. Other industrialized areas had a large Catholic population and hence workforce, but their industrial bourgeoisie included few Catholics. The Rhineland, for example, was largely Catholic but had been part of Protestant Prussia since 1815. It also started with textiles before the immense development of coal and steel in the latter part of the century. These were the principal theaters of intensive and highly successful industrialization in areas of Catholic strength. It will not surprise us that many of the pioneering developments of Catholic social practice — not all — will take place in these regions.

Early Industrial Conditions

What distinguished the first industrialized centers from the kind of industry that had existed previously was, technologically speaking, steam power for the spinning machines and the weaving looms in the textile industry, the increased use of steam engines to increase the productivity of coal mines, and finally the use of mineral coal (coke) rather than charcoal in making iron. Socially speaking, the construction, purchase, and use of steam engines and iron forges, both dependent upon coal, gave the monied bourgeoisie and the rich nobility who did not disdain to do business with them a decisive breakthrough to societal power and influence. Henceforth two new industrial classes would take shape: those who owned the machines and those who worked them — the bourgeois entrepreneurs and the wage earners in their direct employ — capitalists and the laboring class. A concomitant development was the formation of new industrial towns or regions, often apart from the older urban centers of trade and government.

On the face of it, it does not seem self-evident that the entrepreneurs of early industrialization were a new social formation. Had there not been bourgeois businessmen — merchants, bankers — in Europe for centuries? It is true that some of the new industrial entrepreneurs were born to this station of life. But they were not regarded as and were not in fact the typical case. The older bourgeoisie, whether in government administration or political life, whether living off investments or actively engaged in finance or commerce, held aloof for the most part from the pioneering efforts in factory production. They did not make their money available with great alacrity or enthusiasm for such ventures, either. There were exceptions, however, notably in Belgium.

The element that would come in so few generations to wield so much power and influence in Western societies, therefore, had to be formed out of those individuals who defied convention and attempted to make money, often enough succeeding, in ways for which there was no definite precedent. They came from all classes of the earlier society: merchants, of course, but also farmers and artisans who had built up a small capital or could borrow it from a moneylender, or who were of an inventive mind; some were adventuresome aristocrats, some government officials, along with the occasional weavers or smiths who were attracted by the possibilities of machine power in their trade; there were even a considerable number of landless sons of the soil (J.-F. Bergier in Cipolla 1976, 3:397–451).

If they were successful, they became employers, now no longer of a few journeymen in a small shop where the master worked alongside and trained his workers, but employers of workers who differed from earlier wage earners in ways that no one really articulated for some time, least of all the workers themselves. (If they failed, they joined the mass of the poor seeking work from another entrepreneur.) There remained a demand for skilled artisans, handicraft workers, but the skills needed were often different and new. As the handworker saw one after another of the old crafts disappear, it seemed as if soon there would be only two classes left in manufacture, the owners or capitalists with their aides-de-camp and the interchangeable atomized heap of men, women, and children who worked in their mills. (This was not, however, the long-term outcome of industrialization.)

One sign of this change was the worker's passbook, or *livret*. Since 1791, associations of workers had been forbidden in France by the Loi Le Chapelier, an unfortunately archetypical product of bourgeois influence on the French Revolution (Soboul 1976, 3/1:12; Pierrard 1984, 23). Following the Napoleonic Code of 1804, every worker had to present this *livret* to the employer. When the worker left or was discharged, the employer was expected to enter salient characteristics, commendatory or other, in the passbook, which then had to be presented to any other employer or prospective employer. The power this gave any "master" over any worker can be imagined, as well as conferring a class privilege, the very target of the Revolution when it was aimed against the nobility, the church and the monarchy, upon the class of "masters" (including capitalists) over the class of workers. This remained in effect, by the way, until 1868 in France and in Belgium until 1883!

In retrospect it is clear that the early factory workers had the worst of both the old agrarian and the new industrial order. They lived in the miserable and crowded conditions of the poor on the land, except in larger and still unhealthier urban conglomerations or mill towns. Their sustenance was likewise dependent on uncontrollable circumstances, now not so much rain and shine as market conditions. That actual famine conditions were becoming a thing of the past in Europe was no consolation, for who could tell that at the time? When the industrial laborers were employed, they drudged as hard as any farm family at peak output (planting or harvest), but there was no diversity, no slack time for the factory worker, except uncompensated unemployment.

Under the pitiless conditions of the twelve- or fourteen-hour working day, the factory worker was yoked not to beasts of burden but to power-driven machines with their unrelenting and unvarying pace. The same machines that multiplied the productivity of human labor and hence led to a vast increase of wealth, of usable goods and services, were generally exploited one-sidedly for the benefit of the capitalists and their customers. Only by exception, when workers just could not be hired otherwise, were there phases in the first half of the nineteenth century during which wages would be offered above the minimum needed for the basic physical necessities of a short and brutish life.

What industrialization and Adam Smith's division of labor did *for* the masses of the population was allow them to increase. Increase they did, continuing and even speeding up the rate of increase that had spurted ahead before industrialization took off. What industrialization did not do until much later, under pressure from a tardy awareness of the manifest injustices to which labor was prone, was improve the standard of living of the vast majority of the population. However, it must be noted that there was no sharp increase of poverty on account of industrialization. Extreme poverty and Malthusian conditions had long been the rule for many, and the situation was getting worse with increasing populations in many parts of Europe. The regions and countries that failed to industrialize were the ones where this age-old poverty hung on the longest. Not industrialization, therefore, but backwardness has been the reason for the worst poverty of nineteenth- and twentieth-century Europe (Fischer 1972, Abel 1974).

This must be seen together with the particular "brutalization" that the factory worker underwent, comparable only to the conditions of some mines or particularly outrageous treatment of serfs in earlier centuries. Even piecework weavers and lacemakers could take a day off in some circumstances, although in this "iron age" (Michelet, see Pierrard 1984, 49) many could not *afford* to do so if, for instance, they lived in rented quarters: if they did not keep at their work all day every day, they would soon go hungry or be evicted. The typical worst case of this brutalization by factory work was that of the women and children, especially the girls, who all worked, as their mothers had done in the countryside, but now in conditions that hardly bear describing. These conditions are accepted as fact even by historians with no anti-capitalistic axe to grind.

In Lille, one of the industrial concentrations in the extreme north of France, there were twelve thousand women and girls working in the cotton and linen spinning mills at mid-century, as many women as men.

Leaving home at five in the morning and not getting home until eight in the evening, six days a week, earning half the male workers' wage (one and a half instead of three francs per day), laboring at menial but tiresome jobs like flailing, sorting, carding, combing, bundling and tying, constantly at risk of accidents (which were frequent where machines were crowded against each other), solicited by bosses or foremen stimulated by the hot and humid atmosphere needed for working linen and by the resultant state of half-undress of the women workers, these "factory girls" were usually not up to their other tasks as home-makers and mothers.... One of the early industrial inspectors wrote in 1857: "If a women is to raise children properly, she needs some education herself. Does she get it by spending thirteen hours a day in the factory? Too often, before marriageable age, her heart is soured, because the little girls who start factory work at the age of eight, grow even bolder, coarser and wilder than the boys." (Pierrard 1984, 49–50)

In regard to marriage, the previous social strictures that had prevailed in many rural areas against marrying without land and against having children without marrying fell away with no replacement. Indeed, even on the land such customs had been weakened or abandoned since the French Revolution. On the other hand, the French, as the first, started to learn and use methods of birth control to limit the size of their families about the same time. Since no one in the workers' quarter owned any property to speak of, and since one could hope to raise a child or two on the wages of the family members if work was available, the marriage rate rose and even the birth rate rose temporarily or held steady in the cities, where it had always been lower than in the country.

Infant mortality, the main factor in holding population growth back, came down in such poverty settings only with a distinct lag as compared with infant mortality rates as a whole, which began to sink in some populations in the first half of the nineteenth century and went down more steeply in the second half of the nineteenth and the first half of the twentieth century.

Between them both, then, the industrial bourgeoisie and the new working class gave rise to centers of factory and industrial labor, the first generation of those conurbations that industrialization brings in its wake. Like Manchester and Birmingham, the continental cities of Lille, Tourcoing, Roubaix (all in the Département du Nord), Ghent and Liège and the coal-and-iron "Centre" of Belgium, later Zurich, the Ruhr cities in the Rhineland, and Turin in Italy were mostly fairly small towns until coal and iron became the economically decisive natural resources. Some capitals and financial centers grew enormously also, Paris and Berlin notably absorbing a great deal of industry of the new types (cotton, iron, steel, then railroad-connected employment). Other older cities, such as Brussels and Antwerp (to which one could add Mechlin and Leuven in Belgium), grew principally in what is called the tertiary sector, that is, neither directly agricultural nor industrial production, but marketing, transportation, finance, insurance, courts, government, education, and the like.

In the conduct of public affairs, the bourgeoisie made its voices heard more loudly after 1830, but the workers were expected to remain silent and let men of property run things. After all, the argument ran, the lower classes were incapable of forming independent judgments on matters of public welfare and hence were at the mercy of agitators who appealed to their emotions. It was thought appropriate for them to spend virtually all their waking hours at work — otherwise they would merely spend their time, and hence the money that they needed for food, rent, and clothing, in taverns.

It was, of course, the case that both the education and the drinking habits of the mill worker in the early generations of industrialization were very unsatisfactory, the one appropriate perhaps to a stable authoritarian and agrarian setting, the other self-destructive in many cases, "an opiate for the people," as Marx said of religious practices. But frequenting of taverns was also, as some bourgeois more or less clearly recognized, a form of association that could prove dangerous for the status quo so recently achieved. The pressures for a better ed-

ucation, for some schooling at least, for every child, gradually built
up throughout the century. In Western Europe, only Belgium failed
to introduce universal compulsory schooling even by the end of the
century. The anti-tavern campaigns of the churches and certain bourgeois circles who recognized in the tavern culture a dangerous rival
not only to the churches but also to the existing order had their effect. But a sober and responsible working class would not stand to
be treated in demeaning ways, even less so than a drunken and unruly one. The "labor question" or "social question" became more and
more pressing and no one knew how it was to be solved.

Falling birth rates caught up a few decades later with falling mortality rates, especially in Western Europe and hence in the Catholic
populations of Belgium and France. What should also be noticed
is that falling wages in the first half of the nineteenth century were
relieved, again after a certain lag, by falling prices. Textiles, food (especially after the entry of American wheat on the European market
in the 1880s), and manufactured goods for mass consumption began
to come into range for the industrial laborers who made them. Productivity outstripped population growth in the nineteenth century as
a whole. But before these benefits of industrialization would become
evident, a couple of chapters of Catholic response to industrialization
had already been played out.

Alternatives for Catholics in View of Early Industrial Society

The responses on the part of Catholicism to these enormous changes
were spread out over a spectrum of possibilities. They were affected
and complicated by any number of historical factors and conditions.
What were their actual possibilities in the historical setting of the
early nineteenth century?

The Revolution of 1789 to 1813–15 was not just a French affair but affected practically the whole Catholic world and beyond. All
the governments under which Catholic populations lived were overthrown, reformed, or brought into alliances for or against France.
Just to list the headings of the most salient and central vicissitudes
that the church suffered in its most traditional homelands might be
eye-opening (Aubert in Jedin 1980, 7:3–84). In France, of course,
the initial overtures of bourgeoisie and clergy to each other came
to grief by stages in the first years of the Revolution (McManners
1969); a "Constitutional" or national church was set up, resulting in
a nasty split between those who went along with this measure and
those who resisted, with the support of the pope and the emigré bishops; church property of all kinds was "nationalized" or confiscated

and sold at bargain prices to finance the expenses of government; a staunchly Catholic and royalist revolt broke out in the Vendée; efforts were made to supplant Christianity entirely with a philosophical religion; some areas were more or less permanently dechristianized; the Terror brought bloody persecution to church institutions and their personnel.

Only Napoleon's decision to instrumentalize the church with the help of the new pope secured Catholicism a place in the life of the nation, but that place hardly resembled the place enjoyed by the Gallican church before the Revolution, except in some of its negative (subservient, state-church) aspects. The concordat of 1801, which governed church-state relations in France for the rest of the century, with the organic articles that Napoleon attached to it unilaterally, was a remarriage of throne and altar meant to be one of strictly unequal partners.

Revolutionary France invaded other countries. Napoleon's military and dictator's genius spelled the end of the old order all over continental Europe. All the states ruled by abbots or bishops were secularized, the blow befalling the ecclesiastical princes of the Holy Roman Empire in 1801–3 through the treaty of Lunéville (R. Lill in Rauscher 1981, 1:19–28). Only the papal states were restored as a "state of the church," after they too had been suppressed as a consequence of Napoleon's Italian campaign. Not only did the overlordship of numerous rich monasteries disappear, but the temporal power of the prince-bishops of Liège, Trier, Cologne, Paderborn, Münster, Mainz, Worms, Speyer, Strasbourg, Constance, Würzburg, Salzburg, Bressanone, and Trent as well, all told sixty-six ecclesiastical dominions! Millions of Germans acquired new sovereigns.

Except in Bavaria and Austria, higher education, culture, and public administration were henceforth exclusively in the hands of Protestants. Politically and economically as well, the new Germany that arose from the secularization of church territories and the confiscation of church properties was much more one-sidedly Protestant than had ever been the case before. The Catholic clergy was subsidized by the state as partial compensation for all this, but as a whole Catholics counted for much less than before. For some decades they were hard pressed to maintain themselves even in the lower position in society to which they had been relegated in most German states (von Aretin 1970, 33–36; see also E. Alexander in J. N. Moody 1953, 341–65). The secularization of the bishoprics turned out to be a blessing, but it was a blessing in disguise.

The palette of possibilities open to Catholics concerned about faith and life after the Revolution could run from thoroughgoing acceptance of the new conditions, with a will to making the best of them, to total rejection. I leave aside the cases of uncritical jubilation over the changes (for examples see Maier 1969, 78–92), because such enthusiasm always had to do with the potentialities and never with the actual achieved realities, the promise rather than the fulfilment of the Revolution, and faded quickly. Within this broad spectrum of more or less critical minds, several thought-figures suggested themselves.

If, with Charles Davis (1982), one sees the basic stances in regard to nineteenth-century Western European society and culture as being the "radical," the "liberal," the "conservative," and the "reactionary," one has at least a starting place for further analysis. In view of the decrepitude of the old order and the less than self-evident superiority of the Revolution with its concomitants and consequences, a basic division took place between those who viewed tradition, the wisdom of the fathers, as a necessary prerequisite for coping with the world, versus those who regarded it and any appeal to the authority of the past as misguided, a bad habit from which humankind could and must free itself. The watchword of the liberals was emancipation from the traditional. The sociological absurdity of this position — denying the necessity and factuality of tradition as a social reality in all camps including one's own, it denied the condition of its own possibility — should not blind us to the fact that such an outlook lent power and passion to the campaigns of the new class of bourgeois who called themselves liberals and who stood behind the new order of things that was emerging from the shambles of the *ancien régime*.

Hence, in an effort at terminological clarity, I will term "liberal" these persons and causes that tend thus to reject tradition as a positive force in the evolution of society. This means that practically all Christian social movements, at least at the outset, must be called "conservative," since Christianity was the embodiment of the traditional. This is clearly a special determination of the meaning of the troublesome terms "liberal" and "conservative." It is grounded in the usage of the time, however, and it lends itself to a better understanding of where the various parties stood. In terms of value judgments, of course, it has little bearing on our contemporary American usage, which has its own more recent history.

There is an important further distinction to be drawn in regard to both liberalism and conservatism. On the side of those who profess to have no regard for tradition, one can be in favor of immediate revolutionary changes, if necessary by force, or one can rely on the power of individual human reason among those leading classes in which such a way of thinking has been developed by appropriate (logical, critical, emancipatory, scientific-empirical) training. It is only the latter who can be called liberals, while the former come more appropriately under the heading of "radicals." Bentham and Adam Smith were liberals, Tom Paine was a radical. During the French Revolution, Necker was a liberal, the Jacobins were radicals.

Just as important for our present purposes is the analogous distinction on the other side. Among traditionalists one finds not only conservatives of many stripes, but "reactionaries." One decisive difference between them is that conservatives recognized (to a greater or lesser degree and with a longer or shorter lag-time after events and developments had taken place) that the traditionary process essential to societal well-being had in fact brought about changes with the passage of time. Reactionaries, in contrast, are characterized by their refusal to admit that the changes that they hated were not to be reversed, that the time factor in the human condition, unrolling as it does in only one direction, often does not permit a restoration of a previous state of affairs, in this case the *ancien régime*.

Many who perhaps passed for conservatives were reactionaries in this sense. Similarly, those Christians of various confessions who went under the heading of "liberals" were almost without exception conservatives in the sense explained. Within the churches, there was of course a spectrum ranging from conservatives with a comparative openness for recent but well established developments to other less receptive conservatives exhibiting perhaps a tendency to reaction. François René de Chateaubriand (1768–1848) might be considered a conservative, and a rather wishy-washy one at that, even though he pursued an ultra (ultraroyalist) line in the Restoration, whereas Louis de Bonald (1754–1840), however intelligent and principled, was a thoroughgoing reactionary. De Bonald rejected root and branch all that the Revolution stood for.

Another characteristic of the Catholic movement in post-revolutionary Europe cuts across this typology, however. Although committed Catholics could hardly be liberals in the generally valid sense used here, they were more and more committed to the *freedom of the church* from its enshacklement and functionalization on the part of state authority. Insofar as secular liberalism also had to do with freedom and emancipation, there was an intensely problematical and potentially positive overlap of aims.

Pope Pius VII, who came to terms with Napoleon, and his secretary of state, Ercole Consalvi, for example, were conservatives. They were referred to as "politicals," or politicians, in contrast to the "zealots" who preferred another candidate, one who would be firmer in defense of the rights of the church against the state, in particular Napoleon's France. While it is probably true that these *zelanti* at the conclave of Venice in 1800 were reactionaries over against the whole drift of the previous century, their successors in the conclave of 1823 (which elected Leo XII, pope until 1829) continued to be so opposed to state control of church affairs as to begin to contemplate "the fact that the religious division of Europe and its post-revolutionary conditions no longer permitted the traditional solutions which might have been appropriate" in earlier centuries (Aubert in Jedin 1980, 7:97, see also 50–53, 90–100, and Chadwick 1981a, 483, 565).

They were gravitating, in other words, from reaction to conservatism. For the rest of the century, these were the poles between which most leading Catholic thinkers oscillated. However, the cause of the freedom of the church would develop into the issue that would call forth not only intransigent reaction and a variety of conservative responses but also permit approaches along the liberal lines. Here also, as we shall see, it was possible, indeed almost inevitable, that on occasion the extremes would meet.

Chapter 3

INITIAL CATHOLIC RESPONSES

At the height of Napoleon's European domination, even before industrialization was much of a factor on the continent, Adam Smith's teachings were intriguing the administrators and patriots of Prussia and the rest of Germany. At this point, in Dresden, the capital of Saxony, one of the new German kingdoms allied with Napoleon, a young literary light took it upon himself to examine political economy with the same sweep and verve as Adam Smith, but from a position determined by opposition to the French Revolution and its consequences. This work, *Elements of Statecraft* (1809), by Adam Heinrich Müller, was to be the starting point of much later conservative Christian analysis of the new economy.

The next responses fall already into the beginnings of social Catholicism. The figures of Alban de Villeneuve-Bargemont and some followers of Félicité de Lamennais emerge in France; in the 1830s and 1840s Edouard Ducpétiaux starts to work in Belgium, Franz von Baader in Bavaria, Joseph Görres and Franz Josef Buss along the Rhine, and Frédéric Ozanam, Armand de Melun, Maurice Maignen, and most notably Philippe Buchez in Paris. As with their contemporaries, the various "utopian" thinkers and propagandizers, the immediate results of their social efforts were not very tangible. Unlike Saint-Simon, Charles Fourier, or Robert Owen, however, social reform was not the *chief* preoccupation of these Catholic personages. The greater part of church people's active response to the needs of the age was either in the political defense of the freedom of the church or in the age-old works of mercy: direct succor for the poor and for those whose traditional livelihoods no longer supported them. This was done by reconstituting the charitable institutions of the church on a new basis, now that the old one had been swept away.

Adam Müller vs. Adam Smith

Elements of Statecraft arose as a series of lectures that Adam Müller
(1779–1829) gave in Dresden in 1808 and 1809 before interested
members of the court and the diplomatic corps; they were then published in Berlin. They did not come upon the world as a contribution
of Catholic thought, but as a product of Romanticism. Adam Müller's
conversion to Catholicism in 1805 was not generally known. His
sympathetic treatment of medieval and Roman Catholic institutions
evidently did not arouse much suspicion, since Protestant fellow Romantics such as Novalis also struck such tones and the wave of
Romantic conversions was not yet apparent — Müller's was one of
the earliest.

One gets the impression that Müller was offering his ideas to both
Austria and Prussia, but especially the latter, his homeland. Prussia
was in the midst of energetic reforms to bring about a much-needed
modernization in government, the military, education, and the political economy. Both of the leading German states were backward and
vulnerable, as the Napoleonic conquests and the contrast with Great
Britain seemed to demonstrate. There was no question of following
the despised French revolutionary model to power and prestige, but
something had to be done; the English example was avidly examined,
by none with greater interest and fascination than by Adam Müller.
And yet the English way of life could not simply be reduplicated in
Germany, with its different conditions and traditions.

In Berlin, the reforms that were being instituted "from above"
were often represented as being modern and liberal because of the
emancipation of peasants and because many old barriers to trade and
development were to be done away with, just as Adam Smith recommended. However, Adam Müller was not taken in. He saw the alliance
between liberal economic approaches and absolutistic political aims
that was taking place. He urged a more Burkean way, anti-absolutist
and more respectful of historically developed structures. His conservatism predated his Catholicism and even his Romanticism, since he
had read Edmund Burke's *Reflections on the French Revolution* by
the time he was twenty. It fixed his ideas on the Revolution and the
heritage of the Enlightenment for the rest of his life.

Opposition to absolute rule, whether by a king claiming legitimacy
or a totalitarian democracy on the French revolutionary model, was a
central element of Müller's conservatism. Therefore he urged an updating and revitalization of the estates and corporations of the *ancien
régime*, rather than their abolition (as in the Revolution) or further
weakening (as in the Prussian reforms, in the name of effective administration). Confronting Adam Smith's consistently individualistic

and free-trade approach, Adam Müller worked out a Romantic dialectic of freedom *and* constraint, rights *and* duties, agriculture and manufacture, trade and self-sufficiency, even war and peace!

The model was that of the basic human economic and political unit, the (farm) family. One person cannot create a successful economic enterprise. If only for the sake of its survival one needs at least man, wife, and children. In the interdependence of man and woman, of parents and children, is seen the basic pattern of human society. Müller placed this relational structure ahead of the comparatively derivative one of the market, where goods are exchanged (which Adam Smith made so much of in *Wealth of Nations*, book I, ch. ii). As such, it should be reflected at every level of the political economy. By contrast, the haphazard structure of the open market championed by liberals resembled nothing so much as an accidental spatial relationship of unrelated atoms, according to conservatives, including Adam Müller. The necessary difference-in-relation of persons' social functions and the concomitant structure of interdependence furnished the basic pattern of a political economy worthy of human beings.

The element of settled experience in a going society (age/culture/the past, the domain of "the clerisy," represented by the First Estate) must be able to hold its own as well as be challenged by the restless youthful spirit of traders and entrepreneurs with their search for new markets. He coined the phrase "human capital" (*geistiges Kapital*) and insisted that its accumulation in a country was just as important to its economic well-being as the accumulation of material capital. Similarly, in the predominantly agrarian economy that he knew, the vast majority of working people (the Third Estate) stood necessarily in a stable relationship to those who held the resources to work on (the Second Estate, the nobility). This relationship was neither accidental nor a matter of individual preferences, but was organic and basic to human welfare. Müller feared the commercialization of the agrarian economy. His political economics made the case for cautious modernization without abandoning feudal relationships. Hence he played up the different characteristics of property in land and commercial capital. He stressed the reflections in the economy of the archetypal biological relationships of male and female, parent and offspring.

Having originally wanted to create an all-encompassing idealistic system like F. W. J. Schelling's, on the dialectical principle of polar opposition, Müller delighted in relating the most disparate things to one another by opposition, by a *coincidentia oppositorum*. Although this brought him into discredit with the older generation of Enlightenment rationalists as well as with posterity (see Koehler 1980, an outstanding revisionist reading), he remained a source of inspiration to the critics of classical economics in German-speaking countries (Bowen,

IESS 10:522–23; also IESS 4:454–56), and made his way from there into Catholic socio-economic reflection also in France and Belgium later in the nineteenth and even into the twentieth century.

Of course, his rather fanciful (if internally consistent) "discovery" that modern society really should have four estates instead of the traditional three ran head on into the disinclination of the fourth group to be regarded as an estate at all. The bourgeois gave rise to economic *classes* in societies where they were dominant instead of functional-hereditary estates, and they were on their way toward realizing a class society, the hallmark of which would be not interdependence but antagonism between the classes (Gundlach 1964, 2:191–251, and StL, 5th ed. [1929], 3:383–92). That, at least, would be the view, not only of Marx, but before him of the forerunners of social Catholicism, Charles de Coux and F. X. Baader.

The Restoration

Müller wrote his *opus magnum* during Napoleon's hegemony. There followed upon his downfall the "Restoration," a reordering of the map and of the political spirit of Europe. Under Metternich's leadership, a Bourbon king was restored to the throne of France, the papal states were restored to Pope Pius VII, Prussia and Austria assumed the predominance in Central Europe. The map showed a certain reduction in the overextended borders of France and a number of further changes; but the Congress of Vienna confirmed rather than revoked the main changes that had taken place under Napoleon as affecting Catholic areas. The political spirit, however, was increasingly reactionary. Another revolution in 1830 ended the Bourbon rule and the Restoration in France and Belgium, whereas Metternich and like-minded legitimist or quasi-legitimist princes and ministers stayed in place in Central, Eastern, and Southern Europe until the next year of revolutions, 1848. In these circumstances, what is called "the Catholic movement" began to take shape, aiming for freedom of movement for the church and its self-administration, as against the tight oversight and control of its affairs by government agencies and courts. This was the case in Protestant countries, of course, but also in Catholic ones such as Austria and "liberal" ones such as post-1830 France. Church writers often repeated the refrain: whether the regime was royalist or bourgeois, restorationist or liberal, the state apparatus maintained the same close control and expected the same unquestioning support from the clergy as from other civil servants.

All the activists of the Catholic movement between 1815 and 1848 and beyond were concerned about the place of Catholicism in the new society, but most of them, most of the time, evinced little awareness of the epochal economic changes going on around them, upheavals that, in the long run, were to have much greater effects on the history of Christianity than the more obvious political changes, basic as they were: political rights, constitutions, parliamentary government, universal suffrage, democratic institutions. Should we call all these publicly engaged Catholics "social Catholics"? What is the meaning that the term "social" began to acquire in the 1820s and 1830s?

The Emergence of the Social Question

"Social," like "political," is used most broadly in contrast to "individual." Whatever has to do with groups of persons or the comprehensive grouping we call a nation or "the world," is properly referred to as "social." In this sense Catholicism is obviously a social tradition and praxis, not merely a religion of scattered individuals. Another sense of "social," however, more recent, is in contrast to the political. It is in this sense that the expression "the social question" came to be used in the nineteenth century. It has to do with the tensions between groups characteristic of advanced nineteenth-century societies: the difficulty of reconciling the interests of the new classes of industrial bourgeoisie and their clientele on the one side with those of industrial workers on the other. In this form, "the social question" had not existed previously. It was not just a matter of rich and poor, but of a newly dominant mode of production that, though highly efficient, redounded to the benefit of the few, as it seemed, and to the social and economic decline or exploitation of a great number.

"Social Catholicism" has to do, then, with Catholics who concerned themselves with this problem as central. Of course, not only the two new classes were affected by the economic and social changes of which they are at the center. The livelihood of other workers on the land or in the towns, of the middle classes as well as the large landowners all enter into the social question. But industrialization was the dynamic generator of the changes that all groups had to come to terms with. Hence, an increasing concentration on the dynamics of industrialization is a necessary element in the makeup of the *social* Catholic movement and of those to whom we accord a central place in our narrative.

More broadly, a certain degree of economic insight or at least alertness to new conditions distinguishes social Christianity from traditional charitable Christianity. It is not enough for our purposes, even though it be a nobler thing in itself, that a person spend her means and her life in service to the poor. This, as Jesus indicated, is possible in any age of the church's history. Christian charity was not any less necessary in the nineteenth century than before or since. Social Catholicism, on the other hand, had a beginning sometime after 1815. As Duroselle suggests (1951, 9), a necessary condition of social Catholicism is that one regard the misery of the working classes as a state of things that ought not to be and can be changed for the better. As we have seen, before industrialization, with its potential for previously undreamed of productivity, poverty was seen in general as an inevitable plight to be borne by those who were born poor or in other cases made poor by war, accident, or vice. As long as such notions held good within the mental world of a particular Catholic milieu as furnishing an adequate framework for understanding economic distress, one can say that no *social* Catholic awakening had yet occurred there. A particularly striking instance of crossing this threshold is found in the difference between two persons, each admirable in his and her own ways, Soeur Rosalie and Armand de Melun (see the next chapter).

Finally, it is quite possible to be a believing and "practicing" Catholic *and* a socially responsible citizen, while never perceiving any connection between the two roles. It is doubtful whether the activities of this kind of church member belong in a history of social Catholicism. This latter phenomenon was the concern of only a minority among Catholics, an important "elite," since the onset of industrialization.

Forerunners 1815–48: Conservatives, Liberals, and Democrats

At the beginning of the Restoration, leading Catholic thinkers, Romantics and traditionalists, threw their support behind the work of reconstruction of society under the new or newly restored monarchies. Adam Müller stayed in the Austrian consular service almost until his death in 1829, despite differences with Metternich. Another convert, Karl Ludwig von Haller (1768–1854), provided the ideological underpinnings for a counterrevolutionary regime and in the title of his major work also gave the period its name (*Die Restauration der Staatswissenschaften*, 6 vols., Winterthur 1816–26; see R. Lill in Jedin 1980, 7:219–20). With the opponents of the Revolution unambiguously enjoying the upper hand, the uncompromising "ultra" reaction of a Haller and a Louis de Bonald (Aubert in Jedin 1980, 7:88 and 230) seemed for a short while to be riding the wave of history.

Viscount de Bonald (1754–1840), in fact, became the oracle of French Catholic conservatism for the whole nineteenth century. Even more than Joseph de Maistre (1754–1821), Bonald with his philosophy of traditionalism and his counterrevolutionary political theory affected the thought of conservatives, favoring a reactionary trend (Aubert in Jedin 1980, 7:230, 250–51). On the economic front, he lashed out as early as 1796 at the growing modern cities: such gigantism lay more in the interests of bourgeois businessmen than of any humane ideals, which would include the moral and physical health of the working masses (Droulers 1975, 38; Cohen 1969). His son, Cardinal Louis de Bonald (1787–1870), would become archbishop of Lyon (1840). There he did not hesitate to condemn the greed that he saw sanctified by economic doctrine. A human being, he said, counts for "nothing more than a machine that works" (as cited by Droulers 1975, 40–41). "Can they not see how punishing the life of the factory worker is?" Although silk workers in Lyon had been the most restive in all of France during the 1830s, and the clergy had already been criticized for not preaching more strongly on the duty of maintaining order and quiet, he saw the responsibility for worker unrest as lying much more with the employers than with the workers. It is worth noting that the conviction of human dignity was not a liberal monopoly. The conservative spokesmen made much of it and obviously thought that their own proposals would safeguard it, whereas bourgeois individualism would be its downfall for all but the lucky few.

In the further evolution of Adam Müller one detects a clear shift from Romantic conservatism, a reform conservatism that attempted to relate modern freedoms and traditional order in creative tension, to out-and-out reaction, with the aim simply of returning to an earlier notion of group rights and duties and undoing the advances of individual freedoms (Grenner 1967, 201–5). This could lead to opposition to modern factory manufacturing as such (Stegmann 1969, 337). Henceforth an anti-industrial, almost Luddite, attitude could be found here and there among reactionary (as opposed to conservative) and Romantic Christian approaches to the social problem of the nineteenth century. It was not to become a dominant trait, however.

At the other end of the spectrum were the Catholic beneficiaries of the infant industries in textiles, iron and machine-tool manufacturing, mining, the first railroads, and banking. As mentioned previously, Catholic entrepreneurs were found almost exclusively in Belgium and in the north of France, mixed with Protestant and liberal industrialists, who seemed to be the only kind in other parts of early industrial Europe. These two extremes, one seeing in Manchesterism nothing but a scourge of humankind and the other uncritically endorsing the emerging capitalist order, contributed little or nothing to the emergence of social Catholicism, except negatively. The impulses for social reform emanated from those who were deeply disturbed by the "pauperism" of the time and who viewed the prevailing forces in society, in a modern way, as the product of change and as subject to further change.

Hence they proceeded to propose changes — reforms — in the prevailing social order. These tended to cluster around one of three emphases. The conservative emphasis was the most common, indeed, was for a long time a basic presupposition of the other two approaches as well. What was needed was a return to the social bonds that had held Christian society together for so long; only the church, only Christianity supported by political authority, could supply the effective motivation necessary to maintain such bonds. Conservative *social* Catholics — a minority, as were people in any grouping of this epoch who realized that they had a new social problem on their hands — recognized the special responsibility of the propertied classes in readjusting the social order for the benefit of the disadvantaged.

The "liberal" Catholic alternative was to take advantage of the means that, perhaps, lay hidden in the convulsions of the previous quarter century. They accepted certain changes that could not in fact be undone (and in this they showed their basically conservative outlook, in the sense explained before). Freedom and equality were not only natural but Christian values as well; they had taken root even in the consciousness of simple but authentic believers in their new form. There must be ways to realize them in accordance with the changed situation (the passing of the *ancien régime* and the bankruptcy of its attempted restoration). What "liberal Catholics" of the social-reform persuasion (for there were also liberal Catholics, like Montalembert, who were on the whole hostile to social reforms) were after, therefore, was often in the end a new and different replacement for, rather than a repristination of, the social relations of the past. This option appeared to many as an attempt to mix oil and water; in fact, "liberal" Catholics never had more than a precarious foothold in the church in the nineteenth century. Their rehabilitation had to wait until after World War II and the breakthrough of Christian democratic parties in Western Europe.

Finally, there was an option that grew out of the early socialism of the pre-1848 period, among some of the pioneer thinkers whom Marx called the utopian socialists. By placing great emphasis on equality and fraternity, along with the thus far disappointing liberty that the Revolution of 1789 had led to, and by showing how these ideals corresponded to something deep in the bosom of Christ's gospel, one could and did arrive at a "Christian democratic" vision of the world of work. This too was a distinct form of social Catholicism for a brief period around 1848; then it was swept away in one of the periodic red scares that have punctuated the history of the labor movement, only to re-emerge at the end of the century. But this alternative, connected particularly with the name of Philippe Buchez, also deserves a treatment of its own.

These differences were perceived, sometimes with more heat than light, by the historical actors and their contemporaries. Two things, however, were pervasive in all currents of early or nascent social Catholicism. One was the call for reforms that for them followed naturally on the discovery or description of intolerable conditions ("pauperism," proletarian misery) — this belongs, as we have seen, to the very definition of social Christianity or Catholicism in the sense intended here. The other was the conviction that without the church (or the churches), without a leading role in society for Christianity, no reforms would ever succeed in healing society's ills, not even the manifestly secular ills of great wealth and extreme poverty side by side. Villeneuve-Bargemont expressed it once in the following classic formulation, speaking of "the great principle of charity." "Christian love alone, put into action in politics, in laws, institutions and day-to-day practice, can preserve the social order from the frightening dangers that it faces" (Duroselle 1951, 220).

This was a conservative conviction, as I just stated. In an "enlightened," cynical form, it was shared even by conservatives who themselves remained far from the Christianity. For believing, socially conscious Christians, on the other hand, it was an axiom of belief even apart from a Burkean conservative outlook on society. With greater emphasis on the liberation of the working classes, who were not to be treated as the object of charity but as the subject of rights and duties, even Philippe Buchez among the Christian socialists shared a variation of this conviction.

Given this common bond, it will be no surprise to hear Catholic socialists as well as conservatives proclaim that it is necessary for industrial societies as a whole to turn to Christianity as the only salvation for civilized life on earth. In the meantime we have learned that dangerous confusions may lurk in such earnest statements. Religious liberty, for instance, poses insuperable problems to any thoroughgoing "Christian society." The ideal has had so great an attraction, however, that it has accompanied social Catholicism from its birth at least down to Jacques Maritain's "New Christendom" (*Integral Humanism*, 1936) on the eve and in the aftermath of World War II. Before 1848, in any case, especially in France, many social reformers were more or less conspicuously inspired by the figure of Jesus and by his gospel of love and equality. The distance that would open up between conservative ecclesiastical efforts and the labor movement could still be bridged until about 1850 in view of the respect that the gospel still enjoyed far beyond churchly circles.

L'Avenir and Charles de Coux

Charles de Coux (1787–1864) had spent his childhood in America and traveled widely before settling down in Paris in 1823 (Duroselle 1951, 40–59; letter of de Coux to Lamennais, 8 February 1830, in the latter's *Correspondance générale*, 4:627–30). This background helped to make him a liberal Catholic, with the accent on Catholic. Like so many other French during the Revolution, in the emigration or at home, de Coux discovered the societal benefits of Catholicism by contrast with the disasters of its foe, the Revolution, and developed into a fervent believer. The initial impetus, however (as he retold it later), was a peculiarly economic-social concern. Malthus made so much sense to him as a young man that he looked to Catholicism as the only tradition with the potential for spreading a spirit of restraint among the masses, so as effectively to forestall recurring impoverishment and famines.

At any rate, he continued his economic investigations persistently enough so that he was ready, in 1830, to offer his reflections to the abbé de Lamennais for publication in the short-lived but famous *L'Avenir* (16 October 1830 to 15 November 1831; on *L'Avenir* see Aubert in Jedin 1980, 7:271–92). On the strength of that he was appointed professor of political economy in the new university of Louvain in Belgium in 1834. In 1845 he left Louvain to become editor of *L'Univers* under Louis Veuillot. Finding the *Ere nouvelle* more congenial in 1848, he also left the *Ere nouvelle* before very long and was not heard of much thereafter. It is known that he founded a conference of the Saint Vincent de Paul Society in Guérande, where he died in 1864. His articles for *L'Avenir* ("The Future") are the first clear manifestation of social Catholicism in France.

His socio-economic analysis started from a common-sense insight that had struck him even before he read Adam Smith, that all the propertyless worker has to offer in the marketplace is his manual labor. The immeasurable misery of the lower classes, after the liberal reforms in Europe put an end to the feudal system, arose in his view from overpopulation, which by the law of supply and demand (de Coux acknowledged such an economic law) meant an oversupply of labor; this in turn pushed the wages of workers down to the subsistence level. A second factor was the abolition of the corporations of the *ancien régime*. They were supposed to exercise a controlling effect on the supply of labor admitted to the market and hence to raise its price, while constraints on marriage and the celibacy of a fair part of the population kept Malthusian developments at bay. To fill out the picture, he alluded also to the prevailing penal code, dating from the Revolution, which forbade any collusion among workers such as agreeing not to accept work below a certain level of pay. "After the right of freedom of conscience, the most inviolable right is the freedom of labor, and yet, although the penal code does not explicitly deny it to the laborer, it hinders him from taking advantage of it. Workers may neither come together in associations, nor make agreements among themselves, nor walk out [on strike] in the face of the demands of capitalism, without making themselves liable to prison" (cited in Duroselle 1951, 43).

The factory system of industrial production was not yet dominant in France, but Charles de Coux was acquainted with it and with the price it exacted from laborers. While not against machinery, he had no love for "industrialism," as he called it, which perverted the relations between employers (*patrons*) and workers. All the capitalist would see in the laborer was a cost that one must keep as low as possible so as to prosper or at least stay in business.

What was to be done? Here de Coux had only one solution, a "liberal" or populist one consonant with the prophetic spirit blowing so powerfully through the pages of *L'Avenir* in those months after the July Revolution. He noted: "The democratic tendency of Catholicism in the countries where the poorer classes are threatened with imminent misery is assuredly the most remarkable phenomenon of our age" (*L'Avenir*, 21 April 1831). And he proposed the basic mechanism to which this was pointing (*L'Avenir*, 3 April 1831): "Give the worker the right to vote and this undercover warfare that drains our economy will end by itself." The proletarian will always have something to give or withhold independent of the industrialists' conditions — his vote. The industrial bourgeoisie "will need to assure itself not only of the worker's labor, but also of his friendship, in order to carry some weight in public matters."

"Who is against the political freedom of the masses everywhere?" he asked in *L'Avenir* of 21 April 1831 (Duroselle 1951, 42). "The great barons of industrialism! These men fix the level of wages as they please and presume, in place of the bridle of religious beliefs, to hold forth the threat of an individual famine, so to speak, that would instantly descend upon any proletarian dismissed from their workshops. Already the industrial system is producing its bitterest fruits."

De Coux noted the desirability of workers' coalitions (Duroselle 1951, 43) but failed to emphasize the small, painstaking steps that would prove necessary for any real progress in the matter: practical, dogged organizational work and all the rest that a contemporary of ours has called "the long march through the institutions." Instead he proposed one spectacular and perhaps premature move — universal (male) suffrage — that would cut the Gordian knot.

All the same, this was an altogether new departure for Catholic social thought. To focus on the exploitation of class by class inherent in early industrial capitalism, and to do so without simply postulating a return to an earlier form of social and economic development, was the merit of de Coux's pioneering and hardhitting articles. His élan seems then to have been broken by the failure of any populist breakthrough to take place after the July 1830 Revolution and perhaps particularly by *Mirari vos*, the papal condemnation in 1832 of the freedoms espoused by *L'Avenir*. His importance is thus that of a forerunner and of one of those who influenced Frédéric Ozanam, an energizer of the next generation. His ideas, like those of the earliest socialist and conservative critics of industrialism (such as Franz Baader, Adam Müller, Léonard Simonde de Sismondi, and Alban de Villeneuve-Bargemont), are the first expressions of a theme that will be repeated and refined for a century and more: the charge of exploitation of the working class by that other new class, their industrialist employers.

Forerunners in Southern Germany

An avid reader of *L'Avenir* in Munich was the previously mentioned Franz von Baader (1765–1841; see Stegmann 1969 and Grassl 1975). In 1835 he wrote a tract to awaken his contemporaries to the trouble brewing for society in "the present poor relationship of the propertyless or the proletariat to the propertied classes of society," as he entitled his appeal. No legitimist, but a conservative, he analyzed the industrial system and the "moneyed interests" that formed the top of a societal pyramid as resting on the labor of proletarian masses. Liberal freedoms were of no use to them as long as they had no say whatsoever in society and were in fact not really citizens. They must be integrated into the structures of society with the assistance of priests who could articulate their needs and point of view.

This role of social advocacy of priests for classes that were excluded from participation resembles that adumbrated in the pages of *L'Avenir* of 30 June 1831: priests, who in the new society would not be dependent upon the powers that be, could be trusted to serve as connecting links "between the two parties that must come together, the rich who offer land and money to the common fund and the poor who can only contribute their labor" (cited from Gurian 1929, 139, who attributes the article to Lamennais; Duroselle 1951, 57–58 suggests that it is by the abbé Philippe Gerbet, Lamennais's longtime journalistic and priestly colleague and future bishop of Perpignan).

Baader's reputation among Catholics suffered after his death from suspicions that he was not an altogether reliable Catholic thinker, especially because he was not papal enough. However, he has been rediscovered in this century and is now seen as the first Catholic known to have busied himself seriously with economic thought and particularly with the work of Adam Smith (see Grenner 1967, 141–74, and the literature cited there, 141–44). This took place during Baader's sojourn in England and Scotland from 1792 to 1796. He was there in pursuit of a second career, after finding the practice of medicine not to his liking and the writing of philosophy insufficiently remunerative. This second career was the scientific study of mining and mineral products for the ducal Bavarian mines. While in Britain, he not only observed the working conditions in the mines, which Smith himself criticized, but fell in with William Godwin and Mary Wollstonecraft. From this encounter dated the social component in his thinking.

The first documentary record of Baader's objections to Adam Smith is contained in his personal notes and diaries from the 1790s. In various obscure publications from 1801 to 1804, however, he published elements of a critique of Smith's political economy, starting from "the falsehood of the proposition that the common advantage is best promoted by letting each private person look after only his own self-interest" (Grassl 1975, 279). This was therefore a decade before Adam Müller and forty years before Friedrich List, as Grassl exclaims. But then he lapsed into silence on the subject until his notes on countering pauperism in the Bavarian domains in 1832. His British experience was of lasting importance, causing him, as it did, to appreciate the seriousness of the problems that Bavaria too would have to face in time.

Another German Catholic layman, Franz Josef Buss (1803–78), much influenced by French writings (Dorneich 1979, 55–60; Lange 1955; Oelinger 1982) as well as by Friedrich von Schlegel, devoted his one major speech in his first term as elected representative in the assembly of Baden to the problems associated with industrialization — his oft-noted *Fabrikrede* of 1837 (*Fabrik* = factory), the first on such a topic in any German parliament. Neither the government nor the opposition having taken a position on these matters as yet, Buss spoke as an individual legislator. He asked for instance for legislation limiting the workday of factory workers to fourteen hours, with some schooling to be insisted upon for children in the factories. But the problems were not yet pressing or widespread in Baden and the issue was dropped. Buss, it may be noted, was from an extremely modest village background and found his way into the middle class through academics, by becoming a professor of law.

In the Rhineland, Joseph Görres (1776–1848), a flaming liberal from the time of the wars of liberation from Napoleon — he founded the first *Rheinische Merkur* of 1814–16 — and a practicing Catholic from 1821 on, had already started an effective charity organization for those suffering in the hinterland of Coblenz from the disastrous harvest of 1816. Not being government supported, it was a new type of church-related organization (Gatz 1982; Raab 1978; Morsey 1979). It was not a confraternity or any other kind of canonical foundation, either; like any club or association, it required the permission of the civil authorities to exist. It only became unofficially Catholic in its later development, in that Coblenz was in a Catholic region and the officers of the charitable association brought in Catholic Sisters of Mercy to staff the institutions it set up, such as an orphanage and hospital (Gatz 1982, 315–16). Görres was to become the catalyzer of Catholic power in what could be called a civil rights movement for Catholics in Prussia between 1837 and 1848. He represents a group of contemporaries who, in their radical Romantic youth, occasionally caught glimpses of what the misery of the masses would mean to the future of society in Europe, but who after 1815 or 1830 got absorbed in the prior need to free Catholics from second-class citizenship and free the clergy from the smothering embrace of state control.

What continued to characterize the German situation until at least 1848, then, was the priority for Catholics of the church-state question. Baader's influence waned quickly for several reasons. His Romantic style of thinking was going out of fashion; he took up Mennaisian ideas critical of the reaction that set in especially in the papacy of Gregory XVI, and he died in 1841. Görres and Buss turned their efforts to releasing the Catholic Church from the restrictive embrace of the governments in Prussia and Baden. Factory-type manufacturing, as already indicated, would not become a major feature of the German social landscape until the second half of the century, anyway. So it was that, with the partial exception of Peter Reichensperger (see below, chapter 4) and his 1847 book on the political economy, it would take the Revolution of 1848 to direct the attention of German Catholics in the persons of Adolf Kolping and Wilhelm Emmanuel von Ketteler to the demoralization of artisans and the pauperization of the working class as a social and not just a charitable problem.

Belgium

In Belgium, some French-speaking areas were at least as advanced as the industrializing areas of France; by 1830 steam engines were widely used in the coal mines; in one region (the Borinage), for example, coal was brought out of only fifty-five pits by horse power, while steam power was in use in eighty-two pits. Productivity shot up accordingly in the years between 1806 and 1846. In both Liège and Charleroi entrepreneurs expanded iron works and switched over to the new process using coke blast furnaces (Cipolla 1976, 331–41; Milward and Saul 1973, 437–44; Landes 1969, 124–92; Kossmann 1978, 134–37, 176–78, 203–4). Belgian workers seem to have had even less education than in other industrializing countries; at any rate, they put up with degrading conditions with still greater resignation and less protest than their counterparts in France or England.

There was accordingly less attention paid to their plight. It was not clear for a long time that the unemployment and pauperization, if it was even acknowledged, was anything new, or that a virtuous and thrifty way of life in combination with charity for deserving cases would no longer be equal to the demands of Christian morality. Belgian liberal Catholicism was celebrated. Influential "liberal" Catholics had supported the compromise between secular liberals and the Catholic Church in 1828–30, led to the formation of a Belgium independent of the Netherlands in the course of the revolutions of 1830. Among them were a few who did take the economic plight of the lower classes seriously and begin to suggest causes and remedies. Edouard Ducpétiaux (1804–68) would try his best for over thirty years to place the social problem before his peers in the Belgian upper classes (Vidler 1964, 83–86, and Rezsohazy 1958, 10–21).

What he could do, given his times and his proclivities, was a function of his position from 1831 to 1861 as Belgian inspector general of prisons and charitable institutions. He had the authority not to reform or to finance, but to investigate and report, and that is what he did. Beyond his official reports, he started to publish well-documented, sober exposés in 1843 with two volumes "on the physical and moral condition of young workers and the means to ameliorate it" (Rezsohazy 1958, xxix), followed by *Le paupérisme en Belgique* (Brussels, 1844) and other studies still useful as primary sources for the actual living and working conditions of the Belgian working class. After he retired from his office, he became more active in politics. We shall meet him again, trying to inject a social element into the policies of the Catholic party in Belgium while establishing contacts with other concerned circles in Western Europe.

Another Catholic, this one a convert and journalist, had been banished from the Netherlands to France (where he also wrote for *L'Avenir* for a short time before joining the revolution of 1830 in Belgium). This was Adolphe Bartels (1802–62; Rezsohazy 1958, 34–40). In 1842, eager to spread the gospel of French early socialist thought, he published his *Essai sur l'organisation du travail* (a favorite theme of Charles Fourier and Philippe Buchez among others, popularized by Louis Blanc in 1839); from 1844 to 1846 he conducted *Le Débat social,* one of the earliest socialist papers in Belgium (Droz 1972b, 1:535). A weekly, it carried reports and views of all the various socialist schools of its period. (When Karl Marx, no household word as yet, came to Brussels, he called Bartels a "theocrat" [Rezsohazy 1958, 44].) In the period of conservative hegemony after 1848, Bartels slips from the scene, but not, apparently, into the socialist underground. Unlike François Huet, a philosopher and another French-Belgian Christian social visionary, Bartels remained a Catholic until his death.

In Belgium, the compromise or "Union" of the liberals and the Catholics allowed the church to maintain a leading position in education, state schools running a poor second. Whether as a consequence of this or not, there was relatively less progress toward anything like compulsory universal primary education here than in neighboring countries (Kossmann 1978, 200). The children of the new industrial working class were the most disadvantaged. Other undertakings in favor of the working class on the part of the church, beyond almsgiving, also seem to have been extraordinarily slow in coming. Parallels to the *oeuvres* in France (which we will come to presently) appear only after a gap of time, even though industrialization started at the same time as in France and developed faster. Thus the Archconfraternity of St. Francis Xavier was not founded until 1854 in Brussels, whereas its Parisian predecessor had been active already before the 1848 revolution.

Alban de Villeneuve-Bargemont

With the name of this organization, typical as it was of the first large-scale efforts made by Catholics to come to grips with industrialization, we return to conservative social Catholicism. The soil in which it developed was fertilized, just as it was in the case of their "liberal" and socialist coreligionists, by the Christian conviction that charity on behalf of the unfortunate is a duty in some practical sense. If it was necessary to move beyond traditional notions of charity and charitable activity (almsgiving and institutions for the care of the poor) and also pose the question of social justice before one could claim to have a realistic nineteenth-century social consciousness, nevertheless obligations in charity remained a necessary component of all Catholic reflection and motivation, given the daunting quality and quantity of impoverishment in the not-yet industrialized world. To the working class, of course, "charity" increasingly became a red flag, as if they did not earn their living by their labor but had to be eternally grateful to *hommes charitables* and ladies bountiful of the upper classes who distributed food baskets. Some interpreted the whole apparatus of poor relief and charitable organizations simply as society's skin-flinted way of keeping a supply of workers alive so as to be hired when they were needed — at depressed rates of pay. The large element of truth that such interpretations may contain should not prevent us from recognizing that the charitable impulse was often religiously inspired and was also, in the cases we shall examine, directed to the defense and support of human rights rather than to their restriction.

As for the *conservative* French Catholics, there was one personage who was, as Duroselle says (1951, 70), the true initiator of social Catholicism. This was the French nobleman viscount Alban de Villeneuve-Bargemont (1784–1850, see Vidler 1964, 28; Duroselle 1951, 59–71; Bruhat 1972, 377–78; Ring 1935). From 1828 to 1830 he was royal administrator (prefect) of the Département du Nord. As would Ducpétiaux, he took the trouble to inform himself on the realities of life of which the upper classes as a whole took no notice. Then, unseated by the change of sovereigns in 1830, he studied all the economic literature available at that time: Adam Smith, Malthus, Jean-Baptiste Say, Simonde de Sismondi. Writing his *Traité d'économie politique chrétienne* (1834), he contrasted the English and the French economies, as Adam Müller had contrasted the English and the middle European. The French, he counseled, should keep more of its population occupied on the land (which in fact is what happened), rather than going in one-sidedly for urban industry. What one should strive for is a synthesis of English efficiency and a Christian sense of mutual responsibility. Otherwise violence and class warfare would erupt (Duroselle 1951, 63).

Villeneuve-Bargemont analyzed the pauperism of the Nord and of Britain as something new, a by-product of an industrialization that attracts workers from the land and then puts them to work only intermittently and at subsistence-level wages. Hence he ushered in the whole development of the conservative critique of industrialism, as de Coux had done for liberal Catholics, and as Buchez undertook with more persistence for the out-and-out republicans. It is true that Simonde de Sismondi (1773–1842) had hazarded the view already in 1819 that "modern society lives at the expense of the proletariat" (Bruhat 1972, 335). But Sismondi could see no alternative except a return to an agrarian economy. Villeneuve-Bargemont also suggested farm colonies for the excess working population. But he saw a role for the state in alleviating economic distress, unlike the mainstream liberal economists (Bruhat 1972, 377). And he pointed to the necessity for involving the working population in the conduct of their own economic activity, at least to the extent of changing the laws to en-

courage mutual aid societies and something like credit unions run by
workers (Duroselle 1951, 68). Thus timidly he raised for the first time
the issue of the emancipation, the *participation* of the lower classes in
self-administered *associations*, in a search for suitable modern sub-
stitutes for the autonomous corporations of tradesmen in the *ancien
régime.*

Hence also his emphasis on elementary, moral, and religious education for all strata of the population. Left in the condition of their
peasant and serf forebears, workers would not be capable of taking their place in the Christian political economy that he presented.
Only a virtuous and self-denying populace of workers would overcome the scourge of pauperism. Thrift on the part of the poor and
generosity on the part of the well-to-do remained basic remedies in
Villeneuve-Bargemont's view for society's modern ills.

Philippe Buchez

The third stream of French social Catholicism, the social democratic
one that went by the name of "Christian democracy" in 1848, stems
mainly from Philippe Buchez (1796–1865; see Vidler 1964, 13; Duroselle 1951, 80–120; Maier 1969, 201–17; and Bruhat 1972, 381–82).
This son of a Parisian duty collector later worked for a while at the
same job as his father. As a twenty-year-old student, he was disgusted
enough with the Restoration to organize a French branch of the Car-
bonari, a secret (and revolutionary) society. Disappointed in turn with
that, he read Saint-Simon's *Nouveau Christianisme* and joined that
movement, but soon, in 1829, he found the Saint-Simonian disciples perpetrating pantheistic nonsense. This was when he came to
what would be a turning point that would admit of further stages
but no further reversals: he readopted the Catholicism of his childhood. Ten years later, after conscientious examination and study, he
was firmly persuaded of Catholic dogma in its entirety. He would not
take the step of actually participating in the sacramental life of the
church, however, as he explained to Henri Lacordaire, who wanted
him to become a Dominican (Duroselle 1951, 84). For in his situation that would be tantamount to selling out on his companions: the
republicans, the workers, the little people — about whom the church
hierarchy cared hardly at all, as he read the situation.

At the same time that he rediscovered Catholicism, he also discovered what was for him the true character of the French Revolution.
In prefaces to a monumental parliamentary history of the Revolution
(1834–38; see esp. Maier 1969, 201–17), he set forth his interpretation
of it as a product of Christianity. The church, as another socialist said,

if it had not completely hidden the light of the gospel under a bushel, had in no wise caused it to shine out in all its brightness. Nevertheless, the gospel of the poor Christ had supported the hopes of the suffering and burst forth in the Revolution as the message of liberty, equality, and fraternity. The true goals of the Revolution remained to be realized: a democratic republican socialist society of Christian inspiration. Neither the restoration of the monarchy, even in constitutional form, nor the liberal bourgeois regime of Louis Philippe that followed from 1830 to 1848, could be considered the *terminus ad quem* of human progress. That goal was the free association of all humankind as brothers and sisters under God, and there were steps to be taken in its direction that the misery of the majority made urgently compelling.

Like the other socialist thinkers in France up to 1848, Buchez was from Marx's point of view a "utopian." They can certainly be designated as Romantics in the sense in which the greatest of the artists and writers of the period (which lagged behind Germany's Romantic era by some decades) were Romantics. A sense of the whole course that history was taking and of the goal toward which it was progressing generally took priority over painstaking empirical research. Buchez, for one, was certainly more of a moral philosopher than an economist. But that did not prevent him from making some observations in his *Introduction à la science de l'histoire* (1833) and elsewhere that the academic political economists were loathe to express. Since he had a teaching for the workers themselves, an elite of typographers and other workers banded together and put out a periodical called *L'Atelier* to propagate his views. This paper lasted eleven years, from 1840 to 1850, thus representing the Buchezian school of Christian socialism during the heyday of early socialism of the 1840s and the Second French Republic (1848–50). At one point following the February Revolution, during the month of May as the first troubles arose, Buchez was even president of the National Assembly.

Buchez saw the shadow side of untrammeled competition in the modern economy very clearly and very early (Duroselle 1951, 85). In the first pages of his *Introduction to the Science of History*, he pointed out that the most important feature of contemporary European society was its division into "two classes, one in possession of all the tools of labor: land, factories, buildings, stocks — the other owning nothing: the latter class works for the former one." Labor conditions are therefore the chief concern of the vast majority of the population. How are they affected? "The only factor governing labor today is the principle of competition. It corresponds to the existence of two facts: first, the lack of any rule in production, and second, the struggle among the producers to dispose of their goods on the markets." Given this competition, a manufacturer has to bend every effort to supply the markets with the best quality goods at the cheapest possible price. The only way he can do that is to "decrease the price of labor, which he does by the introduction of machines and the reduction of wages."

This makes the entrepreneur "a parasitical being living at the expense of those whom he exploits." His employees "do not have the time to choose; almost from their first day they need to earn their living;... attached like polyps to the soil where they are born, they work and they die" (Duroselle 1951, 86; Bruhat 1972, 382).

The solution, according to Buchez from 1831 on, was to be found in *workers' associations* (cooperatives of production). He was convinced that, once they were started, they would be more competitive than the usual arrangement whereby the manufacturers took more than their share of the workers' earnings in return for providing the stock, the tools, and the marketing. He only proposed this sort of workers' partnership for the crafts and artisans' trades, whereas in factories one would have to intervene by way of government to set up bodies regulating working conditions and minimum wages in the different industries (Duroselle 1951, 92). Profit-sharing was another possibility Buchez mentioned.

The central idea in all this reflection on association was that the division into haves and have-nots, far from being a necessary stage toward a classless society, as Marx would argue some years later, was a blind alley or ditch into which the economy had fallen. It was everyone's duty, in the light of the Christian gospel and the teaching of the church, and hence (according to Buchez) also in the light of the watchwords of the Revolution, not to dig oneself in deeper by stirring up the class struggle but to join hands to get out of the ditch. Liberty without equality had played into the hands of a relatively small possessing class. The remedy lay in associating what had become separated, rejoining laborers with their materials and tools, owners with productive labor, legal freedom with actual participation in society. For the antagonism between different interests, "that leads each party to think only of attacking or defending oneself, can only disappear if equality in interests comes about, in other words, if their mutual association is established. This is in our view the end purpose of Christianity" (Duroselle 1951, 89).

In the years 1828–32 one of those slumps occurred that take place periodically even in an expanding economy: a period of consolidation, to the optimistic economists; a sign of the crisis of industrial capitalism, to the pessimists; hard times for the working class and many an entrepreneur. Earlier, even to some extent in 1817–18, such a crisis was normally a product of poor harvests or war. The terrible crisis of the late 1840s was associated with the potato blight, but that does not explain why whole trades, such as that of the home weavers in Flanders and elsewhere, went under for good. It is well to keep these dates in mind as one examines the growth of social thought in the first half of the nineteenth century. The fact that the three principal French social Catholic forerunners produced their analyses during a time of particular economic hardship, and that the political revolutions of 1830 and 1848 took place in the same circumstances, are connections that bear on the character of the emergent social Catholicisms. The benefits that society could draw from industrialization for the population at large were not being realized, in fact, even in good times. But the hard times acted as an additional catalyst in the midst of general indifference and left their mark — how could it be otherwise? — on nascent social Catholicism.

Chapter 4

TAKING UP THE CHALLENGE,
1830–48

A question naturally presents itself. With the process of reflection on the new economic class development of the industrial age having begun, what changes occurred in the social praxis of Catholic Christians? Clearly, the most notable innovations showed up on the borderline between charitable and social works — the *patronages* associated with the name of Armand de Melun in the milieus touched by Frédéric Ozanam's foundation, the Society of St. Vincent de Paul.

These were not the only responses in Catholic Europe, however, that manifested a positive adaptation in the life of the church to the new challenges. Indeed, the most striking examples of a new consciousness basic to social Catholicism are to be found, as we have already in part seen, in the realm of propagating and refining ideas. Hence it was necessary to direct the attention of literate Catholics, first, to the very existence of a social problem having to do with the world of work and, second, to its serious study.

There is, moreover, an apparent puzzle for historical understanding and interpretation in the extraordinary feeling of solidarity that manifested itself for a few weeks early in 1848 between the Catholic Church and the workers of Paris. Friedrich Engels noted an element of this puzzle when he wrote ([1843] 1975, 399): "It is curious that whilst the English Socialists are generally opposed to Christianity, and have to suffer all the religious prejudices of a really Christian people, the French Communists, being part of a nation celebrated for its infidelity, are themselves Christian. One of their favorite axioms is, that Christianity *is* Communism, *Le christianisme, c'est le Communisme.* This they try to prove by the Bible, the state of community in which the first Christians are said to have lived, etc."

Given the contemporary reports of the clergy to the effect that the

56

working population, especially of Paris, but also in all other French industrial centers, was from the beginning largely unchurched (Pierrard 1984, 14–17 and 52–74); given the little headway and the small number of Catholics who could be qualified as "social" or who displayed any comprehension of the lot of the workingman's family in the middle of the nineteenth century, the initially positive attitude that the revolutionary working class displayed toward the church in 1848 calls for an explanation. In this chapter we wish to see why there was reason for hope in the 1840s as well as why it was so fatally easy, in the event, for the church and the working class in Europe to go their separate ways.

Religious Socialism in France

In the encyclical *Mirari vos* of August 1832, Pope Gregory XVI condemned the political ideas of *L'Avenir* (without naming it or Lamennais; see Aubert in Jedin 1980, 7:289–91; Reardon 1985, 176–206). The principal thing that the pope could not tolerate was the proposal that the Roman Church could and should put itself on the side of popular revolutionary movements like the Irish, Belgian, or Polish struggles for independence. Buchez's impression of the encyclical is indicative of the perspective from which Lamennais was beginning to see things. To Buchez, the papal pronouncement was simply un-Christian: "In vain does one search in this overblown and trite Italian prose for a Christian thought. It can only repeat the phrases of backward minds against freedom, the press and revolutions.... Not a word of encouragement, not a word of pity for those who suffer; no solicitude except for the princes and powers, as if Jesus Christ died to confirm the right to use force on the part of the patricians who condemned him" (Buchez cited in Duroselle 1951, 83). For in the meantime, stimulated by the Polish struggle for independence and freedom, Lamennais himself had discovered the masses as "the people," and the liberation whose hour he proclaimed at hand as comprising not merely political rights but emancipation from economic servitude as well.

In April 1834, when Lamennais's break with the church was not yet validated by Lamennais himself, a book of his came out that would have a tremendous galvanizing and at the same time religious effect in the working class, not just in France but also among German working-class leaders (Schieder 1963, 227–39). It was *Paroles d'un croyant*, a highly charged poetical work that prophesied a new age of democracy and greater social equality. Before it was even published, signs of its power showed themselves. Augustin Sainte-Beuve, who was acting as agent, got this report from the concerned owner of the shop where it was being printed: "It is going to make a big splash. My workers themselves cannot set it in type without going into ecstasy and being carried away. The place is floating on air" (cited in Pierrard 1984, 126). But if that was its effect on the workers, Lamennais's Catholic friends took it as a highly regrettable parting shot at church and society. It was, of course, a distinct move beyond contemporary liberalism, where the assumption prevailed that "the people" must be guided by its betters. All the same, it contributed, in a minor way to be sure, to sensitizing European Catholicism to the labor question (Valerius 1963, 359). From that point on — and it was the point at which Lamennais discovered the social question — his principal role was that of an inspirer of religious socialism as a popular, but not a churchly movement (Bruhat 1972, 379–81).

Buchez and Lamennais were not alone in being religious socialists. A number of followers of Charles Fourier (1772–1837), for example, put out a daily paper in Paris from 1843 to 1850 called *La Démocratie pacifique*. Some of them were Catholic, like Hippolyte de la Morvonnais (1802–53), or became Catholic in due course, like Désiré Laverdant (1810–84). Particularly in the first half of its existence, this paper was on the watch for all manifestations of a social or socialist tendency in French Catholicism and treated them with benevolence.

L'Atelier, on the other hand, after the manner of the earlier Buchez or the later Lamennais, constantly measured the modest initiatives of church circles against the gospel and found them sorely wanting. The one and the other approach testify to the role of Christian images and aspirations in the labor movement on the continent in the decades from 1820 to 1850. *L'Atelier* was a monthly entirely operated and written by workers (typesetters and other artisans), as its masthead proudly stated. It lasted for eleven years (1840–50) and stuck firmly to the Buchezian principles of religious socialism that had inspired its cooperative venture in the first place (Bruhat in Droz 1972, 1:382; Duroselle 1951, 113–20).

Ozanam and the Society of St. Vincent de Paul

The scattered sheep of the *L'Avenir* flock, of whom Charles de Coux stood out for his clearsighted view of system-inherent economic inequalities, coped as well as they could with the official ecclesiastical disapproval, which of course manifested itself earlier and more directly in France, through cancellations of subscriptions, than in Rome. They endeavored at least to keep a periodical afloat, at first *L'Européenne* (1831–32), then the revived *Le Correspondant* (second series, 1843–70), which because of its long life would become synonymous with French liberal Catholicism. Social problems were not conspicuous in its columns, in general. One of its writers, however, Frédéric Ozanam, was a key figure in the short-lived Christian democracy of 1848. His ideas, backed by a selfless and convincingly Christian life, gave the social component a standing in modern Catholicism that at no point entirely disappeared thereafter.

Ozanam, although born in Milan (1813, died in Paris in 1853), belonged to a bourgeois family in Lyon, where he was raised. His father was a physician, with a good position at the city hospital, but he apparently had little in the way of independent wealth (Rivières 1984, 15). The charitable work that called out to a good Catholic doctor willing to climb stairways in tenements found in Jean-Antoine Ozanam and his wife a generous response.

As a twenty-year-old law student in Paris, Ozanam and his student friends, with the help of Emmanuel Bailly *père* (1794–1860), founded the Society of St. Vincent de Paul, from which would spring "conferences" of laymen in hundreds and eventually thousands of parishes across France, the rest of Europe, and overseas. The members of each local conference pledged themselves to visit the poor personally. They would alleviate their needs and sufferings with food and clothing, to be sure, to the extent possible, but first and foremost by breaking through barriers of class and upbringing to establish personal contact. The aim was exclusively charitable and spiritual; it was to be, as Ozanam wrote in 1834 (Duroselle 1951, 174), "an "association of mutual encouragement" in prayer and in Christian living. For French university students in the 1830s who were brought up Catholic and wished to remain so (a distinct minority), "mutual encouragement" was of the essence. Since social reform as such never formed part of the ethos of the St. Vincent de Paul Society, its role in a history of social Catholicism is only indirect. It acquainted substantial numbers of devoted Catholics with conditions among the large marginal population of developing industrial society. It was a seedbed of concerned Catholics, mostly of the middle or upper classes, who would be open to further attempts to analyze and correct problems of gross social inequality.

Of course, there were others who felt the needs of the time, including some Catholic entrepreneurs in Lille with a nascent social conscience (Duroselle 1951, 194–95; Stearns 1978, 142–47). Edouard Lefort and Charles Kolb-Bernard were two of these. Lefort had already founded a "Society of St. Joseph" to provide healthy recreational opportunities for workers (an alternative to the saloons) in 1836. He and Kolb-Bernard were among the founders, then, of the Lille conference of the St. Vincent de Paul Society in 1839.

But Ozanam also played a role of more direct interest in the present connection. Already in 1832, before *Mirari vos*, he had taken part in some conferences organized by Abbé Gerbet and Charles de Coux for students at the university and had even suggested the topic for a course of Gerbet's, the philosophy of history. C. de Coux spoke on political economy several times. Then he came down with the cholera that was raging at the time. The continuation fell victim to the papal disapproval of the Mennaisian movement as a whole. But meanwhile Ozanam wrote to a friend: "M. le Coux has started his course on political economy, full of depth and interest. You should send for the printed version. Large numbers attend; they are full of truth and of life and of a keen grasp of the plague that is preying on society and of the only cure that will succeed" (Duroselle 1951, 46–47).

In 1848, as we shall see, Ozanam will strive again to make sure that Christian charity is not understood in a retrograde fashion, as if it were incompatible with the authentic emancipation of the lower classes.

Villeneuve-Bargemont in the Chamber of Deputies

The main outward characteristic that distinguished conservative Catholics from liberal or republican ones was their legitimism. Whereas a Montalembert or a Lacordaire could see Louis Philippe's reign (1830–48) as a step forward and place some hopes in the bourgeois ideal of the *juste milieu*, conservatives kept thinking that a return to a God-fearing and church-supporting Bourbon monarch was the only truly French solution to the country's problems. Since they were out of power, it was quite possible for them to lend a sympathetic ear to the critics of industrialism. After all, conservatives had comparatively little responsibility for its negative effects. Manufacturing was the domain of the new class of the industrial bourgeois, who were courted so assiduously by the new government.

Nevertheless, few conservative Catholics paid more than passing attention to the spokespersons from their ranks who called attention to the fearful "English" conditions that were unfortunately not unknown in France's industrializing regions. Labor unrest in the 1830s, as when the silk workers of Lyons rioted under the motto "Live by working or not live at all," was seen simply as a result of modern emancipatory ideas and as a challenge to internal security and order. Some few, however, notably Villeneuve-Bargemont, approached such developments from a broader perspective attentive to economics.

The first humanitarian legislation to limit child labor was introduced by circles close to Protestant industrialists in Mulhouse in 1839 at the urgings of Daniel Legrand. They had come to see that gross exploitation of children was not an economic necessity. Having begun to limit it themselves, they were won over to the idea that a uniform standard set by the state might after all be "a first attempt at the regular and moral organization of labor" (Stearns 1978, 162, citing an Alsatian employer's statement of 1840), restraining unlimited competition where its ill effects were most evident. After protracted debates necessitated by the deeply rooted scruples against any kind of state intervention, recognized as such, in the economic sector, a minimal law with slack enforcement procedures was passed in 1841 — the first on a socio-economic issue since 1791! Villeneuve-Bargemont, Joseph-Marie de Gérando, and even Montalembert, among the Catholic legislators, supported it on humanitarian grounds (Duroselle 1951, 228–31). Villeneuve-Bargemont was the only one in the whole debate to raise the full spectrum of social problems associated with industrialization.

As such, his speech (on 22 December 1840 in the Chamber of Deputies, where he was a member for Hazebrouck in the extreme north of France) was the first in a French parliament to advocate social reform (in general terms) as a responsibility of government. Taking place as it did in the parliament of the leading industrializing nation of the continent, it did not remain an isolated episode, as was the case with the 1837 *Fabrikrede* of Franz Josef Buss in Germany. On the other hand, its effect on public opinion lagged far behind that of the Earl of Shaftesbury's parliamentary initiatives on the same question in England in the 1840s. The extent of industrialization and of the social problems it brought in its train were much further advanced in England than in France, as Villeneuve-Bargemont pointed out, hoping that France could learn from England's unfortunate example. All the same, for the continent and especially for Catholic Europe, this marked the first time that attention was focussed on the worker question in general and not just on certain abuses such as child labor. As for the socialists, they had no representation in parliament at this time. Besides, some of their leading theoreticians were no keener on state intervention than were the liberal economists.

The orator's approach was to point to a new kind of poverty that the world had not known before. At the time of the artisans' guilds and corporations, competition was regulated in such a way that one worker did not beggar the other by scrambling for work at any pay. Villeneuve-Bargemont did not urge that the old corporations be re-established. Now, however, the combination of industrial manufacturing with untrammeled and frenetic competition had led to a new kind of poverty, not at all accidental, that "tends to generalize and perpetuate itself in a large part of the population employed in the mills established in our principal manufacturing towns."

To get work in such circumstances, the worker must "surrender himself, his wife and his children to a labor that goes beyond their strength in its demands and in its length, and that for a wage that sometimes does not suffice for the meanest subsistence." Such conditions did not exist everywhere in France as yet, but they did exist: he could vouch for the pauperism in Lille, for example. "I am only doing my duty in this Chamber, gentlemen," he went on, "if I state my conviction that these are the inevitable and long foreseen consequences of modern systems of public economy that have denatured the true purpose and the social destiny of labor and industry." What was needed was the union of what liberal economics separated, "the close alliance of labor and justice, of the moral order and the material order" as Christianity had joined them. It would not do to teach the workers new habits of consumption, on the pretext of increasing production. Mere economic calculation, reckoning the value of workers in terms of their labor only, as the modern economists do, has only led to a result that "no one can want: a portion of the population dependent on certain branches of industry becomes a caste by itself, condemned to unhappiness, as in England; their way of life, health and very existence are a matter of blind chance. This is a situation which no society that calls itself civilized and Christian can tolerate."

Villeneuve-Bargemont praised the industrialists of Mulhouse and the fact-finders who were behind the child-labor bill, but went on to give a gripping description of the plight of the laboring class in general. Outside the large manufacturing companies, in the smaller shops and mills, conditions were still worse. "There, the length of the working day passes all bounds" (indeed, fourteen hours was at this time not an extraordinarily long workday in the textile industry; see Stearns 1978, 58–60 and 199).

As for solutions to such problems, there were various suggestions. Villeneuve-Bargemont did not want to go into them in the very first speech devoted to the labor question. His purpose was, as he said, to attract attention. "For my part, gentlemen, I can consider this bill only as a first step towards a reform that should engage the support of all generous hearts." "The restoration of the lower classes, the working, suffering classes, is the great problem of our times" (Duroselle 1951, 229–31).

Armand de Melun and the *Patronage* Model

It makes sense to have reported this important, if still rather isolated, view of the new social problems of nineteenth-century industrialization in some detail, because it witnesses to the mentality of the most open and informed minds among Catholic conservatives as such issues became publicly prominent. Conservatives formed the most influential group in French Catholicism; their kind of social Catholicism would be the dominant one for decades to come. Where such a social consciousness showed itself, one can characterize it as tentative (not dogmatic) groping, inclined to be suspicious of industrialism and supportive of life on the land, but also, for its time, quite aware of the challenge that economic modernization was posing to society. Not quite sure how this challenge was to be handled, one was nevertheless convinced that it would require massive injections of moral disinterestedness and a return to Christianity.

If we now turn to how that moral generosity was tapped and mobilized for the benefit of the disadvantaged, we find a sprinkling of new developments already at the time of the Restoration. From an article by Lamennais (in 1822, when he was still a legitimist; see Duroselle 1951, 27–36), we learn of an organization set up by "the Congregation," a society of well-to-do Catholics that called many charitable works into existence throughout the nineteenth century. It was for workers and was called the Society of St. Joseph. Abbé de Bervanger took note of the need of the workers for better training and went on to found the first vocational school in Paris, Saint Nicolas, in 1827. The school would weather some storms and prosper modestly over the decades, while the Society of St. Joseph would be dissolved in the Revolution of 1830 as a legitimist front. ("The Congregation" led a sort of double life, one as a respectable private charitable and religious organization, the other, at least until 1826, as an anti-Masonic secret society with ultra-royalist aims.)

The history of this social Catholicism of the conservative main stream between 1840 and 1870 is bound up with the name of its leading figure, Armand de Melun, and with a particular organizational style: what is called the *patronage* (Pierrard 1984, 179–89). A *patronage*, to explain it at once, is a club or organization set up by members of the *classes dirigeantes* or at least by the moderately well-off for members of the *classes inférieures*, who, it will be remembered, neither had the vote (until 1848) nor were allowed to form any sort of organization on their own, even if they had had the leisure or the means. Its novelty consisted in the fact that it was not a charitable institution for residents, nor a distribution point for alms, which were the standard responses of church people to social needs up to that point. Something very like a *patronage* had been started in Paris in 1828. "The Society of the Friends of Childhood" made it their project to find apprenticeships for orphans. Armand de Melun will breathe new life into the undertaking after 1838.

Besides these two documented cases, there was undoubtedly a lot of similar unorganized and unprofessional social work going on in Catholic Europe at large. Some of it was certifiably ill-conceived; such were some of the workshops set up in convents where poor women could do piecework in return for food and assistance. Since the sisters would often take what was offered for the finished products, its net effect was to depress the labor market still further and create an additional hardship for independent textile workers. However, one may assume that many a St. Vincent de Paul visitor, after 1833, took it upon himself to seek and find suitable employment for widows' children as well as unemployed men, as parish priests in their equally limited way also tried to do. Woefully insufficient as all of this was, few took cognizance of it at the time.

There were also the charitable enterprises of women religious, who were at the start of an important revival in terms of numbers and responsibilities. In Paris, one of these was the famous Soeur Rosalie Rendu, a Daughter of Charity since 1802, a member therefore of the congregation of sisters, not cloistered, founded by Vincent de Paul and Louise Marillac in 1633. Begging money as she had to, to support her charitable work among the poor of a quarter in Paris, she impressed a Russian convert to Roman Catholicism, Madame Swetchine, who presided over a famous Parisian salon. Madame Swetchine told Armand de Melun about Sister Rosalie, and with that the first epoch of social Catholic organizations opened.

Armand de Melun and his twin brother, Anatole, were born in 1807 (Armand would live until 1877; see Vidler 1964, 27, 51–53 and 62–63; Duroselle 1951, 209–17). He took up the law and started to practice at the bar in Paris. Then, with the Revolution of July 1830, he retired altogether from professional life (Rollet in *Catholicisme* 8:1134). He was drawn to the Catholic liberalism of Lamennais, Lacordaire, and Montalembert; he considered and apparently rejected the idea of a clerical vocation (Duroselle 1951, 211–17, also for what follows). No hermit, he found his way into Parisian society and soon to Madame Swetchine's, where he was caught up in the brilliant *causeries* of the leading lights of liberal Catholicism and others who also frequented her salon.

When Madame Swetchine spoke to him of Soeur Rosalie, as he recalled later, he had never visited a poor person; his only contact with the poor was with those who begged on the streets. "I left it up to public assistance and charitable offices to acquaint themselves with their needs and to look after them.... In the frame of mind that I was in, the life that Soeur Rosalie led amidst these poor people struck me like a revelation of an unknown and intriguing world."

Soeur Rosalie put him to the test by giving him a list of poor people to visit, which he did, not without trepidation. Soon it became a habit. She also gave him, in 1838, a copy of a *Life of St. Vincent de Paul*. And he wrote to Mme. Swetchine to let her know that he now knew what he would do for the rest of his life. Being able to afford full-time voluntary work for the poor, he would simply be an *homme charitable*. Melun had no previous contact with the St. Vincent de Paul Society, as did so many others with whom he was to be associated in social Catholicism, but through Soeur Rosalie, the historical figure of Père Vincent (1581–1660) was equally present on his way.

Duroselle describes in detail how Melun's "charitable vocation" of 1838 little by little took on the characteristics of a social vocation. He read Villeneuve-Bargemont's book of 1834 and this led him to Adam Smith's classic, *The Wealth of Nations*. Although impressed by the latter, as any serious reader would be, he retained Villeneuve-Bargemont's strictures against the one-sidedness of British economics. He made no real effort to acquaint himself with socialist writers. Although he would perceive the need for a social doctrine from time to time and organize efforts to develop one, he himself was primarily a practical person. His leanings toward the art of the possible would leave French social Catholicism without a doctrine to face the storms of the 1870s and 1880s, but would stand him in good stead in his legislative activity.

All the same, initial experiences enabled Melun to gauge the extent of real poverty and unemployment about him. From his work with the "Friends of Childhood" he came to the conclusion that residence facilities were no answer to the problems of children of the working class. On the one hand, they were simply too expensive and hence could only serve a fraction of those in need. On the other, an enclosed institutional environment was intrinsically incapable of preparing such children for the life they would have to lead as working apprentices and adults. In 1839–40, as we see from a letter of his to Mme. Swetchine (Duroselle 1951, 185–86), he came to see the *patronage* as the form that alone would effectively measure up to the needs of the age.

The terms in which he explained what this vision meant to him reveal a dawning social awareness in his basically charitable orientation. Up to then, he wrote, charity was an individual matter. "Today, we must broaden the horizon. It is not just a matter of filling some gaps, of rendering aid where the dole and the social interest have overlooked someone. One must address the task of making available to everybody the assistance that society is capable of rendering to each. One must become the intermediary between the poor person and the institutions created to feed, instruct and defend him or her." This would be the seed of an "entire system of tutelary action on society," leading to a "present social regeneration not by force nor by science, but by charity."

By 1840, therefore, Melun had formed as much doctrine as he needed to start his work with a clear organizational pattern and goal, that of the *patronage*. This pattern, as has already been stated, would remain the dominant one in legitimist French social Catholicism for decades. It would be fortified by the adhesion of new recruits such as Maurice Maignen and, after 1870, Albert de Mun, and it would not start to fade until the 1880s.

In July 1840 Melun became the director of a *patronage* for apprentices formed under the auspices of the St. Vincent de Paul conferences in Paris. Leaving that in the hands of others, he formed another *Oeuvre des apprentis* with the assistance of Christian Brothers, using their schools as after-hours and Sunday meeting places for the apprentices. This initiative required the permission of the government and was even given some government money. It grew quickly, reaching 470 child workers in 1845 and 1200 by the beginning of 1848. The first *patronage* for apprentices reached perhaps eight hundred. These were for the most part apprentices in artisans' shops, not in mechanized factories (which were not numerous in Paris yet, anyway). Armand de Melun had reason to think he was on the right track. In the rest of France there were parallels and emulators (Duroselle 1951, 193–97).

One of the others who took over the St. Vincent de Paul *patronage* of apprentices in 1840 was Jean-Léon Le Prévost (1803–74; see Fulvi Cittadini 1980). He had joined Bailly and Ozanam at the foundation of the first St. Vincent de Paul conference in 1833 as a young man working in the state ministry of religion and was one of the most tireless collaborators and organizers. Although married, he felt the need for a community for the apostolate, something not unlike what would later be called a secular institute. When a St. Vincent de Paul member from Angers arrived one day in Paris with a similar idea, the die was cast. This was Clément Myionnet (1812–86). In March of 1845 Myionnet moved into lodgings next to the hired hall on rue de Regard where the apprentices met. This is reckoned as the founding date of the congregation of the "Brothers of St. Vincent de Paul." Besides Le Prévost and Myionnet, Maurice Maignen (1822–90), of whom we will hear more later, was the third founding member. Some priests joined the congregation in due course. But all the founding "fathers" remained lay brothers except Le Prévost, who was ordained in 1860.

Meanwhile, Melun became involved in Paris in another line of development, this time in view of adult workers. Since the disappearance of the Society of St. Joseph in 1830, there was no Catholic organization for workers as such at all. In the 1840s this gap was to be filled by the "Society of St. Francis Xavier."

Workers' Meetings in the 1840s: François Ledreuille

The pastoral neglect of the working class and its other side, the indifference of workers by and large toward the church, had various causes. But neither the extent of worker alienation nor its reasons have been studied sufficiently so that accurate and well-founded generalizations can be made as to the actual state of affairs in France, say, in the 1840s. The incomplete picture that we have, however, suggests that the situation was desolate in most cities and towns that had grown considerably with new industry.

Given the contempt for religion of the liberal bourgeoisie itself, one can presume that urban workers were affected by anticlerical republicanism and largely unchurched even in advance of the onset of industrialization in most French cities. The same could hardly be said of other countries in the middle of the nineteenth century, it seems (compare also the 1843 observations of Engels, cited earlier). New parishes had to be approved (and financed) by the government, according to the terms of the Napoleonic concordat that governed church-state relations in France throughout the nineteenth century. Even in periods when church-state relations were good, new parishes were not established in anything like sufficient numbers.

This led to situations such as that in and around Paris, where the old established parishes had to cope with tens of thousands of parishioners each. It is not surprising to hear of a working-class parish in Paris responsible for eighty thousand inhabitants, of whom only two or three hundred women attended mass (Pierrard 1984, 184, see also 15–17).

Thus, around 1840, attempts were made, often stemming from St. Vincent de Paul work, to bring workers' families together in groups for mutual support centered on the parish. In Paris, Armand de Melun noted that one of the Christian Brothers had gathered together a dozen working men for readings and prayers. He and his friend Alex de Lambel won the cooperation of three pastors and organized such meetings with up to 150 workers in attendance.

In December 1840, more workers were coming and two of the most farsighted and zealous pastors, the abbés Haumet and Frascy decided that the meetings could be held in their churches. The name,

Society of St. Francis Xavier, was chosen for the group, after the famous Jesuit missionary. The gatherings of three hundred to four hundred workers attracted the attention of the police, who complained to the archbishop, Denis Auguste Affre. They complained even more when François Ledreuille, a former seminarian, onetime laborer, and now a teacher, started speaking at these meetings around 1843 (Duroselle 1951, 265–71; Pierrard 1984, 183–87). The police had various objections: this was going beyond the religious function of the church; the economic situation of the workers was being discussed by unauthorized laymen (Ledreuille, Raymond Brucker, Théodore Nisard, and Claudius Hébrard, 1820–85, among others); insofar as instruction was being given, the so-called university monopoly was infringed! Then too, a sick fund was being built up through a sort of dues payment. Was some sort of illegal workers' association being formed under the guise of religion?

Archbishop Affre soothed the police and the ministry of religion, shielding the initiative among the workers as best he could (Duroselle 1951, 249–62). Then he ordained Ledreuille, enabling him to speak more freely to the workers, as a priest! His first sermons as an ordained minister were events. In addressing the workers at his first mass early on the Sunday morning of 18 May 1845, he again struck the tone that made people call him *le père des ouvriers*. Having been raised in a worker's family, a rarity in a clergy made up mostly of peasants' sons with a leavening of offspring from the educated classes, he lost no opportunity to speak to workers as to friends and family members.

His second sermon as a priest, however, was at the church of St. Roch, before a well-to-do congregation, on 22 May 1845. It would be 1868 before such tones were to be heard again from a pulpit in Paris.

> If you do not patronize the laboring classes, you will see the gaping abyss of pauperism grow wider and deeper from one day to the next. It will be fine for you to drop coins in the poorbox or donate gold pieces to charity, the abyss will get larger and larger. Believe me, you will never close that gap. It has been growing for fifty years in the deepest part of the vale of tears, in regions where the fortunate never venture. For my part, being a son of the people and coming providentially from the masses, I have kept enough sympathy for them to dare to go down into the chasm. What I have seen, oh God! One man in a thousand manages to feed his family; one family in a thousand finds enough work to feed all its members.

Then he went on to warn his listeners that the people could very well rise up "next year, perhaps tomorrow," throw off its resignation like an ill-fitting coat and march toward the conquest of its unrecognized rights. He reminded them in closing that he considered himself an advocate for the people who "are beginning to despair of the *patronage*" of the well-to-do.

These were plainly subversive sentiments to the guardians of law and order. Archbishop Affre pointed out that they were not addressed to the lower classes, so that there could be no subversive intent or effect. All the same, he had to apologize for Abbé Ledreuille's language. When the state minister of religion charged that Ledreuille was stirring up the people in a working-class area of St. Antoine a few weeks later, the vicar general replied that Ledreuille denied having spoken the incriminating phrase. Speaking of the early church, he was supposed to have remarked, "How far we are from that era of equality!" Had he been a layman, he would have been arrested.

L'Atelier (the Christian worker's paper directed by Buchezian artisans) found Ledreuille's sermon at St. Roch off the mark, however. Guided by their ingrained anticlerical feelings, perhaps, they did not trust him. Their writer, a sharpsighted critic, objected to his interpretation of how the people felt. It was not a question of despair at all, nor did "implacable vengeance" drive them. The people simply

> wants justice; it knows its rights and will gain them. If it is necessary for that end to engage in struggle, it knows the laws of war; it will not resort to the torch of the arsonist or the dagger of the assassin. What the people demands is not alms. It is not philanthropic or religious *patronage*. It is not even bread, if the bread comes with a condition of servitude attached. What it wants is to take its place in the homestead of the great family — the recognition of its formal right. (Duroselle 1951, 271)

Unfortunately, this kind of firm working-class attitude seemed to be possible only at quite a distance from the clericalized church. If Ledreuille himself came to see the justice of such reproaches (which is by no means clear), the paternalists who dominated social Catholicism before 1848 and still more after 1849 were impervious to their appeal.

On the side of social *action*, Ledreuille was also, for a few years, the man of the hour (Duroselle 1951, 272–77). With the help of some rich benefactors, he set up a "Workers' House," *Maison des Ouvriers*, in 1844. Its first task was to put a free placement service in operation, where workers, when they were idled, could be put in contact with employers. By 1847 there was a monthly paper that lasted a few months. The archbishop was planning, clearly in touch with Ledreuille, an archdiocesan-wide Labor Council (*Oeuvre du Travail*), that would provide not only placement services and publications, but also medical and legal services, and mobilize the volunteer work of a ladies' auxiliary.

Since this was a national problem, especially in the form of unemployed workers streaming from the provinces to Paris, Archbishop Affre wanted to harness the rest of the episcopate into a common effort. The Revolution of 1848 and his death at the barricades on 27 June 1848 intervened. But even had he lived, his relative isolation and the resentment against his pretensions to national leadership in the rest of the episcopate, together with the increased strength of "the party of order" in the 1850s, would probably have condemned this particular initiative to ineffectiveness. Nevertheless his archiepiscopal interest in workers' affairs, manifested only partially but all the same distinctly, also helps explain the friendly attitude between workers and church in the first months of the February Revolution.

Melun's "Society of Charitable Economy"

Armand de Melun, we have said, was not a theoretician, and yet he recognized that a body of teaching had its uses and would be indispensable for long-range reforms of society toward a more equitable distribution of the wealth produced by industry. Toward this end, he took two connected steps in 1845 and 1846, founding a journal, *Annales de la Charité*, and then an association to promote the acquisition of knowledge on poverty and its alleviation. This organization was the Société d'économie charitable, which would remain active through the 1860s before giving way to or merging with the school of Frédéric LePlay. Neither the society nor the periodical were exclusively Catholic (Duroselle 1951, 217–27; Pierrard 1984, 187–89). The undertaking was based on the assumption that charity was not, or at least could not remain merely an aggregate of alms and services rendered. The charitable individual or organization had to have a reasoned body of knowledge and analysis of the causes and effects of poverty at hand, in order to shape effective remedies.

The idea was therefore to professionalize and institutionalize communications among the rather haphazard efforts being made in various places to cope with the misery of the working class and the unemployed. It was also the case that the dominant bourgeois tendency did not encourage such investigations in the university. As in most regimes before and to a large extent after 1848, the sphere of legal public action open to private groups was confined to the expression of opinion through newspapers and periodicals, themselves subject to censure. Thus it was to this medium that Melun's thoughts turned.

A full-time managing editor and secretary of the society was hired, Alexis Chevalier. This modest step was certainly necessary; it was only possible because Melun had the necessary contacts in high society to gather a group of restricted membership capable of contributing toward the costs of the salary. Some were eminent contributors to the *Annales:* Frédéric de Falloux, Henri de Vatismenil, Adolphe Baudon, president of the St. Vincent de Paul Society, Augustin Cochin, the prototype of the Catholic bourgeois with charitable-social interests, his uncle, Denis Benoist d'Azy, the viscount Villeneuve-Bargemont, Armand and Anatole de Melun. Others, including Belgians, were prominent names interested in "charitable economy of the Catholic school," as the phrase went, such as Xavier de Mérode, Henri de Riancey, Louis René Villermé, the Duke d'Uzès, Charles de Coux, and Alexis de Tocqueville.

One thing was already clear as the "Society of Charitable Economy" was being founded. Under Melun's leadership, it would work on proposals for social-charitable-humanitarian legislation in the French parliament. Since the first labor law of 1841, no further attempt had been made in this direction. It was not to become a platform for unlimited freedom of the market, therefore, but endorsed a certain measure of government intervention. Another thing was well enough understood and would become clearer and clearer in the future: socialists, especially socialists of Louis Blanc's type, preaching a state socialism brought on by a peaceful revolution, need not apply. Buchez was not approached, one may be sure. Even Ozanam's name fails to figure in the paternalistically conservative Société d'économie charitable. One reason for this may well simply have been that they were not well enough off to support the work of the society financially.

While still in the stage of uncertainty as to the difference between what is charitable and what is social, a feature of social Catholicism appears that will occur again in the most various of settings. That is the search for a third way between economic liberalism and socialism. In de Melun's variation, this third way was the way (not, as he wrote, of force nor of science, but) of Christian charity aided by the practice of association (Duroselle 1951, 221). Oddly enough, the same could have been said of Buchez, with a more democratic, solidaristic understanding of "charity." Instead, what had already taken place was a mutual rejection of the socialist workers' movement and the greater part of social Catholics. Alongside many other mutual grievances, socialists such as Pierre Leroux taxed the "charitable school" with attempting to escape a hereafter in hell by their gifts, instead of devoting themselves to a truly egalitarian (and hence authentic) solidarity (Pierrard 1984, 138).

In 1847, Melun drew up and submitted to the legislature of the July monarchy a *Mémoire...on Various Questions of Public Charity.* He pointed out the need for action on four specific issues: the care of abandoned infants, begging, and reform of the pawn shops (all of a charitable or relief character), and child labor. Reminding the legislators that those concerned have no vote and hence no representatives in parliament to speak for themselves, he pointed out some facts about child labor, even after the first reform legislation of 1841. Interestingly, he had himself probably learned these facts from two articles published in the *Annales de la Charité* in its first year (Duroselle 1951, 232–35). A woman named Eugénie Michel described conditions she had witnessed in a plant where fabric was dyed. Children worked there, in the summertime, from six in the morning until seven at night. Girls starting work at the age of ten normally were pregnant for the first time by fifteen. Their parents were more concerned about the money than about what happened to the children. She commented on a recent official report of the minister of Commerce on the enforcement of the child labor law of 1841 and showed that it was much too optimistic.

Melun used the members of the Société d'économie charitable as a body of consultants, having them discuss his legislative proposal and improve it to the point where it would make headway in the parliament. In fact, a law considerably stronger than the government desired was on the point of passing both chambers, when the Revolution of 1848 intervened. In a little over a year, Armand de Melun himself would be a deputy and would pursue his designs of social legislation all the more effectively.

European Social Catholicism
on the Eve of the Revolution of 1848

As the year 1848 commenced, Karl Marx was about to issue his call to workers everywhere to throw off their chains. Every worker who would hear of it (very few, indeed) would know at once what he was talking about. There was, for one thing, the passbook, which, though not always insisted upon, could always be brought into play against a refractory worker. For another thing, there was the unequal status before the law of employer and employee, another bequest of the Napoleonic Code. There were the new and terrifying business cycles; together with the effects of fierce competition, they left most workers defenseless and, with or without thrift and foresight, completely unable at times to support themselves and their dependents.

The benefits of industrialization were equally ambiguous outside the industrialized sector itself. The lower classes were probably better clothed than before, since productivity had increased so greatly in the textile business. (Here too it was the middle and upper classes who were the prime beneficiaries.) The general wage level had not improved yet. But the masses of rural workers who had drawn or continued to draw a significant part of their livelihood from spinning, weaving, or sewing, now found no market for their relatively expensive and rough products. From Flanders to Silesia (not to mention Ireland), whole branches of preindustrial manufacture went under in the terrible 1840s, while crop failure struck at the population from the other side. Many artisans in the towns were also feeling the pressure, just like their comrades in weaving and spinning. The increased population that might have made more work for skilled workers was instead being just barely maintained by the jobs and products of the new industries. Artisans saw themselves facing the prospect of joining the poorest of the poor in industrial slums (Fischer 1982, 57, 61–69; Stearns 1978, 193–99 for France, and Kossmann 1978, 203–4 for Belgium).

The St. Vincent de Paul conferences were the most notable response from within Catholicism on the international level to these new problems. By 1848 they could be found in Brussels and Ghent, in Munich and Aachen and were spreading quickly in France and abroad (Greschat 1980, 62, 76; Hürten in Rauscher 1982, 2:226; Rezsohazy 1958, 50). Were the phrase not usually meant so pejoratively, one could call this a "Band-Aid approach" to pauperism. Such charity, it is clear, came to grips only with the symptoms and not with the causes of the misery: nineteenth-century demographic, industrial, and economic changes in society. But far from being a retarding factor, something like social consciousness had a hard time developing in the relatively sheltered existence of middle- or upper-class Catholics without the catalyst of direct charitable action, as the paradigmatic case of Armand de Melun shows. The innovation that such volunteer grassroots initiatives represented, after centuries of church-state cooperation and control, must not be underestimated. The spread of St. Vincent de Paul conferences does seem to be the first new organized and more than episodic response of Catholics to the new world of industrial capitalism. Paternalistic structures, within the plants (conspicuously pioneered by Alsatian Protestants, who were the leading capitalists in France), and outside them, as in the *patronages* and *oeuvres*, were the second.

Further faint international aspects of social Catholicism before 1848 were connected on the one hand with the situation of the papacy in Italy and on the other with a first abortive attempt at creating a network of socially conscious *hommes charitables* around Armand de Melun. We shall return to the papacy in a moment. As to the concerned lay circles, Ducpétiaux, the inspector of prisons and poorhouses in Belgium, organized an international congress on penitentiaries in Brussels in 1847. On Melun's initiative, thirty-one of the participants, representing fourteen countries, agreed to form an

"International Society of Charity." The planning was disrupted by the events of 1848 (Duroselle 1951, 225–26). It is not surprising that this project never got properly launched; what is puzzling is that later, in the 1850s and 1860s, when Ducpétiaux got increasingly active and unfolded several important initiatives, Melun declined to offer much cooperation (Duroselle 1951, 624–27).

Other figures who could have contributed to a Belgian-French Catholic connection, so necessary in view of the industrial lead these countries had as second-comers in front of the more backward German and Italian economies, in fact failed to live up to their promise. François Huet (1814–69), a disciple of the philosopher Bordas-Demoulin, was professor at Ghent from 1835 to 1850 (Rezsohazy 1958, 21–34; Duroselle 1951, 78). His Christian socialist writings and convictions were ill-suited to the ultramontanism dominant after 1850, and he became alienated. Charles de Coux was professor of political economy at Louvain from 1834 to 1845. There is no indication that he sought contact with Edouard Ducpétiaux. In fact, his final course lectures on political economy show a distinct turn from a social-economic outlook to liberalism in economics, accepting the "iron law of wages" as inevitable. All in all, it signified a "distinct step backward" (Duroselle 1951, 56).

When de Coux went back to Paris in 1845 to take over *L'Univers*, he was either unable or disinclined to enlighten his readers on the great social questions of the day. In any case, he jumped over to the *Ere nouvelle*, but left that too when it showed signs of departing from the *juste milieu*. As Duroselle judges (1951, 710), he did not develop the confidence or the authority as an economist to influence the public.

German Catholicism, meanwhile, was recovering from the trauma of the 1803 secularization and finding out how to deal with life under new, mostly Protestant, princes. This was especially the case with Westphalia and the Rhineland, which went to Prussia. This region, extending from the Ruhr to Trier and Aachen on the French-Belgian border and including Münster, Cologne, and Coblenz, would play a role of key importance in the further development of social Catholicism. In the 1840s, the Catholics emphasized their loyalty to Frederick William IV while insisting on their equal rights as citizens and as a church body. As part of the settlement of the "Cologne troubles of 1837," Catholics were allowed to found clubs and organizations, some of charitable, some of religious-defense character, with potentially democratic or social effects.

In this atmosphere, Peter Reichensperger of Coblenz (1810–92) published a weighty book entitled *The Farm Question* (*Die Agrarfrage*, 1847), but dealing with the whole of national economy and not just the agricultural sector (see also Becker in ZgLb 5:41–54; E. Ritter 1954, 47–49). His central thesis is that the free sale, heritability, and hence divisibility of farmsteads, customary in the Rhineland and part of the Napoleonic Code, was a solid base from which to modernize Prussia's economy. This was a far cry from Adam Müller and from the Romantic-conservative circles further east that continued to see quasi-feudal estates as the healthiest form of agrarian land use. His basic acknowledgement of the economic need for competition and his general stress on increased productivity set him apart from his Catholic contemporaries. On the other hand, his emphasis on the distribution of goods rather than just on their production allied him with conservative French economists and set him apart from contemporary economic liberalism.

He had read Villeneuve-Bargemont in the 1830s and regarded him as an authority on pauperism (Reichensperger 1847, 267–76); in view of the threat to artisans from factory production, which he saw clearly, he proposed a number of interventions on the part of the state in regulating competition, helping crafts workers to organize their credit, production, and distribution so as to become more competitive, and also in assisting in the care of the poor. The state could and should be helpful in encouraging the formation of associations, he thought; it should definitely recognize the right of workers to form their own coalitions. With care and planning, Germany could lift itself over the hump of a moderate industrialization and provide for a larger, more prosperous population through technical progress (1847, 280–93).

One sees that here a Catholic leader was developing, one who had studied his economics well (at Heidelberg under Karl Heinrich Rau) and who had continued to read and think hard on the problems of his time as did few others. In fact, although he neither aimed at nor achieved any new insights in the field of economics, he was the only German Catholic of his generation, a university study of classical economics behind him, who produced what amounted to a whole treatise on industrialization (Reichensperger 1847, 193–293; Grenner 1967, 231–50, here 247). His attitude was critical but by no means negative. Roughly in the line of Friedrich List, he endorsed protective tariffs until German industry could meet the foreign competition, another example of his mitigated economic liberalism. Unfortunately, his early contribution to the formation of Catholic opinion on economic matters was not very influential. Although he had been, with his brother August, a staunch defender of Catholic interests since 1837, and although he would go on to become a founding member of the Center party and a member of the Reichstag until his death, his critical appropriation of liberal thought must have made his book too exotic a phenomenon for his Catholic contemporaries.

It is worth noting also the main element that Peter Reichensperger had in common with the more conservative Catholics, who were concerned about pauperism and the condition of labor at midcentury. This was his conviction that Christianity had to play a decisive role in overcoming the pathological outgrowths of dynamic nineteenth-century economic development. "The working class must learn in Christian living the virtues of patience, perseverance and moderation.... The employers for their part must learn Christian gentleness and compassion" (*Agrarfrage* 216, cited by Franz Mueller in Grenner 1967, 249). When the conservatives went on to demand a "Christian society" or even a "Christian economic order," however, Reichensperger was no longer with them. What he thought best even for the church was a modern constitutional state in aid of a society based on equal freedom for all.

Further down the Rhine, Adolph Kolping (1813–65); see Göbels, Conzemius 1968, 103–23, E. Ritter 1954, 88–91) was starting an organization for and of journeymen that would make his name famous in many parts of the world after his death. He himself had been a journeyman shoemaker from 1829 to 1837, at which time he went back to school as a twenty-four-year-old among pupils ten years younger. He wanted to become a priest and did, in 1845. More slowly but more surely than Abbé Ledreuille, he drew on his own experience as a journeyman and on that of a group of them gathered together in his first parish by a local teacher, Johann Gregor Breuer.

About two-thirds of the industrial workers in Germany at that time were journeymen, which meant that they had received an initial training in some trade and were free to hire themselves out to masters in that trade or any other employer. However, they were not yet qualified, even if they had had the means, to set themselves up in business, nor could they get married as journeymen. The overcrowded path to factory work or unskilled labor was open to them, of course. Most journeymen could never hope to become independent.

What Kolping saw as the most demoralizing aspect of this whole hideous situation was the lack of any sort of family or social life apart from the taverns. He himself had been terribly isolated during his years as a journeyman shoemaker (and even more so when he went back to school). The master craftsmen, of course, no longer shared their home life with their assistants. Thus the most unruly element in German society at the time was made up precisely of these unmarried, often desperate workers, who moved around a lot and came in contact with subversive and radical ideas in Paris, Brussels, or Geneva (W. Schieder 1963, 82–173; Conzemius 1972, 113).

Kolping let his reflections ripen a little and pulled them together in the leaflet at the beginning of 1848, entitled "The Journeymen's Association: For the Encouragement of All Who Have the True Good of the People at Heart." The Journeymen's Association (Gesellenverein, later Kolpingverein) would be a means by which the unmarried workers could provide each other with company in a healthy atmosphere emphasizing sociability and professional training. The religious element would be present but not so prominent as to turn the clerical host of the group into its only truly active component. At the same time, the organizational structure of the movement would be facilitated by attaching it to the already existing parish structure. For the actual beginnings of Kolping's Gesellenverein, see the end of the next chapter.

When Pope Gregory XVI died in the middle of 1846, the only crisis the papacy faced was in its own back yard, the papal states, and in Austrian-controlled northern Italy (Aubert in Jedin 1981, 8:57–59). Elsewhere no immediately threatening church-state issues were evident. As for widespread pauperism and the industrial revolution, traditional views dominated. The masses would always suffer from poverty; building a railroad would not change that. The problems of widespread poverty and underdevelopment were eclipsed, however, by the question of national unification of Italy and, even apart from that, of a creaking administrative apparatus badly in need of reform. The papal states, where all lay subjects were excluded by law from any position of responsibility in the government, had roughly the reputation in nineteenth-century Europe that South Africa has had in the third quarter of the twentieth century, without any counterbalancing economic successes. The new pope, Pius IX (Giovanni Mastai-Ferretti, 1792–1878) was so eager to please that, despite his own intentions, he gave rise to the most exaggerated hopes on the part of political liberals and fears among the reactionaries. The reactionaries' fears were soon realized.

These dangers might have been minimized, had it not been for parallel manifestations of discontent with the other regimes in Europe that brought the crisis in the papal states to a head. In the meantime, Ozanam in Paris published an article in *Le Correspondant* commenting on the Roman situation (Rivières 1984, 117–18; Duroselle 1951, 296). Whereas Pius IX renewed his predecessor's condemnations of liberalism in his inaugural encyclical of 8 November 1846, adding to it a condemnation of "communism," a brand-new word at the time, he had also lent a ready ear to Padre Gioacchino Ventura (1792–1861), an old friend of Lamennais's who preached the eulogy for Daniel O'Connell in 1847. Given the conflicting signals, Ozanam chose to interpret the signs of the times as indicating an epochal shift in the interests of the Holy See.

His own striking phrase for this was, *"Passons aux barbares!"* Thinking of the papacy at the time of the great migrations of barbarians and of the decision of Gregory the Great to throw in his lot with the Germanic invaders (the Franks) instead of relying solely on the East Roman Empire, he saw Pius IX taking a similar step of great consequence. The rest of us should do the same, he concluded: "Let us go over to the barbarians!" To a friend who reported the offense it was causing, he explained (22 February 1848, as cited in Duroselle):

> When I say *passons aux barbares*, I don't mean "to the radicals." The sovereign pontiff seems to me to be implementing some of our views of the last twenty years. To go over on the side of the *barbarians*, means from the camp of the kings, of the statesmen since 1815, to go to the people. By saying *passons aux barbares*, I am asking that we do as he is doing, that we attend to the people. Our people has too many cares and too few rights; it is legitimately looking for a greater part in public affairs, with some assurances of work and against poverty. Our people has some poor leaders because good ones have not made themselves available; but it is not responsible for the rhetoric of bourgeois books or assemblies, they being outside its ken. Perhaps we will not convert Attila and Genseric, but with the help of God we may win the Huns and the Vandals.

Lacordaire too had just recently, in a celebrated discourse, commemorated Daniel O'Connell (b. 1775, d. 15 May 1847 in Genua), the great Catholic popular leader of Ireland, reviving the hopes of *L'Avenir* of 1830 that Catholicism and the popular masses of the Christian world could make common cause. So it was that at the end of 1847 and the beginning of 1848 there was a spirit of expectation among a number of thinking Catholics in different social and political positions and in several countries. Great tasks were appearing on the horizon of European society. Catholics and Catholicism were called upon to make the perhaps decisive contributions toward bringing civilization into more humane and productive channels after the chaotic and at best spotty progress of the previous century and a half. The hate and distrust of the urban masses for "the Jesuits," the anticlericalists' favorite target, and the church in general, was in abeyance. There seemed to be every reason for hope.

Chapter 5

IN AND AFTER
THE REVOLUTIONS OF 1848

It can almost be said that the election of Pio Nono in 1846 provided the spark that set off the Revolution of 1848. By making concessions to the spirit of Italian liberal Catholicism and patriotism between 1846 and 1848, he had applied oil to one of the most rigidly encrusted joints of the Metternichian system of European states. That system was creaking at *every* joint by the late 1840s. But the papal states were an especial bone of contention. Metternich himself had despaired of pressuring Pius IX's predecessor, Gregory XVI, to make reforms in their antiquated, inefficient, and exclusively clerical administration. Now he saw with alarm that Pius IX was introducing reforms without forethought as to their consequences. By the end of 1847 and the beginning of 1848, lay participation in the government of the papal states was generally permitted, something that Pius IX did not really want and would revoke the first chance he got (Aubert 1978, 5:24–27).

We have seen how Ozanam interpreted this, with a curious mixture of insight into the situation the church was to face for many decades and a generous dose of wishful thinking as to Catholicism's readiness to do so. What was clear was that movement had come into Metternich's Europe at a place and in a way that was hardly expected. In January of 1848 a rebellion broke out in Sicily — it was not put down by the Bourbon regime that ruled southern Italy for over a year. Then followed the February Revolution in Paris and the rest of France, which set off a whole series of revolutions across Europe, especially in Berlin and Vienna. In Paris, Louis Philippe abandoned the throne in a panic over demonstrations that the army tried to meet with force. In Vienna, Metternich took his leave unceremoniously in the middle of March. The key Parisian events might have taken place exactly as they did, even if Gregory XVI had still been pope. But the

79

spectacular papal abandonment of reaction (temporary as it was to be) no doubt contributed to the situation in which so many monarchs and statesmen lost their nerve and abandoned their positions so precipitously in early 1848.

In Paris, the questions of the organization of labor and universal suffrage, both involving the matter of social and economic class concerns, were in the forefront of the revolutionary demands. Moreover, Philippe Buchez became the first presiding officer of the Constituent Assembly elected to frame a new constitution for the Second Republic. A great enthusiasm developed for "Christian democracy," led by Catholics such as Ozanam and the L'Ere nouvelle team. The clergy, two archbishops of Paris, and the group led by Armand de Melun all took prominent roles in inaugurating the hoped-for "new era."

In other countries of Europe, notably in Germany, social issues also emerged and demanded attention in a new way. A young priest by the name of Ketteler would address them in the cathedral of Mainz against a background of economic crisis, especially in textile manufacturing, poor weather for harvests, and the potato blight, all of which, in various combinations, had been affecting German states as well as other European countries since 1846. Hence 1848 forms the threshold of social Catholicism. On the whole, it was a threshold over which European Catholicism slipped — and fell — picking itself up to curse socialism as the offspring of its older revolutionary nemesis, liberalism.

The specter of out-and-out democracy sent a chill up the spines of all those who had more to lose than to gain by revolution. Soon the forces of order in all three countries regained the upper hand. The Second French Republic was hardly established on an anti-socialist basis (November 1848), when the man who was to put an end to republicanism in France for twenty years was elected president (December 1848). Louis Napoleon, supported by Catholics, seized power by a coup d'état at the beginning of December 1851. A couple of months later, after a plebiscite, he was emperor as his uncle had been and the Second Republic was history.

In Germany and Austria, the monarchs (a new one for Austria-Hungary) and their armies gradually subdued the populations in their capital cities. The last uprisings in Germany took place in the southwest in May and June of 1849. The Austrians regained control of northern Italy already in the summer of 1848 and once more, definitively, in the following year. French troops also put down the "Republic of Rome" in 1849, but Pius IX did not return from exile in Gaeta until 12 April 1850. In his mind, as in the mind of so many other Catholics, republicanism, socialism, "communism," and revolution now fused into a single radical bête noire (or rather rouge). It was to be opposed by all right-thinking persons in the name of order (whichever prevailed) and authority.

Only palliative responses to the social problems of industrialization or underdevelopment could flourish in this atmosphere. But other approaches, with more of a future, had also raised their heads for a brief period before being eclipsed by the red scare.

Philippe Buchez and the National Assembly

With the abdication of King Louis Philippe, a provisional government set itself up and moved quickly to declare France a republic, to endorse the main demands of the demonstrators, and to prepare for elections for a constitutional assembly, the *Constituante* of May to November 1848. The socialist writer Louis Blanc represented the more radical wing, while Buchez and his friends were anxious to bridge the gaps between classes and take full advantage of the "spirit of 1848" — not unlike Alphonse de Lamartine, the leading man of the provisional government. Convinced if rather timid republicans, they wanted to bring the majority of the country with them into the Second Republic. Hence they were prepared to negotiate with conservatives — not on re-establishing the monarchy or limiting suffrage, but on the particulars of the decisions in principle taken by the provisional government: the "right to work," the limitation of the length of the working day, the creation of a sort of Labor Department in the government and the establishment of national workshops to alleviate unemployment.

The "national workshops" (*ateliers nationaux*) that were set up to implement the right-to-work declaration could only be one of two things, as it seemed: either workers' cooperatives funded initially by the state along the lines of Louis Blanc's proposals for the organization of labor, which would mean an assault on private property, or *ateliers de charité*, public works projects that would be a continual drain on the budget. Later leading Buchezians would try to get a third way on its feet, but on 26 February the decision was made to set up workhouses for the poor, just as in the *ancien régime*, under the name of *ateliers nationaux*. This was no effective measure against the widespread unemployment and led to meaningless and hence demeaning regimentation of the unemployed with increasing discontent, demonstrations, and finally renewed oppression of the underclasses (June 1848; see Ziebura 1985, 285–88, and Bruhat in Droz 1972, 1:506).

For the ten weeks from the beginning of March until the middle of May, however, the spirit of 1848 seemed to prevail. It was a spirit of mutual goodwill. There was a blossoming of optimism that the interests of the middle and the lower classes were not necessarily antithetical, a spirit that owed a good deal to the concern shown by Archbishop Affre and a number of lay churchmen as to the plight of the working and unemployed poor, especially in Paris. In this atmosphere the Christian socialism of Buchez and his followers could get a hearing. However, once all other classes had united in a war upon the proletariat (as Karl Marx would describe it in the aftermath; see Bussmann in Schieder 1981, 5:84), and Catholic spokespersons had with few exceptions fervently committed themselves to the "party of order" (Duroselle 1951, 413), Buchezian proposals for realizing an equitable economic system by voluntary means lost their actuality.

But for those few weeks it seemed as if the bishops had all become Buchezians in at least one important point. This was that the ideals of 1789 (liberty, fraternity, and equality) were not only admissible but even represented a necessary expression of Christianity (Duroselle 1951, 415–17). They hastened to add that this meant "true, Christian" liberty, fraternity, and equality, but they obviously saw the desires of the little people welling up in February as quite compatible with this true Christian meaning. Buchez, it will be remembered, had first made a name for himself by publishing the multivolume *Histoire parlementaire de la Révolution française* from 1834 to 1838, reissued in 1845–46. Here he had taken the unheard-of step of interpreting the French Revolution in its core and at its beginnings as flowing from and in accord with the gospel of Christ in the Catholic tradition (Maier 1969, 201–7). This interpretation offered at least the possibility that the great gulf between the two modern traditions in France, the one stemming from the Revolution and the other pitted against it (as in the Restoration mentality) could find common ground from which to sink their differences and move forward together. It was a precondition of the spirit of 1848.

So it was that, even though the elections for the Constituent Assembly on April 23 returned a nonsocialist (soon to reveal itself as an *anti*-socialist) majority, Philippe Buchez was elected president of the assembly and another prominent Buchezian, Claude-Anthime Corbon (1808–91), became its second vice-president. Corbon was an authentic if unusually well-read worker, who plied several trades, finally settling on woodcarving, before co-founding *L'Atelier* and again after it folded in 1850. Under Buchez's influence he had been converted to Catholic Christianity, but he would abandon it again over the years. In the provisional government, he belonged to the moderate (*National*) wing with another Buchezian, Jules Bastide (1800–1879), who became minister of foreign affairs for the Second Republic.

Buchez's term as president was short-lived and inglorious. The executive power was held by a body also elected by the National Assembly itself (Lamartine, Ledru-Rollin, and Louis Blanc, surrounded by some liberal but nonradical republicans), until General Cavaignac was called in to quell the workers' uprising in the bloody "June Days" and to become dictator *pro tempore*. The fact that Buchez and Corbon were not elected to the Executive Commission, where no socialists or workers were to be found, but only as presiding officers of the National Assembly, looks in retrospect like a sop thrown to the more popular elements of the February Revolution as the dominant middle classes prepared to veer right once more. In any case, as preparations were made to cope with a protest demonstration on the part of the more radical revolutionaries and their Parisian working-class supporters scheduled for 15 May, the Executive Commission failed to let Buchez know what steps were being taken to keep the demonstrators out of the Palais Bourbon; their wires were so crossed that not even the key army units were called up in time. The demonstrators reached and invaded the assembly because of this confusion (Amann 1970, 62–65). Buchez, thinking that he was responsible for the safety of the deputies, left his seat to order the call to arms for the National Guard, a drum roll audible to all. Then he countermanded the order in writing, in the hope of protecting conservative deputies from the wrath of the populace.

When order was restored, the spirit of 1848 was gone. Buchez, who had served as president of the assembly only for one month, resigned on 6 June. Little or no blood had flowed on 15 May; however, as the unemployment continued and as the assembly turned from republican to conservative to Bonapartist, it also turned to bloody repression for which Buchez had no stomach. He voted against the moderate-conservative majority on the matter of prohibiting the popular political clubs (among them was Le club de l'Atelier, which had to close like the others after 28 July). On other issues he often voted with them, even on the right to work.

At least two other Buchezians were elected to the National Assemblies in both 1848 and 1849, Frédéric Arnaud, called Arnaud de l'Ariège (1819–78), and Pierre Pradié (born 1816). They both voted with the minority to put the right to work into the constitution on 13 September 1848, probably the only Catholic deputies to do so. Arnaud de l'Ariège was to become the focus of surviving Christian democratic forces from 1849 to 1851. But neither of them belonged to the inner circle of longtime disciples of Buchez. This distinction goes to Henri Feugueray (1813–54) and his close friend, Auguste Ott (born in Strasbourg in 1814 and surviving until the late nineteenth century). These were also the two most Catholic of Buchez's followers. Ott's brochure of 1838, *Les associations ouvrières*, began a career of explaining the master more clearly than the original thinker himself. At the time of the February Revolution, he was managing the *Revue nationale* (not to be confused with the better-known republican newspaper, *Le National*, that Bastide edited), spreading Buchez's message among the political class as Corbon and company did with *L'Atelier* among artisans and those particularly sympathetic to workers (Duroselle 1951, 360).

Even though Ott was not elected from the Alsatian district where his name was on the ballot, he was named a member of a commission set up to oversee the distribution of monies to "workers' associations." This was an initiative of Corbon's in the National Assembly following on the closing of the *ateliers nationaux* and the suppression of the rioting workers in "the June Days." On 5 July 1848 a credit of three million francs was authorized "for the encouragement of worker associations" — cooperatives of production — and a twelve-member commission was charged with ruling on applications for the loans. The three or four Buchezians (Corbon, Ott, Dainguy, and, later, Feugueray) tried to establish criteria favoring combinations of workers (like the partnership of jewelry-makers known since 1834 as Leroy, Thibaut & Cie, the only Buchez-type cooperative of production known to have existed; see Duroselle 1951, 361–67), rather than "worker associations" formed by employers. However, they were unable to prevail and they resigned by the end of the year.

Such was the brief appearance of Buchezian Christian socialism on the stage of French politics. Ott and Feugueray used their enforced inactivity to publish substantial works of Buchezian theory in 1851 (Duroselle 1951, 737). On the night of the coup d'état (1–2 December 1851), Buchez was one of the republicans arrested, but he was released shortly thereafter and did not have to go into exile. Ott would publish the last work of the master shortly after Buchez's death in 1866 (Duroselle 1951, 662). A notable chapter in the relationships between socialism and Christianity was closed, but of course the last word had not been spoken.

L'Ere Nouvelle 1848–49

In the last month of his life, Daniel O'Connell, the great leader of the Catholic emancipation movement in Ireland (Conzemius 1972, 15–27), visited France and died in Italy on 15 May 1847. Among the old Mennaisians, this rekindled the enthusiasm for the alliance between popular liberation and Catholicism that *L'Avenir* had once articulated. In the papal entourage itself, Gioacchino Ventura (1792–1861) vividly portrayed the benefits that came to Catholicism in Ireland from the clergy's solidarity with the simple people under the leadership of a freedom-loving Christian and nonviolent agitator like O'Connell.

In Paris, on 10 February 1848, Lacordaire did the same. The effect on public opinion was all the greater when, from the pulpit of Notre Dame of Paris on 27 February, he spoke eloquently of the hopes bound up with the newly proclaimed republic (Aubert 1964, 43). He seemed like the very spokesman of the people, articulating the spirit of 1848. As a man of the hour, he was elected to the National Assembly from Marseilles. For the next three years, he again preached the Lenten sermons at Notre Dame of Paris, where he had first spoken in 1835. At turning points by now familiar to the reader he withdrew from this exposure: just after 15 May he resigned his seat in the National Assembly, seeing an irresolvable conflict between his way of life as a Dominican friar-preacher and the other difficult duties of an elected representative of the people. After the coup d'état in 1851 he appeared no more in the pulpit of Notre Dame.

In the days following the February Revolution, Lacordaire, Ozanam, and Abbé Henry Maret got together with a few others (de Coux, a Buchezian named J.-P. Tessier, etc.) and decided to start a new daily newspaper under Lacordaire's management. It appeared from 15 April 1848 to the 1 April 1849. All three co-founders were "unrepentant liberals," as Lacordaire would say of himself much later (*Catholicisme* 6:1570), true to their past experience with *L'Avenir*. In Lacordaire, however, the commitment to freedom in society went along with a lack of sensitivity toward the problem of social and economic inequality (Aubert 1964, 46). He was not as conservative a liberal in this respect as his erstwhile friend Montalembert, who continued to favor a constitutional monarchy and wanted to keep the broad mass of the people firmly under the protection and guidance of the aristocracy; who, therefore, had to overlook the drawbacks of this imbalance of power even more consistently and deliberately than Lacordaire. But they were both alien to and alienated by the aspirations of the lower classes.

This would lead to tensions within the editorial board of *L'Ere nouvelle*. Ozanam, after all, stated plainly that "behind the political revolution, we see a social revolution, we see the arrival of the working class...." (*Correspondant*, March 1848; see Aubert 1964, 44; Duroselle 1951, 300–308; DBMOF 3:169). He had no proposals as to how to deal with it, but he clearly thought it was a legitimate development to be treated with a great deal of sympathy. Abbé Henry Maret (1805–84) had a similar philosophy of history, welcoming the progressive realizations of human freedom and not stopping at the liberation of the bourgeoisie from the control of the nobility and higher clergy (Bressolette 1977 and *Catholicisme* 8:435–39). When

Lacordaire inserted a one-sided condemnation of the May 15 disorders into *L'Ere nouvelle*, Maret offered his resignation. Lacordaire got him to reconsider by assuring him that he could continue to express his own opinions freely.

Thus, during the "June Days," *L'Ere nouvelle* was able to express dismay at the cruelty with which the laborers of Paris were forced from the *ateliers nationaux* and then butchered indiscriminately when they took to the barricades. Between Ozanam, Maret, and the other writers, the paper became more and more forthrightly dedicated to a brand of "democracy," which, as Montalembert said with more than a modicum of insight, was allied with socialism and claimed to be itself true Christianity. Maret said as much: "What good does it do to refute the pseudo-socialists? Let us make ourselves socialists" without the un-Christian errors (Duroselle 1951, 315). Lacordaire found himself unable to share such a distinctly advanced social line. At the beginning of September, he turned the paper over to Maret, who gave himself to it full-time (Duroselle 1951, 308–20).

Abbé Maret was a theologian who drew not only on the Lamennais and Gerbet of *L'Avenir* but also on Buchez for his social thinking. After 1851, he would try to offset ultramontane Catholicism of the Louis Veuillot (*L'Univers*) stamp as best he could behind the scenes, eventually by making common cause with elements in the government of the Second Empire whom he considered responsible and friendly to the church. But for the present, he turned *L'Ere nouvelle* (which Veuillot persisted in calling *L'Erreur nouvelle*) into a model of Christian advocacy for the lower classes in a country otherwise turning more and more to conservatism and even repression (Aubert 1964, 53). He let Charles de Coux go and recruited Pierre Pradié and Frédéric Arnaud, as well as their friend Eugène Rendu. Another Buchezian, Feugueray (with Ott the leading Buchezian theorist), filled, as it seems (Duroselle 1951, 315), the theoretical vacuum that Ozanam and Maret more or less consciously left open. *L'Atelier*'s columns were packed with reports and discussions of worker associations and various public or church welfare projects. It published an investigation on the working class (Duroselle 1951, 314). Maret had in mind the idea of forming a school of social thought and action around *L'Ere nouvelle*. But the opposing forces, especially within the clergy, were too strong and gaining strength daily. Soon *L'Ere nouvelle* fell into financial problems and had to be sold, not quite a year after it had started publication.

Among the blows suffered by Christian democracy was the death of Archbishop Affre on a peacemaking mission to the street barricades on 27 June 1848. Felled by a bullet fired to the dismay of insurrectionists from no one knows where, his death deprived Maret and other democrats of *L'Ere nouvelle* of one of their strongest supporters. Ozanam would still be able to write a few strong articles, but from the beginning of 1849 his health deteriorated (he died 8 September 1853) and he was no longer able to fight the good fight at Maret's side (Aubert 1964, 47, 50).

Christian Democrats of the Second Republic

At this point, however, Arnaud de l'Ariège emerged as the chief spokesman for "the right to live by working" and became the new focus of the Christian democratic movement in the Second Republic (Pierrard 1984, 159–65; Duroselle 1951, 374–83; DBMOF 1:108–11). Arnaud was a lawyer who had sought out the meetings and writings of those interested in the plight of the working class: Fourierist humanitarians, Buchez, *L'Atelier*. In 1846 he penned an appeal in the *Démocratie pacifique* to Catholics to take a good look at socialism. A fervent Catholic (like so many of the other Christian socialists we have seen in this generation in France), he founded a St. Vincent de Paul conference in his hometown at the end of 1847. Elected from his home district (hence Arnaud "de l'Ariège"), he took a consistently republican stand in all his votes. Maret brought him onto the administrative board of *L'Ere nouvelle* at the beginning of September 1848, as mentioned.

During the debate on social rights (the right to earn one's living by working and the right to subsistence) from 11 to 15 September 1848, Catholic spokesmen such as Montalembert and Tocqueville allied themselves with secular bourgeois in the nascent "party of order" and turned the fire of their rhetoric explicitly against the social component of the 1848 Revolution, which Ozanam and others had underscored and welcomed. In stark contrast, Arnaud's address made him the undisputed leader of the Christian democrats from that day until the day three years later when Louis Napoleon pulled off his coup d'état. (Maret found a place for Arnaud to hide from the police and helped him escape to Belgium for several months.)

Arnaud had no better solution to the problems than Ozanam or the Buchezians, but he was equally concerned about them. He (rightly) foresaw that if the first demand of the Revolution, the acknowledgment of the right of every human being to live by working, was left out of the preamble to the constitution of the Second Republic, then the February Revolution would have brought virtually no change in the status of the laboring classes. And to accept that, he knew, was morally wrong. He may be seen as a consistent Catholic defender of the ideals of 1789. Not only was liberty a central value for him (Duroselle 1951, 378–79), but so were fraternity and equality (DBMOF 1:108–11). If by nature all share the same human dignity, then the organized collectivity that is a state has the duty to see to it that one class is not particularly discriminated against and disadvantaged. The corollary of this collective duty, as Arnaud saw it, was what was meant by "the right to work" (Pierrard 1984, 160).

Shortly after the June days, when upper-class Parisians as a whole were less inclined than ever to go into the workers' quarters, one young but very well-to-do Catholic, Augustin Cochin, brought Arnaud to a meeting of the Society of St. Francis Xavier in the faubourg St-Jacques (9 July 1848). There Arnaud stated that it was a mistake (of Louis Blanc's in particular) to expect the state to "organize labor," i.e., to administer the economy. "Only by freedom," that is, by free association, can the labor of human beings be effectively organized (Duroselle 1951, 378). And this requires mutual forbearance and other Christian virtues.

Despite the lack of attention on Arnaud's part to economic (as opposed to moral or political) factors, his commitment to and rapport with the working class, given the lack of other possible leaders, brought Arnaud to the head of the remaining small band of Christian democrats after his strong support for the right to work in the assembly made him stand out. He and Pradié were the only Catholic representatives in the National Assembly whom workers could count on to uphold their interests. (Pradié would realize around the beginning of 1851 that workers as a class were not going to be spared a class struggle or an ongoing series of class conflicts. Therefore he abandoned the idea of workers' productive cooperative associations for the right of labor to organize in unions to represent workers in a militant way against the counterpressures of employers; see DBMOF 3:251–52 and Duroselle 1951, 331–36.)

Outside the National Assembly a series of small journals served as rallying points for Christian democrats after the sale of *L'Ere nouvelle* (April 1849) and the demise of *L'Atelier* (July 1850). Pradié himself founded *La République universelle* (see Duroselle's *Index des oeuvres* and bibliography for these publications). Abbé Paul Chantôme (1810–77) brought two shortlived journals into existence, the more interesting one being the *Revue des réformes et du progrès*. It served as a sort of continuation of the *L'Ere nouvelle* for Arnaud, Rendu, Feugueray, and others. Victor Calland, a Christian socialist writer of Fourierist proclivities like Chantôme and Abel Transon, wrote for it and then started yet another monthly, the *Revue du socialisme chrétien*.

All these propagandists remained Catholic to the end of their lives, even after the Second Empire put an end to their republican journalistic activity. The same applies to the most notable convert from Fourierism, Désiré Laverdant (see Duroselle 1951, 379–83; DBMOF

2:449–50). He had been a principal editor of *La Phalange* and had been largely responsible for the friendly attention of *La Démocratie pacifique* to social Catholicism from 1846 on. He became a Catholic at the beginning of 1848 and gravitated to Arnaud's camp. Along with Arnaud, he endeavored to provide an organizational network for the scattered Christian democrats of France in early 1850, called the "Catholic Democratic Circle" (*Cercle de la Démocratie catholique*). But there was no follow-up from the man to whom the whole group looked. Even before the coup d'état took place, this venture fell apart.

What then was this "first" Christian democratic movement? As is clear from the circumstances of its birth and decline, it was the work of those who looked beyond the political preoccupations of 1848 to the socio-economic realm and declared their solidarity with the new class of urban industrial proletarians. They were not content to take advantage of the spirit of 1848 merely to advance political and civil freedom, but took seriously the human dignity and aspirations of the working class in the cities as well; a sufficient measure of equality between the classes was not guaranteed simply by the right to vote (although that was necessary and not to be restricted again as happened in 1850). As distinguished from "the charitable school" of a Melun, they declined to look upon inequality as merely or even in the first place a challenge to the generosity of well-to-do Christians. What they insisted upon was the need to promote political *and* social-economic participation (although they did not use the word) in all classes of society.

The issues they faced were thorny ones, requiring patient trial and error and receiving at best half-hearted and highly provisional attention from leaders in politics and economics. Just as with contemporary socialists, of which they were a fringe, or rather a subset, there was a great deal of idealism among them and a shortage — how could it be otherwise? — of experience in trying out the bright ideas that surfaced.

The sum total of their passionate commitment might seem to have amounted only to a scattering of generous words and actions, admirable but futile lives. Charles Chevé, for example, was a bookbinder who threw himself into the Revolution of 1830, turned to Christianity under the influence of Buchez a few years later, became a Proudhonian and communist, and founded his own journal, *Le Socialiste*, after the February Revolution, all the while never ceasing to profess the Catholic faith. Another was Hippolyte de la Morvonnais (Duroselle 1951, 383–91), another Fourierist Catholic who tried so hard to set up a self-sufficient "Christian commune" in Brittany as an experimental model for the future organization of labor. Or, as in the case of Emmanuel d'Alzon (Duroselle 1951, 339), the founder of the Assumptionists, and many another priest during the Second Republic, one tried one's best to defend the cause of the workers but then resorted to a "charitable-economic" (paternalistic) approach in the face of socialist excesses and respectable persons' aversion to Christian democracy.

Paternalistic social Catholicism was going to grow while Christian democracy faded away to all appearances after the middle of the nineteenth century. However, ideas and attitudes reflecting realities do not disappear altogether as long as the realities from which they stem remain. The watchword of Christian democracy would be proclaimed again most loudly two more times, after *Rerum novarum* in the 1890s and after World War II in the Christian Democratic parties. Finally it would become an accepted part of the modern Catholic social outlook.

Rich and Poor in 1848: Ketteler's Initial Public Stands

Wilhelm Emmanuel von Ketteler was an unlikely candidate for historical fame as the great educator of German Catholicism and Pope Leo XIII's "great predecessor" in the social question. He himself was a scion of a Westphalian family of lesser landed nobility. He considered the relationship of a squire with his tenant farmers to be something quite normal. He knew from his own experience growing up on the family's lands near Münster that such a relationship could be quite a worthy and humane one on both sides, given a constant effort, in a spirit of Christian respect and simplicity of life, to meet the mutual responsibilities involved. The upshot of his brief lay career as a civil servant was a determination to emancipate the church from the tutelage of the state. He shared, that is, the preoccupations of the German Catholic movement of his time as a whole, with its emphasis on questions of church and state rather than of church and economic society.

Hence nothing in his background would directly suggest that Ketteler (1811–77; see Roos 1980 and 1982; Iserloh 1975; Langner 1974; Lenhart 1966–68; Grenner 1967, 206–30; Alexander 1953, 410–17, and Vigener, translations of his pertinent works in Ederer 1981) would become the foremost spokesman of social commitment in his age for Catholic Germany and beyond its borders. When he did notice and begin to pay special attention to the social question, especially in the form of the subsistence wages of factory workers, his first steps in coming to grips with it took off down a path that he eventually had to abandon. But from 1848 on, it was already clear to him, on the one hand, that here lay a great need of the time, an evil to be remedied;

and on the other, that the Roman Catholic Church was called upon to make a determined effort in response.

The year 1848 catapulted him into celebrity from obscurity as a country pastor (there was hardly any other kind in the diocese of Münster). First, the farmers of his area narrowly elected him to the Frankfurt parliament, or constitutional convention; then, by speaking at the funeral of two other delegates who had been ambushed and killed, presumably because of their conservative political line, he found himself in the public eye for the first time. Violence and disorder, he said in effect, were no help in establishing free institutions (Ketteler, *Sämtliche Werke und Briefe*, 1/1:10–16).

In October and during Advent he made two more notable public appearances, both in Mainz, the city to which he would return as bishop in 1850; in these he called attention emphatically to the social question. After this, he would be silent on the matter until 1864, as things political and social moved into a new stage in Germany. To stay with 1848 for the present, he made an impromptu declaration at the first general assembly of Catholics from all over Germany, predominantly representatives of the lay Catholic clubs and organizations that were shooting up everywhere in that year of new departures. (Together, they submitted more petitions to the authorities and to the parliament than any other constituency.) As a delegate in Frankfurt, he realized that people would expect him to address one or more of the burning constitutional issues that occupied everyone's attention.

Instead he directed the attention of the Catholic assembly (Katholikentag) to "the social question," by which he meant the gross inequalities of wealth and poverty and the immense growth of the latter (*Sämtliche Werke und Briefe* [henceforth cited as SWB], 1/1:17–20). The Frankfurt parliament might arrive at the best conceivable form of government for a newly united Germany, he said, and yet this would in itself contribute little or nothing to putting an end to economic distress and inequality. For his part, he was convinced that not the state, but the Catholic Church had the solution to this question, which was the most urgent problem of the age. He hinted that Thomas Aquinas had examined the problem of inequality of wealth six centuries before and had outlined the solution.

At this point, an assistant pastor at the cathedral of Mainz, Johann Baptist Heinrich (Vigener 1924, 283–84), got to know Ketteler and exerted himself to engage him as preacher of the Advent sermons in the cathedral. Who knows, perhaps he had even mentioned Thomas Aquinas's teaching about property to Ketteler before the latter's improvised remarks of October.

At any rate, he undertook the task of preparing the resulting sermons for publication in Ketteler's first book, *The Great Social*

Questions of the Present (Mainz, 1849; critical edition in Ketteler, SWB 1/1:23–87). It was Thomas's formulation of the doctrine of property that Ketteler then presented *in extenso* in the first two of his Advent sermons. As the most recent editor notes, it is most likely that Heinrich, co-editor of the Mainz *Katholik*, future dogmatics professor of the seminary and one of the future bishop's closest co-workers, called his attention to the passages from the *Summa theologiae*.

In the first two sermons, then, Ketteler portrayed the gap between the well-to-do and the poor as having become an explosive situation primarily because of the entirely negative influence of "liberalism." With the use of this term, he did not have in mind only or even chiefly the Manchester school of economic liberalism. He does not even seem to be acquainted with what the economists as such were teaching. To him, as to other Catholic conservative spokespersons of the time, individualism was the essence of modern liberals' views. Each human being would then be nothing but an autonomous individual, at best related to others only by freely chosen bonds or connections. In practice, what could that mean but an atomized or monadized collectivity of human organisms, indifferent or antagonistic to one another, and entering into combinations primarily to encroach ("gang up") on another individual's freedoms and property-holdings? Private property, on this view, is as sacred as the private "free" persons to whom it belongs. As with his conservative contemporaries (of whom more in a moment), Ketteler viewed liberalism primarily in its connection with the deist or atheist Enlightenment and with the French Revolution that it spawned. Liberalism rejected revelation and with it any sense of obligation to one's fellow human creatures that went beyond respecting their "freedom."

Besides this liberalism and often enough mixed up with it, Ketteler acknowledged a "historical," prerevolutionary tradition of human freedom and dignity as reposing on God's will, power, and goodness. In later years Ketteler would admit that there was or had been a strain of liberalism sharing common ground with this tradition of freedom. But in his sermons of 1848 he defined liberalism as rejecting the authentic tradition; hence all religious persons had to be opposed to liberalism, especially in view of the devastating social consequences of its outlook in practice.

Ketteler counted the dreadful spread of abject misery among these consequences, since liberal doctrine insisted only on the sanctity of private property and encouraged the notion that it was strictly up to each individual to satisfy his or her own wants. The resultant gross inequalities had also called forth an equally mistaken reaction, "Communism." Marx was of course still virtually unknown. What Ketteler understood by communism was the continuous redistribution of property (SWB 1/1:31), i.e., the abolition, in effect, of private property. He cited Proudhon's dictum that "Property is theft." Indeed, he granted it an element of truth, if one were talking about the inviolable, utterly private property of individualistic liberal doctrine.

Then Ketteler restated the traditional teaching on the providential purpose of poverty and wealth, such as Groethuysen found it in the eighteenth-century preachers in France. Rich and poor are mutually dependent on each other in God's disposition of the matter. Mutual dependence was, on this view, exactly what liberalism revolted against in its exaggeration of the legitimacy of private property.

Thomas Aquinas had worked out the golden mean between the extremes on the property question. Basically, of course, all of creation belongs to God. No human ownership of anything can be absolute, for it has the character of a loan from the Creator, as it were. Particular human families or persons may and should own property of their own, but as it were in stewardship, as the caretakers and managers upon whom it has devolved. Horizontally, as regards other human beings and authorities, what belongs to one private owner does not belong to any other and hence may not be reappropriated by force, legal or illegal. This was based on the common-sense observation that property not belonging to a particular person, family, or corporation tends to be neglected and become unproductive.

Between ownership (stewardship) and the *use* to which property is put, however, there is a distinction (SWB 1/1:30, citing Thomas Aquinas, S. th. II, q. 66, art. 2). The produce of private property is to be regarded as there for the benefit of all, for the use of all. How is this right of all to the produce of private property to be accomplished? Neither Thomas nor Ketteler went beyond the hallowed Christian duty of almsgiving as a mechanism for the proper distribution of produced wealth (above and beyond the market, he might have said, if he had been acquainted with Adam Smith or even Adam Müller). But Ketteler was convinced that in this cardinal point of the modern social question, the Catholic tradition contained a practicable moral alternative to the liberalism and the communism of his day: Christian charity as the practical expression of the social responsibility that goes with even private ownership of property.

Theoretically, he furnished a rationale on which Catholics could build and assert themselves on a basis independent of liberalism and communism. His proposed solution remained the traditional one of change of hearts and charity. But he had called emphatic attention to the social question and began to define it as best he could (as a Christian conservative, battling both liberalism and communism/socialism as mirror images of each other's errors), without as yet taking into account the novelties of capitalist economics or the industrial mode of production.

The influences on Ketteler's thinking at this point were not, at least not directly, Adam Müller or Franz von Baader. He evidently had not come across Peter Reichensperger's book, nor did he know of the previous work of Villeneuve-Bargemont, Ducpétiaux, or de Coux, not to mention Buchez or Ott. His political thought was well within the Christian-conservative realm typified by a periodical he certainly did read, the *Historisch-Politische Blätter* published in Munich (Stegmann 1965, 7–11; Lill in Jedin 1980, 7:333–34). The "Historisch" in the title reminds us of the Romantic interest in the historically developed pre- and anti-revolutionary institutions of Catholic Europe. In fact, the conservatives were beneficiaries of Romanticism in both Catholic and Protestant circles. Ketteler was receptive to both Catholic and Protestant conservative writers (Langner 1974, 69–82).

On the Catholic side, one of the foremost collaborators of the *Historisch-Politische Blätter* was Carl Ernst Jarcke, a former professor of criminal law in Berlin but otherwise very like a successor of Adam Müller: a convert (1825), a restoration publicist for Metternich after 1832, a conservative appalled by the social tensions feeding into the outbreaks of 1848. Like his co-editors, Guido Görres and George Phillips, he was a theorist of the "Christian society," agrarian, traditional, authoritarian, monarchical, such as also appealed to King Frederick William IV in Prussia and his Catholic adviser, Joseph Maria von Radowitz (E. Ritter 1954, 49–52).

The most influential proponent of this conservative politics of Christian inspiration, however, was the Protestant Friedrich Julius Stahl (see Bussmann in Schieder 1981, 5:101–3, and Langner 1974, 62–93). Himself a convert from Judaism to Lutheranism and subject to Romantic and idealist influences (Schelling), he built on the foundations laid by the so-called historical school of jurisprudence founded by the Calvinist Friedrich Carl von Savigny in Berlin. All these Christian jurists made common cause against the spirit of the French Revolution, i.e., against what they called liberalism.

This is the thought-world which Ketteler found congenial and whose assumptions he shared for a long time. What distinguished him from them was his sense of the times in which he lived. He exhibited a conservative respect for the past without becoming its prisoner. A practical Christian above all, a man of action, he always was on the lookout for what would be for the good of Jerusalem, not in some other age but in his own. Some have taken his use of Thomas Aquinas as evidence that Ketteler, like Pope Leo XIII, regarded Thomist thought as the God-given instrument by which the Roman Catholic Church would prove its worth to the nineteenth century. Actually, Ketteler, who was not of a scholarly cast of mind and who had not been trained in Thomism (the Neo-Thomist revival in Germany had started in Mainz earlier in the century, but Ketteler had studied theology mostly in Munich), merely regarded Aquinas as a particularly representative and clear spokesman for the common Catholic tradition on the relations of the propertied and the propertyless.

From the modern conservative school just mentioned, which had not yet rediscovered Thomas Aquinas's possible special relevance to the modern age and which cannot be regarded as neo-scholastic by any stretch of the imagination, Ketteler absorbed and retained a preference for the Germanic corporative organization of society. He would move beyond this position in the late 1860s, as we shall see. Other German Catholics would find it harder to do so. When neo-scholastic natural law doctrine became dominant after Ketteler's death, it did so in part by entering into a symbiosis with the conservative corporatist strains in German Catholic social thought. Thus the two wings of the German Catholic social movement in the early twentieth century, roughly the trade-union wing and the vocational-order (corporatist) wing, both claimed Ketteler for their own and both regarded him as more Thomistic than he was. But his own further stages will occupy us in a later chapter.

This later development was to be of great importance for the Catholic social movement in Germany and beyond. When he embarked on this voyage in 1848, he in no wise suspected where it would carry him in terms of new perspectives and concrete recommendations. Like a rower pulling his oars, he concentrated his gaze on where he had come from; he provided an emphatic restatement of classical Catholic doctrine on the mutual relations of rich and poor in the scheme of a merciful providence. What he hardly glimpsed as yet was that the agrarian society, to which that traditional teaching was a Christian pattern of response, was about to yield, even in Germany, to a process of industrialization. In a world dominated by the relationship of capital and labor, traditional solutions would no longer be effective. They would have to step back and form a second line of defense, yielding the first place to new approaches.

The Working-Class Artisans in 1848: Kolping

Meanwhile, downstream from Frankfurt, Mainz, and Coblenz in the Prussian Rhine Province, Adolph Kolping (1813–65) was laying the foundations for what would soon become a large movement of and for young, unmarried workers. It would incorporate in an effective way the broadly articulated need for association: for mutual assistance, for self-help and self-improvement. And it would bring it about for the segment of the German working population that was the hardest hit in the middle of the century: the artisans and craftsmen. Most of them were *Gesellen*, journeymen (Neitzel 1987). After a more or less impoverished apprenticeship, and with diminished hope of ever being able to establish oneself as an independent master, journeymen in the various trades still wandered from town to town. They found employment wherever and under whatever conditions they could, and tried to maintain their pride in being after all not mere laborers but skilled artisans.

Their dismal prospects were due to the widening gap between population growth and economic backwardness in the Germany of the 1830s and the 1840s. More and more workers took up trades that, on the whole, catered to steady or diminishing demand. There was not enough work to go around and factory work, besides being a cruel alternative inasmuch as it spelled certain proletarization, was not as yet widespread enough to take up the slack. The factories that did exist, such as the weaving mills in parts of the Rhineland, had little need for workers trained in most of the traditional crafts; nevertheless about two-thirds of their male workers were journeymen. If Kolping had been easily impressed by the predictions of both socialist and conservative commentators around 1850, he would have given up his movement: many saw the end of the independent tradesman and the small crafts shop as just around the corner. As it happened, however, the industrial development that was coming would directly and indirectly open continuing employment opportunities for craftsmen, even though many of the individual trades would disappear or be agonizingly transformed. The organization of artisan workers, therefore, filled a crying need for a long period of difficult adjustment.

Kolping's highly successful idea was a chain of clubs with largely educational and social activities ("social" here also in the sense of passing time in pleasant and morally respectable company), designed to give the demoralized and uprooted journeymen some mutual support under the mantle of the church. These meetings in church rooms or eventually in their own clubrooms gave them something of the family atmosphere that they sorely lacked and helped them to become "proficient journeymen now and excellent masters and fathers of families later," as the statutes of the first Journeymen's Association in Kolping's first parish, Elberfeld, stated at the end of 1848.

The freedom of association grasped so energetically by German Catholics and others had already resulted in a mass of so-called Piusvereine, named after the new pope. They were mostly of a charitable or quasi-political character, championing Catholic interests in the ferment of new beginnings and hopes for a freer and juster society. They too contributed indirectly to a network of informal self-help or mutual-aid connections that were often centered around a church and that would become, after the anti-Catholic *Kulturkampf* of the 1870s, the basis for Germany's highly developed set of formal associations that crisscrossed Catholic society and undergirded the Catholic political party's electoral efforts.

The relatively early success of the Kolping clubs of journeymen made it a sort of paradigm for German Catholicism's effective organizational work among less favored strata of society. Adolph Kolping himself came from the most modest background — he was the fourth of five children of an illiterate small farmer in the hinterlands of Cologne. By exception, because he was not particularly strong, he received a good elementary school education; but then he had to go into apprenticeship to a shoemaker at an early age. He practiced that trade as a journeyman for seven years until he made up his mind to escape the milieu that later he was to affect so signally. At the age of twenty-two or twenty-three, he announced his attention to become a priest. The first priest to whom he confided this is supposed to have said, "Cobbler, stick to your last" (Conzemius 1968, 222; see also Conzemius 1972; Franz 1914, 111–46, and E. Ritter 1954, 88–91).

After learning some Latin and Greek from a more sympathetic priest, as a twenty-four-year-old he sat down beside boys ten years younger in a *Gymnasium* in Cologne. The next year he got a scholarship and managed to finish the five years he was lacking in three-and-a-half years. In 1841, with the help of a benefactress, he was off to theology studies at the University of Munich. There he got to know the leading members of the Görres circle as well as Professor Döllinger, probably the most impressive theologian and church historian of the Munich faculty.

There he also met Wilhelm von Ketteler, of such unlike social standing but like him a "delayed vocation." If the report given by Albert Franz (1914, 120–21) is to be trusted (it is based on only one recollection and seems anachronistic), Kolping spoke with Ketteler while they were both students in Munich of the distressed situation of the journeymen and of his wish to help them by the oft-invoked means of "association." He naturally thought of a religious association like the medieval guilds with their churchly affiliation. Ketteler suggested however that the religious or pious element should not be in the forefront; let the association pursue social aims first and foremost, let it be an organization devoted to the economic betterment of the Kolping's class. Thus it would have a better chance of attracting independent-minded workers. All the same, this should take place under the auspices of the church; then the religious dimension would quite naturally assume its rightful place.

Whether this exchange took place just as later recorded or not, it corresponds to the strong agreement of the two men, Ketteler supporting Kolping when he could, as to the complexion that the Catholic Journeymen's Association assumed and maintained. It was an organization with clerical leaders, to be sure. Nevertheless, it was not to be a sodality of all the Catholic bachelors of a place, but specifically of artisan journeymen, a particular group subject to its particular moral, but also social and economic, problems. Focussing on these problems, it developed institutions to meet and alleviate them, all aimed at raising the economic and spiritual status of its members.

After finding and trying out his concept at Elberfeld in 1848, Kolping lost no time in asking for a transfer to Cologne. He wanted to establish a whole series of Journeymen's Associations in all the major German-speaking cities where journeymen flocked from all over. He got the second one started in Cologne by workers themselves, before he arrived there. In short order, there were such clubs established in Berlin, Munich, Vienna, and a dozen other places. By 1855 there were 104 such local clubs with 12,000 members; one or two larger centers already had their own facilities: not only rooms for the many courses in reading, writing, and arithmetic (few journeymen had the excellent elementary education that Kolping had received) and continuing education in the trades, business, religion, and civics, but also room and board for the travelling journeyman who just arrived in town and had not yet found work.

The clubrooms where the local members came to study or socialize also served as a sort of clearinghouse on job information for those who needed work. Such intensely practical services were organized by the priest head with increasing participation by the worker-members themselves. Financed by outside donations, such facilities could also rely after a while on the considerable holdings of the accumulated small savings of the members in a credit-union-like institution such as the pioneers of social consciousness had called for but rarely realized. Activities on this scale seemed hardly legal to some police authorities, but they merely made use of the possibilities that still remained from the failed Revolution of 1848 — they would hardly have been possible before then.

By 1865, when Kolping died, there were 24,000 Kolping journeymen, and the association's growth was not over. Even with the advance of factory work and the declassification of factory workers, there were still a half million master artisans in Prussia alone at that time and probably about as many journeymen (Nipperdey 1983, 210–14). The impetus for the phenomenal growth of the movement was twofold: Kolping, with enormous effort, found the means and the freedom to undertake propagandizing tours to advocate and assist in the grounding of local branches; and the wandering members of the first big club in Cologne spread the word very effectively among their fellows. From 1851 on, Kolping became a feature of the annual Katholikentage, thus stirring up or rekindling interest and support for the Association throughout Catholic Germany. Despite an effective organizational scheme, closely linked to the church by way of the priest heads of each club, Kolping had to support himself by religious journalism. Here he filled another gap (Catholic reading material with a popular touch) while educating broad popular strata on the rudiments of Catholic views on labor and solidarity; but what he could have done with a salary and an assistant or two paid by the church is an open question.

Kolping, *der Gesellenvater*, had hit upon the right combination, for his times and circumstances, of pastoral guidance and initiative (the strength of the paternalistic approach) and the educator's respect for one's students, sharing their wish for equality and full participation. The connection with the institutional church and the traditional parish system through the diocesan clergy proved to be an economical and effective way to provide the project with stable organizational support (see Roos in Rauscher 1982, 2:70–71). It was designed for and only worked for what we might call the endangered blue-collar middle class (not for the industrial proletariat), but there it did take hold, as we shall have occasion to observe later.

The comparison with France is significant (Conzemius 1972, 231). There, as also in Belgium, a practically unmitigated paternalistic approach dominated Catholic efforts to cope with working-class problems for decades after 1850. Abbé Ledreuille, who was also a workers' priest of humble origins, did not seem to have the energy and iron persistence of Kolping, or perhaps he was traumatized by the wave of reaction that followed the June days in Paris. Once 1848 had passed, the *compagnons* of France were certainly less responsive than the Catholic *Gesellen* of Germany to clerical efforts on their behalf, if a helping hand had been extended from that quarter. But the latter was lacking in France. Somehow, in Germany, Kolping had started a tradition among the clergy that some of them would devote a good part of their pastoral efforts to the working class, at least in the form of the Journeymen's Associations. The relatively few French priests stationed in population centers had their hands full, as it seemed, with the conventional duties of pastors.

In 1853, Kolping was invited to a meeting of Armand de Melun's Charitable Economics Society in Paris (Duroselle 1951, 607–9). As Kolb-Bernard of Lille admitted, the French *oeuvres* were a holding action at best: they exerted little or no attraction on workers who were not already attached to the church. Kolping could point to the great progress that his movement was making in Germany and saw as the key element to that success that a priest be found to head every local group, since "only he would enjoy the necessary authority." Passing over that point, a long-time member of the Melun circle picked up another one: Kolping had also indicated that the journeymen were better served if one could create an after-hours environment away from their employers. Now the very principle of the *patronages*, as they had been reactivated after the Revolution of 1848, was that of paternalism. The Christian employers supported and actively engaged in the after-hours programs put on for the benefit of "their" workers. Without them, said the Frenchman, there would be no one familiar with the industrial world to aid and assist the workers, for example, in placement. In France, therefore, he concluded, it would be better to involve all the Christian entrepreneurs in the workers' clubs.

Kolping responded that he did not involve employers in his associations for two major reasons. In the first place, workers much preferred to be out of sight and out of earshot of their bosses when not at work. The second reason was the informal atmosphere that prevailed and that was so attractive to the members; the presence of higher-class, possibly rich or influential personages in such an atmosphere would make the workers keenly aware of their lower status in society and would inevitably turn them away. (A third reason, unmentioned, was that often enough the factory-owners were non-Catholics.)

As Duroselle comments, Kolping knew intuitively, or rather, from his journeyman's experience, that the paternalistic approach so dear to Melun and his friends was bound to be offensive to a worker's sense of self-respect. A priest could still get away with a certain degree of "authority," but a factory owner? This vignette goes a long way to explain the relative success of the Kolping movement in German-speaking countries and the very limited effectiveness of paternalistic social Catholicism in France and Belgium.

Chapter 6

ECONOMIC AND INDUSTRIAL DEVELOPMENT AFTER 1850

Starting in the 1850s, two decades of accelerated economic development took place in France, Belgium, and Germany. A combination of setbacks had hit hard in the 1840s (Landes 1969, 190) — the potato blight, the collapse of the traditional, unmechanized linen industry in Flanders and Silesia, the economic depression, the pauperization, and, on top of all that, the revolutions and ensuing political instability. Now there followed a period not just of recovery but of unprecedented growth in the countries and regions that had the resources for industrial development and enjoyed a balanced economy (Milward and Saul 1977, 514, 528–33). By that I mean regions where agriculture, industry, and services such as education and banking could support one another, supplying or finding markets for their goods while employing a workforce more productively because of technological innovations. For example, the railways that were built in the 1840s and 1850s in all Western European countries had a decisive dynamic effect upon the economies of Belgium, France, and Germany and a decidedly beneficial effect on Austria-Hungary a little later, but were economically impotent in Italy until the end of the century; in Spain, they amounted to a misallocation of resources.

After a downturn in 1869, particularly noticeable in France and immediately aggravated by the Franco-Prussian War of 1870 and its aftermath in the 1871 Paris Commune, there was a long economically sluggish period from 1873 to the 1890s, sometimes referred to, particularly from a British perspective, as the great depression of the nineteenth century. This was, in Landes's view (1969, 231–37), primarily a matter of deflation. Goods became cheaper throughout the nineteenth century, since they were produced and distributed to markets more and more efficiently. In the 1873–96 period what has been variously characterized as a crisis of overproduction or of insufficient demand made itself felt. But all agree that the 1850s saw at least six or seven years of boom times that constituted an important step up for the more advanced industrializing nations of the continent, each in its own way.

The socio-economic context, in which social Catholics and others operated, includes the triumph of liberal capitalistic and individualistic theory and practice, the growth of populations, their migration within and across national boundaries in search of employment, and the changing relative weight of agriculture and industry over the period. One must also take into account the stages of development of modern industry in its main branches and geographical locations. Each country (Belgium, France, Germany) had its own combination of opportunities and problems in terms of internal economic development as well as with regard to each other, to Great Britain, and to the wider world.

Economic Theory and Practice

Economic Thought

The classical economics of the free-trade tradition of Adam Smith and David Ricardo received a further and equally classic expression in two volumes that appeared in the fateful year of 1848. These contained *The Principles of Political Economy*, by John Stuart Mill, the moral and social philosopher (see Heilbroner 1953, 119–26). It was to be an enormously influential work for decades to come, summing up as it did all the recognized economic theory of the time, cast in a progressive form that took humanitarian viewpoints and concerns seriously. The economic laws, those that gentlemen of finance, commerce, and industry generally agreed upon, seemed to make sense while not necessarily condemning the greater part of the human race to an incessant struggle for subsistence. Mill thought that it was within the power of society, not to change the laws of *production* of goods, but to modify their *distribution* in more humane ways than his predecessors suggested. Mill, in short, did not think that conventional private property relationships were necessarily "sacred."

Was there a second Adam Müller to respond to Mill as he had responded to Adam Smith? Did some gifted Roman Catholic student of economics, perhaps from Louvain, where Charles de Coux had taught political economy, rise up to baptize Mill? Did the respect for St. Thomas Aquinas that had led Ketteler in 1848 to hazard the view that private property was indeed a useful institution, but not an absolute right, stimulate such a one to legitimate Mill's opening?

In fact a two-volume counterpart to Mill's *Principles*, written by a political economist at Louvain and dedicated to Charles de Coux, did appear in Paris in 1861: *De la richesse dans les sociétés chrétiennes* by Charles Périn (1815–1905; see Jedin 1981, 9:199). The book was destined to form a most influential paradigm of economic reality and morality for Roman Catholics in the ensuing period. In his economics, he quoted Mill respectfully and showed himself at least equally appalled at the destitution of the common people in otherwise prosperous times and countries. But Périn had a different and directly religious set of preoccupations, in tune with most concerned Catholics of his time. Only in small part did he set out to answer or exploit Mill on economic questions; in fact he merely used him where he seemed useful to support a point of his own; as for criticism of him, that took place only in the most indirect fashion in those long stretches of his work where he insisted that only a restoration of morals on the lines of the Catholic Christian tradition would have any appreciable effect on humane economic progress. A soulmate, Frédéric Le Play (1806–82), furnished him with empirical descriptions of actual conditions of life of the European worker in his early work, *Ouvriers européens* (1855). Le Play's influence had only begun to be felt at this point in social Catholic circles.

Périn's religious convictions, together with his view of the failings of modern society, led him to teach, not unlike Ketteler, de Melun, and other social Catholics of both conservative and socialist leanings, that the widespread exercise of personal Christian virtues out of love of God would be equal to the task of re-establishing the solidarity of classes, as in more Christian times. His particular emphasis was on the necessity of Christian self-denial (hence willingness to forego gratifications) as the basis of prosperity. Not only did those frugal Christian classes and populations, which practiced self-denial, create the conditions for the accumulation of capital and hence of greater prosperity and less want; but a spirit of abnegation, possible only (as he saw it) within the household of the Catholic faith, also inclined the prosperous to come to the material assistance of the needy, through charity. A further important benefit of self-denial would be in holding Malthusian developments at bay through parental sexual abstinence among the masses.

De la richesse dans les sociétés chrétiennes therefore starts with the social and economic value of abnegation and culminates with the benefits of charity. It calls on Christians to realize these benefits through personal commitment on the part of the well-to-do classes. Even in the chapters ostensibly devoted to themes such as the interaction of labor and capital or mechanisms of exchange, there is a good deal more apologetics than economics; nevertheless, the economic doctrine, as far as it goes, is absolutely unexceptional, safe, conventional, hence (this is 1861, after all), "liberal." In no point is this so clear as in his explanation, or should I say moral valorization, of (private) property. He derives the right to own property from the origin of economically worthwhile goods through labor: the workers are entitled to the fruits of their own labor. Since all property rights were supposed to have originated in this fashion, once growing population and scarcity had rendered the primitive "finders keepers" stage passé, the ravings of socialists such as Proudhon were not worthy of a refutation: in attacking property, they were attacking the foundation of a just and ordered society, depriving lawful beneficiaries of their own or their ancestors' labor of their rightful due. (This was also the view of Périn's contemporaries in Roman Catholic moral theology; see Beutter 1971, 76–83 and 116–33.)

Thus (Périn asserted) the two principles on which advanced societies repose are each the legacy of centuries of Christian culture, namely, the principles of *freedom* and of *property!* Personal freedom depends necessarily on the ability of all individuals to keep and dispose legally of what they have gained through their own efforts, after the model of the settler who clears unclaimed ground and makes it fruitful by cultivation. Societal intervention through governments has its place here, but it is a restricted one, properly exercised primarily to maintain, enhance, and assist freedom, including freedom of association in natural (hierarchical) forms (see esp. Périn 1861, 1:164–69 and 283–87, with recapitulation of the thought in 2:4).

The critique of modern society that emerged was aimed directly at the weakness of doctrinaire anticlerical political liberalism, rather than at capitalism or economic liberalism. Ironically, however, voluntary charity and the formation of free associations, the remedies suggested for the undoubted economic evils of the nineteenth century, were themselves a curious mixture of the individualistic and the paternalistic. They had a certain theoretical affinity to the economic and, to some extent, political mentality of an increasingly conservative bourgeois Europe. The elements for a rapprochement of Catholicism and bourgeoisie seemed to be falling into place in the third quarter of the nineteenth century. At any rate, an option for any kind of socialism was clearly not even considered.

A Period of Free Trade

In the middle part of the century, the liberal doctrine of free trade was widely put into practice for a couple of decades. The German states under the leadership of Prussia already had a customs union (*Zollverein*, 1834), creating a large internal market; France constituted another large market — it was still the most populous country on the continent. Both were compelled to protect their own textile manufacturers from the overwhelming competition of British exporters; and German industry needed protection from the French as well. But in the early 1860s an extraordinary explosion of free-trade agreements took place (Landes 1969, 199–200) and lowered all these barriers.

This expansion of markets was a godsend to Belgium, with its weak internal market and its need to export if it was not to decline. As soon as the railroads that Belgium had built in the 1840s were connected up with German and French lines in the 1850s, its economy had the transport facilities it needed for an expanding international trade. Then, when the customs barriers went down in the 1860s, it seemed as if the last hindrances to its iron, steel, glass, and even linen exports had been removed. Prussia was still far from having caught up with France economically in 1862, when these two countries agreed to lower their tariffs. But France's relatively advanced position was no longer such as to cripple German efforts at industrial investment. Even the agreement between Great Britain and Prussia in 1865 proved satisfactory to both sides. In 1879, however, the grain growers of East Prussia and the heavy industrialists of the Rhineland prevailed upon Bismarck to reinstate protective tariffs. (Imports from America, not just cotton but food grains and iron products as well, were becoming a factor. This is one of the several features that set the thirty years before World War I off from the third quarter of the nineteenth century.) When the expansionist mood characteristic of the 1850s set in again around the turn of the century, it did not bring the prevailing tariffs down again.

Other, more inhibitive barriers to capitalistic development had fallen permanently, however, and the effect was most pronounced shortly after 1850. The last remnants of noncommercial ("feudal") relationships of peasants and owners to agricultural land had fallen in East Prussia and Austria-Hungary. France had not encouraged joint-stock companies until then; before their wide use was permitted in the Second Empire (1852–70), it was difficult to assemble the capital that big projects such as steelmaking and large-scale mechanization of industry or exporting required. Railway building was a special case in which government participation in one form or another was common. Difficulties of transport itself diminished abruptly in two stages, first when trunk lines were established and then when the network of national connections was completed. The 1850s saw the first wave of stimulating effects from railway transport (earlier in Belgium); the French market was completely accessible by the 1880s, in time for a new period of commercial and industrial development. The internal unification of Germany, promoted by the Zollverein for decades, finally became a fact with the wars of 1866 (with Austria) and 1870 (with France).

This defeat of France and the loss of the industrialized region of Alsace to Germany, combined with Germany's own increasing coal, iron, and steel production, presaged the eclipse of France by Germany as the leading industrial nation of the continent. Later on, by the 1890s, it was clear that Great Britain itself had lost industrial predominance to Germany and the United States, at least in heavy industry. There was a whole new phase, a "second industrial revolution," that Germany, but not Great Britain, was poised to exploit in a leading fashion: I need only mention further great advances in agricultural productivity; the use of electricity in lighting, tramways, and many industrial sectors; the internal combustion engine; the beginnings of the automobile industry; and the use of oil fuel in shipping. But of course none of this was foreseeable in the generation of Ketteler and Maignen. Lighting with gas made from coal was what the most modern figures of the following chapters worked by until at least the 1890s.

Growth and Development

The Heyday of Iron — From Iron to Steel

If the hallmark of early industrialization was the exploitation "of vast sources of inanimate energy" (Cipolla 1976, 8), then coal supplies were an indispensable condition for getting started. The first industry in which coal, through the medium of steam engines, could be put to use on a broad scale to satisfy an actual demand was in textiles, especially cotton spinning and weaving. Another application was in iron-making through the use of coke rather than the traditional charcoal for smelting of the ore. The problems inherent in this long-known technique were such that stupendous production increases were not attained until the 1840s and 1850s, even in Great Britain. Only in the 1880s was it possible to produce steel in great quantities at a competitive price. Until the discovery of effective new methods of producing steel, iron remained king.

On the continent, Belgium had iron ore and plentiful supplies of coal that could be used for coke smelting. Since its independence in 1830, coal and iron constituted the leading sector, rather than textiles, as was more typical elsewhere. Growth was considerable already in the 1840s under the impetus of railway building (Milward and Saul 1977, 154), though rail and locomotives were imported at the beginning. The coal, iron, and associated machine-building industries were located in the Wallonian or French speaking area of Belgium, especially around Liège, where the leading Cockerill Company, named after its English founder, still has large plants. Ernest Solvay, a Belgian but no Catholic, founded the Solvay Company in 1863 as a portent of the great subsequent development of a new industry: chemicals.

The Ruhr area in western Prussia (Rhineland-Westphalia) had some blackband ore ("where iron ore and coal were found together in the same formations," Milward and Saul 1973, 199). This accounts for the early development of coke-smelting operations east of the Rhine. In other Prussian coalfields (Saar, Upper Silesia), the state-owned mines were the largest. But it was the development of a process by which the local coal and ores could be combined in coke smelting that really made the Ruhr into the industrial powerhouse it was to remain for over a century.

Without the hindrances of a quasi-mercantilist bureaucracy, as had prevailed before 1848, many entrepreneurs founded various combinations of coal- and iron-producing firms in the Ruhr in the 1850s. William Thomas Mulvany (see Treue 1975, 133) was among the most interesting and far-sighted, but having been rescued from Romanism by his Protestant schoolmaster in Dublin, has little claim to a place in an account of Catholicism and industrialization. The demand for wrought iron for rails and the equipment and construction that went with railways was there. A remarkable take-off occurred. Despite difficulties (local ores ran out, coal became more difficult of access), the Gilchrist-Thomas process of making basic (as opposed to acid) steel in the 1880s opened up such large opportunities that, in that later part of the nineteenth century, a major migration of workers from the eastern provinces of Prussia (including many Poles) was necessary to man the works.

Agriculture in France and Germany

It is a matter of controversy among economic historians whether it is more appropriate to speak of the nineteenth-century development of the French economy in terms of retardation or even stagnation (relative to Britain, to be sure) or to see it as a process of steady modernization from an already relatively advanced starting point (Kemp 1985, 49). Certainly the wars of the revolutionary and Napoleonic period had left France (like the rest of the continent) at a huge disadvantage and with a huge lag in comparison with the British industrial revolution of the same period. But France had distinct advantages over its continental neighbors. Its manufacturing tradition was broader and more advanced. Moreover, its revolution had resulted in the complete dismantling of the traditional ("feudal") patterns of ownership and use of land in the countryside. The French Revolution was not only the victory of the Third Estate but also a uniquely successful peasant revolt.

Throughout the nineteenth century and even down to the Second World War, France had a numerous peasantry owning their mostly small farms outright. During the Second Empire about 53 percent of French workers were employed in agriculture — not a high figure for the time. In the industrial recovery of the 1890s, there was a noticeable but moderate shift to urban occupations. Until World War I, however, agricultural workers still constituted nearly 40 percent of the active population. On the "retardation" view, this large rural population constituted a drag on the economic development of the country, holding back its potential for productivity and hence higher income. This was particularly true at the very time when Germany surged forward. It seems that the agricultural stagnation of the 1880s in France was such as to put a crimp even on the industrialized sectors of the economy. Apart from the 1880s, productivity improved considerably, but seemed until then to rest on changes introduced a long time previously, such as switching from the traditional three-field rotation to crop rotations without a fallow season, using clover or newer food crops such as sugar beets and potatoes.

The increase in agricultural productivity and income per capita could have been much greater, at least by the end of the century, if a much greater proportion of the population had left the land and had left it earlier on. This would certainly have been possible, through the consolidation of small parcels into large contiguous holdings apt for labor-saving machinery and other modernized farming methods. As it was, the three million peasant families with their all too stable rural incomes depressed the total gross national product. Furthermore, the French peasants' discipline in not having as many children as their landless counterparts in other countries (so as not to divide small holdings even further), deprived the industrial labor market of the oversupply that would give it a competitive edge.

Defenders of the "appropriate modernization" line reply that there is little reason, at least at this late date, to set up the British experience as the standard model for all others to follow. Mobilizing practically the entire rural population for wage labor can perhaps only be rationalized as a necessary response to unprecedented population pressures, which the French countered in a way that was on the whole more humane. It avoided the scale of proletarianization that characterized the industrializing of Great Britain. It held down the necessity of large-scale emigration with all the heartbreaking separations and upheaval it entailed. Moreover, it preserved an economic base from which, despite the ravages of wars, present-day France has drawn up to and surpassed Great Britain, even on the basis of per capita income.

The comparison of France with Germany and its peasantry is more à propos than with Great Britain, since Germans also continued to believe that agricultural production was an important segment of the economy, not to be sacrificed for foreign trade. (Of course, only the western provinces of Prussia and the southern German states resembled France in this regard; the eastern provinces with their huge grain-growing estates, though important in many ways to Prussia, may be left out of consideration for present purposes.) The German peasants were much better educated and thus better prepared for change than the rural French or Belgians; 16 percent of French males and 25 percent of females in the 1880s could not sign their own marriage license (Milward and Saul 1977, 109, 115). There was no encouragement from the French government to set up rural credit unions under Louis Napoleon's Second Empire nor indeed from any of the governments of the Third Republic until the 1890s. The German peasantry, however, started to organize itself after 1848 and combined in educational and financial cooperatives, prompted by such leaders as Friedrich Wilhelm Raiffeisen, the Protestant founder of popular credit unions (1818–88; Milward and Saul 1977, 58), the prominent Catholic peasant leader Burghard von Schorlemer-Alst (1825–95; see Köhler in Jedin 1981, 9:220), and the aforementioned Peter Reichensperger. Germany also retained a fairly high proportion of its labor force in agriculture: about 35 percent in 1913, as compared to 37.4 percent in France and 17 percent in Belgium (Milward and Saul 1977, 20, 71, 145).

If France did not keep its centuries-old lead over Germany, this stood in relationship to its natural resources, which were less rich in coal than its eastern neighbor and provided an iron ore that could not be commercially exploited until the 1880s. In the nineteenth century, this was a disadvantage that could not be overcome directly or immediately. When agriculture all over Europe found itself undersold by American exports late in the century, this was another crisis to which France, and to a lesser extent Germany, responded with protectionist tariffs. One more factor, however, in the overall French change of position from being the dominant economic actor on the continent in the Second Empire to playing catch-up to Germany was its long-delayed modernization of agriculture. Only in the prosperity of the *belle époque* of roughly 1896–1914 with its again thriving industrial and financial sectors was any considerable investment made in mechanization, use of artificial fertilizers, and other means of increasing productivity on the land. By that period, a late date for a country in the cultural vanguard like France, one also sees credit unions and other rural self-help organizations spring up, as often as not under Catholic auspices.

Developments in the Textile Trade

The textile industry, even though it had grown by leaps and bounds in the earlier stages of the industrial revolution, was poised for still greater growth after 1850. It remained a major industry in terms of value of its product and especially in the number of employees right down to World War I. If it was second to iron and steel in Belgium, it was the larger of the two branches in France; in Germany it easily rivalled iron and steel, even after cheap steel making made the Ruhr valley into the most heavily industrialized area of the whole region of heavy industry that stretched over the coalbeds from the Pas de Calais to east of the Rhine. One reason for this was the fantastic demand for cotton, a nineteenth-century miracle fabric that lent itself so well to mechanized spinning and weaving and that fashion-conscious businessmen could market so adeptly both within and outside their national boundaries to the growing world population. Other fabric industries either went into decline from the competition of cotton, notably linen, or contented themselves with much smaller market shares, preferably at the high-quality end of the price scale (wool, silk).

Where coal was, there were textile as well as metallurgical factories in great abundance: the three French cities clustered near the Belgian border in the Département du Nord (Lille, Tourcoing, and Roubaix) in particular had a kind of ruling class of practicing Catholic textile industrialists. This makes them of particular interest for the development of social Catholicism. But cotton was an imported raw material; with it one could set up shop in a more scattered pattern, nearer to markets, transport, labor pool, or alternative power sources (especially watercourses). Alsace was France's most industrialized region until 1871, when it was occupied and then annexed by the newly formed German Empire; thereafter (until 1918), its leading industry, cotton processing, swelled German economic statistics. The Rhineland, Bavaria, and other parts of Germany already had large cotton manufactures; they expanded with the general trend of increasing cotton consumption and export. Even Flanders recovered somewhat by bringing its textile industry, centered in cities such as Ghent, under power and under factory roofs.

Cotton spinning was fairly well mechanized by 1850, but the use of power machinery on other materials (wool) and in other processes (especially weaving) was to be achieved on the continent only in the ensuing decades (Milward and Saul 1973, 316; Treue 1975, 177). The old putting-out system, whereby the contractor distributed material and paid for the spinning, weaving, embroidery, and sewing done at home, survived, often under frightful conditions of exploitation, mainly in operations such as making garments or hats. In 1896, a French industrial census counted 141,000 homeworkers just making lingerie, no doubt largely in and around Paris and Lyon. Even after the first phase of mechanization was complete (around 1870), there were still major technological improvements to be introduced, heightening productivity and competitiveness in the vast world market (Landes 1969, 159–61, and 188–89; Milward and Saul 1973, 396–404, and 1977, 80–86).

In this major industry, employing such a large part of the working class, two unusual industrialists emerged who were also leaders, indeed movers and shakers, of social Catholicism (Jedin 1981, 9:222). Léon Harmel (1829–1915) belonged to the third generation of Harmel Frères, a wool-spinning establishment between Reims and the French Ardennes (at Warmériville). When he took over the firm in 1854, his father had already supplemented a modern hydraulic turbine with a steam engine for the spindles and looms; his brothers and he would continue to modernize their plant, employing several hundred workers. The Harmels did not come from the *grande bourgeoisie*, in that the grandfather, like many a founding entrepreneur, started out as a blacksmith. Like some of the forward-looking Protestant entrepreneurs in the Alsace, Léon's father had set up some modest social institutions for the welfare of his workers: a "friendly society" for cases of sickness, a savings program. He took a personal interest in his workers and was known as *le bon père*, a title that Léon would inherit (Trimouille 1974, 1–19).

The Harmels were a typical French family firm, with the peculiarity of being staunch Catholics, ultramontanes in religion and legitimists in politics. Or rather they were untypically successful in their modest way, in that the firm survived the foreign competition, wars, and successive downturns in business by dint of technological innovation and development of new products (one of Léon's brothers, Jules, was a gifted inventor), aggressive marketing (including a costly attempt to set up an affiliate in the United States), and enlightened management practices based on a maximum of worker stability and participation (brother Ernest looked after these affairs with Léon until 1885, when the next generation started to come up through the ranks after a thorough training). The firm, in fact, was the only producer of woolens in the Reims area to make it into the age of Orlon.

Not much more than 250 kilometers northeast of Val-des-Bois in Germany, Franz Brandts (1834–1914) heard of Léon Harmel and, inspired by him, founded an organization for Catholic workers in 1880, of which more later. Brandts likewise belonged to a line of textile manufacturers, who got their start by "putting out" raw material or yarn to the weavers of the countryside around Mönchengladbach. As an entrepreneur's son, Franz Brandts toured the British industry in the 1860s; he realized that there were important innovations to make in the family plant (probably self-acting looms); he introduced the production of mixed fabrics of wool and cotton in 1865 (NDB 2:534) and set up his own plant in 1872. An upstanding bourgeois patriarch to the core ("How can we be afraid of becoming too rich? We are only beginning!" — Jedin 1981, 9:222), he also had the social responsibility to set up a workers' committee independent of the foremen to manage the workers' funds (sick leaves, savings, etc.) and to discuss matters of common interest with himself (in 1873; see Roos in Rauscher 1982, 2:124).

Social Changes — Societal Responses

Formation of the Working Class

With the growth of the industrial sector that we have described went the enhanced prosperity of the industrial bourgeoisie and the professional classes catering to them as well as the increase of the urban proletariat. Besides factory workers and their families, this comprised many who were forced out of farming or the traditional crafts and trades that had employed the greater part of townspeople in preindustrial Europe. Population growth in the developing countries (except France) and inner-European migrations from less to more developed regions assured an ample if not particularly adept workforce, even in boom times. In the period 1850–70, as before, industrial development had no evident positive effects on the mass of the population. For example, real wages for industrial workers reached their low point in the late 1850s, before stabilizing (Grebing 1985b, 34; Bruhat in Droz 1972, 1:511). A noticeable improvement, with the working day cut to below twelve hours, would have to wait until around the year 1900.

We have noticed that the early approaches undertaken in the tradition of social Catholicism concentrated on young workers, child apprentices, or still unmarried workers, and that they reached mostly apprentices in the crafts, "artisans" in the work-shops, rather than "workers" in factories (as with de Melun and Maignen in Paris and Kolping in Germany). In fact, at this stage of industrial development, the artisan problem, especially among apprentices and journeymen, was much more widespread than "the labor question" concerning factory workers. Certain crafts, such as weaving, had virtually been industrialized out of existence; all the others were overcrowded and could not support the number of workers who wanted and needed to earn their living with a skill, by the work of their hands (Treue 1975, 100–108). Of course, there were some skilled trades in the new industries, like the puddlers in iron making or the machinists, making up a small new labor aristocracy.

But it seemed there would be no place left for the mass of middle-class *Handwerker* to ply their trades with only a modest accumulation of capital for tools. The ability of a master artisan to sustain a workshop with a few employees was more and more confined to the business of repairing items made in factories. This changed only with the development of the electric motor (and electric power supply networks), which gave skilled tradesmen's shops a new lease on life.

As in agriculture, it was in Germany rather than in France that an efficacious attempt was made to organize the hard-hit segment of the working population that was made up of urban crafts workers. Kolping and Ketteler organized and publicized on their behalf. Raiffeisen and others (Victor Aimé Huber, Hermann Schulze-Delitzsch) did the same on the Protestant and liberal sides. Enough political pressure was exerted to see to it that free vocational corporations (*Innungen*) and craft guilds (*Zünfte*) were expressly recognized in law, even though their exclusive rights to control access to their trades were suppressed (*Gewerbefreiheit*). This in contrast to the French situation, where all coalitions of workers were felonious and prosecuted as such from 1790 until 1848 and thereafter again until 1864 (Bruhat in Droz 1972, 1:521).

Industrial Labor and Socialism, 1850–75

If master artisans were forbidden or only grudgingly permitted to form organizations for their mutual support and economic assistance, journeymen, apprentices, and factory workers were expected all the more to avoid all associations except those set up and controlled by their benevolent betters. Nevertheless, while most of the "schools" of early socialism in the 1850s totally disappeared, the cooperative movement did not; and the birth or rebirth of a labor movement can be discerned in the 1860s. In the succeeding decades it continued to gather strength under adverse conditions. It took on the lineaments of modern socialism to the accompaniment of internal struggles between anarchist and Marxist-authoritarian and democratic tendencies. The First International Workingmen's Association (1864 to the early 1870s) and the Second International (1889–1914) reflect these difficulties, external and internal, as well as the virtual identification of the European labor movement with socialism and its close alliance with socialist political parties.

The fruit of June 1848 in France was a bitter disillusionment on the part of workers as a class with what passed for "society." One expression of this was contempt and loathing for the church whose representatives so quickly switched from praising brotherhood to backing the forces of "order" in their unrestrained repression of the National Workshops and every other expression of concern for workers' rights. Anticlericalism entered into a new phase and became inextricably connected with the self-image of the working class. The theorists of the "mystical school," as its detractors called it, i.e., Buchez, Leroux, and all the religious socialists, fell into disrepute and eclipse. The biblical element in the outlook of others such as Proudhon and Corbon fell away in keeping with the post-1848 mood of disillusionment.

Workers in Germany found a first champion of their political rights in Ferdinand Lassalle (see Grebing 1985b, 34–37). From 1862 until his death in a duel in 1864, he galvanized the labor scene in Prussia and Saxony. He founded and led a workers' association to achieve, by peaceful means, the granting of universal direct suffrage in all the German states. His organization was thus essentially a political one, not at all a labor organization in the sense of the British trade unions. It was the forerunner of a labor party, which of course could not be constituted as long as the principle of one man, one vote was so far from realization.

Lassalle popularized the slogan the "iron law of wages"; this was the notion drawn from Malthus and David Ricardo, according to which the wages of the working class in a capitalist regime cannot exceed the minimum needed for subsistence for any significant period of time. He shared much of the outlook of Karl Marx and even hoped that Marx and Engels would support his program from London. His view of history and society was communist, in that he expected a revolution to bring about the end of private ownership of land and capital. A Hegelian like Marx, he did not think that that revolution could be planned in advance, but only shaped in the occurrence. Meanwhile, and this is where he differed from Marx, he looked to the state as a useful structure, necessarily to be brought into the service of the Fourth Estate. Nowhere did Lassalle indicate that he thought the good society of the future would do without its state or states.

Thus a theory of social-democratic reformism aimed at winning the state to socially revolutionary purposes through mostly legal means (above all through the ballot box) was propagated successfully among potential labor activists in Germany before the Marxian brand of international, revolutionary socialism was widely known. (The first volume of *Das Kapital* came out in 1867, the other two volumes only after Marx's death.) There were Marxist strains in a party founded in 1869 by Wilhelm Liebknecht and August Bebel, to be sure, but also Lassallean approaches. This party joined forces with Lassalle's party in Gotha in 1875, to form the German Socialist Workers' party.

From 1862 on, at any rate, the efforts of some conservatives and liberals (such as Schulze-Delitzsch and the Progressive party, to which Lassalle had belonged up till then) to come to the aid of the working class faced the deliberate resistance of a new breed of workers, led by Lassalle, Liebknecht, and Bebel. They were not prepared to take guidance from even the progressive bourgeoisie, oriented as they were at best mainly to educational and self-help schemes. Catholics, for the most part, stood apart from all these groups, off by themselves.

The development of labor unions themselves was a spottier affair outside of Britain. Although Lassalle himself did not encourage them, the First International did after 1864; in any case, craft or trade unions were a natural outcome of workers getting together for the political purposes in Lassalle's Association (Grebing 1985b, 67). In France, a rash of strikes broke out in 1862–64, particularly among miners and typesetters (Droz 1972, 1:521). The law against "coalitions" was becoming unenforceable and was softened. A large number of workers' (producers' or consumers') cooperatives were formed. Emperor Napoleon III always wanted to be regarded as protector and promoter of the popular classes; now that his support from the most conservative elements in the party of order was becoming somewhat precarious, he sought to strengthen his "plebiscitarian Caesarism" among the working classes.

It was in 1864 likewise that the International Workingmen's Association was called into existence in London. The French government had sent a delegation of workers (artisans) to the 1862 Exposition in London, where they came into contact with some British trade-unionists. That led to an international workingmen's congress in September 1864. Karl Marx was invited at the last minute and decided more or less reluctantly to attend. He ended up taking a leading part (though by no means an unchallenged hegemony) in the life of the First International (Kriegel in Droz 1972, 1:605–16). In the "Inaugural Address of the International," which he wrote, he noted: "It is a fact of great importance that the plight of the mass of workers has not lessened at all from 1848 to 1864, in a period that stands out in a class by itself by reason of an unprecedented development of industry and an unheard-of growth of trade."

The First International succeeded in setting up local centers in Belgium, France, and Switzerland. The German Social Democrats of Liebknecht and Bebel also joined, although the larger Lassallean group remained aloof. One of the First International's stated goals was to encourage the formation of trade or labor unions. In fact, the time was ripe. Often, an ad hoc union of sorts, perhaps based on an older traditional corporation or guild (where, as in Germany, this kind of body had not been completely forbidden), would stage a strike action (most often illegal). A notable wave of strikes occurred in France and Belgium in 1869. The International would then signal its existence, if there were members in the area. By 1870, its activities were notorious and, in bourgeois papers, exaggerated and pilloried. To the charge that it was driving workers into strikes, the valid reply came back: "The strikes are driving the workers into the International" (Kriegel in Droz 1972, 1:613). In all events, the International soon became synonymous with strikes and workers' organizations. This brought the hostility of the governments down on it and provided the excuse of "outside agitation" for renewed repressive measures. After the 1871 Paris Commune, the First International was on its deathbed and breathed its last in 1876. It could have struggled on, were it not for the opposition between Marx's emphasis on central authority and the anti-authoritarian principles of, among other comrades, the French Proudhonians and the anarchist group around Mikhail Bakunin (1814–76).

Nationalism

Political and military events in the years 1870–71 changed the map of Europe in a way that would hold good down to World War I. The redrawn maps were, moreover, increasingly symptomatic of the renewed hostile pressures under which the Catholic element in Europe labored, after the (in many respects deceptive) position of strength that it seemed to enjoy in the middle part of the century: toleration and even respect in Prussia, a highly favorable concordat with the Austrian Empire, a supposedly dependable ally in the Second French Empire.

After this respite, in quick succession, the blows rained down: Italy found its path to national unification at the expense of the papal states (loss of territory in 1860, fall of Rome in 1870); another Polish insurrection was repressed without quarter (1863, as in 1848, as in

1832); Austria suffered ignominious defeat to "Protestant" Prussia in the war of 1866; "Catholic" France went down to still more ignominious defeat in 1870; and the unification of Germany in the second Reich took place under Prussian domination, excluding Austria and co-opting largely Catholic Bavaria.

Prussia, with its western provinces and its considerable Polish population in the East, was about one-third Catholic; but its traditions and ethos, emphasized ad nauseam by the circles around King (now German Emperor) William I and especially by the "Iron Chancellor," Otto von Bismarck, were pronounced to be supremely Protestant. Bismarck had a penchant for high-risk politics. In the aftermath of the Franco-Prussian War, he thought he could prevent the Catholics from playing any cohesive role in Prussian or imperial affairs; he set out to stamp the new Center party as an anti-national, particularist, clericalist party, which patriots should not have to tolerate. Thus developed the *Kulturkampf* (ca. 1873–83).

The French Third Republic labored under great difficulties of legitimacy, in all senses. It was born in defeat at the hands of Germany. The republican form of government was associated with the revolutions of 1789 and 1848. This was the same revolutionary tradition to which the leaders of the seventy days' Paris Commune appealed. Thereby republicanism, like everything else associated with the revolution, was discredited anew in the eyes of many "respectable" citizens. Legitimacy was also involved in a very particular sense: the "legitimists" had a considerable following, especially among conservative Catholics who were never friends of the Orleanist "usurpers" and who were now left high and dry by the disgrace of the Napoleonic scion as well. There was a legitimist pretender to the throne of France, a descendent of Louis XIV and grandson of Charles X. The Count of Chambord lived in exile in Frohsdorf, Austria; at a critical juncture he made himself ridiculous with his insistence on the white fleur-de-lis flag instead of the French tricolor. When he died in 1883 without heir, it can be plausibly conjectured that Pope Leo XIII heaved a sigh of relief. In 1889, the pope would discreetly send up a trial balloon and urge French Catholic legitimists to accept (or "rally to," *Ralliement*) the Third Republic (Jedin 1981, 9:96–107).

The fires of nationalism burned all the more fiercely in the second decade of the twentieth century, of course. It is no coincidence that the Second International dissolved in 1914, as the First had been crippled by 1870 — nor that the efforts of popes were of little avail when they collided with nationalistic passions.

Industrial Labor and Socialism, 1875–1914

With the crash of 1873 and the long period of deflation and consolidation that followed, given the continuing population increases in most European countries, the condition of the industrial proletariat looked even more desperate than before. Marx's interpretation of what was going on had more than a semblance of verisimilitude: the competition of capitalists with one another must lead to an ever-increasing concentration of wealth and power into fewer and fewer hands, forcing the impoverished small businessmen, shopkeepers, artisans, and professionals into the ranks of the proletariat. Among the spokespersons of socialism, however, endeavoring as they were to spread their ideas among the workers and gain their adherence, the Marxist program was not yet dominant (Droz 1974, 2:7–9). Since this increased concentration of capital in an industrial economy was inevitable, and since the ultimate revolution presupposed the actual class tensions being heightened to an unbearable degree, Marx opposed seeking ameliorative, "reformist" measures, such as social legislation, within the present system. His dictate was to let history take its foreordained course; then be prepared to influence it when conditions were ripe and the capitalist order had crumbled!

The most formidable opposition to this Marxist strategy within the socialist camp in this period came from proponents of direct action. Fed by the French revolutionary tradition, by the anarchism of Bakunin, by the anarcho-syndicalist strategy of plant takeovers, general strikes, and the seizure of power by labor unions, this wing of socialism was still prominent in the early years of the Second International (1889–1914), and remained a factor to be reckoned with for some time to come, at least in the Latin countries. But in the 1896 congress of the Second International, Marxist predominance was acknowledged; henceforth socialist parties and labor movements would be organized on the basis of Marxist orthodoxy.

At once, *Richtungskämpfe*, skirmishes between different interpretations of Marxist orthodoxy, broke out. Eduard Bernstein was decried as a revisionist by his friend, Karl Kautsky. Rosa Luxemburg rose up on the left to preach insurrection within the bounds of Marxist theory. In France, the leading socialist politician, Jean Jaurès praised the size and cohesion of the German Social Democratic party, but criticized their inability to achieve anything politically with all their seats and backers. During the same period, as we shall see, parallel skirmishes over orientation raged with equal vehemence among social Catholics. Orthodox doctrine having been set forth in the encyclical *Rerum novarum*, the "school of Angers," preaching unregimented goodwill as the only solution to the social problem, admitted limited state intervention on issues such as child labor. Meanwhile, the radical corporatist school, seeing nothing salvageable in modern capitalism, continued to develop their strict alternative, while the Christian democratic movement took up the cudgels for labor participation in the political and economic decisions of (existing) society. This hardly exhausts the parallels that might be drawn between the history of European socialism and that of social Catholicism. The differences were no less significant, as will be clear.

Between the First and the Second Internationals, speaking chronologically, there fell a period of formative-disformative importance for both Catholics and socialists in the German Empire. I have briefly mentioned the *Kulturkampf*. As the German Socialist Workers' party managed to put thirteen deputies in the Reichstag in 1877 and showed promise of much more in the immediate future, Bismarck pushed through his anti-socialist law. The law forbade socialist agitation to overturn the existing order of state and society. It was used to suppress party organizations, newspapers, meetings. Perhaps fifteen hundred persons were punished by imprisonment, including terms at hard labor, under the law (Grebing 1985b, 59; 1985a, 66–87 and 149–51). Others were exiled or forced to emigrate. The party was driven underground in most respects. The Reichstag seated the socialist deputies who continued to be elected, however. In 1890, the law was not renewed (the Center party never supported it, even though the rivalry between Catholics and socialists was unremitting). In the twelve years it had been in effect, the socialist vote more than doubled, from 9 percent to almost 20 percent. Labor unions, though prohibited, had continued to exist in various disguises — choral societies were a favorite front. The great strike of 1889 in the Ruhr mines (Grebing 1985a, 9–35) brought to light a certain reluctance in high places to continue Bismarck's all-too-partisan policies.

After embarking on a "struggle over culture" with organized Catholicism, therefore, Bismarck threw the German state into the class struggle against organized labor. This systematic denial of equality to workers solidified their class consciousness and made them feel part of a movement that would triumph one day, but not necessarily through playing by rules that were so disdainfully twisted to their disadvantage. They wrote off any party but the socialists as having their basic human interests and dignity at heart. When the Great War came, however, their desire to prove themselves as good patriots despite everything gained the upper hand over their internationalism (as was also the case with churchgoers).

With the hope of undermining worker support for the socialist party, Bismarck turned away from the National Liberals and toward the conservatives and the Center party; in 1883–84 the first social legislation of the latter part of the nineteenth century passed the Reichstag. A scheme of insurance funds to cover sickness and accidents was set up with mandatory contributions on the part of employees and employers. In 1889 an old-age and disability insurance (social security, as Americans would call it half a century later) followed, with state participation in pension payments. After Bismarck's departure in 1890 from the chancellorship, the new Emperor, William II, pressed for an international conference on labor questions and for further legislation favorable to workers. He too hoped to wean workers away from socialist leadership, which did not happen. But the real possibility of gaining majorities for labor reform measures was the cause of grave perplexities for the German Social Democratic party (as it was known from 1890 on; Grebing 1985b, 74–86).

With the exception of Austria and Switzerland, other countries lagged behind Germany's pioneering social legislation. In 1874, the French Third Republic replaced the innocuous 1841 law on child labor with one that forbade factory work for those under ten years of age, limited it to half time between the ages of ten and twelve(!), and prohibited work at night and on Sundays for males under the age of sixteen and females under twenty-one. Half time was six hours a day, much to the consternation of factory owners who could not envisage a morning crew and an afternoon crew of child workers (an exception was promptly made for factories operating on continuous steam). Furthermore, funds were set aside for the first time for inspectors to check on the observance of the law and report on conditions (Pierrard 1984, 86).

It was certainly only a modest measure: there were only fifteen inspectors at first for all of France; small shops were excepted. In two more stages progress was made, however: schooling was made obligatory for children from the ages of six to fourteen in 1882; and inspection was stepped up while loopholes were closed in 1892. Although socialists were present in the parliament as a significant minority since 1893, the decisive advances in the condition of labor came from the labor unions, which were finally authorized by an act of 1884, and from the revival of economic prosperity that set in around 1900. Strikes and labor unrest became more and more common and better organized.

Social legislation in Belgium came still more slowly. It was in 1883 that the interdictions of the French Revolution and the Napoleonic Code forbidding labor unions were overturned. A socialist labor party was founded, becoming the chief opposition to the Catholic party. Desperate strikes broke out in waves, starting in 1886 and leading to more firmly organized labor unions and a stiffening of anti-labor sentiment among the bourgeoisie. Belgium still had no adequate public schooling, since the Catholic conservative party that was in power was opposed to compulsory universal education. The vote was extended to all classes in 1893, but in a discriminatory and unequal manner that would be remedied only in 1919. As late as 1896, all that the Christian Democrats and socialists could get through the chamber in the way of labor legislation was a provision that industrial employers had to consult with workers' representatives when drawing up factory rules. Much more significant in terms of workers' welfare was the pension plan set up by the state: although it was neither obligatory nor subsidized, its payments were guaranteed and privileged (Rezsohazy 1958, 303). Rezsohazy (310–15) sees a breakthrough in the law on industrial accidents of 1903, in that responsibility for the minimum security of workers was assigned to the employing firm by law and hence removed from the vicissitudes of individual contracts. In the year 1907 there was more in this vein and a token representation of the Christian Democrats was appointed to the cabinet.

Conclusion

The main effect of this overview will have been to fix the principal stages of economic development in the period, with special attention to some regions of strong Catholic presence, and to correct impressions perhaps gathered from learning about the industrial revolution in Great Britain. On the continent everything took place differently and later. A great shift in most respects is evident after the boom years of 1850–57 faded and before *la belle époque* around the turn of the century dawned. Whether in industrial development, character of capitalism or of socialism, degree of urbanization, class consciousness, or population shifts, whatever the perspective, the difference between the early and late parts of the period are manifest. In this chronological setting, *Rerum novarum* (1891) did not come too late, as is often said from a not particularly historical perspective; it came right before the rise of economic activity that would for the first time permit a modest rise in the standard of living of the ordinary worker in industrialized societies.

During this whole period, the Catholic response to the social questions arising from unprecedented population growth and industrialization would fall short of success, as would the contemporary liberal and socialist efforts. The basic challenges were to come to grips intellectually with the dynamic economic and social reality of an industrializing world (in the realm of theory or doctrine), to recruit and to communicate with other agents willing to play a positive role (propaganda, publicity), and to act on this reality in appropriate ways (organizational practice). In this period and in the continental European theater, social Catholics more than met their match in the schools, unions, and parties of Marxist inspiration. The anticlerical milieu of labor found Marxist approaches more suitable than anything Catholics or Protestants offered. But the social Catholics did not give up. They persevered, wrestling with paternalistic assumptions, learning from repeated attempts to "go to the people," and created islands or beachheads of Christian labor culture in the working class. Here and there, by 1914, the Christian labor movement would even establish something more significant than mere beachheads for future operations.

Chapter 7

SOCIAL-CHARITABLE
CATHOLICISM AFTER 1850

Corporations, Mutual Aid, Patronages, Christian Factories

Although the Revolution of 1848 did not spread to Belgium, the lurid
glow from across the border in France discredited anything "socialist" or "communist" with equal effectiveness throughout the Catholic
world. Social Catholicism entered into an almost exclusively charitable phase. Although this would perdure in many minds down to
World War I and beyond, its decline is usually dated from the 1880s
and 1890s, when reliance solely upon charitable beneficence would
be increasingly regarded as not rising to the level of authentically
social Catholicism at all. Until then, however, there were only faint
echoes of a voice like Chevé's, pointing out that the basic deficiency
of the purely charitable approach was simply the insult it added to
the injury of belonging to the working class.

   As a result, it was mostly young and dependent elements in the
workforce who benefited from the good will and dedication of the
more fortunate. The gulf between social Catholics and adult workers of independent spirit widened in proportion as anticlericalism
grew. Only a few particularly flexible activists gradually grasped the
implications that respect for the human dignity of workers should
have for the latter's active involvement and leadership in organizations founded for their advancement. And only much later (with
the notable exception of Ketteler) would even these exceptional figures in the movement be able to accept autonomous labor unions
as an appropriate form of organization to deal with economic class
inequalities.

   In the meantime, however, the main story of social Catholicism
is the story of associations and *oeuvres* formed, not of or by, but for

the most part *for* the workers. Beside the purely charitable works, as in the St. Vincent de Paul Society, there were three other types of organization widely utilized by social Catholics in the generations following the Revolution of 1848 and the Commune of 1871. The traditional confraternities encompassed various categories of the faithful for explicitly religious purposes, especially prayer and the spiritual edification of its members; when such an organization existed for the members of a specific trade or skill (the hatmakers of Brussels, for instance), it took on the features of an occupational guild. Here and there it *was* the continuation, in a voluntary and more or less disguised form, of a trade corporation of the *ancien régime*, with its patron saint, its annual religious celebration, and so forth.

The liberal nineteenth-century state frowned upon these organizations and suppressed them for the most part, insisting that they keep strictly to "religious" activities and not discuss economic conditions or, still less, plan any common tactics in their common economic or political interest. But mutual-aid or "friendly societies" were generally legal, as were savings clubs. Some vocational groups formed their own fraternal or benevolent associations, which could and on rare occasions did function as workers' associations under their own direction (Scholl 1966, 31–35, 138). Such was the first labor organization of factory workers in Belgium, the Fraternal Weavers and Spinners of Ghent (1857). More often mutual-aid associations were two-tiered benevolent societies, with bourgeois or noble protectors incorporating them and serving as the legally responsible board charged with administering the funds.

From the friendly society of this kind to the third form of religious outreach to workers, the *patronage*, was not a large step. The difference was mainly in the more elaborate program of the *patronage*, with an emphasis on education, "moralization," and general self-improvement of the workers. This necessitated a much more intensive involvement of the upper-class and clerical leadership at the helm of the organization. In France, Maurice Maignen provided the leading example of a fully developed *patronage*, with his Montparnasse "circle" in Paris. In Belgium, there was a Société de St. Joseph, based in Liège, and a remarkable Flemish movement of *patronages* started in Brussels in 1854 by Louis Van Caloen, S.J., and called the Archconfraternity of St. Francis Xavier (like the earlier Parisian organization). This reached a membership of eighty-three in 1879; there were still sixty-seven thousand enrolled in 1908, mostly in the less industrialized sectors of Flanders (Rezsohazy 1958, 51–56). In 1867 (reorganized in 1870), the leaders of the different *patronages* in Belgium formed the Fédération des oeuvres populaires chrétiennes. In thirty-nine conferences or "congresses" from 1868 to 1891 very little of significance took place, however (Scholl 1966, 135). The French counterpart, L'Union des Associations ouvrières catholiques (1871; see Duroselle 1951, 593), was destined for a more turbulent history in connection with the initiatives of Albert de Mun during the Third French Republic (see chapter 8).

The toughest problem on the horizon was that of labor in big industry (textiles, mining, metallurgy): their wages, their working conditions, their housing, their terms of employment and experience of unemployment, sickness, old age, their hopes for their children. The persons who had the power to act effectively in regard to this "labor question," as it came to be called, were the industrialists, the factory owners who still for the most part managed their own enterprises. These persons, if they were conscientious Christians, found themselves in an unenviable position. Open to moral appeals, they were inclined to follow Charles Périn's views on the humane character of modern capitalism, *if* it were supplemented by the Christian moral virtues of self-control (all bourgeois wanted to see the working class emulate their own ideals of discipline and sobriety), but also of self-denial and generosity on the part of the well-to-do. This was no more than could be expected of Christian employers, in whom the spirit of charity would give rise to a sense of solidarity with the poor. The problem, of course, was how to be sufficiently generous to one's workers while one's competitors operated seemingly without compunction and hence economized on the charity. The solution most often offered was to set up *patronages* under company auspices.

As Périn pointed out, there were some examples of family firms (and he could have pointed to some in major industrial firms, except that these were in Protestant hands) that invested substantially in ameliorative schemes (education, insurance, housing) and remained competitive. One of these that he did not mention, Harmel Frères of Val-des-Bois, made use of the whole gamut of charitable, educational, and associative approaches known to the Christian world in the middle of the nineteenth century and gradually developed something approaching a "Christian factory" on a voluntary basis. Since this experiment was to be much lauded if not widely imitated, and since its driving force, Léon Harmel, was later to become a leader of worker emancipation in the sense of self-government of labor organizations, its early stages in the period 1850–70 deserve our brief attention.

Another approach that enjoyed a passing flurry of attention, this one especially in Germany, is also named after "the Christian factory," this time under the direction of religious sisters. If, on the one hand, mass poverty and the demoralization of the young for whom there was no work on the land or in rural villages cried out for a remedy, and if, on the other, it was possible to keep afloat factories that employed easily trained young workers, why not open factories under Christian auspices? They could be located away from big cities and employ young country people, particularly young women, with suitable structures for their education and their moral and physical well-being. The attempts of a Swiss Capuchin, Theodosius Florentini, to do this in German-speaking areas of Central Europe are most closely associated with this more or less natural, though foredoomed, option.

By far the most influential pathbreaker of social Catholicism in the 1860s, however, was Wilhelm Emmanuel von Ketteler, bishop of Mainz from 1850 until his death in 1877. His programmatic discussion of 1864, *The Labor Problem and Christianity*, still moved within the sphere of Christian charity and interclass cooperation under clerical guidance, out of the conviction that only Christianity could effectively unchain the forces needed to solve the problem of the modern worker. But already by the following year, he saw that there would be no way to avoid invoking the power of the state as well. And in 1869, he endorsed the British trade-union model: workers would have to organize in their own associations to assert their claims in society.

Before examining these manifestations of social Catholicism after 1848, it is well to notice an approach taken in papal Rome shortly after Pius IX's return from Gaeta in the early 1850s. Distinct from both Périn's and Karl von Vogelsang's (see chapter 9) approaches, it was not much noticed at the time and had little immediate impact. It had a good deal in common with Ketteler's "associationism," however, and would play a background role, as did Ketteler's thought, during the gestation period of *Rerum novarum*.

A Roman Answer to Socialism:
Corporations of Tradesmen and Workers

In the aftermath of the revolutions of 1848, the possibility of a Christian socialism vanished from the churchly horizon. It now seemed clear that Christianity had not just one new adversary to contend with (liberalism), but two (liberalism and socialism). Liberalism had given rise to the chief demon of the modern age, the Revolution. Socialism was its plebeian offspring. That, at least, was the point of view on socialism that came to the fore after 1848. It settled in very quickly and became standard in the Catholicism of the second half of the nineteenth century.

The still darker name of communism, holding all things in common, occurred for the first time in a papal document in Pope Pius IX's 1846 encyclical, *Qui pluribus* (DS 2786; Carlen 1981, 1:280). But it was not taken seriously as a threat likely to assume politically powerful shape, whereas socialism was. The ex-liberal Juan Donoso Cortés (1809–53; see Graham 1974, 275) put it in a nutshell in a book title of 1851. His *Essay on Catholicism, Liberalism and Socialism* would influence the Catholic view of the alternatives at hand for Europe and America for decades. Catholicism inculcated social solidarity (a word he himself put in high relief). Liberalism cultivated only individuality, even isolation. Socialism, for its part, having caught the infection of materialism from the liberals, reacted against the prospect of savage competition with anarchism or alternatively with regimentation and collectivism. Bishop Ketteler maintained a similar view (see SWB 1/4:27).

This interpretation was akin to the view taken in papal Rome after the Revolution of 1848 was put down. No doubt with a view to confronting the spirit of revolution more effectively in Rome, Pius IX appointed a commission of three cardinals and another prelate to look into the economic organization of the papal states (Martina 1986, 2:20–21). The artisans' guild organizations or "corporations" had been suppressed in the wake of the French Revolution. In 1801 Pius VII had confirmed their suppression in his own right. The new commission's work led to the *Motu proprio* of 4 May 1852, *I gravissimi mutamenti*, in which Pius IX permitted and encouraged the formation of primarily religious associations along vocational lines. Employers and employees working in the same trade (e.g., furniture makers or apothecaries) could join together and develop occupational associations with representation to the governing bodies of the city of Rome.

Charles Périn (1861, 2:344–47) saw this measure as significant, as did the cardinals' report and the *Motu proprio* itself, in the light of the struggle on two fronts against liberalism and socialism. Périn did not have to force himself, against his better economic judgment, to hold up the Roman associations as models of modern legislation — they were not the monopoly corporations against which the Physiocrats and Adam Smith had directed their charge. Artisans (masters and men) in Rome could now join together in workers' associations, which the liberal influence had forbidden; but they were perfectly free not to do so, without any professional disqualifications. This reflected a distinctly voluntary or "liberal" principle of association. It was not a matter, then, of "closed" corporations, but of voluntary and nonexclusive ones, with the permission of the civil authority of the pope. As the cardinals' report stated, a middle way was to be trod, vindicating "the *freedom* of association in opposition to a regimenting socialism" and "free *association*" in opposition to the chaotic liberty of individualism (Langner 1975, 199, 204).

This is perhaps the first time that the term "socialism" occurs in the usage of the Roman curia; and it is an interesting illustration of the same placement of the concept (as the rebellious, equally mistaken, offspring of liberalism) that we see becoming standard Catholic understanding in these very years following the 1848 debacle.

In the pages of the *Civiltà cattolica* one finds further evidence of a reflection on a Catholic tradition of life in economic society. The *Civiltà*, the Jesuit periodical that was to be so close to the Vatican down to the present time, was founded in 1850 in the Kingdom of Naples, moving to Rome shortly thereafter (DSMCI 1/1:277f.). The most prominent members of its team at the beginning were Carlo Maria Curci (see Mucci), Matteo Liberatore, the principal drafter of *Rerum novarum* in the last years of his life, and Luigi Taparelli d'Azeglio. Taparelli could draw on the major work he had already completed in the early 1840s, his *Theory of Natural Law Based on Fact* (*Saggio teoretico*, Palermo, 1840–43). He was the leader of the as yet small Thomistic revival that later, under his admirer Pope Leo XIII, would become the prevailing philosophy informing all ecclesiastical studies. The *Civiltà cattolica* would be the most powerful voice in the Catholic world promoting the sound philosophy and right reason of Thomas Aquinas as the remedy for the modern world's ills.

From the first number of the *Civiltà*, Taparelli and the others addressed the social question in principle and in its various aspects (Droulers 1982, 97–121, here 109). The *Civiltà*'s articles examined all modern developments in the light of its central message: whatever form of government a country may have, disorder will prevail in society if it is not firmly rooted in the sense and practice of morality that the Catholic Church provides. All social Catholics of the era would heartily agree; to this extent the gradually growing prestige of the *Civiltà cattolica* could only lend weight to their weak and scattered efforts. The Jesuit periodical was also typical of social Catholics for decades to come in the intransigent front it maintained against modern liberalism in its individualism, a front articulated without nuances in the Syllabus of Errors of 1864. All social Catholics henceforth would be ultramontanes, and ultramontanism was characteristically critical of the social abuses of liberal economism. They conceived liberalism as based on the doctrine that reality is limited to the material and hence "all moral discipline and integrity is to be related to piling up and increasing riches by whatever means" (DS 2958). All this was standard Catholic discourse. The specific contribution that the *Civiltà* alone made to the future development was that it drew consistently on a Thomistic personalism to ground these conservative or even reactionary judgments on contemporary society.

By "Thomistic personalism" (Droulers 1982, 119) is meant an insistence on the human dignity of every person, even among the masses, who struck enlightened liberals as practically bereft of reason. Curci and Liberatore sounded the theme from the beginning (104–7); Taparelli contrasted the common human vocation to live by working with the terrible conditions inflicted on working people by liberal capitalist economic principles and practices (111–14). To the Thomist, the class struggle thus conjured up was merely a logical consequence of an egocentrism and individualism hostile to all societal bonds. When the *Motu proprio* of 14 May 1852 re-established the corporations, Taparelli took the occasion to underline the social dimension of personalism. Surely associations of those engaged in the same line of work are the natural counterbalance to the cupidity of the individual, always prone to take advantage of a weaker neighbor. "It is clear that, given charity, given economic exchanges, and given the love of self that tend to distort them, associations of workers in the crafts ought to arise from the very nature of the human being and from the law of mutual love" (115). Such "professional communities" bear only a superficial resemblance to the "workers' societies" of a new type, which, according to Taparelli, were but the first step toward socialist materialism.

In the French Second Empire

Some of France's "notables" began to return to the practice of the faith shortly after the French Revolution. Not only unrepresentative types such as de Coux and Buchez reconsidered their alienation from Christianity; a stream of legitimists and conservatives, aristocrats and bourgeois, quite thin at times but in the long run substantial, contributed to the vitality of the churches in an uneven rhythm throughout the nineteenth century. This was particularly the case at the beginning of the Second Empire (1852–70; Cholvy and Hilaire 1985, 1:197ff.). Raymond Cummings (in HDFSE 631) speaks of a "flight of nominal Catholics into the church, which they viewed as the bulwark of order." A side-effect of this was to retard the further development of social Catholicism during the Second Empire and Third Republic.

Nevertheless some gains were made. Louis Napoleon had a pronounced personal concern for the working-class poor — he wrote a short work called *Extinction du paupérisme* in 1844 — and even though he was unable to accomplish a great deal along these lines

during the Second Empire, it was a constant theme of his programmatic discourses. It is no mere coincidence that Frédéric Le Play's
period of greatest public prominence was precisely that of the Second Empire. Armand de Melun worked closely with Napoleon III
in the preparation of the decree of 25 March 1852 encouraging the
establishment of mutual aid societies for workers (HDFSE 631, see
327–28, and Duroselle 1951, 498–507). There were about 2,400 such
societies with a membership of 260,000 in 1852. With government
support, the number of communes with such a society went up to
6,000, benefiting some 900,000 workers (the ones in less desperate
straits, to be sure). The benefits were significantly increased by the
government subsidies added to the members' small dues, so that some
real help could be expected in cases of sickness or injury or toward
funeral expenses. Melun succeeded in stipulating a role for the parish
priests in the mutual aid societies, in providing for a possible linkage
with *patronages d'apprentis* and in extending their benefits to women
and children workers. But many another idea of his did not find its
way into the decree, such as his desire to give public status to the
church's charitable organizations. The resistance of the bureaucracy
against enhancing the clergy's official role was too strong. Besides, all
socially ameliorative programs had to be seen as emanating from the
personal good will of the emperor, as this was an essential feature of
"bonapartism."

The *patronage* movement drew support from a sense of responsibility for the poor seemingly more widespread than in the previous
generation, paired with a conservative fear of revolution, in a voluntary, paternalistic mode. Many St. Vincent de Paul conferences supported these programs and organizations for young workers. Under
the presidency of Adolphe Baudon (from 1847 to 1886), the St. Vincent de Paul Society reached a total membership (of benefactors, not
beneficiaries) of 32,500 in 1861 in over sixteen hundred parishes. One
patronage they supported in Paris was no doubt exceptionally well
maintained: already in 1851 they donated 6,500 francs to the *patronage* in the rue de Regard, of which 800 francs went to pay Maurice
Maignen as director, the rest for food, library, a rent assistance fund,
etc. Every Sunday there was a dinner for the hundred apprentices and
separate small groups of young workers; in the winter the kitchen distributed 100,000 "portions" to needy folk. Such organizations, and
the benefits and sums connected with them, increased greatly from
the 1850s on (Maignen 1927, 1:171).

Maignen, for his part, was not yet satisfied that he had found
the right approach. For one thing, the "graduates" of the *patronages d'apprentis* rarely had much further connection with the church
or, as far as one could tell, with the life of faith in any form. Re-

sponding to the advice of a visiting abbé, Joseph Timon-David of Marseilles, Maignen cut back on the hectic Sunday activities after 1855, balancing them with a more earnest emphasis on the life of prayer and forming an elite in the traditions of nineteenth-century devotions.

Maignen also recognized that the tendency of the St. Vincent de Paul gentlemen and indeed of the clergy active in the *patronages* to "do for" the boys and to expect a deferential attitude was frustrating their maturation process; at the very least, it discouraged more independent types from coming back as they got older. Later, in 1867, after Kolping's death, he paid a short visit to Cologne to see for himself how the Rhinelanders did it. He was positively impressed, but his ways were set by then, and the Kolping model had no particular influence on the Cercle des Jeunes Ouvriers of boulevard Montparnasse that he founded in 1864 (Maignen 1927, 1:305–7; see also *Catholicisme* 8:170–72 and Duroselle 1951, 553–57 and 586–94). Unfortunately, he had not been present in 1853 when Kolping himself visited Paris and the main encounter between him and leading French social Catholics took place.

As related at the end of chapter 5 (above, pp. 99–100) Kolping insisted on the need for workers to run their own associations. Above all, when they were gathered in their meeting rooms, there must be no bosses around. Maignen was all for the presence of deeply spiritual chaplains and even for entrusting leadership positions to workers in their associations. But in contrast to Kolping's advice, from about 1860 on he came to regard the presence and interaction of employers and industrialists (not merely bourgeois from the liberal professions) as the one thing necessary for a real solution to the social problem (Maignen 1927, 1:238–41). He saw the need to bring the working class back to the church as quite different from the German situation. Severe damage had been done to the relationship between clergy and workers in France; the goal of overcoming that rift was regrettably distant; it was this that called for the aid and assistance of capitalists. They at least should realize better than most what a re-Christianized working class would mean for social peace, prosperity, and order.

Maurice Maignen, himself raised in genteel but desperate poverty and alienated from the church until coming into contact with Le Prévost in 1843, raised the social question among directors of oeuvres, when others still thought exclusively in terms of preserving the faith of the youth whom they could reach (Duroselle 1951, 586). Although he did not see his way clear to imitate the Kolping model, he was spurred on by its successes to intensify his search for a form of *patronage* that would be equally effective in France. In this he was encouraged by his confreres in the Institute of the Brothers of St. Vincent de Paul, Le Prévost and Myionnet, while relying on the spiritual guidance given to the young people by Emile Hello. This priest was the brother of the journalist Ernest Hello; soon after his ordination in 1853 he became chaplain at Maignen's *patronage* and stayed there until his death. Maignen himself never became a priest, so as to be able to go in and out of workshops more freely and not attract attention by the way he was dressed.

Patronages also multiplied in other parts of France during the Second Empire, most often under the direction of priests. Cholvy and Pierrard, while noting the particulars of their proliferation, also stress the countervailing force of anticlericalism (Cholvy and Hilaire 1985, 1:236–45; Pierrard 1984, 173–257). In some cities (Paris, Lyon) and among some artisan elites the anticlerical stream ran particularly deep. Working populations that were not anticlerical were the exceptions, on balance, even apart from socialist influences. In Roubaix-Tourcoing, for instance, with its many Belgians, the majority of the workers were *pratiquants* up till 1870; in certain parishes at least two-thirds of the inhabitants made their Easter duty (Cholvy and Hilaire 1985, 1:243). That could hardly be said of most French parishes, except some strictly rural ones.

A case in point was the woolens mill that Jacques-Joseph Harmel moved from the Belgian Ardennes to Warmériville near Reims in 1840. A core group of worker families came with the Harmels and kept practicing the faith as was expected of them. By 1854, however, in the same period of time in which Jacques-Joseph turned over the active management of the firm to his son, Léon, it was clear that local nonpracticing custom had gained the upper hand. The Harmel workforce stood out by attending mass and by its relative freedom from abuse at the hands of its foremen; but only a few women ever received communion; the exceptional male workers who "made their Easter duty" did so in a remote parish. To Jacques-Joseph, this was an ominous development in itself and in its consequences for the enterprise. Without the religious practice of the Ardennes years, he evidently foresaw not only eternal damnation for his workers, but their brutalization such as Le Play found in the surrounding villages and towns (Trimouille 1974, 38–40). They would become antisocial and lose whatever chance they and their children had of a better education and place in society.

During Lent one year Jacques-Joseph, who never let slip an opportunity to encourage his workers to know and love God, persuaded four of them separately to go to confession and communion. One came back and told him it was the first time and would be the last. "I thought I would be by myself.... The confessing was all right, nobody saw us; but at the communion I saw the other three and they saw me too! I can hardly show my face in the shop, they're going to give it to me for six months over this! I'll never do it again!" Small wonder that in Léon Harmel's demonology, "human respect" came right after immoral and deceitful foremen at the head of the list.

The "Christian Factory"

Women religious and, in the case of the Harmel establishment, male chaplains were as indispensable to the *atelier chrétien* in the Val-des-Bois as they were to the Theodosian *christliche Fabrik* in Switzerland or Bohemia. It appears that three Christian Brothers were at work in the Val-des-Bois since 1858, followed by three sisters of St. Vincent de Paul in 1861 and by the intermittent presence of a Vincentian priest from the mid-1860s (in permanent residence after 1870). This was in addition to the priest-educator of the Harmel children in the main house. In this respect, the Christian-factory project (it would be exaggerated to call it a movement) was an activity overflowing from the immense educational and charitable accomplishments of the great nineteenth-century resurgence of religious orders and congregations. One may note also the strange coexistence of *les deux France*, clerical versus anticlerical, churched versus unchurched. From the France that remained Catholic, repeated assaults could be launched against the positivist bourgeoisie as well as sorties out into the great hostile portions of the working class.

Jacques-Joseph was not only a religious entrepreneur; he also put into practice the more advanced ideas for attracting and keeping a capable workforce. Thus he encouraged social institutions connected with the plant such as a sick fund, a savings club, and a company store where foodstuffs were available at a discount. Building on this platform of decent treatment, Léon Harmel worked out by trial and error a further four steps toward the Christian factory, or, as it was called later, the Christian corporation (in the sense of a replacement for the medieval corporations suppressed in 1791). First he would create a hard core of practicing Catholics, a few in each age group; around them he would form religious associations to draw in the others; the third stage was to found "economic institutions" (social institutions building on those already in place and managed largely by the workers themselves); and the fourth was to cap it all off with a worker-management organism to administer the whole complex (Trimouille 1974, 41–45).

This substantial allocation of resources and dogged effort led in time, at the Val-des-Bois, to a considerable success. Whereas in 1865 the whole workforce was religiously apathetic or hostile, by 1878 three-quarters belonged to the religious associations, including the St. Joseph Society for adult males. By 1894 the number signed up in it was 313 or practically all the men workers. Léon Harmel attributed this to "the action of like on like" exerted at first by the small number of converted workers and then snowballing. Trimouille suggests empathetically that the first "converts" came from the fifteen families imported (again) from the Ardennes in the 1860s, when the growth of the plant necessitated an intensive recruitment of workers.

The situation of Father Theodosius Florentini (see Bünter 1985, Gadient 1944, Stegmann 1965, 43–45, and 1969, 352–59) was quite different inasmuch as he stumbled on the idea of the Christian factory not from the angle of a businessman but from that of an organizer of charitable institutions. Theodosius was the most dynamic figure in Swiss Catholicism after the Sonderbund "war" of 1847 that left the Catholic cantons in a position inferior in every way to the Protestant industrializing cantons under liberal governments. By organizing the slender resources of backward Catholic areas, especially (one might say) by organizing young women with little education and less wealth into communities of religious sisters, he contributed mightily to the bootstrap operation by which Swiss Catholics eventually withstood a *Kulturkampf* and achieved equal status with other Swiss. His main efforts were directed to the education of rural youth and the alleviation of the worst effects of poverty.

In the pursuit of these aims he also found opportunities as early as 1849 to promote cottage industry in a remote poverty-stricken area. Seeing the need of unemployed and nearly unemployable mountain boys and girls may have prompted him to buy several small textile mills to run for socially beneficial purposes; moreover, he set up a printing shop at the motherhouse of a group of Sisters of Mercy he was setting up at Ingenbohl. In 1860, the same year he was appointed to be vicar general of the diocese of Chur in Switzerland, he also bought a textile factory in Oberleutensdorf in Bohemia. All these investments had several purposes beside taking advantage of a market niche. He described them in a programmatic speech he made to the German Katholikentag of 1863 in Frankfurt am Main.

He was conscious of making a new thrust in an age-old Christian concern for labor and for the poor. He was also aware that he was not alone in the church in his unease over the social question. Citing his German companions in the struggle, Kolping and Ketteler above all, he cited also the principle he shared with them that "all of society can only be saved by what is Christian" (see Gadient 1944, 281–93 for this address, here 284; see also Stegmann 1969, 357). The ordinary human being has a right to work, according to a Christian social outlook; moreover, the principle of association is necessarily involved in the fulfillment of this right. But work and association must not be bent to purely material results: Christian charity must hold sway and turn them to more humane ends.

As far as the traditional trades were concerned, what this kind of association can do in modern conditions is clear from the Kolping experience, he went on, provided that the necessary previous schooling and apprenticeship are available. The condition of factory workers is much less salvageable, however. "Should we therefore work against factories? No...factories as such are no sin." What is sinful is the exploitation of workers by masters who place no limits on their exactions. What is needed therefore is a corps of "lords of the factory" with an enduring relationship to their workers and a code of responsibility reminiscent of the Christian "lords of the manor" of an earlier day. Such entrepreneurs can organize labor on a humane and Christian basis, as Theodosius was doing.

Theodosius had nothing against the idea of productive associations run by the workers themselves, quite the contrary (Stegmann 1969, 353). But with the dependent and poorly educated population with which he was faced, such ideas were not readily realizable. Thus he described how one could run a "Christian factory," a "factory convent," with but a half dozen nuns in charge (357f.):

> Since factory managers are expensive people..., I sent Sisters of Mercy there (to Bohemia) to transform the factory into a convent. There are ten sisters there now, one is in charge of the whole operation, the second and third are in charge of the accounts, payroll and correspondence, the fourth and fifth supervise the shopfloor. A manager, an engineer and several workers who know the business work under them. And how does it go? This is the way the place operates: at six in the morning — we don't start at five — when the workers assemble, we do morning prayers and the Angelus in common. Then the work starts, with the sisters going up and down on the floor and taking care to see that the work is being done properly. At eleven, after assembling once again and saying a short prayer, everybody goes home to eat, comes back at one and departs again at seven, after another common prayer session. No one is hired who is not Christian or at least promises to become Christian.

As a result, reported the Capuchin, "124 workers are gainfully employed and treated like Christians." Furthermore, in a desperately poor town, the factory made possible an infirmary and an organized program of care of the sick at home as well.

Theodosius Florentini did not shrink from new departures in the religious life so as to meet the new demands of industrial society on the pastoral care of the church. Unfortunately, like so many of the other experimental enterprises of that or any era, his factories did not survive his death and the sisters were saddled with many of the debts and costs of liquidation. Harmel ran a successful family firm *and* a model Christian factory, but it too was not a model that could be reduplicated at will. The perplexity of the concerned Christian over the social question deepened, fortunately not to the point of utter discouragement and apathy.

Ketteler, Sower of Seeds in a Time of Perplexity

Posthumously, in the wake of *Rerum novarum*, Bishop Ketteler became a figure of mythic proportions in European social Catholicism. Nowhere was this more the case, and more justifiably so, than in Germany itself. After all, he was not only a pioneer of Christian involvement in the labor movement but also a political guide for German Catholics in the tumultuous years in which Otto von Bismarck welded together the German Reich, in the process declaring war on organized Catholicism as an anti-national force (above, chapter 6).

During the 1850s, as later during the 1870s, Ketteler was preoccupied by his large diocese of Mainz and by church-state issues. He had not forgotten his social concerns, all the same. His pastoral experiences would not allow that, even if the growth of industrialization in the Main-Rhine area did not take off until around 1870. In the Catholic press of the era (according to Stegmann 1969, 342) the problem of pauperization was commonly seen purely as a result of a breakdown of morals, a lack of benevolence on the part of the well-to-do. One theological writer, however, a layman in the line of Müller, Baader, and Görres, did make the connection between the social question and prevailing political-economic theory and practice.

This was Friedrich Pilgram (see Stegmann 1965, 14, 51–58; 1969, 345f.; and Langner 1974, 81), who wrote for the influential Catholic periodical, *Historisch-politische Blätter*. Purely moral appeals to swim against the stream of modern economic structural realities would not be effective, he realized. Instead, one must try to think of ways in which capital and labor could be reassociated without, as in the liberal political economy, subjugating labor entirely to capital. Departing from the common conservative apprehension of government interference, he also realized that the power of the state would have to be mobilized behind such a pervasive reorganization of economic society. His 1855 book, *Social Questions in the Perspective of the Principle of Church Fellowship* (Freiburg, 1855) and his article on "Pauperism" in the 1856 *Kirchen-Lexikon* (edited by J. Wetzer and B. Welte) were far ahead of their time (see Bernhard Casper in Fries and Schwaiger

1975, 2:222). Most probably they influenced Ketteler's thinking a decade later.

In the years 1862–64 German Catholicism crossed a threshold to greater awareness of the problems of labor and capital. We have seen how the question was brought to the fore at the Katholikentag of 1863 by Father Theodosius, nor was he alone. In 1862 Bishop Ketteler published his first longer work, an attempt to bring some clarity into public opinion about questions prominent in the journalism of the day: *Freedom, Authority and the Church* (now in Ederer 1981, 103–303, and SWB 1/1:222–364). Since the Catholic presence in Germany was systematically ignored by the national press, he called for a forthright representation of Catholic views on all matters of importance to the public in a more substantial Catholic journalism. Although he accused the reigning liberals of striving for a most illiberal, absolutist sway over public opinion and hence over politics and society, he made distinctions that opened the way for a possible understanding between liberals and Catholics. If both would consistently be on their guard against the absolutist tendencies of modern statecraft and reclaim their common ground in the dignity of the human person and his or her inviolable rights, then the ancient antagonisms between Protestant and Catholic Germany could be overcome. Only by putting Christianity first and material gains and power second, however, could such an entente have a lasting foundation.

Ketteler called for a campaign of Catholic assertiveness (in the first place through the press), to put this point of view across. In the process, however, he dispensed two bits of advice that were not typical of nineteenth-century ultramontanes. First, he said (Ederer 1981, 114),

we Catholics have to avoid conveying the impression — and the Catholic press ought to be especially alert to this — that we are satisfied with things as they once were, that we regard the social and political institutions of a bygone era as beyond improvement, and that our only ambition is to praise them whenever the opportunity presents itself as the only and best design for the future. The truths we have expressed are certainly relevant to the moral well-being and progress of humankind. However, the manner in which these come to bear in the area of social and political well-being cannot be predicted in advance, just as we cannot tell beforehand what civil and social institutions the spirit of Christianity may give rise to when it has again permeated all of humanity.

Secondly: we have to distinguish between those currents of our time which are justified and those which are not.

This sense for historical process, for the legitimacy of what has become and is still becoming, is a legacy from the Romantics. It seems to have had more influence on his thinking than the natural-law think-ing of the Neo-Thomists (Langner 1974, 69). At any rate, Ketteler displayed an unusual latitude for fresh thinking as he turned to the problem of labor in the following year. He examined the latest propos-als of Hermann Schulze-Delitzsch (1808–83) and Ferdinand Lassalle as they were put forth early in 1863. Schulze-Delitzsch was a liberal (free market, free trade) social reformer and champion of workers' cooperatives; he made the case for worker self-help, including cooper-atives of production. Ferdinand Lassalle was the socialist leader who countered with an attack on the "free" labor market that flourished by the "iron law of wages." He also took up the idea of productive as-sociations of workers (ultimately from Buchez), but with the demand that they be started up with government financing.

On 16 January 1864 Ketteler sent an anonymous proposal to Las-salle with a post office box return address. Lassalle was then at the height of his fame; Ketteler asked him for assistance and advice with a project for the founding of perhaps five productive associations, for which he could make a 50,000-florin capital available. For a so-cialist leader, Lassalle enjoyed an unusual respect in certain Catholic circles (e.g., Ketteler, the *Historisch-politische Blätter;* see Stegmann 1969, 397). Then in April 1864, Ketteler published the book that discussed all these proposals for coming to the aid of the industrial working class in the light of Christian principles. Taken together with his 1869 utterances, this book, *The Labor Problem and Christianity*, constitutes the most important step forward between 1848 and 1891, in terms of social Catholics coming to terms with industrialization on the European scene.

Ketteler made direct reference to the proposals of Schulze-Delitzsch and Lassalle, thus focussing on productive cooperatives as possible instruments for social progress. He makes his own the cri-tique of economic liberalism that Lassalle had formulated (Ederer 1981, 321–23; SWB 1/1:377–80).

> The provision of all the necessities of life for the worker and his family rests, with so few exceptions that they only prove the rule, on the worker's wage. And the wage rate in our time is determined by subsistence in the strictest sense of that word, i.e., the minimum food, clothing, and shelter that a person needs to sustain a bare physical existence. The truth of this proposition has been so well established as a consequence of the well-known controversies between Lassalle and his opponents that only an overt intention to deceive would lead one to deny it....
>
> This is the condition of the working class. Workers are dependent on the wage paid for their labor, and this wage is considered just like the price of any commodity. Its price is determined daily by demand and supply conditions. The level around which it fluctuates is subsistence. If

supply exceeds demand, then the wage falls below subsistence. The general tendency, however, as with all commodities, is toward ever cheaper production. Here the cheapening of production means reducing the necessities of life. Thus, in terms of this totally mechanical, mathematical process it becomes inevitable that at times the price of labor does not even cover the barest minimum needed for subsistence; and large segments of the working class and their families are destined for eventual starvation. What a state of affairs!

As he said in 1869 (Ederer 1981, 451): "What good are the so-called rights of man contained in constitutions — which are of little relevance to the typical workingman — when the moneyed interests are in a position to contemptuously disregard these social human rights?"

What was to be done? The association of workers among themselves is a necessity. For the trades, voluntary cooperatives such as Schulze-Delitzsch proposes would certainly be advantageous. Continuing education and development of skills is another matter where the social liberals are on the right track (Ederer 1981, 333–54). But why exclude any participation or influence on the part of Christianity? And how will self-help benefit any considerable part of a working class on the edge of subsistence? When Lassalle, for his part, proposes employee ownership of enterprises with consequent profit-sharing, he must also propose a government fund to purchase or set up the cooperatives and turn them over to the workers, which Schulze-Delitzsch opposes. Ketteler also considers this coercive redistribution of wealth by the state to be impermissible. Does this leave him without alternatives, since "Lassalle is right against Schulze-Delitzsch, and Schulze-Delitzsch is right against Lassalle" (Ederer 1981, 355)?

There is an alternative, in Ketteler's view: where the state and its coercive power are incompetent, the church still has resources. Just as Christianity championed the human dignity of all against slavery in the ancient world and eventually prevailed, so it could gradually transform the wage-system into something that would serve human beings and not merely greater production of goods (Ederer 1981, 383–87, citing "the excellent Périn"). The church can provide long-term remedies in traditional ways: charitable institutions for the sick, poor, and aged; Christian marriage and home life; education not only in economic skills but in the realm of culture and values; and associations of every kind, promoted by the innate Christian communitarian tendencies (387–410). Only genuine Christian devotion can maintain such forces and institutions in the long run, as the liberals will find out. Their efforts to supplant church organizations with secular ones can draw on natural human inclinations up to a point, but is it not the residual Christian selflessness in their members that accounts for such life as they enjoy?

Besides the above four services of Christianity to society, it has a "fifth aid" to offer to the working class, "the advancement of producers' cooperatives by special means which only Christianity has at its disposal" (Ederer 1981, 411). Instead of Lassalle's mode of implementation "through capital subsidies provided by the state," Ketteler proposed a vast collection. Christians could levy voluntary taxes on themselves to create the funds necessary to try out this experiment! After all, he reasoned (415), if Catholics all over Europe could contribute twenty-three million marks to the Holy Father in the newly expanded Peter's Pence, should Christians not "be able to come up with the necessary remedies for the plight of the working classes"? First, of course, the idea would have to be propagated and examined critically.

When this showed no signs of happening, despite the attention his book received, Ketteler took the next step in his thinking. While dropping the proposal of the Catholic fund-raising campaign for the financing of cooperatives, he did not relinquish his analysis of the problem, pivoting on the insight that labor was treated as if it were just another commodity. Hence the law of supply and demand had to be reckoned with in the labor market. His first undeveloped response was to cross a threshold that up till then he had religiously avoided. He admitted the necessity of governmental intervention along with the factors of religion and morality, self-help and association. This he did first in an address at a celebration of the Kolping Journeymen's Association in Mainz, 19 November 1865 (SWB 1/1:685–88), and more publicly in 1869.

Ketteler is a nodal figure in social Catholicism just because he did not abandon his traditional positions of 1848 — and did not resist change and forward movement either. He carried forward most of what his predecessors in social Catholicism had arrived at. All parties to the internal controversies in later social Catholicism could also appeal to him, if sometimes only selectively, to support their cases. But this would have been much more difficult for Catholic trade unionists at the turn of the century, had Ketteler not crossed another threshold publicly in two decisive pronouncements in 1869, just before the Franco-Prussian War took center stage in everyone's attention. At the end of July, he took the first step in a sermon to thousands of workers gathered around a shrine church (Liebfrauenheide bei Offenbach across the Main from Frankfurt; translation in Ederer 1981, 439–63; see SWB 1/2:406–28).

In this sermon Bishop Ketteler deliberately drew near to the independent labor movement such as it was at the time and endorsed several of its main features. In effect, he invited his listeners to make contact with the union movement, to organize and be organized, while putting them on guard against political or other misuses of unions and emphasizing certain concerns of Christian morality. His expectations in regard to the role of the church in solving the labor question had grown more modest; in the hope of being more effective, he called for governmental social policies that would favor the worker. After posing the social question from the point of view of the choices that the worker was called upon to make among the various "currents that are stirring" in modern Europe, he restated his basic principle in the new context (Ederer 1981, 440): "Whatever is good and legitimate in the labor movement of our time can only be realized to the extent that it remains firmly tied to religion and morality." He then articulated the basic aim of the labor movement ("its very essence") as "the effort to unite, to organize workers so that by solid united effort their interests may be promoted."

This was in his view not only legitimate but an imperative need. Here Ketteler's acceptance of the liberal idea of individual freedom went further than ever before, but only in close conjunction with the right of workers to organize and thus to withstand "the concentrated power of high finance" (as exemplified by the wealth of James Rothschild and his heirs, Ederer 1981, 442). A breath or two later, Ketteler again referred to "the power of centralized capital," which required a corresponding concentration of forces in a "collective effort" on the part of workers to "protect their rights and interests." Hence it is clear that Ketteler did not fall back on a nostalgia for the age of Christendom after his new thrusts of 1862–64 met with no success. Instead he retained the new insights that Lassalle had mediated to him about the question of capital and labor and cast about for more practical remedies than the cooperative movement seemed to offer at the time, hitting upon the trade union movement of British provenance.

In this newly conceptualized scheme of the problem to be dealt with, Ketteler reinculcated the primacy of "religion and morality." With a topical reference to the controversies going on between the successors of Lassalle's movement and the rival tendency under Bebel and Liebknecht that summer, he made some pertinent connections (Ederer 1981, 443).

> You see before your own eyes how often bitter hostilities break out among the very men who hold the leading positions in the labor movement — something that is occurring right at the present moment. Note how these men then become guilty of the same selfish tactics of which they accuse the capitalists. How could it be otherwise? Without religion, we all fall prey to egotism; it makes no difference whether we are rich or poor,

capitalists or workers. We will take advantage of our fellow man as soon as we have power to do so.

No matter how justified the aspirations of the German workers to organize may be, real benefits can only be expected if the leaders of the labor movement will cease their hatred of Christianity and adopt a position which is at least respectful and amicable toward religion and the Church. That ought already to be clear to us when we observe the great difference in the results achieved by the labor movement in England and in Germany. Even though the English working class was in worse shape than the German, so far as the dire consequences of modern economic philosophy are concerned, the efforts to organize the working class in England are vastly superior to our own. That is due first and foremost to the great respect shown in England toward the significance of religion in solving social problems. In Germany, on the other hand, the spokesmen for labor make a public display of their hatred for religion.

One does not quite know what to make of the bishop's seemingly naive homiletic assumption that people loyal to religion would not "fall prey to egotism" and on the contrary would always be loyal to each other. A more precise statement of the relation between Christianity and social ethics remained elusive for generations of social Catholics. All the same, it was surely a timely warning that the anticlericalism of the German labor movement would be counterproductive (Tenfelde 1977, 471).

How mild Ketteler's own paternalism or clericalism was can be gauged by the support he gave in the rest of the sermon for the most "striking" demands of the labor organizers: a substantial increase in wages, to be gained by strikes if necessary (Ederer 1981, 444–48), as well as a reduction in hours of work (448), regular days off, especially Sundays (449–52), and the elimination of (the need for) women in factory work, especially girls and mothers (453–58). The sermon closed with appeals for frugality and sobriety, out of a sense of responsibility for one's own family and future.

While visiting the parishes of the Frankfurt/Main area in July, Ketteler also completed a report to the upcoming German bishops conference, held in Fulda at the beginning of September 1869 (SWB 1/2:429–51, English trans. in Ederer 1981, 469–93). This was a task he had volunteered for at the previous meeting of the bishops conference in 1867. Preparations for the First Vatican Council, where Ketteler opposed the definition of papal infallibility, the Franco-Prussian War, and finally the hard-pressed situation of the Catholic minority in the new German Reich, all took precedence over the labor question for the next decade and more. The analysis he made for his fellow bishops in 1869, therefore, and the proposals he submitted for their approval, were the last major contribution he could make to the development of social Catholicism.

It was a contribution that would not lose its actuality for many a long year, even after *Rerum novarum*. He proceeded on the explicit assumption that there was no way to abolish or replace the factory system of industrial production with something entirely different. There were even "blessings" that came with the system, increased production, for instance. The challenge, therefore, was to find remedies "to soften its ill effects...and see to it that the workers also share" in its benefits (Ederer 1981, 478). After going through a string of social institutions that enlightened factory owners had already set up and that had proved effective in reducing the suffering of their employees, Ketteler also listed eight or nine issues that needed legislation for the protection of workers. Basic rules of fair play between employers and workers and among competing employers had to be established *by law*. These concerned, in his listing, a minimum age for child workers in different kinds of work, their schooling, the separation of sexes in the workshops, hygienic conditions, hours of work, Sunday rest, accident insurance, the legally recognized legitimacy of workers' associations, and an official industrial inspection system (Ederer 1981, 485; see SWB 1/2:447f. and 1/4:242–45). Although Ketteler did not offer an argumentative rationale for these proposals, what they signalled was his conversion to the conviction that without laws, without the state setting basic standards, that is, without a political consensus on a certain level of regulation, the social question could not be solved (Roos in ZgLb 4:30) — just as it could not be solved without individual responsibility, without the beneficent influence of religion, or without an effective organization of labor to confront the power of concentrated capital.

What Ketteler did argue in detail was the proposition that the church must get involved in the problems posed by factory work *for the workers* (Ederer 1981, 474–78). "The church cannot exercise its proper ministry toward millions of souls if it ignores the social problem and is satisfied to confine itself to the traditional pastoral role." And, as Victor-Aimé Huber, the leading social-policy writer on the Protestant side, noted, the Catholic Church, with its greater numbers of laborers in the vineyard and with its closer relationship to the ordinary people, could be potentially much more effective than the Protestant state churches (SWB 1/2:434; on Huber see *Evangelisches Staatslexikon* 3184 and Shanahan 1954, 282–96). True as it is that the church's central mission is to announce the saving spiritual truths of Christianity and not to proclaim any doctrine about capital and industry, the social problem nevertheless "touches on the deposit of faith" (Ederer 1981, 475)! There was a materialistic, entirely self-centered principle at work in modern economics that "stands in flagrant opposition to basic humanity, let alone Christian dignity, just as it stands opposed to the destiny of material goods, as intended by God, to serve the needs of all humankind." It is certainly within the competence of the magisterium to condemn the theory of human labor that sees in it no more than a commodity and the worker no more than a machine. Even slavery was better than this, as Lassalle claimed, since the relationship between master and slave was acknowledged to be one between human beings.

Pastorally, it was of the greatest moment for the church to bestir itself. Inaction was tantamount to abandoning vast numbers of the working masses to a "proximate occasion of sin." To preach other-worldly rewards while not lifting a finger to help the working masses would lead predictably to mass alienation from Christianity. Already they were turning to other sources of support that were "indifferent to Christianity or downright hostile to it (as Schulze-Delitzsch or the Social Democrats)."

Ketteler spelled out for his brother bishops a seven-point program that could guide the church's efforts in Germany in propagating "worker associations and protective measures on a wide scale." As is obvious, he was pragmatically interested in effective social change. The clergy should not establish labor organizations themselves, certainly not as church organizations. But the church (1) could promote them "by offering benevolent encouragement, support, and recognition, and by providing instruction and educational programs" (Ederer 1981, 486). That meant (2) that the clergy, in its training, be familiarized with the social problem, with certain young priests being given the opportunity for specialized training (travel) and experience. (3) Not just any priest should be assigned to parishes in industrial areas. (4) The bishops should endeavor to create the conditions in which a new Kolping could arise, this time for the factory worker. "It is well to note that Kolping, as closely as he wished his organization to be bound to the church, nevertheless rejected any proposal to establish it as a canonical confraternity; this applies *a fortiori* to the establishing of workingmen's organizations" (Ederer 1981, 489). (5) Each diocese should start by designating a priest for factory workers without delay. One should utilize (6) the press and (7) the Katholikentag for publicity, especially in industrial areas.

Germination of a Catholic Labor Movement

Ketteler mentioned the *Christlich-Sociale Blätter* of Aachen as an already existing periodical devoted to the social question and ready to assist the bishops in promoting the proposed program. His whole report soon appeared in its pages. This was of emblematic significance. A few young priests in Aachen, in fact, formed the most visible leaders of a Christian-Social movement that actually gave rise to pioneering labor organizations and had a certain impact on the regrouped Center party in Prussia for the next few years (Brose 1985, 37–44, 47–58; Sperber 1984, 177–84, 263–67). Aachen and Essen were the two centers of this movement in the vast Cologne archdiocese. Both boasted large concentrations of Catholics; Aachen was so Catholic that even the factory owners were Catholic, making it unique in Germany as Lille was among French industrial cities. Lassallean and other antireligious, socialist labor "agitators" were becoming active in both places in the late 1860s (Lepper 1977, 17, 58–60). The response of some of the clergy was notable enough to make Karl Marx resentful. In a letter to Engels of 25 September 1869, Marx reported on his trip out from London (*Collected Works* 43:354):

> During this tour through Belgium, stay in Aachen, and journey up the Rhine, I convinced myself that energetic action must be taken against the clerics, particularly in the Catholic areas. I shall work in this vein in the International. Where it appears suitable, the rogues are flirting with workers' problems (e.g., Bishop Ketteler in Mainz, the clerics at the Düsseldorf Congress, etc.). In fact we worked for them in 1848, but they enjoyed the fruits of the revolution during the period of reaction.

One of the founders of the *Christlich-Sociale Blätter* in 1868 was an admirer of Ketteler named Joseph Schings. When he died in 1876 at the age of thirty-nine, another priest, Arnold Bongartz, took over the editorship until 1883. But the real founders of the labor movement were Eduard Cronenberg (1836–97), assistant pastor at St. Adalbert's in Aachen, and Johannes Laaf (b. 1840), fourth assistant at St. John the Baptist. Another young priest joined them in their efforts after gaining a doctorate in theology; this was the third assistant at St. Foillan, Hermann Joseph Litzinger (b. 1839; see Lepper 1977, 67–80). Cronenberg organized the Paulusverein for workers in this westernmost, and most Catholic, of German Catholic cities in 1869. He was also elected to head it, while Fr. Laaf served as vice president. Herbert Lepper has chronicled the rapid rise of this labor organization of "Christian socialists" to its peak of some five thousand members in 1875 — and then through its equally rapid decline in the next three or four years.

As long as it was vigorous, Aachen remained a "black stronghold" where socialist labor organizers could not gain a foothold, even though 30 percent of the population was directly dependent on factory work. In 1872, Cronenberg supported a strike in Eupen (now across the border in Belgium). The Paulusverein organized subgroups and activities of many sorts. Its amateur theater group even traveled to Liège to give a performance for the *patronage* de St. Joseph. It put up an imposing headquarters, the *Paulushaus*, the debt for which figured prominently in its decline (along with the slump after the so-called *Gründerboom* of 1870–73). Perhaps of importance for present purposes are two items about its "red priests." When Cronenberg endorsed the strike in Eupen and ran for the Reichstag in 1873, even Schings recoiled. Archbishop Paul Melchers was prevailed upon to transfer Laaf in 1872. At his new assignment in Essen, Laaf promptly breathed new life into the Catholic labor organization that was already in existence there (see E. Ritter 1954, 76 for a list of early Catholic labor organizations; see also Brose 1985, 48–51). It proved too strong for the bourgeois and aristocratic Center leaders to do without: despite the best efforts of the latter, a Catholic labor candidate, Gerhard Stötzel, who came out of the Krupp metalworks, was elected to the Reichstag in 1877. He joined the Center party fraction there and was repeatedly re-elected as the Center's only labor member until the turn of the century.

Meanwhile, the *Kulturkampf* raged, with unpredictable but finally negative results for the embryonic Catholic labor movement in Germany. The leader of the Center, Ludwig Windthorst, although a political democrat, was out of touch with economic developments and inclined toward Manchesterism (M. Anderson 1981, 207–18, here 208). He appointed the young Georg Baron von Hertling (1843–1919; StL 2:1257) to be the Center's expert for social and economic questions without expecting him to be very active on this front (see Brose 1985, 50; the future Reichskanzler Hertling's prior concern, in any case, was with Catholic backwardness and discrimination in the academic world; see Becker 1981a). From Windthorst's political perspective, initiatives regarding the social question were a parliamentary luxury that the Center could ill afford and was ill-equipped to promote; he welcomed such initiatives from the Social Democratic deputies, however.

This is the context in which the famous Galen motion of 1877 must be seen, the first effort at social policy by any party in the Reichstag (as Anderson 1981, 210 remarks). Launched by the conservative rural magnate, Burghard Baron von Schorlemer-Alst, the "King of the Peasants," it was introduced into parliament by Count Ferdinand von Galen. Galen (father of the cardinal famed for his resistance to the Nazis) was thoroughly acquainted with the thought of his uncle, Bishop Ketteler, even if his sense of the politically advantageous was not so keen. The motion called for the kind of legislation for the protection of the working class that Ketteler had outlined in 1869. After the parliamentary debacle, Windthorst wrote to Canon Christoph Moufang of Mainz, the co-worker and legatee of Ketteler in the labor question, that "we were somewhat too doctrinaire" (Brose 1985, 52).

The following year, 1878, saw Bismarck take cynical advantage of two attempts to assassinate the emperor to push through the Socialist Law. Thereafter the only representatives of labor who could propagandize, hold meetings, or express themselves with any freedom whatsoever were the elected labor — i.e., Social Democratic — deputies; and they were often in jail on trumped-up charges, just as refractory Catholic priests were, in consequence of the *Kulturkampf*'s muzzle laws. For twelve years, not just socialist but any and all labor agitation was legally impossible. Windthorst consistently voted against the Socialist Law and its renewal, finally seeing it expire in 1890. But until then the Center party, and with it the bulk of Catholicism in Germany, had neither the means or the inclination to pursue labor organization or legislation. The prevailing tendency was to decry Bismarck's proposals for accident and old-age insurance as "state socialism" (see further on, chapter 10).

A promising beginning of social Catholicism in the German Reich gave way to the cold blasts of political opposition. But with the lifting of the Socialist Law in 1890 the season of growth would set in again.

Chapter 8

SOCIAL CONSCIENCE AND COUNTERREVOLUTION IN FRANCE: KNIGHTS OF THE SYLLABUS

The first permanent effect of the Franco-Prussian War was the withdrawal of French troops from Rome, where they had been defending papal rule. Italian forces consequently took Rome on 20 September 1870. Shut up in the Vatican precincts as he was, Pope Pius IX experienced a bitter winter in 1870–71. It was equally bitter for two French officers named Albert de Mun and René de la Tour du Pin. They spent it as prisoners of war in Aachen, after their army, penned in by German troops, surrendered at Metz at the end of October. In their defeat, and while seeking an explanation for it, the two officers — each Catholic and of the nobility, La Tour du Pin an heir to large land holdings as well — became friends; they read a book lent to them by a local Jesuit, a Father Eck, on the pope's Syllabus of Errors of 1864. They heard about Bishop Ketteler's taking the side of workers from Dr. Joseph Lingens, a prominent local Catholic politician and St. Vincent de Paul man. Then, on their return to France, they were immediately confronted by the civil war between the National Assembly at Versailles and the Commune of Paris (19 March to 28 May 1871), put down in a week of bloodshed by the regular army. All this stirred them to profound reflection. It all seemed to come together when they met Maurice Maignen, who indicated to them the way in which France could, by the grace of God, be redeemed.

The movement that they started at Christmas 1871 is known as the Oeuvre des cercles catholiques d'ouvriers (henceforth OCCO). It became one of the best known collective efforts in the history of social

Catholicism. Each of its two principal founders are also well known for other initiatives: de Mun for his political activity (he was a deputy in the French assembly from 1881 till his death in 1914) and for founding the Association Catholique de la Jeunesse Française (ACJF) in 1886 (B. Martin 1978, 47, 63; see HDTFR 661f. and *Catholicisme* 9:847ff.); La Tour du Pin for his theoretical work in Catholic social thought in the *Revue de l'Association catholique* (see chapter 9) and in the international Fribourg Union (chapter 10; see HDTFR 512 and *Catholicisme* 6:1906ff.). In this chapter, the orientation imprinted on the OCCO by its founders' ultramontane Catholicism must be considered, before recounting the further activities of de Mun, La Tour du Pin, Maignen, Harmel, and their colleagues in the ranks of the social Catholics (McManners 1972, 81–93).

The Encyclical of 1864 and the Principles of 1789

When Pope Pius IX issued the encyclical *Quanta cura* (Carlen 1981, 1:381–85) and its attached "Syllabus of [Modern] Errors" (DS 2901–80), the secular press of the Western world had a field day. Félix Dupanloup, bishop of Orléans, responded with his renowned "liberal Catholic" interpretation of this compilation of condemnations of nineteenth-century liberalism (Jedin 1981, 8:293–303). He noted how each of the condemned propositions were excerpted from documents having to do with highly particular cases, where the long-standing rights of the church, its property, and its institutions were taken away by guile through anticlerical publicity campaigns and hostile legislation on the part of self-styled liberals. Thus, when the famous proposition no. 80 (DS 2980, the last in the list), was condemned, to the effect that the Roman pontiff could and should come to terms with "progress, liberalism, and modern culture," Dupanloup argued that the context should be borne in mind: particularly Italy's annexation of parts of the papal states in 1860 and the dissolution of ecclesiastical institutions in that territory. Besides, it was a breach of logic to reason that if the Vatican condemned proposition 80, it was proclaiming its contrary, as if to say that in the pope's view everything modern or progressive should be rejected.

Dupanloup's brochure came in handy for papal diplomats, who after all had to deal on a daily basis with "liberal" governments. But it did not reflect the views of a stronger segment of Catholic opinion, that of intransigent Catholicism. An adroit spokesman for intransigence was an Alsatian Catholic member of the French national legislature in the Second Empire. Emile Keller (*Catholicisme* 6:1392f.) had already made a name for himself by calling on the imperial government to defend the papal states unconditionally, no matter what such a policy would mean for French relations with the Kingdom of Italy. It was his book *L'Encyclique du 8 décembre 1864 et les principes de 1789* that made such an impression on La Tour du Pin and de Mun when they read it in captivity in Aachen. After Alsace was taken by Germany, Keller was re-elected to the Third Republic's assembly from Belfort. Having been associated with the Society of Charitable Economy of Armand de Melun in the years 1857–62, he became one of the founders of the OCCO at the end of 1871.

His book (Keller 1865) was a formidable indictment of the French Revolution and its offspring, liberalism, as codified in the Declaration of the Rights of Man. The fault lay not just in 1793, with the Terror, but in 1789 and indeed, even further back. The *ancien régime* was far from the Christian society that the church could inspire; not even the Middle Ages necessarily contained the model for which one should strive (Levillain 1983, 171–74, 272, 623, and Molette 1970, 183). In this last point Keller showed a disinclination to go along with the Romantic glorification of the Middle Ages so prevalent among Catholics and certainly influential in the circles of Maignen and de Mun. Keller actually had a "historicist" approach (Levillain) to the question of how church and society should relate to each other, in the sense that he saw the matter as never definitely settled, but requiring changes as times changed. Combined with that insight, however, was the conviction that the rights of the papacy are to be asserted in season, out of season, and that society will be healthy only to the extent that its members freely consent to be guided by the truths confided to the Petrine church (see, e.g., Keller 1865, 289).

This would include the Christian teaching on relationships between labor and capital (more precisely, between employers and workers). The Declaration of the Rights of Man contained (not inadvertently) an Article 17, declaring private property to be an inviolable and sacred right. "If neither religion nor rule are sacred, why should property alone have this privilege," he asked indignantly (Keller 1865, 253) — was it not simply to preserve the control of property owners? A first consequence of liberalism in the social domain, therefore, was that, where before traditional or hereditary authority had the command, henceforth it would be wealth.

The results of this "principle of 1789," as of the rest of the liberal political economy, were devastating for the people. The election manifesto of the Parisian workers in 1864 did not exaggerate when it claimed that civil liberties, such as equality before the law and universal suffrage, were powerless to give birth to "social emancipation" (cited by Keller 1865, 261). In considering the remedies proposed in liberal circles, Keller's fixation on 1789 and its principles as the essence of liberalism (Keller 1865, 263–72) prevented him from crossing the threshold that Bishop Ketteler stepped over at this same time. For if Ketteler and Keller were each opposed to both absolutism *and* nineteenth-century liberals with every fiber of their being, Ketteler nevertheless recognized a humane thrust in the emancipatory strivings of liberalism and was able to distinguish this from the unfortunate historical alliances that it made during its rise to power. Keller too admitted that, "as in all the modern ideas, there was a vague and noble instinct of truth" in the right to association, mandatory education, and factory legislation. But:

> Unfortunately one thinks that [these ideas] must be placed under the patronage of 1789. It is forgotten that it was the Revolution itself that killed association, representation and education — by creating individualism, unitarism [or totalitarian democracy, to use Jacob Talmon's phrase] and the proletariat. Freedom all by itself will hardly cure the wounds that it has inflicted, or satisfy the aspirations that it has proclaimed. By invoking only more and more freedom, one condemns the most efficacious solutions to utter powerlessness.

True freedom ("social liberty"), by contrast, can come from no other source than "social truth" (as the title of his chapter 17 proclaimed, Keller 1865, 274). The economic laws that have been discovered form part of that social truth which no one can ignore. In a manner reminiscent of Périn, but seen more from the perspective of labor than of the property owner, Keller invoked moral as well as economic law and virtue. In the circumstances of a fallen humanity, he insisted, it will take a corps of specially dedicated guides, renouncing property for themselves, to inspire the mutual forbearance and deference necessary for capital and labor to work collaboratively instead of exploitatively with each other (see *Quanta cura* 4 in Carlen 1981, 1:383).

After all, Keller maintained (Keller 1865, 287f.), economic activity does not take place independently of the beliefs one brings to it. Every economic system conceals a religion; one can distinguish four types in European history. The Catholic system founded corporations or guilds based on the free combination of capital and labor, aided and abetted by persons living under the vow of poverty. Since Philip the Fair, another school had contested the terrain, the legists. "Without denying original sin, they claim that only legal jurisdiction can cope with it, regulating commerce and industry and organizing labor, education, the common weal." Then there is the Protestant school; its dogma is the free expansion of individual forces, the absolute domination of capital, the exploitation of the worker, every kind of financial speculation and usury. Finally, the "revolutionary school" denied original sin outright, eliminating that explanation for social inequalities and injustices. For the protection of property only naked power was left, at best mitigated by plebiscitary caesarism, really "the worst of tyrannies." The Revolution of 1789 at least made the alternatives clear: either rapacious individualism offset by totalitarian regimes, or Catholicism (Keller 1865, 289).

Are Catholicism and freedom then irreconcilable forces? By no means. Keller limited the church's weapons to persuasion (and prohibition), whereby people must come to terms with each other and with the guidance of the church freely, voluntarily. As in the first centuries of its existence, force might well be used against the faith, but not on its behalf (Keller 1865, 289f.). It seems Keller could square this stand with the Syllabus of Errors on the assumption that the French (and Italian, etc.) *people*, after all, were still Catholic — only the liberal coterie of the propertied class had duped a certain number of them against their better judgment. This is perhaps one of the reasons why Ketteler's German Catholic defense of the freedom of the church and attacks on liberalism contained some nuances missing from Keller's denunciation of the Revolution. Ketteler lived in a country where there was no denying that Catholics were a minority.

Maignen and the Founding of the OCCO

Maignen's flourishing Cercle des jeunes ouvriers on boulevard Montparnasse was laid low by the war and the Commune. He was on the lookout not only for benefactors to replace the ones he lost during the interruption, but precisely for army officers to take an interest in the *patronage*. First he got La Tour du Pin to speak to the circle, then Albert de Mun. In the months after the Commune, there was a new recognition that something had to be done to repair the relationships of the working class with the rest of society. Maignen aimed to take advantage of the opportunity; but he could hardly have suspected that these noble officers, speaking to workers for the first time in their lives, would be the spearhead of a new movement with pretensions of revolutionizing the system of *patronage*.

De Mun (in *Ma vocation sociale*, 1908, 20–22) has described unforgettably the impression made on him by a worker casualty during the bloody suppression of the Commune. De Mun himself was not involved in the fighting, but was handling press relations for the military government of Paris. One day the general whom he was accompanying came across a group of soldiers carrying off a wounded man. The general asked who he was. " 'It's an insurgent, sir,' said the troops. At which the nearly dead form raised itself up on the stretcher, pointed a bare arm at us and, looking us in the eye, rasped, 'You are the insurgents!'" "The accusation seemed to echo across an abyss, from another world" (McManners 1972, 81). After his visions of a "social regeneration" of France based on a post-liberal mobilization of religious and traditional resources as described so persuasively by Keller, the Commune convinced him of the extent to which the rot had sunk in. Not that it was the fault of "the lower orders" who were in revolt.

It took several months for Maignen to find de Mun and entice him to the Cercle des jeunes ouvriers; in the meantime, beside his military duties, de Mun, with La Tour du Pin, paid visits to eminent Catholic figures and devoured authors such as Joseph de Maistre, Louis de Bonald, Jaime Balmes, Juan Donoso Cortés, Louis Veuillot. Through La Tour du Pin, he also discovered Le Play and his rejection of the Revolution, based as it seemed on empirical studies (Mun 1908, 47–56). But in September La Tour du Pin visited the club and spoke to the young workers; several weeks later, Maignen showed up at the Louvre, where de Mun, a general staff officer with the rank of second lieutenant, was still part of the military government. Maignen, of course, spoke of the Montparnasse club; he was still trying to get it back on its feet after the Commune had shut it down. Perhaps sensing the desire of de Mun to get involved in effective social action toward "a Christian and social rebirth of the country," he spelled out the lines of responsibility for the hatred which seemed so prevalent, in the same sense as Keller and the dying insurgent. He assured de Mun that there was still a chance to restore good interclass understanding, on condition that "the rich, the great, the successful" acquaint themselves with the people and their needs. "I live with the people, and I tell you that for their part they do not hate you; they simply have no contact with you nor you with them. Go to them with your heart open, your arms extended, and you will see that they will understand you" (B. Martin 1978, 13; Mun 1908, 62).

With some trepidation, de Mun arrived at the door of the club on boulevard Montparnasse on the evening of 10 December 1871, dressed in his light blue uniform with silver shoulder knots, a saber at his side. An implausible apparition this, an army officer addressing edifying words to Parisian workers within a few months of the "Bloody Week." All the same, the reception he got let him know that his destiny was settled, not yet as a "fixed plan," but in the sense of "an irrevocable engagement" (Mun 1908, 66). He had discovered not only a remarkable charism for public speaking in himself, but in the Cercle des jeunes ouvriers he had found the very means and model by which the gulf between "society" and the working class was to be healed (Mun 1908, 74).

What he thought he saw before him was in good part an illusion conjured up by his paternalistic instincts. He contrasted the young workers' club with the conventional *patronage* in the following passage (Mun 1908, 57–58):

> In the *patronage*, made up of children and very young people, the director and those who assist him in his work retained the administration and the internal affairs in their own hands. In the *cercle*, whose members were workers beyond their apprenticeship, the director kept only a mission of fatherly oversight: the president of the club was a worker chosen by his comrades; a council of workers, also elected, governed it and administered the dues.

Each circle, like Montparnasse, would have clubrooms, a chapel, and a chaplain, reflecting and promoting its conspicuous Catholic character. Following Maignen's central intuition, each circle would also have a committee recruited from the *classes dirigeantes* and divided into four sections: publicity, club activities, finances, and studies. From the interaction of the two levels, that of the workers and that of the upper classes, under the benign guidance of religion, would result the restoration of the social health of France.

One of Maignen's volunteers and intimates, Paul Vrignault, a bureau chief at the Quai d'Orsay who roomed at the Cercle Montparnasse, suggested a vision worthy of the young officer's ardor: to reproduce the club of Montparnasse in every one of the twenty arrondissements of Paris (Levillain 1983, 256–64). By Christmas 1871, Vrignault, Maignen, and de Mun had gathered nine prominent Catholic men, including Emile Keller, to launch a new organization dedicated to this end and to be called the Oeuvre des cercles catholiques d'ouvriers. An "Appeal to Men of Good Will" was drawn up by Vrignault and published in several newspapers by the middle of January 1872. The organizing and expansion of Maignen's design could begin.

In the "Appeal" (Mun 1908, 72–75) and more soberly in the statutes worked out during the early part of 1872, the paternalistic character of the OCCO comes through clearly. They regarded the working class as a whole as "children," at best as younger "brothers" (73) prone to join revolutionary clubs. The statutes (*Bases*) defined the aim of the OCCO to be "the devotedness of the upper class to the working class." Its principles were "the definitions of the church on its relations with civil society" (291; what was meant was the encyclical *Quanta cura* and the Syllabus of Errors; see 105). Its form was to be the Catholic workers' club (*cercle*), a needed response to the republican or socialist workers' clubs.

De Mun's Strategy for the OCCO

Soon Albert de Mun was putting the organization in place that would be necessary to carry out this bold plan. A secretariat (or executive committee) was formed with La Tour du Pin at its head, Albert de Mun in charge of founding new clubs, and Count Robert de Mun, his older brother, in charge of finances. Maignen was as before the director of the Cercle Montparnasse as well as member of the board, with other persons distinguished for their charitable activity or contributions. Both La Tour du Pin and Albert de Mun combined their intensive OCCO work with duty as active officers of the French army for the first three or four years (Robert de Mun apparently could devote full time to the organization, especially in setting up its headquarters). They also combined a spirit of Christian mutual deference and brotherhood with habits of command formed in the military. According to Levillain, Albert de Mun followed a policy of asserting his authority from the first, counting on his brother's unfailing support in any question that came up within the secretariat. Beyond that threesome, his energy, initiative, and spellbinding oratorical gifts were largely, but not completely, equal to the task of molding the fledgling organization to his views. The earliest notable frictions arose when de Mun called on older established *patronages* and Catholic workers' clubs to fall into line with the new order of the day (Mun 1908, 150f., 215, and Levillain 1983, 332–30). Although Maignen was happy to receive the new support that de Mun brought to his *cercle*, his superior in the Brothers of St. Vincent de Paul would not tolerate it becoming a mere appendage to an upstart lay group. This was to be only the first of de Mun's takeovers and attempted takeovers in the name of the greater cohesion and effectiveness of French social Catholicism under the aegis of the OCCO.

By midway through its first year of existence, the OCCO had expanded modestly beyond the initial Montparnasse circle. From the start, the will to penetrate the working-class quarters from where the Commune had drawn its most persistent support led de Mun, his brother, and Vrignault to Belleville (Mun 1908, 85–87; Levillain 1983, 288–301). This was the neighborhood that de Mun had tried to reconnoiter during the Bloody Week in May, the day that he heard of the execution of Archbishop Georges Darboy and the other hostages taken earlier by Communards. With the assistance of the local pastor (one parish for a population of sixty thousand), the pioneers of the OCCO managed to create a workers' circle and its corresponding committee of patrons by April 1872. Present at the inauguration were several young ladies, relatives of members of the Paris committee. Their teacher accompanied them and brought a friend from Lyon along, a certain Mademoiselle Dissart, who taught at a girls' school. On her return to Lyon, she promptly sold the idea of a workers' club to acquaintances and soon had a group of men ready to undertake such a project in Lyon (Mun 1908, 131f.). Then she wrote to let the OCCO in Paris know about it, much to de Mun's surprise. He visited the group after some initial hesitation, since at that early date the founders had not really thought of a national network. Thus was started the campaign throughout the provinces that got under way when de Mun took over the position of OCCO general secretary from La Tour du Pin in 1873.

The third new foundation was in another Parisian neighborhood, Montmartre, on 16 June 1872. It was preceded by a publicity coup on the part of the OCCO, when the exiled bishop of Geneva, Gaspard Mermillod (*Catholicisme* 8:1232f.), preached on behalf of the new cause at the society church of St. Clothilde (14 April 1872). This victim of Swiss liberal hegemony, the son of a working-class family, would found the international social Catholic Union de Fribourg in 1884 (see chapter 10 below; Paulhus) and the Catholic University of Fribourg in 1889. He had already caused a sensation once in Paris, at the same church, in 1868, when he denounced the indifference of the rich in tones seldom heard since the days of François Ledreuille's outspokenness. Now he offered them one more chance to redeem themselves (Mun 1908, 116ff.). This time, after the horror of the Commune, his upper-class audience was chastened. As *Le Monde* commented the next day, "There is a great difference between a speech before and a speech after the explosion." With this act, not only were the OCCO coffers bulging with the proceeds of the collection, but the whole Catholic and conservative upper class took notice of the OCCO.

The OCCO was not the only sign of the renewal of social Catholic activity in the wake of the Commune. On the one hand, there were the *Comités catholiques:* like the Katholikentage in Germany, they brought local lay leaders together once a year in a general assembly and sought to promote and coordinate Catholic organizational life of all kinds. The OCCO used the good offices of the Comités catholiques of Paris, and seems to have been linked to others through what one might call interlocking directorships. Even more geared to a political defense of the church against the liberals was the idea of a Catholic League (Levillain 1983, 339–44), propagated by certain Assumptionists; it stood in parallel with the Opera dei Congressi in Italy (see chapter 13). On the other hand, there was the Union des Associations des oeuvres ouvrières catholiques (Levillain 1983, 333ff.). It served as a kind of meeting ground for all the Catholic workers' clubs of France. It was reorganized after the Franco-Prussian War at a congress held in Nevers in 1871. Three possible orientations were proposed for the organization at this meeting, without any of them finding general favor. The abbé François Courtade, of Paris, stressed the importance of a national Catholic workers' association that would link the workers themselves; the clerical directors would be more on the sidelines of such an organization, or backstage. Maignen and a like-minded colleague from Nantes pointed to the need for a federation of the autonomous local clubs, so that journeymen doing their tour de France could find a Catholic workers' club to which he belonged, by virtue of his membership elsewhere. (This would resemble the Kolping journeymen's associations.) Others, finally, called for the creation of a major apostolate of the press and lectures, with the assistance of capable representatives of the working class.

When this Union met again in Poitiers in August 1872, Albert de Mun was ready with a bold proposal. He introduced the new OCCO to the assembled directors as the comprehensive answer to all the needs brought to the fore in the previous meeting. The workers' club should develop into the means and the occasion of a constant interaction between the estranged social classes. It should lead to the formation of employers' and employees' associations ready to cultivate mutual contact. The clubs would be affiliated and constitute the network of a Christian journeyman's association, perhaps primarily from now on for the draftees who found themselves all over France without contacts (Maignen's idea). Since they would all be parts of the national OCCO, they would fulfill the function of the workers' union that Abbé Courtade has asked for. The organization of appropriate instruction for the workers would be facilitated by the national model, much as the third party desired.

De Mun was not deferential before his predecessors in the social apostolate. For lack of a central organization, the workers' clubs had not had the impact on society that society needed. The individual oeuvre and its director must venture forth from under the church tower and join hands with the upper-class men whom the OCCO was mobilizing. They could just as well abandon the loose union in which they had hitherto gathered and join up under the banner of the OCCO. In fact, in time, this organization, with one foot in the upper classes and the other planted firmly among the working class, could become a veritable Catholic League (Levillain 1983, 339ff.)!

La Tour du Pin and de Mun were the honored houseguests of Bishop Louis Pie, the great intransigent champion of the church's rights, while they were attending the meeting in Poitiers. They also had the favor of Msgr. Gaston de Ségur, the head of the Union itself. That did not prevent their proposals from being sharply attacked in the course of the meeting. Finally they were voted on, favorably; but, as de Mun wrote (1908, 151), it was more out of "sympathy for our effort, and the desire not to discourage us, than out of conviction." The vote was not binding on anyone in any case. Its main effect was to secure some sort of status or recognition from their senior peers at a very early stage.

Harmel into the Mix

Léon Harmel, when he surfaced on the OCCO's horizon in 1873 (Mun 1908, 243ff.), displayed another dimension of the labor question, that of factory workers and their families. He proposed another working model, one that would challenge, or at least distract, the OCCO's leadership for years to come. What we have called "the Christian factory" (chapter 7) may also be called the Harmel model; in its era people referred to it as la méthode Harmel (Trimouille 1974, 41). It came from the world of industry, of the family-owned manufacturing firm, which was as foreign to the de Mun brothers and La Tour du Pin as the world of the Parisian poor had been. It was crucial to the beginnings of social Catholic corporatism, a quest for that will-o'-the-wisp, the Christian corporation.

It cannot be said that the challenge was taken up in the most fruitful, self-effacing way, as one might expect of the dedicated knights portrayed in de Mun's memoirs (Rollet 1947, 1:56–65). A sort of corporate egoism led de Mun, after some brief oscillations, to a strategy of coopting Harmel without letting him or his model call into question the bases of the OCCO as they had been fixed in 1872. This took place by reason of a sudden decision at the end of 1875, one taken largely for organizational considerations connected with de Mun's ascendancy in the leadership of the OCCO. Though de Mun constantly called for reflection and research on Catholic social doctrine (Molette 1970 passim), the study commission that he set up did not function until well after a disagreement with La Tour du Pin over de Mun's political ambitions in 1876. De Mun's own reading never included a single work of the liberal or socialist adversaries against whom he felt called upon to do battle (Levillain 1983, 444).

In 1875, La Tour du Pin, under the impact of the Harmel model, made the central committee of the OCCO face the question of factory workers, married workers and their families, and hence women. The Maignen model was tailored for single men establishing themselves in a trade. Its idea was that, having been preserved by the workers' cercle from the shoals of bachelorhood and having saved enough money, they could then get married and join the class of petit bourgeois artisans, some of whom served on OCCO committees here and there (Levillain 1983, 401). By failing to reassess critically the model with which they started, the leaders of the OCCO severely limited their potential for addressing the social problem of industrialization in its full scope. The much-invoked social teaching of the church was in fact hardly more substantial than the perfervid anti-liberalism of authors like Keller and Donoso Cortés. That may be why de Mun thought it was all already contained in the encyclical and syllabus of 1864 (Levillain 1983, 580; Molette 1970, 167; Rollet 1947, 1:63). The idea that more serious investigations in the social sciences — economics in particular, and the rival schools of social thought — were going to be necessary, if one was to accomplish the grand design of social regeneration in the age of industry, did not hit home. Nor did the idea that a lay association like the OCCO might have a special warrant for sponsoring such secular studies in the service of the church. Even apart from the fact that the gentlemen of the OCCO were not academics, such a prospect labored under the drawback that it would mean paying serious attention to authors who were indifferent or hostile to the Catholic tradition. It could never appear as attractive an undertaking to these Catholics as a direct retrieval of traditional theology and social philosophy.

Both La Tour du Pin and de Mun were at first bowled over by the new and different possibilities for social Catholicism represented by Harmel. In the case of La Tour du Pin, lasting bonds of respect for and friendship with the factory owner resulted, a case of opposites attracting. It even seems that La Tour du Pin gave Harmel the name for what he had created: "la Corporation" du Val-des-Bois (Trimouille 1974, 40). Though Le Play had been a formative influence on both Harmel and La Tour du Pin, he did not have much to say about guilds. His watchwords were patronage and association. And when Périn alluded to the revival of professional associations in papal Rome, they were different enough from Harmel's plant associations that he did not yet appropriate the term "corporation" for them. La Tour du Pin, however, with his legitimist family background, would have been keenly aware that the medieval corporations were linked with the medieval monarchy and that they both fell victim to the Revolution together — even if Keller and Maignen had not recently reminded him. Harmel, with a more detached reverence for the monarchy as such, was delighted to find out that the complex of associations that his father and he had nurtured so painstakingly was but a modern version of the trade guilds of the ages of faith. He had discovered his approach by trial and error; now he was energized to propagate it all over France, within the OCCO and apart from it. He wrote and published a capital Manuel d'une corporation chrétienne (Tours: Mame, 1877; 2d ed.

1879; see Trimouille 1974, 206, and Levillain 1983, 578), which was an instruction book for employers as well as the main source for the history of Val-des-Bois itself.

In the bosom of the OCCO La Tour du Pin's shift of interest from the Maignen model workers' club to the Harmel model corporation raised hackles. Creating the necessary associations not just for men but for women was seen as encroaching on the clergy's prerogatives by the Jesuit chaplain of the Paris committee as well as by Maignen. The latter deemed the idea of a laymen's organization setting up women's associations to be tantamount to flouting church discipline. La Tour du Pin summed up Maignen's objections under two heads (cited by Rollet 1947, 1:59)

(1) The Corporation is impossible outside an industrial agglomeration.
(2) It is necessarily based on confraternities or associations that cannot be formed without the good offices of the clergy, which is not likely in present circumstances. I feel the full force of these two objections, but I cannot believe that providence has uttered its last word for the reconquest of our country at the Montparnasse club. It is an admirable gathering place, but it is not rekindling anything yet.

Not that there were no objective reasons to be soberminded about the Harmel model as well. Maignen could point out that the Harmelian "Christian corporation" worked at Val-des-Bois because of a rare combination of factors. One precondition was that it constituted a self-contained community with a stable workforce. In any good-sized city, however, factory workers constituted a drifting population, independent to a fault, whose fortunes might not be tied to any particular plant or firm (Maignen 1927, 1:482–500). Maignen thought that if there were to be any way to re-Christianize urban workers, it would have to start outside the workplaces. The first stage was the *patronage*, the second the cercles des ouvriers, the third would be an association of employers geared to convert them to a Christian view of the relations between master and workers. Only then, after these parallel organizations had taken root, could one proceed to resurrect the guilds proper. Thus he welcomed an initiative by Harmel to form an association of employers in Paris who would be encouraged to care for their workers the way Harmel did and also participate in the evening and Sunday activities at the Catholic workers' club (Levillain 1983, 428).

Maignen could therefore welcome an adaptation of the methods of Harmel, such as an association of employers affiliated with the club, so as to strengthen the club. Beyond that, however, he doubted that consumers' cooperatives and the other economic institutions, which were an integral part of the Harmel model, could be transferred to urban settings. Harmel of course found it difficult to appreciate Maignen's reservations about the factory corporation. Encouraged by La Tour du Pin, he failed to see why his model and Maignen's could not be applied in different settings under the common roof of the OCCO. Still as paternalistic in his way as other OCCO activists at this stage, Harmel called upon employers to take advantage of their unparalleled position to imitate him to whatever extent that would be possible. He found admirers but disappointingly few imitators.

Maignen's guiding vision had always been the reconstitution of the trade guilds ("corporations"). In 1876, under the provocation of the Harmel alternative, he took up the theme for serious consideration once again (Maignen 1927, 1:504–35). By the end of 1877 he had completed a proposal spelling out what a corporatist labor policy would look like (Levillain 1983, 595–603). The key provision that alarmed the Catholic industrialists of the Nord was that the 1791 abolition of all guilds should not only be revoked, but that every worker must receive certification from a guild before he could be employed in that trade. The so-called "guild property" was the right of the guild to determine who was qualified to work and at what level. It was clear that Maignen's anti-liberalism was consistent. It would revoke the freedom of workers to enter any trade they liked, to take any job offered to them — and more significantly, it limited the pool of workers to whom employers could offer jobs.

To this conception of a closed corporation, Harmel opposed his of a "free" or open Christian corporation. Apparently he did not object directly that a closed corporation, set up by public authority, would infringe on workers' freedom of religion — a general right of this type was not yet acknowledged by Catholics in the nineteenth century. But Harmel did object that the corporation was evidently intended to include all those engaged in a particular line of work or branch of industry; hence it would have to include nonreligious, perhaps antireligious members; hence it would necessarily fail to be inspired by Catholic principles of social and economic life.

Harmel, strong in his Périnism, emphasized the voluntary character of membership in the Christian corporation, based as it was on membership in one of the confraternities or prayer groups. Maignen's difficulty was not with the Christian character of the corporation, of course; he envisaged it as the culmination of Christian action in *patronages*, circles, and associations over a long period of time. He did not, however, wish to sacrifice what he considered the heart of the Christian organization of labor, namely, that both employers and workers would be subject to corporate or corporatist discipline. The unlimited freedom of the Revolution must yield to the interdependence of capital and labor, employer and employee. Harmel was a veritable apostle of the factory milieu, in his eyes. But the factory milieu itself could hardly be regarded as any sort of a Christian ideal of work. And as for nineteenth-century feudal lords of the factories like Harmel, his was a paternalism no more ideal than that of the medieval barons. True freedom and meaningful equality could flourish only under legitimate kings: the Christian monarchy was the keystone of the whole organization of labor and of society, as the unrepentant and thoroughgoing anti-liberal Maignen saw the matter.

These debates in the first years of the OCCO illustrate some of the ambiguities under which the organization labored. Despite all its strenuously asserted ultramontanism and intransigence, liberalism had made inroads in Catholicism by way of the bourgeoisie, for good or ill. De Mun's instinct was generally to avoid theoretical questions and exhort the troops to the practical dedication of the upper to the lower classes. But now that he was a deputy in parliament, the thought occurred to him and others that he could be "the deputy of Christian labor" (Levillain 1983, 605). Besides, he was torn between making the OCCO into the gathering place of all social Catholic orientations, which would mean a certain diffuseness in its thrust, or shaping it into the spearhead of a veritable Catholic movement for the reconquest of France, with a well-defined social and political program. If the latter, he would have to choose one or the other of the two ideas of corporatism that were present in the OCCO (his political base) since the advent of Harmel. He had tried to finesse the problem since 1876 and it had not worked. In 1878, he came out definitely behind Maignen's position, since it alone seemed to him to do justice logically to the anti-liberal line of the Syllabus and of Keller. The move was ill considered, however, and saddled the OCCO with additional problems as France became more and more anticlerical.

Counterrevolution as a Doctrinal Stand

Meanwhile the OCCO was growing to about 375 circles in 1878, with 38,000 working-class members and 8,000 upper-class committee members (*Catholicisme* 9:847 and DHGE 18:134). This growth coincided with a period of right-wing monarchist strength in the early years of the Third Republic, which however started to yield ground to a republican majority after the elections of 1876. When the new republican government, to consolidate itself, shifted to the more anticlerical stance characterizing the 1880s, it became more difficult to keep the Catholic workingmen's-club movement growing. Through his 1878 option for counterrevolution, despite his intentions, de Mun identified social Catholicism with the legitimist cause until at least 1883, when the pretender to the throne, the count of Chambord, died (for Henri, comte de Chambord, see HDTFR 178f.).

Several changes that would affect the OCCO's future course took place around the same time. Albert de Mun was forced to choose between his military career and his social action; he resigned from the army in 1875. He did not have much to live on; this was a factor in his running for a seat in the assembly in 1876 and succeeding in 1877 (B. Martin 1978, 23–30). La Tour du Pin was transferred to Avignon in 1876 and was offered the position of military attaché in Vienna in 1877. He accepted on condition that he could visit the count of Chambord in exile in Frohsdorf, near Vienna. In 1881 he retired to his estates with the rank of lieutenant colonel and with full time to devote to his social Catholic interests. The pope of the Syllabus, Pius IX, died in 1878 and was succeeded by Leo XIII, who continued to show signs of appreciation to the OCCO.

In these circumstances, as has been often said, the OCCO, which had been a movement, became a school. Perhaps it would be more accurate to say that it gradually lost the dynamism it had shown in its founding years — its paternalistic methods were losing their efficacy — whereas the effort of doctrinal reflection on Catholicism and society finally came under the strong and persistent guidance of La Tour du Pin. To prevent this from happening, and in an attempt at synthesis that would fulfill the OCCO's modest need for an operative doctrine to inspire its program, Albert de Mun simplified the legacy of Emile Keller and summed up the orientation of the OCCO in the ominous term "counterrevolution."

Chartres, 8 September 1878, was the setting chosen to catapult this petard into the public (B. Martin 1978, 36). This was not the first time that he had used the word *contre-révolution* (see, e.g., Mun 1908, 285), but it was the occasion on which he targeted economic liberalism in particular. He intended to launch an attack against the Revolution in a domain where its evil effects were not widely recognized: in the world of work and business. And Maignen's resolutely intransigent interpretation lent itself more readily to that purpose than did Harmel or Périn's adaptation to prevailing economic reality (Levillain 1983, 609–17). What was then the root error of the Revolution in regard to work? Nothing other than its principle of the absolute freedom of labor. Of course the liberal heirs of the Revolution would say that that was its greatest benefaction, to have given the people liberty (cited in Poulat 1977b, 275–80, here 277).

> Freedom, gentlemen? Where is it then? I hear it spoken of everywhere, but I only see people who confiscate it for their own profit! If I try to

pick up the trail of freedom in an area where it makes a difference for you, namely in this great question of labor, the problem that involves all the others and sums up the whole social struggle in our time, what shows up there more than anywhere else is — the lie of the Revolution! I hear the absolute freedom of labor proclaimed as the very principle of the liberation of the people, and I see it end up in practice as the servitude of the workers! Gentlemen, you are artisans, you are men of the trades, tell me if I am wrong.

Absolute freedom of labor is the formula of the Revolution, the implementation of the Declaration of the Rights of Man in the economic order. It is based on the autonomy of reason and the native goodness of man. It posits one's personal interest as motivation for one's efforts. By depriving the sovereign power of the duty of protection that is the foundation of its right, by suppressing in one fell swoop every tutelary intervention, it has delivered the weak without defense to the mercy of the strong. By creating the individualism that makes the weak and the strong face each other in isolation, and by opening the door to free competition, that is to implacable war, the Revolution is like those gargantuan riverboat duels they have in America: each goes at the top speed that its engines will attain, until they explode and dump crew and passengers.

You are this crew! The passengers are France!

De Mun took care to reject any imputation of socialism or lawlessness: such developments were to be seen as the result of liberalism, not of Catholicism.

No, no, we are not and we will never be socialists! Socialism is the denial of the authority of God, whereas we are its affirmation. Socialism is the affirmation of the absolute independence of man, whereas we are its denial. It is the passion of possession, whereas our passion is justice! Socialism is the logical Revolution, whereas we are the irreconcilable counterrevolution! We have nothing in common with it — and between these two terms there is no room for liberalism.

The mission he confided to the members of the OCCO was simple and practical (Levillain 1983, 616): they were to struggle against liberalism with legal means and for what he called "the professional association." This was to be "neither a trade union nor an arbitration panel, but a home of Christian activity where professional interests would come before individual interests, where the antagonism of boss and worker would yield to the religiously proffered and freely accepted *patronage*, where the rights of the one and the other would find their legitimate realization in the performance of their reciprocal duties." Implicit here is the key element of Maignen's idea of the corporation, namely a labor regime in which owners and workers have rights spelled out by the corporation, hence not entirely subject to the will of the individual parties to a labor contract.

Charles Périn might seem the least likely person in the world to challenge a call to counterrevolution. After all, he belonged to those ultramontanes who were more Catholic than the pope. His career at Louvain came to a tragicomic end in 1881, when the pope felt forced to disavow him because of his inopportune attacks on the liberal government in Belgium (Jedin 1981, 9:199). Hence de Mun was not prepared for Périn's declaration on the following day. It came as a regularly scheduled address on the first day of the meeting, also at Chartres, of the Union des Oeuvres (also called the Union des Associations ouvrières catholiques — Msgr. Ségur's federation). It was prepared without knowledge of de Mun's discourse, against the background of the divergence between Harmel's and Maignen's respective notions of guild-like associations. Périn proceeded in five well articulated points (Levillain 1983, 618f.; Molette 1970, 57–61).

(1) The inherent difficulty of doing good in this world is exacerbated today by the radical individualism of revolutionary provenance. Inasmuch as individualism is viewed today as the very principle of social harmony, instead of charity, Christians must rise up in opposition. (2) Liberalism is vicious in principle, and Christians must oppose it with their own set convictions and clear principles; nevertheless, "the way of principles is long." An unfortunately common mistake is hastily to endorse solutions that seem to have tradition behind them. It may instead merely be a matter of changeable custom. (3) "Catholics are the natural sustainers of tradition; but they are not, as one would like to think, the born adversaries of all change." It will not do to talk of restoring the old legal relationships between employers and workers, or of re-establishing guilds when the trades they represented are a thing of the past. Big industry is developing in a striking fashion and with it the importance of capital, the concentration of labor, a market economy. When Pius IX encouraged corporative associations in 1852, he did not re-establish them on the basis of the old system of mandatory guilds. (4) The old Catholic spirit is not one of return to outmoded forms of the organization of labor, but of the revival of charity. The true Christian corporation of our age is one in which charity "provides for everything by *patronage* combined with association." (Notably absent: guild discipline!) (5) What is necessary above all is "the combined action of the church, to inspire and sustain charity, and of the state, to lend the support of its laws to the church."

Périn allowed no opening for an accusation of liberalism to be brought against him. Indeed, he made a point of condemning "those honest, but dangerous persons who would like to be for God, but cannot bring themselves to be against the Revolution." Nevertheless his reading of the Revolution is nuanced differently from de Mun's. Périn remarked: "We cannot dream of joining battle against the vices and disorders of revolutionary society if we repudiate the conditions of civil liberty and equality under which we have been living for a long time and which, in themselves, are not at all revolutionary. The modern nations have come to their present [flourishing] state by reason of centuries of social toil aided by the church and the Christian royalty. Such liberty and equality are the law of our epoch, just as the permanent bonds and the restrictions on the freedom of labor were the law of another time." Lamennais would recognize this line of thought.

Another heir of Lamennais's manifold legacy soon stated his opposition, Count Alfred de Falloux. But the warning shot that Emile Keller fired across de Mun's bow (Molette 1970, 182f., 62–64; see Levillain 1983, 623f.) was one that he tried to take very seriously, in that it pointed out to him how ambiguous his chosen slogan was. Keller wrote:

> You have stated once more that you are the "irreconcilable counterrevolution." Very well, but I miss an explanation, particularly from the mouth of Count de Mun, to wit, that you are not the *ancien régime*, the nearly pagan monarchy from before 1789.... Please give this point your full attention, because I have heard any number of fears and apprehensions raised by your statement. *Neither Ancien Régime nor Revolution*, but the *Christian society* — that is the true watchword.

Shadow and Light of the Social Conservatives

Not all OCCO members were swept up in the firm new line of the general secretary, of course. But by this time de Mun had become *the* spokesman of the OCCO and to a large extent of social Catholicism in France. Later he would rally to the Republic, at the behest of Pope Leo XIII. But his unambiguous and undifferentiated rejection of the whole liberal tradition was fateful for the subsequent development, all the more so because of the late date when he renewed it so forcefully. At mid-century Donoso Cortés and Ketteler could still plausibly think of the re-Christianization of Western Europe over the incumbent corpse of failed liberalism. But after the "modern schism" of ca. 1870 (Martin Marty 1969) it was more counterproductive than ever to dream restorationist dreams. After nearly a century there no longer was any neat division between "the Revolution" and the tradition. French Catholics were left with the task of differentiating between the good and the bad, the valid and the harmful, the living and the dead elements in their two traditions, the religious one of Catholicism and the modern national one of revolution and counterrevolution. Albert de Mun blocked this process to the best of his ability by locking Catholicism together with his counterrevolutionary pathos.

All was not reaction and defiance, however. In the years leading up to the French labor legislation permitting unions and associations in 1884, de Mun and the OCCO made a breakthrough by endorsing governmental intervention and modest regulation of the conditions of labor in industry. Charles Périn mounted a stubborn opposition, but the columns of *L'Association catholique*, the review that the OCCO published from 1876 to 1908, were full of arguments demonstrating the permissibility and the necessity of labor legislation.

The problem that Périn posed to the OCCO on this cardinal point was like the reluctance Ketteler experienced before the question of social legislation, only aggravated. It was the church that had always provided the social services and moral guidance conducive to the social welfare of Christendom — the state will make a mess of it, as it had made a mess of education. The aggravated situation in France was that the state was not in the hands of anti-Catholic Protestants, who after all were Christians, but of Voltairean anticlericals, who could be counted on to try to destroy the last vestiges of Christianity. Nevertheless, La Tour du Pin replied sharply to Périn (Molette 1970, 82): what a travesty, "what a mockery of the cry of distress that has been coming forth from the morass of capitalistic hegemony for a generation," to quibble about an issue of competence! One could hardly turn down all assistance "until it can come forth *exclusively* from the spiritual resources of the church. It is hard to repress the suspicion that these dilatory tendencies come from a conscious or unconscious complacency with the capitalist system, especially when one surrounds them with these fuzzy appeals to 'Christian liberty' that have no concrete reference."

This was an issue on which Maignen, Harmel, and de Mun could agree with La Tour du Pin, if not all for the same reasons. The Study Council of the OCCO (Molette 1970, 80–88) put out a succession of *avis*, platform planks of its social policy, as it were, from 1879 on. They called in principle for social legislation: limiting the length of the work day, setting up accident and retirement insurance, enabling professional associations to exist and own property, etc., all much in advance of what the current governments were willing to undertake. In early 1884, de Mun summed up the consensus in the OCCO in his parliamentary utterances and proposed a bill with the following two points.

> The Chamber invites the government:
> (1) without delay to take the [administrative] steps necessary to promote the principles of association and of professional solidarity between employers and workers.... (2) to prepare the adoption of international legislation enabling each state to protect the worker with his wife and children against excessive work.

The idea of an international convention limiting working hours had come up before. The primary practical objection to such legislation on the national level was that the national economy would be crushed by competition from other countries, unless they too would agree to pass similar legislation. Previously, social Catholics thought in terms of an international conference convened by the pope in his capacity as "advocate of the poor" (Molette 1970, 76). But the pope's diplomatic elbow-room had been limited for centuries and was especially crimped after 1870. Adjusting to the realities almost despite themselves, the OCCO "discovered that it belonged to their own responsibility" as citizens to be the spokespersons or the conscience of their fellow citizens (Molette 1970, 87), even if they had to make use of assemblies and procedures dating from the Revolution to do so.

They received some at least indirect encouragement from Leo XIII's encyclical *Humanum genus* (Carlen 1981, 2:91–101), dated 20 April 1884. While condemning freemasonry, the pope came to speak of "association or guilds of workmen," which he exhorted the bishops to sponsor (par. 35), a harbinger of his 1891 encyclical, *Rerum novarum*. Perhaps more to the present point was what he did not say, namely that secular governments, even Masonic ones, should stay out of social policy. In that light, Albert de Mun endeavored to state precisely the viewpoint that had been adopted in his address at the close of the twelfth general assembly of the OCCO in June 1884. True, a Christian social order could not exist without a Christian government; but still, even if and as long as that would not be the case, two duties remained (Molette 1970, 88). One was to create professional associations and work to make them vigorous. The other would be to deploy all possible political forces "to wrest from the de facto government imposed on us the maximum of justice that it is capable of giving to the people, and to force it in the measure of the possible to accomplish the social mission" for which it had taken responsibility.

Surely this stand, although still controversial, helped prepare the way for the position favorable to governmental intervention that Leo XIII took in *Rerum novarum* in 1891.

Chapter 9

THE CORPORATIST STRAIN
IN AUSTRIA AND FRANCE

Soon after René de la Tour du Pin arrived in Vienna as the French military attaché, an anti-liberal government was installed there for the so-called Taaffe era, 1879–85. The new envoy found a group of Christian-social conservatives pressing that government, with some success, to pass corporatist and other labor legislation. The "Christian economics" that they embodied struck him as far more advanced than anything that one could point to in France, he wrote with malice aforethought to Maignen (Levillain 1983, 602, 582). Thus was forged a relationship between social Catholics from the Vogelsang school in Austria and what became the school of La Tour du Pin in France. Bishop Mermillod was the initial link between the French and the Austrians and between them and Rome (Weinzierl 1961, 108f.). In addition to the different corporatist visions of the Thomists in papal Rome and of Harmel and Maignen in France, this central European version would play a leading role in social Catholic thought during the 1880s.

Vogelsang and Labor Legislation in Austria

Karl von Vogelsang (StL 5:765, KSL 3266, De Gasperi 1931, 20–21, and Boyer 166–80) was a Protestant baron from Mecklenburg in northeastern Germany. He had hardly entered the civil service in Berlin when the king of Prussia granted the populace a constitution under pressure of the events of 1848. Vogelsang promptly resigned in protest and headed back to his possessions in Mecklenburg, though they seem to have been insufficient to support him and his family appropriately. He took up journalism, at first with a conservative paper in Rostock, which soon followed the mood of the Junkers into reaction. When it supported the return of serfdom, he looked for an alternative.

He came to believe that Catholicism, with its communitarian bent, was a more apt form of Christianity than his native Protestantism to guide modern Europe back to social health. He consulted Ketteler, who was at that time pastor of St. Hedwig's in Berlin; Ketteler in turn introduced him to the circle of Catholic intellectuals in Munich connected with the *Historisch-politische Blätter*. From here he was directed to the Jesuits in Innsbruck, Austria, where he became a Catholic in 1850. There followed years of going back and forth between journalism, agriculture, and even a bit of rural industrial entrepreneurship, as well as a period of two years (1859–60) when he was tutor and traveling companion to Prince Johann II of Liechtenstein. He acquainted himself with the Romantic social thought of Adam Müller. The stock market crash of 1873 and the subsequent economic tailspin caught him in an exposed position: the company to which he had leased his cement factory went bankrupt and saddled him with huge debts (Boyer 1981, 168). In 1875 a Bohemian count, Leo von Thun, offered him a position as editor of *Das Vaterland*, a newspaper representing a conservative, provincial opposition to the current liberal, centralizing, and German-national government in Vienna.

In the *Vaterland*, then, Vogelsang developed his views on the social question, thereby becoming the figure around whom all social-minded Austrians gathered. For more thorough investigations, less subject to ephemeral politics, he also founded the *Österreichische Monatsschrift für christliche Socialwissenschaft* (Austrian Monthly Review for Social Science, 1879; the title was changed in 1883 to *Österreichische Monatsschrift für christliche Socialreform;* see R. Knoll 247). In the Austrian parliament, a group of social-minded conservative noblemen represented ideas like Vogelsang's. Prominent among them were the counts Egbert Belcredi and Gustav Blome, a friend of Mermillod. Born in Hannover, Blome entered the Austrian diplomatic service in 1852, became a Catholic in 1856, and was appointed to the Austrian House of Lords for life in 1867 (KSL 307). Prince Aloys von Liechtenstein (KSL 1673ff.; Weinzierl 1961, 112) also lent his prestige and his emphatically corporatist or populist leanings to the cause. Much taken by the Christian socialists in England, his wife's homeland, he sought and received a seat in the lower house of the Austrian *Reichsrat* in 1878.

Vogelsang's basic thought and emphases can be summed up in the following way (see Erika Weinzierl in KSL 3268f. and Josef Oelinger in StL 5:766). The social question of the nineteenth century simply reflected the shambles to which individualistic and rationalistic liberalism had reduced the architecture of society. Instead of an organic commonwealth, there was left only a mechanical state coldly embracing atomized individuals. This state, under the influence of capitalism, emancipated property from the social duties ownership once entailed, gave free rein to the competition of private egoism, and held up the maximization of profit (e.g., "unearned" interest) as the highest aim of economic activity. The social harm all this caused could be overcome only by a comprehensive social reform ("Christian socialism," culminating in a "social monarchy"). Such reform in turn must arise out of faith, Christian morals, and organic thinking.

To dislodge economic liberalism, one needed to develop the foundations of charity, justice, and solidarity. In practice, this would mean decentralization and self-management of enterprises, be they urban or rural. A corporatist organization of society would develop out of links formed from the bottom up, by entrusting the trade groups (always including representatives of the employed as well as the employers) with responsibility for policing their own operations and products. At the top level, these would become "offices of national labor" for the formation of "national, common, ideally shared property" in contrast with the capitalistic notion of private property. In Vogelsang's day the most urgent reforms had to do with farming and the small artisan shops. He repeatedly proposed energetic measures to eliminate the indebiture on land being farmed by smallholders (favorable conditions for cooperative savings and credit unions, for instance). Further proposals were for guildlike coalitions of those practicing the same trade and participation by qualified workers in both the organization of the work process and its proceeds.

In a word, "Vogelsang's ideal society was one in which horizontal class divisions would be replaced by vertical, hierarchical divisions of various broad economic sectors, the three most important being large industry, the small craft trades and shops, and agriculture" (Boyer 1981, 177; see Paulhus 1983, 36). This would eliminate the proletariat by integrating or absorbing its components into the three main economic Stände or "estates." It would also eliminate or restrain usury and bureaucracy by the workings of self-management. Finally it would largely replace the "artificial" modern institutions of the liberal, constitutional state. A monarchical head with defense forces and courts remaining under the royal sovereignty seemed self-evident to round out the scheme.

One can also glimpse the vision of the way this better future will come about: not through violence or another revolution, but, as in the saying attributed to the Russian prince Peter Kropotkin (IESS

8:463ff.), by building up a new society within the shell of the old. This vision was opposed to social Darwinism: it saw mutual aid as the necessary basic paradigm so devastatingly neglected by "the liberals."

A special feature of the Vogelsang school was its condemnation of usury, comprising under that term also the interest that entrepreneurs pay on the capital they borrow. He was encouraged in this especially by two Dominican friars, the Bavarian Albert Maria Weiss, who would later be a professor of moral theology at the University of Fribourg, and Andreas Frühwirth, at the time the provincial of the Order of Preachers for Austro-Hungary, then head of the order in Rome, and finally cardinal in the curia (R. Knoll 1973, 124–33). Vogelsang and some of his disciples would remain convinced for decades that the Jesuit and curial authorities in Rome still held, as they themselves did, to the condemnation of usury by the Fifth Lateran Council in 1515 (DS 1444) and by Pope Benedict XIV in 1745. Although the question was hotly disputed, evidently no Catholic except the pope could state authoritatively that the earlier condemnations were no longer in force, and the pope issued no such pronouncement (see above, p. 20). All the same, a close associate of Vogelsang, Count Franz von Kuefstein, because of his Roman connections and sojourns, had a much less hostile attitude toward capitalism. At least he did not appear to notice the discrepancies between the Roman Neo-Thomist positions of a Matteo Liberatore, whose book he translated (KSL 1565; see R. Knoll 1973, 121f.), and his revered master, Vogelsang.

During the early years of the conservative Taaffe ministry, members of this group took the initiative and managed to get a series of bills passed that offered Austrian workers a measure of protection matching that legislated in England and Switzerland (Ebert 1975), which were at that time the leading nations in this respect. Even before that, in 1877, the young Aloys von Liechtenstein, the "red prince," addressed the first Austrian Katholikentag in Vienna on the social question and published a brochure on "The Representation of Interests in the State," thus bringing prominence to the themes that Vogelsang was taking up in the *Vaterland*. A reform of the trades law of 1859, which declared absolute freedom of labor in typical liberal fashion, was overdue. When the conservatives became the majority in 1879, Count Belcredi got himself appointed to the appropriate committee to shape that reform (Ebert 1975, 138f.; see R. Knoll 1973, 111–17). In stages, from 1883 to 1888, the statutory length of the working day was shortened, first in the mines (to ten hours), then for children and other categories, thus placing certain limits on the freedom of the parties to a labor contract (*Dokumente* 79–82).

The problems that this legislation was meant to deal with were concentrated in Vienna itself. The city had grown from 520,000 in

1857 to 705,000 in 1880, and would count 1,100,000 inhabitants by 1890, with annexations. Jews as well as Christians flocked to the capital from villages in outlying parts of the Dual Monarchy: in 1880 Jews constituted just over 10 percent of the city's population (Boyer 1981, 79); they would become the target of much "Christian-social" anti-Semitism in coming decades. Industrial development was relatively late in coming to Austria, but now was all the more rapid and upsetting. When the *Vaterland* took up the grievances of the urban lower class, it was disconcerting, to say the least, for the more radical or democratic liberal politicians. How could a mouthpiece of the rural aristocracy pretend to represent the needs of "their" constituencies? The resulting controversy served to make the *Vaterland* and its social-reform ideas much better known than it had been heretofore, especially in Vienna itself, where it counted.

The 1883 law established limited protections or privileges for the handwork trades, threatened as they were by better capitalized industry and by foreign imports. However, it also permitted a broad array of production in the so-called free trades, which included all factories and retail and wholesale commercial establishments. Secondly, "entry into a craft as a master artisan now required a proof of competency," accorded only to those who had worked in the trade for a number of years (Boyer 1981, 65). In practice, the law did not offer much protection to crafts which were otherwise under pressure, since their competitors were still "free." But it did make membership in the trade associations and chambers mandatory for small tradesmen, set standards for apprenticeships, and in general encouraged artisans to look after common interests in an organized fashion.

Another reform act of 1883 created labor inspectors for all workshops and factories to check on the working conditions, the training of workers and their safety, and especially the employment and treatment of children in the plant (Ebert 1975, 270–72). That it was possible to pass such a relatively far-reaching piece of legislation so quickly was partly due to an *enquête* of the material conditions of life of the working class, with statistical material provided by a former mechanic and future member of parliament, Ernst Schneider, and a former radical, Franz Motz (Ebert 1975, 29; R. Knoll 1973, 112f.). These shocking data were supplied both to Belcredi and Blome in the legislature and to Vogelsang, who published them in four installments in the *Monatsschrift* with Liechtenstein's financial assistance. (For an earlier report of this nature, in the first volume of the *Monatsschrift*, 1879, see *Dokumente* 50–78.)

Another example of Christian-social exposure of inhumane labor conditions was supplied by one of the younger clergy who began to feel the magnetic attraction of Vogelsang. Rudolf Eichhorn (KSL

501f.) was assigned to a Viennese industrial area in 1881 as assistant pastor and religion teacher, then pastor from 1887 to 1889. In 1888 he was elected deputy from a country constituency and henceforth served rural parishes. During the 1880s he studied the labor question, reading Marx and Lassalle before coming into contact with Vogelsang and his circle. In contributions to Vogelsang's periodical from 1884 to 1886 he described the plight of workers. To report on the working conditions of workers in the Danube shipping industry, he signed on as a deckhand on a river barge convoy to the Black Sea. One particular article was also printed separately and attracted a great deal of attention: "The White Slaves of the Vienna Tramway Company" (1885, reprinted in *Dokumente* 91–132; see Boyer 1981, 159). Eichhorn reported how the conductors worked fourteen to sixteen hours on normal days, on their feet, with only fifteen or twenty minutes away from their post during the middle of the day, and with never a Sunday or a holiday off. The coachmen worked just as long, trying to keep their overworked horses from falling and injuring themselves. Longer penalty shifts were common.

These reports were not for the most part what one would refer to as muckraking, in a bad sense, or yellow journalism. The *Monatsschrift* was not an apt vehicle for that, anyway. All the more noteworthy then is the massive stereotyping of "Jewish-liberal" capitalists as responsible for these conditions (*Dokumente* 92 and passim). Not that Eichhorn did not have some personal experience with liberal politicians who were also Jews and directors of the Tramway Company (121–26). Jews had finally been fully emancipated from legal disabilities in Austria in 1869, a measure for which the liberals took credit. Many Catholic people expected a "Christian" government to revoke this equality and roll back its effects, just as many German Austrians expected the same of a Germanic hegemony. Nevertheless, the ease with which Vogelsang equated Judaism with economic liberalism-cum-exploitation in an editorial note on Eichhorn's investigative reporting was a bad omen for ensuing anti-Semitic developments in Christian-social propaganda (132).

> The reverend author, who has already put us in his debt for casting so much light on social conditions in his area of observation, here describes the lot of the lower ranks of service personnel in the Viennese horse-trolley company. These conditions are typical of the behavior of large stock companies (which are mostly in liberal and Jewish hands) toward those persons who — literally by the sweat of their brows, in horribly long and arduous shifts — bring in their rich dividends and inflated directors' fees. The workers, expending their entire human effort, their whole existence as they do, are confronted with an unfeeling, impersonal something, a stock company with its exclusive orientation toward

the highest possible return on capital. The only immediate remedy for the economically disadvantaged in a case like this is the regulation and oversight of the state; step by step, however, the whole harsh capitalist system can be made to yield to more humane and Christian institutions.

The 1885 law, under the guise of revising the provisions of the law of 1859, set a maximum working day of eleven hours in factories and ruled out factory work for children under fourteen (Ebert 1975, 273–83; see also De Gasperi 1931, 22–24; one may note that Alcide De Gasperi served in the Tyrolean legislature before World War I and on the Imperial Council in Vienna and hence was acquainted with Austrian law and administration at first hand). No child labor at all was permitted under the age of twelve, or at night; all workshops were to be closed on Sundays and holidays; special provisions that created new precedents were made for women workers, e.g., no work for four weeks after childbirth. Contrary to expectations, the factory inspectors found that the new work schedules were introduced immediately almost everywhere, causing few problems for the firms and providing real relief for the workers (Ebert 1975, 254).

This relatively happy result was the result of a combination of social-conservative initiative, careful study of previous labor legislation in all the industrialized countries of Europe, the publicity given the 1883 inquest, and the factor of political compromise in parliamentary processes. By virtue of this last factor, the Christian social conservatives gained substantial backing for the (mitigated) reforms in liberal and even socialist circles. The factory owners felt their interests had not been totally ignored. Socialist papers pointed to the insufficiency of the measures enacted, of course, but some welcomed them as steps in the right direction. The petty bourgeois tradesmen, according to Boyer, would feel disappointed in their hopes for what the reform would bring, and they would become the primary political allies of Vogelsang's disciples. Perhaps this disappointment aggravated the negative attitude fostered by some of them toward parliamentary bodies and processes. But that would be a development of the 1890s. For the moment practical considerations took precedence over doctrinaire positions. For example, associations were encouraged by the law of 15 March 1883 to collect interest on their funds, despite Vogelsang's hostility in principle to "usury."

La Tour du Pin's Corporatist Theory

One thing Vogelsang did not lack was ideas, often controversial even among his supporters. La Tour du Pin was deeply impressed by his conversations with Count von Blome and his discussions with the count of Chambord over articles in the *Vaterland*. He returned to France with his own corporatist thinking vigorously stimulated. Already in 1878 the Austrian influence midwived by La Tour du Pin was becoming apparent. In the pages of the *Association catholique* one could read the presentation by Aloys von Liechtenstein on "The Representation of Interests in the State" (Jarlot 1938, 69). And among the visitors from Vienna to France in the summer of 1878 was Rudolf Meyer (*Dokumente* 79), a writer for the *Vaterland*, who helped persuade de Mun to launch his head-on attack against the much-vaunted "freedom of labor" in his Chartres speech (Levillain 1983, 613ff.).

Meanwhile, in France, the research council (*Conseil des études*) of the OCCO was trying to determine and formulate some firm principles of Catholic social teaching. Led by Félix de Roquefeuil, members such as ex-diplomat Count Antoine de Bréda and Louis Milcent (after 1884 Milcent was active in founding Catholic rural associations and cooperatives; see Rollet 1947, 1:599–601), toiled to produce authoritative opinions or *avis* on social questions from the point of view of a Christian, moral social order. In trying to formulate only what was authoritative for Catholics, of course, they were hamstrung by the quasi-liberal views of Charles Périn and others, who were considered to be at least as Catholic and as well-versed in economics as the anti-capitalist corporatists in central Europe (Levillain 1983, 662–76).

Until La Tour du Pin came back to France, therefore, the deliberations of the council tended to be frustrating oscillations between, for example, the strong doctrine on justice found in St. Thomas and the prevailing insistence on charity (Talmy 1963, 46f., 69; Jarlot 1938, 88–89). When du Pin took over the *Association catholique* and the internal newsletter of the OCCO in January 1882, however, he lost no time in freeing himself of the necessity of always speaking on behalf of the church. Statements framed in the first person plural, he announced, "will reflect the views of the OCCO leadership;" but when the singular "I" appeared, that would be a personal commentary. La Tour du Pin asserted himself in the first person singular regularly thereafter, stating his own views without seeking to wrap them in the mantle of the theologians or of the OCCO.

That these should be counterrevolutionary views was never in question. But that they should also be made politically effective in the present generation was of comparatively little consequence to him, in contrast to de Mun. First the doctrine must be retrieved in all its purity; only then would it be prudent to haggle over its application in the concrete. The two old comrades also disagreed about the role of the OCCO Conseil d'études. De Mun supposed that a very little doctrine went a long way, provided that it was the strong, assured doctrine of the church. La Tour du Pin retorted that just as the Revolution had a social doctrine (liberalism), so the church's social doctrine needed to be developed into a consistent counterposition; otherwise the traditional wisdom would not effectively engage the prevailing deleterious doctrine.

In his initial analysis of the situation in 1882 in the *Association catholique*, La Tour du Pin noted that his social Catholic compatriots were divided between Le Play and Périn. But there was no need to follow either the one or the other exclusively. A wider perspective revealed the existence of another master, Bishop Ketteler, with his own disciples on the banks of the Rhine and the Danube. From them one could learn a valuable lesson. That is (and the emphasis was in the original): "The Christian corporation of Harmel must be complemented by *the corporative regime* in the Christian state." He went on to point out on every occasion how any particular social-reform proposal, if it made sense, would live up to its potential only if it was contained within the enabling and sustaining framework of a "corporative regime." The corporative system was to be not only economic but religio-cultural and political as well (Jarlot 1938, 89f.).

> Hence the restoration of the corporative regime is a perfectly obvious need, with all the reforms that it involves in the realms of politics and finance. Just because it is necessary, however, does not mean that it will be purely spontaneous or voluntary....A hands-off attitude on the part of public authority will not suffice for it to play its role in the state again. Abuses of power in this world do not get corrected by freedom, but by constraint, when persuasion fails. True, the restitution of the corporation could not be the result of legislation alone, since something that has disappeared cannot be simply decreed back into existence. One prepares its rebirth by appeals, however, and accords it legal recognition when it reappears in fact, and strengthens it with privileges.

The Conseil d'études abruptly, surprisingly, adopted this point of view in early 1882. Of course this resuscitated the controversy that Maignen's guild ideas had raised earlier in the OCCO (and between the OCCO and the Catholic jurists and Le Playsians) about whether membership in the reconstituted "corporations" was to be voluntary or obligatory. Since the corporative regime was far from realization, there was plenty of room for maneuver. La Tour du Pin proposed using the organizational freedom granted by the law of 1884 to establish voluntary corporatist organizations. He always maintained that the corporative regime of his imagination would limit freedom much less than the prevailing liberal-bourgeois constitutional regimes, that it could in fact confer the freedom to participate meaningfully in public affairs to most people for the first time. But he never cleared up this equivocation between freedom and obligation or other like puzzles to outsiders' satisfaction.

In the late twentieth century, we are certainly no better placed to understand the corporatist outlook of Vogelsang and La Tour du Pin than their contemporaries were. When we read of "representing interests," we necessarily think of "pressure groups," normally portrayed as lacking all sense of the common good or the national interest and pursuing single-issue, hence irresponsible, politics. To correct for possible anachronistic bias, it is necessary to remind ourselves that in fact the societal spheres of the economy, culture, and politics are in fact arenas in which conflicts of interests must be carried out. In this perspective, the corporatists can be regarded as puncturing the bourgeois illusion that the latter all by themselves represent "the general interest," whereas all other formations have only Rousseau's special interests at heart. With a dose of good will, one can even see corporatism as a conservative opening to societal pluralism (StL 5:258). Of course, it must be recognized at once that it labored under an immobilist presupposition; to speak with Vatican II (*Gaudium et spes* 5), corporatists (and others) had not yet made the transition "from a rather static concept of reality to a more dynamic, evolutionary one." Hence the acknowledgment of pluralism was never clearly articulated or conscious.

A similar difficulty arises from the historical experience of those post-liberal regimes that exploited corporatist thinking for their propaganda before and during World War II ("fascist" regimes, generally speaking). Corporatism in this actualization meant regimentation, totalitarianism. Yet it must be recognized that the corporatist theorists within nineteenth-century social Catholicism charged the liberal regimes of their day with totalitarian tendencies, not without reason — and thought of the corporative system as the necessary bulwark in defense of "public freedoms." Was it a mixture of acute social criticism and nostalgic illusions that they served up for their readers?

Perhaps a key lies in their views on "the representation of interests" (the subject came up for repeated discussions, including an essay by Vogelsang in the September 1887 issue of the *Association catholique;* see Jarlot 1938, 145). They were prepared to admit that universal suffrage was a relative improvement over political participation limited to the property-owning classes. Their ideal was, however, one of real participation and real responsibility of *all* elements of society; this ideal was undercut, in their view, by the asocial and unrealistic individualization of societal procedures in modern liberal regimes. In regard to religion, each individual was encouraged to participate or not in a cult of his own choice (or her husband's or father's choice). Economically, the same applied in the great free market of all commodities, including the very skills that one had acquired to take part in the life of society. Politically, one could vote for "representatives" proposed by others; after voting for them, they were entirely unaccountable to anyone until the next election. To La Tour du Pin, nothing could be more chaotic and subject to the worst abuses of irresponsible power (Jarlot 1938, 151: *"le parlementarisme, voilà l'ennemi"*). Given the tradition on the continent since the French Revolution of what has been called "totalitarian democracy," this critique, as a view of the underside of liberalism, was not so far off target. A Churchillian judgment, that (parliamentary) democracy is "the worst form of government, except for all the others," was a beneficiary of hindsight.

Even the most doctrinaire liberal, however, could not dis-organize society so thoroughly as to ignore economic interdependence. In the family, as La Tour du Pin had learned from Le Play, but also in the world of work, those natural, organic groupings could be found from which a sound society could be built up again. Farmers must farm, tradesmen must trade, mechanics must ply their craft, factory workers must tend mills, entrepreneurs must construct them, if any are to prosper or even survive. Why not base the political order on these natural vocational groupings? One would have the policy-makers of the land elected by colleges that are themselves made up of delegates of all the interest groups of the country. All this presupposes, of course, "a rather static concept of" social "reality."

In a sketch of an "organic law" (not to be called a "constitution," since that was identified with parliamentarism), La Tour du Pin stated the basic rules that would prevail (Jarlot 1938, 154). Every citizen would be reckoned to a category by the economic role he or she performs. The basic principle was that no one would be left out: some substitute would be found for the normative connecting role of the paterfamilias for widows, single persons, and children. Only drones (coupon-clippers) would have no access to participation in the political process. People of the same occupation would elect regional delegates, who would formulate the platform of the regional "estate." These in turn would elect their own delegates to the National Assembly, with instructions and a specified mandate. When new questions arose, there would be no doubt whose advice would be most significant: that of the electoral college, which of course would still be in existence and which the delegate would take pains to represent. No specific mention need be made of the executive branch of government, since that would be an emanation of the royal power, the indispensable keystone of the corporative system. However, La Tour du Pin wanted it understood that he was not thinking of any kind of absolutism or any monistic notion of the state. Neither Louis XIV's "*l'état c'est moi!*" nor the principle of sole parliamentary sovereignty would do. The "natural" occupational formations would have their irreplaceable role in opposing statist pretensions and defending the "public freedoms."

It goes without saying that the first step in this scheme, the enrollment in a corporation or (in this electoral sense) *corps d'état*, would be a corollary of one's line of work. But actually joining a functioning corporation of one's occupation could still be voluntary and optional. Thus La Tour du Pin (in 1893; Jarlot 1938, 162) summed up his thought in the phrase *la corporation libre dans le corps d'état organisé*. This insistence on the organization of the people, not just in unions or associations but as a nation at work and participating in its own government, was the main legacy of the corporatist period of the 1880s to the Christian democracy of the 1890s. It seems La Tour du Pin saw a three-tiered arrangement as typical, wherein a factory "corporation" like Harmel's would be the first level, a regional mixed commission or union of half employers and half employees of the same industry would be the second level, and a "corporative senate" elected by the mixed unions would represent "the organized people" at the national level (Rollet 1947, 1:123f., 129). In contradistinction to any liberal parliamentary regime, the chosen delegates would not represent individuals, but groupings. Individuals would belong to such groups on the basis not of home address but of occupation in a certain sector of the economy.

Those sectors would be formed around four leading functions: (1) religious and moral interests (education, arts, family, and personal nurture); (2) public interests (public services and authorities); (3) agricultural interests; and (4) industrial and commercial interests. At the provincial level, each of these could form an estate and maintain communication with their counterpart estates in other provinces (Jarlot 1938, 155f.). Free corporations in each of these sectors could be organized in anticipation of the full-blown corporative regime. La Tour du Pin especially urged the foundation of agricultural and then industrial corporations and federations which would be as it were so many corps d'état-in-waiting (158). In these cases, so as to implement the guiding principle of enabling every class and condition of person to participate, it would be appropriate to found distinct interest groups of employees only and employers only. They would then delegate representatives to a mixed commission, half and half. There were, after all, certain "democratic" features in the corporatist project, which did not recommend it to paternalistic industrialists.

Even though these hopes and ideas were never realized, it is worthwhile to fix them in the mind's eye. The corporatist strain in social Catholicism suffered an eclipse, but far from a total one, in the period between 1891 (*Rerum novarum*) and World War I. It constituted a significant element in the thinking of social Catholics for decades to come. Its heritage was split, as it were, between the Christian democratic and the more authoritarian tendencies of the movement. Then it would enter another period of some notoriety before and after *Quadragesimo anno* (Pius XI, 1931).

It served to open an additional breach in the prevalent Catholic distrust of governments and governmental action; in this at least it prepared the way for *Rerum novarum*. But Leo XIII's simultaneous call to French Catholics to put aside their legitimist dreams and work within the republican framework fell on stone-deaf ears in La Tour du Pin's case, relegating him thereafter to an honored spot on the periphery of French social Catholicism. The monarchism of the Action française attracted him, whereas its proto-fascist nationalism of racist character did not seem to repulse him, sad to say. "Economic" anti-Semitism was after all perfectly respectable in large parts of the social Catholic movement, especially in Austria and France. Thus was prefigured the mésalliance of the two anti-liberalisms, the idealistic, socially conscious one of Vogelsang and La Tour du Pin and the nihilistic-positivistic one of Charles Maurras, in the fascisms of the 1930s.

Toward the Modernization of Social Catholicism

When German Catholics began to breathe more freely again as the *Kulturkampf* let up, the beginnings of the earlier Catholic labor movement in Aachen and Essen and a few other Rhineland towns lay in ruins. It was impossible to revive them as they were in the face of the Iron Chancellor's anti-socialist law. The focus of Catholic labor concerns shifted to industrial *patronage* for workers and with it to a new locale as center of gravity, a place to the north of Aachen and Cologne, not far from the Netherlands. Mönchengladbach, also written at the time as München-Gladbach or M.-Gladbach, became the mecca of German social Catholicism — initially simply because the textile factory of the exemplary Franz Brandts was located there (see above chapter 6). Not only were his employees better paid than the going rate, they also worked shorter hours (ZgLb 3:93 and Klinkenberg 1981, 141). His fellow industrialists waited for his operation to fold after he went ahead on his own and reduced the length of the working day from fourteen hours to twelve for men and ten and a quarter hours for women. With its small size (three hundred workers), its advanced human relations, and its market niche, however, the plant prospered.

The possible influence of Léon Harmel on Franz Brandts is suggested by various indications. Harmel's portrait hung behind Brandts's desk. Dr. Lingens, the lawyer in Aachen who mediated Ketteler's thought to La Tour du Pin and de Mun in 1871, propagated the Harmel model in 1877 at the Katholikentag in Würzburg; the *Christlich-sociale Blätter* did likewise in 1879 (Klinkenberg 1981, 142). On the other hand, Brandts's social innovations in his own factory predate this publicity by way of Aachen and differed from Harmel's in characteristic ways, reflecting the different starting point in Mönchengladbach. Here the majority of workers were still Catholic and voted for the same political party as did the few Catholic industrialists, namely the Center party. In the factory itself, though, no religious practices or political pressures were allowed, since Brandts employed not only Catholics, but also Protestants and socialists. No one ever was to inquire about these allegiances; the rule was merely that no talk or agitation disrespectful of religion was permitted. Brandts and Harmel were both conspicuous for encouraging worker self-management of the social institutions of the firm; at least in this respect one would conjecture that Brandts followed Harmel's example. But the fact is that Brandts had started on this course in 1872 or 1873, before Harmel was widely known in France, much less in Germany.

The story of the workers' committee at the Brandts factory in Mönchengladbach exhibits Brandts's practicality and his rare gift for not standing on ceremony or supposing that workers were after all just children. It started with a sick fund. This in itself was nothing new; to a concerned Christian employer like Brandts it was a matter of course that in his own factory, when he opened it in 1872, a fund for sick workers would be available. A little more than 1 percent of every worker's pay was withheld for this purpose; as the head of the firm, Brandts contributed 50 percent more and paid five percent interest on the current balance. When workers fell ill, they got free medical treatment and medications and half of their wages for up to six months. The fund was administered initially by the factory owner, the chief engineer and the board of four workers elected by their peers.

By 1880, however, all six members were workers, of whom at least two were women. According to the statutes, the agenda of each board meeting was to be approved beforehand by the proprietor, who could also take part in the meetings. Brandts made a point of never attending, so as not to hinder free discussion. For by this time, the sick-fund board had already developed into a workers' committee that took up any and all questions connected with the plant, except pay. In the course of the 1880s, even this sacred cow fell without much resistance on the part of Brandts. What Brandts now had and commended to other industrialists, therefore, beside a panoply of self-administered welfare arrangements, was a workers' committee in every plant, free to range widely over the entire territory of employer-employee relations, house policies and benefits, and grievances — and discuss them with the owner. It also functioned in a disciplinary role. Not only did it make recommendations on fines or firings for incidents that took place in the shop, such as fighting or lewd advances (one surmises that there were very few!); it also brought to the employer's notice undesirable activity outside the factory. One young woman was dismissed on the committee's recommendation for failing to break off a relationship with a shiftless good-for-nothing who never came around the plant.

The only respect in which Brandts might have undertaken something solely because of the influence of Harmel seems to have been in missionizing his fellow factory owners by promoting the association called Arbeiterwohl, started in 1880 (ZgLb 3:94). It was the editor of the *Christlich-sociale Blätter*, Arnold Bongartz, who suggested that the time had come for the concerned Catholic industrialists of the Rhineland to join forces in order "to work for the amelioration of the condition of the workers' estate on the basis of Christianity." Harmel was at the organizational meeting as a consultant and of course Franz Brandts came as a leading Catholic industrial patriarch in the region. As a result of the conference, Brandts returned to Mönchengladbach as president of the new association. Soon the headquarters of the organization, together with the editor of its periodical, were located on the factory grounds in Mönchengladbach. Brandts had just finished the construction of the St.-Josephs-Haus, with room for kitchen and eating facilities and all the plant organizations on the ground floor, along with the Brandts family quarters upstairs. Evidently he built generously, for when Franz Hitze, as a young priest, arrived to serve as editor of the Arbeiterwohl's magazine (also called *Arbeiterwohl*), there was room for him to live and work in the same building (ZgLb 1:53–64, here 58; see Schoelen 1982, 267–300).

Unlike the typical liberal of his time, or the typical conservative, for that matter, Brandts was not overly concerned to keep the worker in his place. On the contrary, his efforts were bent on encouraging the participation of the workers in everything that affected the life and well-being of themselves, their families, and the Brandts "company family." Brandts worried about socialism just as others did, but in local politics his main constituency was the Catholic working-class population (he served on the city council in the minority). This meant that he was not disposed to fear the rising influence of the popular strata, but would have welcomed a voting system that would give them political clout in proportion to their numbers — at least in

Mönchengladbach. To judge by the official shop policies that were published in 1882, he was inspired by "a patriarchal spirit" (Löhr in ZgLb 3:94; Klinkenberg 1981, 142). But it is now clear that this aura stemmed largely from the priest (Dr. Peter Norrenberg, 1847–94) who composed the opening considerations on moral values to be promoted in the workplace. Here the traditional emphasis on the mutuality of duties between unequals predominated. The superiors were expected to "show good example to their subordinates in the fulfilment of their moral and religious duties." Workers were called upon to "dress neatly, act modestly and behave toward each other in a cooperative and harmonious manner." They were reminded that they "owed loyalty, hard work and prompt obedience to the proprietor [*Fabrikherr*] and his representatives." For Norrenberg, the social problem was remediable by religious, charitable means. Difficulties could be overcome by serious meditation on the spirit of the gospel, "which is still the only prescription for the lacerated social body." Little was to be hoped for from the modicum of self-administration of which the workers were capable. His motto was "Everything for the worker, but with and through the proprietor."

Brandts, even at the age of forty-eight, was not inclined to contradict a respected spiritual guide, so he let these considerations be printed without additions or corrections. But his own practical convictions were like Harmel's, to wit (Guitton 1927, 1:299; see also Trimouille 1974, 9): "The worker's welfare — by and with the worker; so far as possible never without and certainly never despite the worker." This did not mean that he ceased to think of his workers and their families as part of the company family with himself as Christian patriarch. Having built the Josephshaus and garden as an amenity for the workers and as his own family's residence, he pursued the matter of workers' quarters with great diligence at the municipal and private level. Eventually he had a housing project built around the factory with a neo-gothic chapel in the middle. Workers could buy these houses under favorable conditions. Members of his own family were involved in the Josephshaus programs, starting with his wife, who was in charge of the midday meal served in the dining-hall; she also supervised the child-care program and the sewing classes, with a view to training the young women workers in the household arts. Here in the Josephshaus, and in the parish church, the mutual religious edification of workers and entrepreneurial family that was out of place in the factory could be carried on in a freer atmosphere.

The efficacy of Brandts's social undertakings was not confined to one small factory, however. He spearheaded social Catholic undertakings in two larger concentric circles: Arbeiterwohl and the Volksverein für das katholische Deutschland (of this more in chapter 14). Both organizations had Franz Hitze as a kind of general director, until he went to Münster as professor for social ethics in the Catholic theology faculty in 1893. The mutual influence of these two men during the years that Hitze lived in the Josephshaus with the Brandts family was decisive for the future of social Catholicism in Germany and to a great extent beyond its borders. Indeed, in Hitze and his priest associates (like August Pieper, see StL 4:395, and Heinrich Brauns, see StL 1:874), one could see the successor of Kolping to whom Ketteler had looked forward, one who would help educate and organize factory workers as Kolping had done for Catholic artisans. Although the Volksverein would overshadow the Arbeiterwohl, a few details on Hitze and his collaboration with Brandts in the earlier organization are certainly in order.

Arbeiterwohl was an association, not of workers, but of employers and priests (it attained a membership of about a thousand, mostly in the Rhineland). As such, the first number of its publicity organ struck a tone of welcome to industry and industrialists that seemed quite new in German social Catholicism, despite Reichensperger and a few relatively isolated comments by Bishop Ketteler. This is all the more surprising because Hitze had just written a tome of sixteen lectures, *Kapital und Arbeit und die Reorganisation der Gesellschaft* (Capital and Labor and the Reorganization of Society, Paderborn: Schröder, 1880). This was thoroughly Vogelsangian in conception and approach. It called for nothing less than a radical reform of economic and political society along corporatist lines, since economic and political liberalism was a source only of misery, sin, and more misery for the bulk of the working class. Now, nevertheless, in the new periodical of which Hitze was the editor, appeared a manifesto endorsing modern industrialism without a word of criticism for the one-sided control exercised over it by capitalists. It called for a more intensive paternalistic involvement of industrialists in the welfare of their workers, however (Focke 1978, 44–50; see De Gasperi 1931, 31–33). As a recruiting brief for new members in the organization, it appealed to the enlightened self-interest of bourgeois entrepreneurs and clergy.

It also ushered in a development of great importance for the future of social Catholicism, namely, the basic acceptance of the modern industrial system of production under capitalist auspices, combined with efforts to mitigate its untoward effects and "abuses." That this came wrapped inextricably with clerical and bourgeois paternalism may be regretted. Anything bearing the features of a Christian socialism as an emancipatory labor movement was to be greeted with horror for decades to come. However, that it offered a foothold for an effective contemporary approach to the social question on the part of Catholic thinkers and activists is generally booked to its credit.

Hitze's lifelong goal was in fact the integration of the "Fourth Estate" into society. First he thought that a corporatist reorganization of society would be the only way to achieve that end. Then, when given a chance to take immediate practical steps with the backing of Brandts, he tried it, found it congenial, and left behind not only Marx's but also Vogelsang's ideas of complete societal overhaul. In the real world of workers and bosses, one could hardly achieve much against the embittered resistance of the latter; whereas some improvements that employers could accept were possible and would actually benefit some workers. Hitze foreswore utopian ideas after he was ensconced in Mönchengladbach, so much so that he was never the first by whom the new was tried. But he was not simply satisfied with proven paternalistic formulas. Thus, in 1884, after Pope Leo XIII had advocated workers' associations, he propagated them throughout Germany with some success (Aretz in Rauscher 1981–82, 2:16ff.). These were neither the feisty politically involved unions of Fathers Cronenberg and Laaf nor joint employer-employee groups, but church organizations for factory workers only, with priest-presidents and lay secretaries, patterned after the Kolping organization for journeymen. By 1889 they encompassed sixty thousand members.

A famous pan-German meeting of social Catholic figures took place in 1883 at Haid Castle in Bohemia, the estate of Prince Karl zu Löwenstein (StL 3:954; Anderson 1981, 312–14). This scion of a noble house (not to be confused with the Liechtensteins, although the two families were related) was the most eminent lay dignitary of German Catholicism, throwing himself into one Catholic or papal cause after another (Buchheim 1963). He became president of the central committee of German Catholic organizations in 1868 and thereby permanent chairman of the annual Katholikentage. In 1883 he decided to form a grouping of Catholics interested in social policy (Freie Vereinigung katholischer Sozialpolitiker) and invited members of the Vogelsang school and a few other disciples of Ketteler to the estate where he had been born, Haid, for an exchange of ideas. What he proposed was a meeting of minds on some basic issues of economic policy that could be proposed to Catholic politicians and others as guidelines for social policy. In France, this was the same need de Mun wished to meet with the study council of the OCCO, though not on the scale desired by La Tour du Pin. However, the prince's illusions were different from those of the typical French Catholic nobleman, in that he saw no Catholic monarch in the future — if there were a void there, the pope himself could fill it. Instead, never very far in the background of his various schemes and proposals was the idea that Catholics must take charge of the modern nations by accepted parliamentary or republican means. Inasmuch, he wrote to his confidants, as "we cannot prevent the social republic any more, we must at least make ourselves its master" (Jedin 1981, 9:202).

Löwenstein was an avid reader of Vogelsang's work, starting with the *Vaterland*. He considered the Vogelsangian alternative to industrial capitalism to be "at last, the modern concept" he had been looking for to seize the initiative from the liberals and socialists (R. Knoll 1973, 134; for what follows, see Knoll 134–39). He hoped an agreed-upon labor program could come forth from the conference as a basis for a Catholic "league of workers."

In June 1883, then, the invited parties conferred for several days at Haid. Present were Blome, Kuefstein, and Fr. Weiss, along with a number of other aristocrats and moral theologians from Austria and Germany. Franz Hitze was also there; Bongartz had sent a discussion paper on the labor question with the intention of presenting it himself; but his death intervened. Plans had been laid to discuss three issues: usury, artisans, and (factory) workers. It soon became apparent that Vogelsang's extreme position on interest payments would not be endorsed by even a majority of those present, although they did agree on the principle that society should be reorganized by cooperatives. The second point also soon raised the same difficulty that created divergences between Maignen and Harmel: should craft guilds be optional or obligatory? Fr. Weiss carried the day with his *plaidoyer* for obligatory guilds. (This was one issue which newspapers in Germany would play up, giving the Haid theses and the Freie Vereinigung a reactionary image.) Bongartz (by testament as it were) and Hitze weighed in on the third question, strongly defending the legitimacy of the ordinary wage contract between employers and workers, which Vogelsang considered morally flawed simply because it was individualistic, not merely because the agreed-upon wage was so often inadequate. Thus Vogelsang's specific ideas about the wage contract were not adopted; but in recommending the corporative organization of big industry and the social insurance programs that should be created for its workers, the final document followed the outlines of his reform program.

Hitze had obviously been a fast study under Brandts's tutelage and in the framework of Arbeiterwohl. And yet, when the "theses of Haid" became known, with the understanding that Prince Löwenstein wanted to present them at the next Katholikentag as policy directives for Catholic politicians, Ludwig Windthorst took action to neutralize them. In his view, far from giving the Center party a socio-economic platform on which it could stand united, they could only divide the wings of the party and cripple its effectiveness. The Freie Vereinigung met annually until 1888, but its influence on German Catholicism was not great. Eventually the Austrians decided to pull out and tend to their own affairs or find more congenial international Catholic contacts.

Within two years, Hitze was a deputy in the Reichstag (he was already a member of the Prussian Landtag). The social platform that the Center party developed in the next few years was a compromise between the anti-interventionist approach of Ludwig von Hertling, Windthorst, and the other more "liberal" Center politicians, on the one hand, and the anti-capitalistic tradition represented by Löwenstein and Vogelsang, all appealing to Ketteler's pronouncements. Hitze soon dropped all "reactionary corporative ideology" (A. Pieper cited in De Gasperi 1931, 39), placed himself firmly on the terrain of current economic institutions, and sought to achieve those gains for the workers that were possible without a thoroughgoing recasting of the structure of society. This was a posture that would stand German Catholicism in good stead as Germany overtook France and came to rival Britain as the leading European economic power.

Chapter 10

NEW PROBLEMS AND NEW HORIZONS, 1886–91

For social Catholics, the faith itself gave rise to the conviction that the Catholic tradition possessed the key to the solution of the nineteenth century's most pressing moral problem: so much misery, so much poverty alongside so much wealth and prosperity. In retrospect, one must acknowledge that they were right not to place their hope, with positivists, in scientific progress alone — as they were right not to resign themselves to the indifference all too typical of liberals and even conservatives. Surely both responses were out of harmony with Christian moral teachings.

Yet no one had an adequate grasp of how to apply church teachings positively and effectively to remedy the prevailing economic inequities (Köhler in Jedin 1981, 9:207f.). That is why a two-pronged approach of practical experiments on a trial-and-error basis on the one hand with, on the other, book learning (as Ketteler suggested for German seminarians in 1869) and empirical research (as in Ducpétiaux's projects) was a fully justified provisional response. Catholics, like others, had to prepare themselves patiently and with persistence for the still new and poorly comprehended changes of industrial society. Insufficiencies in the responses of the social Catholics were many and inevitable. The insufficiencies most to be regretted, however, were those that blocked or unduly limited the process of trial and error. Among them was that self-same conviction that the Catholic tradition held the key to the solution of the social question, when twisted slightly in the mood of resignation, as if to say: "The church has always known and taught how employers and employees, rich and poor should behave toward each other: honestly and uprightly and with doses of discipline and generosity as needed; if people would

189

simply conduct themselves as Christians, all these problems would be alleviated."

These insufficiencies and blockages made themselves felt painfully the longer the century wore on. They came to a head just about the time when Pope Leo XIII was finally ready with his long-awaited encyclical "On the Condition of Labor," *Rerum novarum* (15 May 1891). This papal declaration would give "a great fillip" to social Catholicism all over Catholic Europe (to use an expression of Vidler's, 1964, 146). It stimulated the further theoretical elaboration of Catholic social thought and provided fuel for many attendant controversies. It also inaugurated a first great wave of Catholic social practice by encouraging practical applications of what came to be called, especially in France and Italy, "Christian democracy." All this we shall consider in subsequent chapters. Here we look into the matrix in which *Rerum novarum* took shape.

The Catholic Congresses of Liège (1886, 1887, 1890) produced remarkable signs of a new resourcefulness in Christian approaches to the social question, reflecting and stimulating an international ferment that is to be re-evoked in its national variants. The pattern of oppression by so-called liberal governments was an experience common to both clerical Catholicism and the proletariat. In this characteristic three-sided pattern of forces, intransigent social Catholics faced off against both organized socialism and governmental liberalism or conservativism. The possibilities of mobilizing Catholic forces in electoral politics varied from country to country; inevitably, voting patterns were a factor, in different combinations, in the struggle for social justice. Against this background, the international study group of corporatist Catholic social reformers known as the Fribourg Union (1885–92) labored to provide the pope with their proposals, in view of his forthcoming encyclical. "Liège" and "Fribourg" advocated a degree of governmental intervention in the labor practices of industry that was highly controversial within the *classes dirigeantes* in the 1890s. This provoked a countermovement championed by the bishop of Angers. In these social, economic, political, and ecclesiastical circumstances, Leo XIII judged that the time had come for a detailed treatment of the church's wisdom on the social question.

The Pivotal Years 1886–91

Liège in Context

As one looks back from more than a century later, the year 1886 marks a turning point in the social question of the nineteenth century.

It was the year of the first Catholic Congress of Liège, to be sure; but this was only symptomatic, as an event, of the context with which it was grappling; it has only become significant in view of the further developments that followed.

In many ways, Europe in 1886 seemed to be caught in a deadlocked situation. The long depression dragged on. National imperialisms promised power and glory abroad, but the vision of fame and fortune in exotic lands beguiled aristocrats and merchants more than it did the working classes. Their lot's improvement was slow and painful and did not give them much cause for confidence in the plans and policies of their betters in society (see chapter 6). Karl Marx's explanation of just why there was no hope for workers short of a violent revolution or collapse of capitalistic society was beginning to make an impact. Marx himself had died in 1883, but the publication of the second volume of *Das Kapital* in 1885 seemed to stimulate interest in the first volume (1867), which saw both English and Italian translations in 1886.

Workers were resorting more and more to strikes. There was one wave in France in the early 1880s, which reminded the nation that although the Paris Commune had been crushed, labor peace was not thereby achieved. A further severe series of strikes and riots in March and April of 1886, starting from the Liège region and spreading throughout industrialized Belgium, lent a new social urgency to the deliberations of the Congress of Liège in September of the same year (Gérin 1959, 81-87). With the pickup of economic activity around 1890, strikes multiplied still more, also in Germany and Britain and elsewhere, becoming part of the industrial landscape. The patronizing methods of Christian employers had not made much impact up till then — one could hardly expect that they would succeed in big industry after they had such a limited success in family firms.

In England, Cardinal Henry Edward Manning was declaring that the time was past when the favor of princely rulers was effective; the time had come when the peoples would exercise dominant influence in European society (Köhler in Jedin 1981, 9:136-38). A few years later this was a refrain to be heard all over papal Rome. In 1889, he served as arbitrator of a famous dock strike, lending much-needed support to the dockworkers' demands. The question of the organization of labor reached the Vatican and hence the European news services in 1886 from as far away as the United States of America: Cardinal James Gibbons of Baltimore had to mount a campaign to keep Rome from condemning the Knights of Labor as a proscribed secret society (see now G. Fogarty 1982, 87-92). When such dignitaries weighed in on the side of labor in a widely publicized way (Wangler 1982, 370-74, and Weber 1981, 62, 74-77) and carried the day in the Vatican, precedents were created that could not be ignored when it came to the drafting of *Rerum novarum* in 1890–91.

The Congress of Liège attracted Harmel, de Mun, and Bishop Gaspard Mermillod from Francophone Europe. The Jesuit moralist August Lehmkuhl was there from Germany along with other German-speaking Catholics from the Alsace and Austria. Bishop Edward G. Bagshawe of Nottingham, England, author of the recent anti-capitalist work, *Mercy and Justice to the Poor: The True Political Economy*, came and lent his support on the issue of state intervention (Rezsohazy 1958, 106; Jedin 1981, 9:206).

Léon Harmel had by now abandoned the opposition, which he had had in common with the much admired Périn, to governmental regulation of labor contracts and certain other economic matters. He was destined to become the most important pacesetter of the second "Christian democracy" in France. Already he was looking beyond *patronages* and even beyond the type of factory council that he had set up in Val-des-Bois. Optimal Christian management scheme that it was, it was evidently not the whole answer. He had begun to cast around for other answers and to envisage them in the form of labor associations or unions run exclusively by the workers themselves (Guitton 1927, 1:102, 138–45, 259–67). His thinking threatened the paternalistic and authoritarian control of labor by the owner of the enterprise; as his mind became known, his fellow industrialists knew instinctively that his influence was to be feared (Guitton 1927, 2:49–75). Meantime, he started to organize workers' pilgrimages to Rome in 1887, to Leo XIII's immense satisfaction.

It was dawning even on Albert de Mun and René de la Tour du Pin that the counterrevolution (in 1889 there were commemorations and counterdemonstrations) was not getting very far, along the lines they had pursued to date. In a new departure that can also be dated to the year 1886, de Mun founded the Catholic Association of French Youth (ACJF), a student association that would indeed play a substantial role in twentieth-century social Catholicism. For the rest of the nineteenth century, however, its role was largely defensive and political rather than social. It was to serve as the training school for a largely extra-parliamentary opposition. De Mun wanted to prepare the ground for the political dominance that, he thought, Catholics deserved in France. In a regime of universal manhood suffrage, such as France enjoyed, why were the Catholic people, heirs of all the glories of French history, not overwhelmingly represented? Although the OCCO went on, it was a holding operation; evidently de Mun no longer reposed much hope in the workers' circles as seedbeds of the Catholic revival under their prevailing upper-class leadership (B. Martin 1978, 63; Levillain 1983, 898–903; Molette 1968, 51–54).

As things stood in France (McManners 1972, 58–67), political power in the assembly was divided fairly evenly into three groups. The moderate Republicans or (1) "Opportunists" stood in the middle and held the reins of government, drawing support habitually from the (2) Radical Republicans on their left as long as an anticlerical course was maintained. The conservative grouping (3) contained, like the others, heterogeneous elements, but was generally supportive of the historic Catholicism of the French. By 1886, the anticlerical legislative program of the Republican middle and left had been rounded off with a laicization of all state institutions, including the army and the public schools. The aggressive phase was over; the possibility of cooperation between moderates and conservatives beckoned.

Likewise in Germany and Rome during the 1880s the *Kulturkampf* was being laid to rest. In 1886, negotiations between Bismarck and the pope's diplomats led to the principal piece of legislation that put an end to the *Kulturkampf*, basically on Bismarck's terms (according to M. Anderson 1981, 321–35). Bismarck and Pope Leo XIII could turn their attention to another pressing matter, the rise and growing influence of socialism (above, chapter 6).

In Belgium, wonder of wonders, the conservative Catholic party was in power, but not inclined to do anything about the social question under the leadership of Charles Woeste. At the third Catholic Congress of Liège in 1890 (Gérin 1959, 96–101), the Catholic political establishment was audibly dismayed to hear the greetings that Cardinal Manning sent to the Congress (Rezsohazy 1958, 106):

> I do not believe it ever to be possible to establish pacific relations between employers and workers without acknowledging, setting and establishing by public act a right and proper measure to regulate profits and wages, a measure by which all free contracts between capital and labor would be governed.

Similar suggestions came from the dais, along with proposals for government regulation of working hours, Sunday labor, and accident insurance plans like those broached in Austria or Germany.

These were all pernicious notions, long refuted by political economists, and now they were being propagated right under employers' noses at a Catholic congress! The silence of one prominent participant at the congress, however, was to be ominous for Woeste's chances of shaping the mentality of the upcoming generation of Catholic politicians, many of whom passed through Brants' seminar at Louvain or belonged to his study circle in Brussels. Victor Brants (Meerts 1982, 1983) was Périn's chosen successor in the chair of political economy at Louvain and a disciple of Le Play as well as Périn. His liberal economics was already coming into question, the more he investigated the situation of industrial workers in Belgium. He was also in touch with Schorlemer-Alst in Germany, had visited Harmel's model plant at Val-des-Bois, and corresponded with Toniolo in Italy (Spicciani 1984). He still hesitated before embracing governmental intervention regulating labor practices; but when *Rerum novarum* came out, he became the only notable economic liberal to be converted to the positions characteristic of the 1890 Congress of Liège. These were put forward, as we shall see, by Abbé Antoine Pottier of the major seminary and Professor Godefroid Kurth, who taught history at the University of Liège.

And Archbishop Doutreloux encouraged them! It does not take away from the credit due Cardinals Manning and Gibbons to note that it is one thing to defend the cause of labor when your flock is overwhelmingly poor and immigrant and another thing altogether to do so when you belong undeniably to an anti-labor establishment and workers rarely darken the door of your churches.

Such was the origin of the "School of Liège." This designation would become practically coextensive with the new departures of the Christian democrats in Belgium and France in the 1890s.

Secularism, Socialism, and the Church in Europe

Would it be fair to bring the whole development affecting the history of social Catholicism in Europe after 1886 under the heading of "opposition to socialism" (Wallace 1966)? It would not be more misleading than many another helpful simplification, as long as one remembers that the Catholic opposition to continental *liberalism* very often involved tensions with conservatives as well. At this juncture, "conservatism" and "liberalism" were often joined in "liberal conservatism." It requires some explanation to make clear what such terms conveyed in late nineteenth-century Europe and where the social Catholics and Christian democrats of the 1890s stood in relation to other forces. The point is, authoritative Catholics often viewed an alliance of Catholic with conservative forces with almost the same repugnance as an alliance between Catholics and socialists. Socialists were not the only and perhaps not even the principal ideological threat to a good social order in the demonology of intransigent Catholicism.

Culturally and politically, the relations between church and society in the whole period of European history from 1789 to 1914 or 1920 were characterized by church-state tensions, intensifying at times into outright persecution (see, e.g., Becker 1981b). The dramatic highpoints — the separations and concordats — can be compared to episodes in a whole clanful of unhappy marriages, destined, as we now know, to end in divorce. The situations of divorce finally arrived at, or, in cases like Germany's, the separate but connected households maintained by church and state, we may call secularity. It was all part of the process referred to as secularization. From a sufficient distance, we may look upon the results with equanimity and regard the de facto process as not necessarily either good or bad on the whole. At the time it was hard for church people to see anything good coming out of it, whereas secularist liberals deemed progress to be obtainable only by blocking off the public influence of the clergy, monks and nuns who were so active in the cause of backwardness.

Martin Marty (1969) has pointed out that there were three main "paths to the secular," all taken within a fairly short time about two-thirds of the way through the nineteenth century. One was the moderate and decorous, but ultimately quite thorough process that took place in Great Britain. A second form developed in the United States, where there was an early emphasis on religious freedom and pluralism and where neither the state nor any of the churches really had to fear that they would come under the domination of the other partner (a most friendly divorce, all things considered, and one where the poet's word holds true, "Good fences make good neighbors"). The third path was that followed by France to "utter secularity." A most bitter divorce this, and one that continued to poison the atmosphere at least down to the *union sacrée* during World War I. This continental type, where anticlerical liberals wielded state power and clerical intransigents spoke for the church, played itself out in Belgium, Austria, and Germany before it reached its radical conclusion in France with the official separation of church and state in 1905. In Italy, the liberal state had to take over the territories that remained to the papal states (1860, 1870) on its way to secularity. In Spain, the pot boiled away well beyond 1920 in a virulent fashion. Here the old alternative of an authoritarian state either imposing Catholicism or persecuting it came back for a reincarnation in the age of totalitarian states (fascist and communist) with no pretensions to liberal progress whatsoever (Lannon 1987).

Seen from the perspective of the late twentieth century, two things at least are clear. There are few who would seriously wish to return to the condominium over public life shared by church and state from which the process of secularization took its departure: No one wants to see church and state rejoined in anything resembling the bonds of that matrimony that was known as the union of throne and altar. Nor does anyone wish to see all sectors and levels of society operating only at the beck and call of the state. And why not? Because the freedom of all members of society is too tightly straitjacketed in such regimes. A sounder strain of liberalism than that represented by the continental anticlericals has been the vehicle for a serious challenge to the authoritarian presumptions of both public powers, hierarchy and civil government, in the name of a "free society."

What Marty studied was the break-up of church-state union. But state is a more limited concept than society. Even where the state is "utterly secularized," it does not follow that the population of the country is. There can be islands, even large ones, that resist or escape the pressures of even a hostile government, as McLeod (1981) reminds us. To a large extent, the story of the Christian democratic and Christian labor movements between 1890 and 1914 is the story of how such islands were preserved in every country of Western Europe and in the working class as well. The Catholic Church did not "lose" the whole of the working class to socialism nor the whole of the middle class to anticlerical liberalism. There were examples of solid Christian culture across the class strata that remained bulwarks of Catholic influence on society until at least the cultural revolution of the 1960s.

But to the extent that the church-state struggle was fought on authoritarian presuppositions, it seemed inevitable that either the church or the state must emerge victorious, to protect the freedom of the one against the designs of the other. The battle lines were drawn between the "liberals" fighting to their last breath for freedom from Jesuitical domination and "clericals" contending with equal determination for the freedom of their flocks to provide a religious education, with public assistance, to their children. In Belgium and France in particular, the church's influence in the education of the young became one of the hardest-fought theaters of the cultural struggle (*Kulturkampf*).

It is important to bear this in mind, for otherwise it is hard to credit the good faith of that horror of liberalism that affected most Catholics, even and especially the "Christian democrats." In the 1830s and 1840s, some "social Catholics" had also been "liberal Catholics," while some were conservatives, even legitimist reactionaries. Under the combined blows of the increasing anticlericalism of secular liberals who dominated politics and culture and the reactionary, defensive stance of an increasingly ultramontane clergy, liberal Catholicism (never a large movement) became more and more restricted to a few small circles. At least from the time of the Syllabus of Errors in 1864 to the 1930s, it was unable to give rise to any vital strivings that would take root within the Catholic body at large. The most that can be said for liberal Catholicism in this period is that it survived among a few educated and sometimes even devout Catholics and that it supplied a few writers who could remind the Catholic world again of the values of Montalembert's anti-absolutism, when individuals such as the abbé Lemire proved receptive.

Hence it is important also to realize that when Christian democrats went radical, it was not under the influence of liberalism but because of their intransigent anti-liberalism! For the most part, except for the extreme anticlerical wing that eventually prevailed in France, the liberal bourgeoisie was defending the status quo and in that sense was conservative. Inasmuch as the prevailing power arrangements and outlook favored positive scientific and technological progress and decried aristocratic or clerical privilege, liberalism was "established." The expression "liberal-conservative" was therefore much used.

What would prevent the church from cooperating with such persons in power so as to hold socialism at bay, assuming some readiness in government circles to cooperate in matters concerning education and church? In fact, one can point to many examples of such coalitions, the Méline cabinet in France in 1896–98, for example, or the so-called *clerico-moderati* in Giolitti's government in Italy in the early 1900s. Belgium's Catholic party, in power since 1884, was basically clerical-conservative in orientation. Indeed, as late as 1883, German Protestant conservatives, who were still distinct from the German national liberals, with the help of the Center party, responded to Bismarck's initiative for social legislation. The German Center, a de facto Catholic party, always voted with socialist deputies to repeal the law against socialist parties and organizations, however.

The Constellation of Forces

A Three-Cornered Contest

This last example illustrates a recurrent characteristic of Catholicism in public life of the period in question. As is notorious, in a three-party setup of any kind, as in a *ménage à trois*, any combination of two against one is possible. The interesting thing to note is that henceforth coalitions of Catholics and conservatives yielded little or nothing that could qualify as consulting the interests of the "people." In earlier years, a de Melun or a de Mun could achieve something for the working class on occasion by appealing to conservatives' sense of social responsibility, *noblesse oblige*. Leo XIII launched these appeals regularly, also in *Rerum novarum*. However, the indifference with which it met was not lost on him. When there were signs that an alternative approach might be crowned with success, therefore, he did not hesitate to urge priests to "go to the people" (Brugerette

1935, 2:377; see also Cholvy and Hilaire 1986, 2:79). In the 1890s he sometimes sounded like Cardinal Manning himself.

A factor that is often overlooked in the rise of this Christian democracy is the predisposition against liberalism in the sense described. If socialism was to be condemned and opposed, so also was liberalism (see Poulat 1975, 1977a, and 1977b, 173–205; also Mayeur 1986, 17–45). The two were opposed to each other on one level, to be sure, as to the ownership of capital; but they were both in error and their errors were closely related, as social Catholics (Cathrein 1890, 2:200–206) and Christian democrats saw the matter. Socialism is the natural offspring of liberalism, vindicating for the proletariat what liberals claimed for the bourgeoisie: political dominance based on economic achievement. Without the prior false option of the liberals for a positivistic materialism mobilized for class selfishness, the rallying cry of the socialists for workers to unite and organize would have been deemed basically sound.

In Leo XIII's eyes, for instance, the great battle to be waged was that of Catholicism against "the Sect," meaning in the first instance the Freemasons (*Humanum genus*, 1884; see Jarlot 1964, 84–99, and Mayeur 1986, 49). To this international secret fraternity was attributed the success of liberal laicist and anticlerical campaigns all over Europe and Latin America. These were a continuation of the assaults against the church and Christian civilization that first took constitutional form during the French Revolution. This kind of liberalism (really "totalitarian democracy," Murray 1953a, 1–7, and 1954, 21, citing Talmon) was also responsible for the proletarianization of the masses. Here Leo XIII picks up themes already familiar in social Catholicism. Liberal social doctrine left the people to shift for itself and broke up the confraternities and guilds of the Christian civilization without providing any replacement except unrestrained individualism.

So the workers' resentment was well founded, as long as the liberal bourgeois classes dominated the governments (as in France, Italy, Belgium) or at least influenced them powerfully (as in Germany and Austria). An aristocratic populism, one that would relegate the bourgeoisie to a more modest place in society, was a solution that appealed to many an intransigent. Socialism, for its part, hardened the class differences made so noxious by sectarian liberalism. Instead of appealing for interclass justice, it wished to despoil the well-to-do of their property and proletarianize everyone. By contrast, in Catholic book titles, an opposition on two fronts, against both liberalism and its congenitally defective offspring, socialism, sounded from Juan Donoso Cortés with his *Essay on Catholicism, Liberalism and Socialism* of 1851 to Heinrich Pesch's

Liberalism, Socialism and Christian Societal Order (1893–1901) and beyond.

Rerum novarum itself would illustrate perfectly this three-cornered structure of the social Catholic worldview: Christian civilization or social-ethical outlook in the lists with *both* liberalism and socialism. The interpenetration of modern Catholicism and liberalism (see chapter 6 on Périn), which seemed to be making its way from the outer reaches of the institution, in countries or strata where modern, Protestant, or lay elements could get a hearing, was rejected by Leo XIII. Social Catholicism and even "Christian democracy," as we shall see, had their rebirths during his pontificate precisely where this double opposition was taken most seriously.

"Intransigence" is the term, first and most commonly used of the "unyielding" or "die-hard" champions of papal rights and territory in Italy, to designate this attitude toward the liberal establishment (DSMCI 1/1:20–28). It entailed a stance of opposition to the modern, secular state and very often also to the modern economic development that such states fostered. In Italy itself, not all clerics, and certainly not all cardinals of the papal curia, qualified as "intransigents." That an ostensibly forward-looking movement like Christian democracy could emerge from such antecedents may appear paradoxical, so much so that many accounts (e.g., Vidler 1964), used to overlook the connection.

Electoral Politics

German and Belgian Catholicism developed reputations as models for coping with the labor question in a relatively advanced way — and the activity of a strong Catholic political party in these two countries had something to do with that. Why did these Catholics resort to electoral politics so successfully, whereas others did not or could not do so? (Another question will be dealt with as the story unfolds, namely, what impacts "political Catholicism" and social Catholicism had on each other's development.)

A prior condition of any political organization of Catholics for electoral purposes is the existence of a constitutional state (monarchy or republic) that is professedly "indifferent in matters of religion" (to use Lamennais's phrase); a further stimulus is present when electoral politics has become an instrument of anticlerical policies (Mayeur 1986, 115–23). Thus there was no need for a Catholic political party in the *ancien régime*, since the power rested with the throne and political issues had to be taken up with the court through royal advisers or diplomats. Likewise there was no need for a Catholic party in the United States, where full and equal religious freedom was effectively guaranteed by the courts of law, or more precisely, by the common law or rights that were every citizen's and group's birthright.

Of course, tiny minorities cannot normally form effective political parties; thus, Catholic parties were in fact formed in nations of overwhelmingly Catholic populations such as Belgium, Austria, and Italy, where a substantial number of Catholics could be found to support political organization against hostile liberal regimes, or in Germany or Holland, where the Catholics were a strong minority overall with strong regional concentrations (as in the Rhineland province of Prussia, or in the Polish East around Breslau).

Following the example of Daniel O'Connell's Catholic Association in Ireland, Belgian Catholics split from the liberals already in the 1840s over the school question. First the clericals (Aubert in Jedin 1980, 7:306), then the liberals overplayed their hand in securing control of the schools in Belgium (Kossmann 1978, 206–9). Waging their own version of the *Kulturkampf* without a Bismarck, the Belgian liberals lost the elections of 1880 to the Parti catholique, which remained in office until 1919, facing the mounting opposition of the Labor party instead of the declining forces of the liberals. It was in this setting of a predominantly conservative Catholic party in power, with its signal plusses and minuses for their cause, that the social Catholics waged their struggles in the period under consideration here (Köhler in Jedin 1981, 9:109–12). A major political issue was the franchise, still quite limited by property qualifications. In 1893 a compromise between universal suffrage and the previous system, involving plural voting on the part of those with higher status, went into effect. The next year the "clerical" Catholic party, with its Christian democratic (labor) component, won a smashing victory. Not until the eve of World War I was the government prepared to move to a "one man, one vote" system that included certain women in the electorate as well.

The German Empire's Catholics were obviously ahead of the Belgian Catholics in many respects, even though the Center party could not hope to be a majority party, even under universal suffrage. (Belgian social Catholicism was stuck at the level of *patronages* right up to the Congresses of Liège and *Rerum novarum*. It resembled France more than Germany in this respect.) In its initial forms, the Center party predated the hostile measures of the *Kulturkampf* and was formed to make sure that the clauses of the Prussian constitution of 1850 protecting religious freedom were carried over into the new constitution of the Second Reich (1871–1918). Its failure in this matter, together with the growing signs of Bismarck's disaffection with minorities deemed suspect of disloyalty (Poles, Catholics, and others), spurred the growth and consolidation of the Center party as a necessary political defense of the rights of Catholics and other minorities.

Ludwig Windthorst showed inexhaustible resourcefulness in electoral and parliamentary tactics in this democratic cause. A network of associations grew up around the parishes, flourishing particularly in traditionally Catholic areas. Hence the typical *Vereinskatholizismus* that characterized the milieu in which social Catholicism would thrive. Of course, a Catholicism knitted together in a plethora of active associations, especially when these were at least loosely co-ordinated as in the German case, would also provide a firm basis and support for a Catholic political organization.

Suffrage in the Second Reich was universal, direct, secret, and equal for every male citizen over twenty-five years of age (Schieder 1975, 146), whereas the twenty-five states that comprised the Reich had their own systems for elections to the various assemblies (Landtage). The Prussian plural voting system was also one that the Center party came to grips with successfully.

In Italy, meanwhile, the electoral situation could not be more of a contrast. In protest against the annexations of the papal states to the new unified Kingdom of Italy (since 1870), the word went out that staunch supporters of the pope would boycott national parliamentary elections. They would not stand for office and they would not vote (*né eletti né elettori*; see De Rosa 1966, 61 and 144). This policy was confirmed by the Vatican in the phrase *Non expedit* (i.e., it is not expedient to vote in the prevailing circumstances; in 1886 this was officially interpreted, after some tentative moves toward relaxation of the ban, as a flat prohibition). Thus, for over a generation, Catholics were vigorously discouraged from any "political" activity (i.e., participation in elections on the national level). This effectively ruled out anything like a political party. Since diplomatic relations between the Holy See and the Kingdom of Italy were also in suspense, Italian Catholics fell back on voluntary associations of various kinds in the so-called Catholic Movement, headed by the Opera dei Congressi (1874–1904), an adaptation of the German *Vereinskatholizismus* and Katholikentage to the newly unified Italian national scene.

It is only in France (and Spain) that royalism played a leading role in impeding the development of political Catholicism. (Needless to say, monarchy held little charm for Italian *intransigenti*, who already had a Catholic but "liberal" king on the throne.) In retrospect, it is clear enough that as long as Catholic political leaders confined their electoral appeals only to the anti-republicans among their coreligionists in the Third French Republic (1870–1939), they could make no headway and exert little or no influence in the National Assembly or with the government. Nevertheless, a substantial part of the potential Catholic political leadership was royalist of one stripe or another (legitimist, Orleanist). When Pope Leo XIII suggested indirectly that all

Catholics should come to terms with the Republic as a practical matter and carry out their battles within the existing system, they were
deaf to his appeals (McManners 1972, 64–75). De Mun and some
others — Harmel of course — did come over, as did still others, when
the pope finally issued direct instructions in a "Letter" or "Encyclical
to the French" of 16 February 1892, *Au milieu des sollicitudes.* But
the continuing "refractory" behavior of the royalists, abetted by the
unfortunate coalition of Catholics and other anti-republicans during
the Dreyfus affair, dealt the pope's *Ralliement* mortal blows.

Parties of Catholic inspiration had a considerable future before
them in twentieth-century Europe. The Italian Populist party of don
Luigi Sturzo would join the earlier organizations in other countries
after the *Non expedit* was revoked in 1919. A new Christian democracy of a less clericalist character, capable of carrying elections, had a
remarkable resurgence in Western Europe after World War II. But
except for the few years of the Mouvement Republicain Français
(1945–47), social Catholicism in France had to make do without the
support of a Catholic political party. In this respect also, therefore,
they were at a disadvantage in comparison with their Belgian and
German coreligionists and with the socialists.

Radical Reconstruction vs. Liberal Conservatism

The Fribourg Union: Zenith of Corporatist Thought

It was also in the years just prior to *Rerum novarum* that the various corporatist schools of social Catholicism intensified their efforts
at solidifying the theoretical bases of a Christian social order in the
industrial age. Largely at the prodding of La Tour du Pin with his
contacts in Austria and Switzerland, Bishop Mermillod convoked a
number of leading Catholic students of the social question, all strictly
anti-liberal in economic outlook, to internationalize the study of the
social question.

Thus in 1885 the Union catholique d'études sociales et écono-
miques came together for the first of its seven annual meetings (Jedin
1981, 9:207f.). It is referred to simply as the Union de Fribourg after the city in Switzerland, Mermillod's place of residence, where
they met. Principal members besides La Tour du Pin and Mermillod were Stanislao Medolago Albani (DSMCI 2:366–71) in Italy,
Franz Kuefstein of the Vogelsang school, and Kaspar Decurtins (KSL
397f.), a Swiss Catholic politician from the Romansh-speaking area
of Switzerland. Prince Karl zu Löwenstein embodied the aristocratic-
traditionalist "Haid theses" school of German Catholic social think-

ing. Because of this longstanding interest and because of his preeminent rank in the Catholic aristocracy of Austria and Germany, he was invited to become honorary president of the Fribourg Union alongside Mermillod as actual president.

One can piece together a fair picture of the accomplishments of the Fribourg Union and avoid most of the legendary embroidery that the secrecy of their deliberations engendered by consulting three or four books. Alcide De Gasperi wrote the first of them, *The Times and the Men That Prepared "Rerum Novarum,"* partly in the eighteen months he spent in Mussolini's prison in 1927–28, and published it in 1931 under a pseudonym (now available in a reprint of 1984). The 1983 dissertation by Normand Paulhus, "The Theological and Political Ideals of the Fribourg Union," is based on the unpublished minutes, reports, and some other files of the group preserved at the Catholic University of Fribourg. Finally, Robert Talmy's study of "the school of La Tour du Pin" (1963; see Molette 1970, 261–77 and passim) is valuable in indicating how much of the work of the Fribourg Union is simply a reproduction or parallel to the study projects of La Tour du Pin's Parisian research council after 1881.

This is not to say that the Austrian influence was negligible (see chapter 9). The recent work of John Boyer, *Political Radicalism in Late Imperial Vienna* (1981), along with the still more recent one by Richard Geehr (1990), contains much fascinating detail on the political aspects of the Christian social movement in the imperial capital. They also fill us in on another turning point of these pivotal years just before *Rerum novarum*. It was in 1887 that a populist politician of considerable local stature, Karl Lueger, offered himself to the Viennese Christian Social party and adopted a program worked out with their leading theoretician after Vogelsang's death, the priest-professor Franz Schindler (he also became a member of the Fribourg Union; see Boyer 1981, 339). A politician seeking a program beyond mere anti-Semitic and anti-industrial resentments encountered a well-formed theory that itself was seeking some kind of realization in practice. It proved to be a potent political combination.

La Tour du Pin was now able to elaborate his corporatist inspiration on a broader international scale and in the more sympathetic milieu that Mermillod created in the Fribourg Union. Under the marquis's persistence and drive, the active core of the group grappled with the difficult problems that had faced traditionalist social thinkers ever since the advent of industrialization and the ascendancy of the Manchester interpretation of economic reality. They spent no time, however, at least as a group, in studying the classical or socialist economists. After all, they were convinced that liberalism (individualism) in both the political and the economic realms had brought about nothing but grief. What they wanted to get at were the applications of associationist principles that would enable the twentieth century to enjoy the benefits that they thought the prerevolutionary guilds and other professional groupings had conferred upon medieval Christendom.

By dint of preparing reports, discussing them, and assigning further work on specific questions at the annual meetings of their small group (never more than sixty on the rolls or thirty-two actually on hand for a meeting at any one time), the Fribourg Union was able to develop a number of positions that represented the common thinking of corporatists in the four major countries from which it drew its membership. (As far as Belgium was concerned, Mermillod did invite Charles Périn in recognition of his status as a Catholic economist, probably counting on the invitation being declined, as it was. He then recruited Léon Collinet of Liège and Georges Helleputte of Louvain, as well as the duke Jean d'Ursel, a relative of de Mun's; but none of them appear to have been very active participants.)

When Leo XIII requested a report on their labors in an audience in early 1888, they were able to provide him with a précis in a few days (Paulhus 1983, 73; Talmy 1963, 55; text in Molette 1970, 271–74). It dealt chiefly with the dignity of labor and the laborer, property ownership, and market speculation. The ills of the prevailing (capitalistic) system were laid at the door of the Reformation and the liberal revolution, which falsified the idea of human nature and existence. The upshot? "This system has destroyed the economic and social equilibrium. It has favored the accumulation of riches in the hands of a few and has brought about the impoverishment of the masses" (cited in Paulhus 1983, 74).

More detailed reports were appended to this memoire to the pope. One was on morally appropriate minimum wages for labor by the German Jesuit moral theologian August Lehmkuhl; another was on credit and interest by Henri Lorin, who was a well-to-do young Parisian layman and devoted practically full time to La Tour du Pin's social studies and later to the Semaines sociales in France. The third, on the corporative organization of society, probably by La Tour du Pin (De Gasperi 1931, 85), was in an earlier stage of elaboration. Besides Lehmkuhl, who also spoke at Liège and was evidently very much at home in the French language used in all these international meetings, two other theologians should be mentioned as exerting influence on the work of the Fribourg Union, one at a distance and one in the inner circle. Albert Maria Weiss, O.P. (Jedin 1981, 9:204) taught at Fribourg after 1890 and made great use of the social question in his apologetics to knock the emancipated modern world's self-image down to size. Father Georges de Pascal (a Dominican until 1880, when he was displaced from teaching by the Ferry laws), by contrast, was the closest collaborator of La Tour du Pin in Paris as well as in the Fribourg Union. In the early 1890s he would speak before Christian democratic assemblies; fifteen years later he addressed a Semaine sociale while fraternizing at the same time with the reactionary Action française. He and La Tour du Pin always remained monarchists, Leo XIII or no Leo XIII.

Kaspar Decurtins was the only member (besides Mermillod himself, who was of working-class origins) to bring other, nonaristocratic experiences to this process. Already at the meeting of 1886, he impressed the others present with his intellect and acquaintance with the issues — he knew his Fathers and his Aquinas and he alone of this illustrious group had taken the trouble to study Marx. First and foremost, though, he was "the true Christian democrat" (Louis Milcent) or ultramontane man of the people, despite his mother's family traditions (Molette 1970, 211; Fry 1949, 1:17, 41, and 139–42; Jedin 1981, 9:80 and 9:207).

The corporatism of the late 1880s was in fact something like a waxing moon heading for eclipse. Perhaps encouraged by a reference to the benefits of corporative workers' organizations in the important encyclical against Freemasonry of 1884, *Humanum genus*, ultramontanes everywhere sought to develop or redevelop such groupings. In Belgium as elsewhere, there occurred what Rezsohazy refers to as a "corporatist parenthesis" (1958, 109–21; Vidler 1964, 144–46) between paternalism and Christian democracy in the years 1886 to 1891. Georges Helleputte was professor of architecture at the Catholic University of Louvain, a man with many irons in the fire and time for still more. One of the university colleges asked him to head a major building project in 1878. Instead of taking bids from contractors and awarding the whole project to one of them, he approached masons, plumbers, carpenters, painters and other skilled craftsmen to carry out his plans on their own. When the building was finished, there was a banquet. Helleputte recalled the guilds of old, probably under the direct or indirect influence of the French movement around de Mun and La Tour du Pin. That was enough to start a small movement. Helleputte talked about this experience at the Liège Congress of 1886 and again in 1887 in the context of corporatist theory and interpretation of economic history. Now that the Le Chapelier law had finally been repealed, tradesmen and other workers were free to organize. Guilds like that in Louvain were founded in Brussels, Bruges, and elsewhere, predominantly in Flemish-speaking Belgium.

In retrospect they look like (and were) a transitional form of association between the *patronages* and the labor unions that the clerics Pottier and Rutten would promote. But at the time they seemed to

Helleputte and others to represent the embryo of an alternative social and economic order, worlds apart from liberalism. Hence the
corporatists only endorsed guilds or workers' associations in which
employers (master craftsmen or shopowners) and their employees
were both included. Separate organizations were calculated to foment adversary relations, one thought; they were organized for the
class struggle, as socialist organizers frankly avowed. *Rerum novarum*
would not settle the matter definitively (although it actually encouraged both kinds, the "mixed" as well as the separate associations,
depending on the circumstances, while remaining opposed to class
struggle). Hence this issue would loom large in the subsequent history
of social Catholic controversies.

The corporatists represented in the Fribourg Union realized of
course that a total and fundamental restructuring of economic life,
such as they envisaged, could not be carried through without a
supportive state apparatus. Indeed, if their ideal of far-reaching autonomy for the various professional associations, each in its own
sector of the economy, were to become reality, it would be at the expense of government bureaucracy, which they found too overbearing
already. They realized too that the times were not propitious for finding such support. While working out their long-term plans, therefore,
they also had a short-term project to remedy some of the worst effects
of liberalism as it was practiced in the 1880s. That was a matter of
international labor legislation, or more precisely, a multilateral treaty
or "convention" by which the signatory nations would undertake to
pass certain minimum labor legislation (Molette 1970, 265-66 with
275-77).

The thought was that if all industrialized nations would, for example, introduce similar limits to the number of hours in a work day,
or similar mine-safety standards — and if they undertook to enforce
them by law, then the cut-throat competition for each others' markets would not force entrepreneurs to pay starvation wages for work
in life-threatening surroundings. But it was easier to promise not to
connive at the slave-trading of certain African countries, as Cardinal
Charles Lavigerie got several colonial nations to do in the Act of Brussels in 1890 (see Renault 1971), than to have them pass legislation
against unfair labor practices at home.

The Fribourg Union also had what might be called an ulterior
ultramontane motive. As head of an international church with traditional claims to sovereignty but without a national economy of his
own to worry about, Pope Leo XIII could be called upon to serve as
a neutral arbitrator of the international agreement. Leo continued to
protest against the unlawful occupation of his territories. He regarded
the papal diplomatic corps the internationally accredited represen-

tatives of a provisional government in exile. He could be counted upon to show an interest in diplomatic measures that demonstrated the positive influence of Christian morality on world affairs, as when Bismarck asked him to arbitrate the Caroline Islands dispute between Germany and Spain in 1885. Hence, this was an aspect of the proposal that interested all intransigent or ultramontane Catholics (see Buchheim 1963, passim). In the sequel, the new Emperor of Germany, Wilhelm II, did convoke such an international conference in 1890 and invited the pope to send a representative, a rather unusual step. However, nothing much came of it in the concrete.

"The corporative system" faltered when the attempt was made to bring it to bear on modern industrial conditions (Paulhus 1983, 127–31). This was the test case for the future, as persons like Harmel knew. His *Conseil d'usine* at Val-des-Bois inspired La Tour du Pin and his co-workers in the Fribourg Union, but it was not applicable to larger joint-stock corporations managed by nonowners. It is true that Louis Milcent got so far as to ask the crucial question of industrial finance in an 1888 study: "Why must the means of production belong to an association of investors rather than to those who actually use them? Would it not be completely natural the other way around?" (Paulhus 1983, 127). But no real consensus among social Catholics obtained in regard to this question or any of the more daring theses of Vogelsang or La Tour du Pin, even in the select company of the Fribourg Union.

Perhaps Vogelsang's strictures against lending at interest prevented them from seeing the only way it could be done. Workers would have to form a modern business corporation and themselves borrow capital from investors, instead of just putting themselves out for hire to the management owners or borrowers of capital. At any rate, despite good timing and excellent contacts, none of the Fribourg Union's inspirations were taken over undiluted into *Rerum novarum*. As it happened, Pope Leo issued no general affirmation of "the corporative system" at all (Aubert 1978, 150). On the other hand, neither did he frown upon such ideas, which persisted and helped fuel the debates of the 1920s and 1930s about "vocational order."

What did come through from both international social Catholic forums, the public one in Liège in Belgium and the highly confidential meetings in Fribourg in Switzerland, whether from more forward-looking or more traditionalist spokespersons, was their shared opposition to economic liberalism and hence their willingness to call upon the state for governmental interventions to correct the outcome of the free play of market forces. Brutal labor practices had not diminished with the maturing of industrial production techniques or the expansion of markets. The state, they agreed, must step in to render such practices justiciable. On this point, however, they were far from carrying with them the whole body of Catholic public opinion.

The "School of Angers"

Given the church-state tensions (to put it mildly) that characterized the European Catholicisms in the late nineteenth century, it is not surprising to find an influential body of Catholic thought that was skittish about state control of any sector of society. Add to that the influence of classic economic liberalism, as mitigated through Christian self-denial and charity in Charles Périn or as coopted into an authoritarian, counterrevolutionary perspective by Frédéric Le Play (Pierrard 1984, 247-50), and one finds the ground prepared for the charge of "state socialism" (as opposed to revolutionary or anarchist socialism) levelled against the "school of Liège" by the "school of Angers."

These ephemeral "schools" represented in reality two broader currents. The Angers tendency was sustained particularly by an association of professors of law teaching at the Catholic Institutes of Paris, Angers, Lyons, and Lille, with their own scholarly journal (Pierrard 1984, 363) as well as by the Le Playsian *Réforme sociale*. Together they constituted as it were the socially conscious part of the cautious, middle-of-the-road body of Catholic opinion that was otherwise not particularly concerned with the plight of the masses. Thus, as if to implore the pope not to issue any more pronouncements touching on political and social matters, a Catholic Orleanist deputy wrote in the *Revue des deux mondes* in 1890 (De Gasperi 1931, 65): "Haven't we already drawn the church altogether too much into our political battles? Would we like to see her compromised further by taking stands on economic questions beyond her competence? Let us not bother her to take sides on the freedom of labor or of competition.... All these issues come and go, and she remains."

The Angers "school" found an episcopal patron, like Doutreloux for Liège only more assertive, in October 1890 (that is, a month after the Congress of Liège). Charles-Emile Freppel (DHGE 18:1257-61) issued a resounding declaration at the Catholic jurists' annual conference. Bishop of Angers in the Catholic west of France since 1869, an elected deputy in the National Assembly since 1880, extremely ultramontane, Bishop Freppel opposed all legislation that would affect the ability of employers and employees to come to terms by themselves on wages and working hours. He called the Congress of Liège the "socialist Catholic" congress and its recommendations "state socialism." Shortly thereafter, he helped found the "Catholic Society of Political and Social Economy." This society formulated its stand as follows (De Gasperi 1931, 65):

Individual freedom;
freedom of association with all its legitimate consequences;
intervention of the state limited to the protection of rights and to the
    repression of abuses.

Freppel, like the Le Play school and the *Patrons du Nord* (Pierrard 1984, 348–52), had corporatist leanings himself and was no liberal in politics. However, on the question of whether there was an interventionist or merely a constabulary role for the government to play in industrial relations, he clearly aligned himself with the teachings of economic liberalism. Were Freppel and his school "social Catholics"? The question should be answered with a yes, not only because he and they were actively concerned about the "condition of labor," but also because they saw the remedy to the problem as coming about through associations (preferably "mixed" ones), not exclusively by means of labor contracts entered into on a one-to-one basis plus charity. In other words, there has also been a school of social Catholicism that was, in a limited nineteenth-century sense, "liberal." Besides, as the discussion after *Rerum novarum* would show, there was room for a convergence of the two tendencies toward a common center. One could broadly interpret the category "protection of rights and repression of abuses," to open it up a bit toward the moderate interventionists.

The "liberal" school of social Catholicism, therefore, disciples of Périn and Le Play in Francophone Europe and of Peter Reichensperger and Schorlemer-Alst in Germany, are to be distinguished from the larger apathetic, do-nothing, and stand-pat element in the Catholic leadership, the likes of Charles Woeste, the Belgian leader of the Catholic party, or Martin Rutten, Doutreloux's vicar general and successor (in 1901) in the archdiocese of Liège. In Germany, the most prominent such social Catholic was Georg von Hertling (Becker 1981a, 3, ZgLb 1:43–52, and E. Ritter 1954, 111–33). A philosophy professor at the University of Munich from 1882–1912, one of the few Catholic Thomists or Aristotelians to seek a university position outside of the concordatary theology faculties, he entered public life in the mid-1870s by being elected to the German parliament from a Rhine district. At the same time, he stimulated the formation of the famous Görres-Gesellschaft for the promotion of scholarship in the minority Catholic culture of Germany. His political career flourished in the bosom of the Center party, ending with a bitter breakthrough: he was named chancellor of the Reich in 1917, just as it headed into its precipitous defeat and collapse.

What makes Hertling centrally important to the history of social Catholicism is that he was a Neo-Thomist natural-law theorist who managed, under the pressure of political responsibility, to "deromanticize" Catholic social thought (this at least is the interpretation of Bauer 1931, 37–43; see Roos in Rauscher 1982, 2:97). That is, facing squarely the impossibility in the foreseeable future of replacing industrial capitalism with an (undesirable) socialist or (perhaps theoretically desirable) corporatist system, Hertling consistently pursued a moderate reformist course of social policy that was acceptable to Windthorst and most of the elected Catholic parliamentarians. His "natural law" was less affected by its medieval avatars than that of the Catholic corporatists. Although somewhat more willing than his coreligionists in the French school of Angers to countenance government interventions in business affairs, he remained allergic to anything that smacked of "state socialism." This included not only Lassallean proposals for government-owned workshops, but also the milder suggestions of the so-called academic socialists (*Kathedersozialisten*). To Hertling, those parts of Bismarck's schemes for industrial insurance that included a tax-supported contribution to the funds constituted state socialism (as Bismarck himself avowed; see Gall 1980, 604–7).

It has been argued by Bauer and Roos that the relative head start that German social Catholicism came to enjoy over France and Belgium in the 1890s had to do with Hertling's influence (Bauer 1931, 41–43, and Roos in Rauscher 1982, 2:96–108). It cannot be attributed directly to Ketteler, since the *Kulturkampf* had intervened since Ketteler's time and all of German Catholicism's forces had to be concentrated on the defense of the Catholic minority in the new empire, leaving no time or attention for other serious matters. The man who would become Hertling's younger colleague in parliament and the leading galvanizer of the social Catholic movement in Germany, Franz Hitze, had gone to Rome for postgraduate studies as a young priest "with a copy of Marx's *Kapital* in his bag" (E. Ritter 1954, 58; see Alexander in Moody, 1953, 426–28) — and came back with a thoroughly corporatist reply to it in the form of his *Capital and Labor and the Reorganization of Society* (1880). The title aptly indicates that he was thinking in grandiose terms of a total restructuring of economic and even political society that would require a dedication and energy only to be found in the sources of Christian life.

As related in the previous chapter, the exposure to the outlooks and experiences of Hertling, Brandts, and others (rank-and-file Center politicians, the textile workers in Mönchengladbach) had brought him around to a more practical assessment of what was for the common good in Germany's age of intense industrialization. In Vogelsang's view, he would have passed for a "liberal." In the terminology of his new view, which came to prevail in Catholic Germany, Hitze had come around from an advocacy of thoroughgoing or total "social reform" to the pursuit of a more just and human "social policy" *within* the capitalist economy (*Sozialpolitik anstatt Sozialreform*). Social Catholics, like their socialist counterparts, had to withstand the contention between revolutionaries, radicals, and revisionist reformers.

Cracks in the Positivist Wall

In France, starting in 1886, signs of what was to be a "Catholic revival in literature" (Griffiths 1965) and philosophy (Daly 1980) appeared, supporting Catholic social efforts with a renewed religious and cultural vitality. Paul Claudel's famous conversion started emblematically in Notre Dame Cathedral on Christmas Eve of 1886 and was completed by 1890. Paul Bourget's took place in 1887 (McManners 1972, 113–14), a second pearl in a string that was to include Léon Bloy, Joris-Karl Huysmans, and (shades of Philippe Buchez!) Charles Péguy. Mayeur writes (1968, 47–48):

> Suddenly everything seems to move. At the same time as the socialist menace gives rise to disquiet among "respectable people," the certainties born of science and progress are challenged by a new generation. The positivist age comes to a close. The convergence of dates has often been noted: in 1886 E. M. de Vogüé publishes *La Roman russe* [a "call for soul-searching" instead of naturalism and decadence, McManners 112], then in 1889 his nine articles in the *Revue des deux mondes* entitled "A travers l'exposition"; in the same year, Paul Bourget writes *Le Disciple*, and Edouard Rod *Le Sens de la vie*. At the end of the novel, the hero comes back to the faith and murmurs the Our Father. Likewise in 1889, Bergson, with his *Essai sur les données immédiates de la conscience*, puts in question the assurances of positivism.... The *Revue bleue*, in January 1891, is able to diagnose a "revival of the religious idea in France."

Mayeur goes on to report:

> The new countenance of the church seems to come from beyond the seas: American [or "Americanist"] Catholicism reconciles the church and freedom. Like Lacordaire or Tocqueville before him, Viscount de Meaux, Montalembert's son-in-law, holds up the transatlantic bonding of Christianity and democracy. To the younger clergy, Cardinal Manning, Cardinal Gibbons, Bishop Ireland are so many examples to be imitated.

One such priest, nearing forty at the time, was Jules Lemire, professor at a minor seminary in the diocese of Cambrai in the north of France and the subject of Mayeur's most illuminating biography.

Lemire had visited Cardinal Manning in 1888 and set about writing a book on him "and his social action," which appeared in 1893. Lemire, even though he was the most "liberal" (in our prevalent American sense of the epithet, roughly equal to "progressive") of the *abbés démocrates*, exemplifies as well a more general point I have been endeavoring to make. The new generation of social Catholics, like most of their forebears, came to their social commitment out of a clearly intransigent or (in the nineteenth-century sense) anti-liberal, anti-establishment, clerical mindset. This is as true of the laymen who predominated in social Catholic ranks up to 1890 as of the clergy who emerged from obscurity after *Rerum novarum*, notably in the guise of so-called democratic priests. The lay Decurtins turned out much too "black" (i.e., clericalist) for his mother's satisfaction; and although Abbé Lemire became what Decurtins always was, a thoroughgoing republican who asked for the church and its clergy no more than equal status before the law of the land, that was more than laicist "liberals" of the time were willing to grant.

Chapter 11

THE ENCYCLICAL
RERUM NOVARUM
AND BELGIUM, 1891–1902

After the brief flowering in the Second French Republic of a school of social Catholicism called "Christian democracy" (chapter 5), this expression went into eclipse. In 1891, the Ligue démocratique belge resurrected the term (Aubert 1978, 150–64). The orientation that it represented fit remarkably well with the directions encouraged by the encyclical *Rerum novarum*, which came out later that year. Pope Leo XIII and his new secretary of state, Cardinal Rampolla, showed many marks of favor to those who struggled under the banner of Christian democracy in Belgium and France, such as Léon Harmel and the *abbés démocrates*. This virtual identification of the papal directives with a concept — democracy — that already had a number of common secular usages became a ticklish issue from the Vatican point of view. This was particularly the case in Italy, where it led to a disavowal of the contemporary political meaning of the term (in a papal letter of 1901, *Graves de communi*). This only served to heighten tensions between the democratic element among social Catholics and the "integralists," who believed that Catholicism was intrinsically bound up with an authoritarian social structure (as developments in the pontificate of Pius X will show).

For the Christian democratic movement posed some very serious questions. Although not answered satisfactorily at the time, they remained knotted up in the vicissitudes of social Catholicism right down to World War I and beyond. There was the issue of state regulation of the labor contract: even though *Rerum novarum* might seem to have settled this in principle for Catholics, each fresh legislative proposal raised the question of the correctitude or at least wisdom of

213

that solution. There were the issues of labor unions and their *ultima ratio*, strikes: should one not strive rather at all costs to form joint trade associations or house "unions" of employers and employees? And then there was the question that *Rerum novarum* had not even raised, because Leo XIII, no less than Pius IX or Pius X, could not admit its presupposition: if secularization had proceeded so far as to be irreversible, what stance should the Christian adopt vis-à-vis secularized society? This was the core question of French Christian democracy of the era, especially as embodied in the abbé Lemire, deputy from Hazebrouck, and in Marc Sangnier, founder of the Sillon. The Belgians also played leading roles in the rise of the Christian democracy of the 1890s; they must be considered first.

Rerum novarum

Leo XIII's *modus operandi*, when it came to one of his numerous encyclicals, was to consign the matter to a trusted author in papal Rome with some oral instructions. Then he would have it revised and rewritten until it corresponded to his intentions. In the case of *Rerum novarum* (translation in Carlen 1981, 2:241–61; cited as RN with section number), it was long known in informed circles that the pope was preparing to address himself formally and at length to the social question, "the condition of the working classes" (RN 2; on the following see especially Mayeur 1986, 47–65). He entrusted the task of writing a first draft to another eighty-year-old pioneer of the Neo-Thomist movement, the Jesuit writer Matteo Liberatore. Liberatore had just published a work on the moral bases, or principles, of political economy in the columns of the *Civiltà cattolica* starting in 1889.

The encyclical, as the first major statement by one of the old established forces of order in nineteenth-century society to take up and endorse the grievances of the working class against their betters, could be expected to make waves. It did, despite the efforts of some liberal-conservative commentators to downplay any new departures that a reading of the encyclical might suggest. This is the context in which to understand the powerful defense of private property and the corresponding condemnation of socialism and anarchism placed right at the front of the document (RN 4–15). Although it was certainly heartfelt (and adapted from Liberatore's draft with little substantial alteration; see Antonazzi 1957, 40), this rejection of socialism was not calculated to conceal the still more basic antipathy to economic liberalism. Both materialisms were the inevitable result, in Roman eyes, of "eliminating religion from public affairs and repudiating the teaching and authority of divine revelation," leaving "no other aim for human society than that of amassing wealth." (Pius IX had put it this way already in *Quanta cura* of 8 December 1864, DS 2890.) While there was no special section devoted to a sustained description of social conditions at the end of the nineteenth century, repeated remarks from beginning (RN 3) to end (47, 61) expressed, for a broader public in the church and the world, the views of social Catholics on the intolerable inequities of the modern capitalist regime. The antagonism of rich and poor was not legitimated, rather it was decried (19); but its existence was clearly acknowledged and the blame for it laid at the door of the powerful and well-off.

The greater part of the document has to do with remedies to economic liberalism more likely to bear good fruit than attempts at regimentation, whether socialist or corporatist. Recognizing that human beings are equal before the state as to basic rights and interests (RN 33–37) but not equal as to possession of property, the pope first laid out the reciprocal duties owed to each other by employers and employees as such (RN 17–25). Here already is enunciated the principle of the dignity of the human person (*dignitatem humanam*, 20, 40), which is to be acknowledged and respected in all workers and without regard to social status. A kind of "option for the poor" is expressed (Dorr 1983, 12), for example where the state's duty to protect the rights of individuals is mentioned (RN 37): "The poor have a claim to special consideration.... The richer class have many ways of shielding themselves, and stand less in need of help from the state; whereas the mass of the poor [*miserum vulgus*] hardly have resources of their own to fall back upon and must rely on public policy. The mass of wage earners number among the poor and hence should be the special object of governmental concern."

Governmental intervention was the burning topic of the moment among social Catholics and others. Leo's teaching on this matter (RN 31–47) was highly nuanced and hedged about with many conditions. The state in question could be set up along monarchical, parliamentary, or even democratic lines, according to the Thomist principles of his 1888 encyclical, *Libertas;* but in any case it must be limited and respect the claim of the church to play a public role. Its own role is a secular one, to provide for the common good and, as a major part of that task, to promote the well-being and interests of the working class (rural and urban). The first duty of rulers "is to act with strict justice — with that justice which is called *distributive* — toward each and every class alike" (RN 33; see Hollenbach 1979, 148–52, and Calvez and Perrin 1961, 158–61). It is a matter of political authority "distributing" the duties to and the claims on society so that all benefit and no one class is sacrificed or exploited for the advantage of another.

Distributive justice is distinguished from "commutative" justice as public goods and transactions are distinguished from private goods and transactions among individuals or legal persons.

Commutative justice between, say, unemployed workers and a factory owner with jobs to fill, was often formally observed according to the "law" of supply and demand, but given the absence of equality between the economic standing of the contractants, it might well lead to outcomes so unequal as not to provide even the basic subsistence needs of the workers. But this would violate "a dictate of natural justice that wages ought not to be insufficient to support a frugal and well-behaved wage-earner" (RN 45). Where wages are insufficient to provide this minimum, the state must intervene to support the natural order. It does so as a matter of "strict justice," but not the commutative kind (according to which each individual is treated alike). This is the "justice called distributive," which can take notice of class contexts. As far as the justice-vs.-charity debate was concerned, the pope came down firmly on the side of justice without in any way diminishing the need for alsmgiving and charity besides.

Pope Leo also treated, but more briefly, other examples where some kind of governmental intervention might be appropriate: child labor, hard or excessively long hours, work on Sunday. In terms of the Catholic discussion of the time, the mere fact that he spoke of justice as well as charity and hence of legitimate public-policy concern as undoubtedly appropriate seemed to ally him with the school of Liège. It did mark a definite departure from the teachings of Charles Périn, with his emphasis on voluntary austerity and charity alone as the remedy for inequalities. But by speaking of the state's right to intervene as a matter of last resort and by explicitly preferring a government's indirect encouragement to direct regulation, the pope was actually in line with the mitigated liberalism of the school of Angers. "The law," he said (RN 36), "must not undertake more, nor proceed further, than is required for the remedy of the evil or the removal of the mischief."

Further on (RN 45), he brought up what must be considered his central suggestion for coping with the conflicts that bedeviled labor relations in a liberal regime:

> If through necessity or fear of a worse evil the workman has to accept excessively hard conditions, this is nothing but unjust force unwillingly endured. Here, however — in questions such as, for example, the hours of labor in different trades, the health and safety measures that should prevail in factories and workshops, etc. — to avoid undue interference on the part of the civil authorities (especially as circumstances, times, and localities differ so widely), it is preferable that recourse be had to associations or boards (*collegia*) such as We shall mention presently, or to

some other mode of safeguarding the interests of the wage earners; the state being appealed to, should circumstances require, for its sanction and protection.

Out of a diffidence toward the governments that actually held power in fin-de-siècle Europe, as well as from fears of a possible socialist or communist future, the successive drafts of *Rerum novarum* progressively toned down those elements of Liberatore's proposals that called for direct governmental action, thus at the same time moving away from a marked tendency of the Fribourg Union (Mayeur 1986, 58–60; Jarlot 1964, 213–15). Effective regulation was needed, all the same, and would be best provided by intermediate bodies, freely formed according to the diversity of circumstances and then sanctioned by framework legislation. Thus *Rerum novarum* achieved a certain balance between Liège and Angers, on ground common to them both, by sketching a preliminary form of what would later be called the principle of "subsidiarity." The modern replacement for the old corporations and guilds would be voluntary, unlike the former ones, and would make its crucial contribution to the solution of the social question by bringing together capital and labor to work out their problems under more equitable and fraternal conditions, with the guidance and encouragement of the church (nos. 3, 48–61).

A last-minute addition to the text (in italics below) providentially put the church on record as advocating a means of carrying out labor conflicts that would eventually become the main vehicle of the whole labor movement. The pope wrote (RN 49): "It is gratifying to know that there are actually in existence not a few associations of this nature, *consisting either of workmen alone, or of workmen and employers together;* but it would be desirable that they grow in number and impact." Jarlot hypothesizes that considerations brought forward by Cardinal Gibbons and perhaps also by Giuseppe Toniolo were influential here. However that may be, encouragement for labor unions organized for the representation of "workmen alone" was clearly stated as admissible, at least in unusual cases like the United States. *Rerum novarum* thus offered a dual option for the solution of the class conflict of capitalist society: either trade associations of corporatist ("medieval") inspiration, but formed on a voluntary basis as private associations, or Christian trade unions.

This stood in a certain tension with the overall seigneurial or paternalistic logic of the pope's teaching, no doubt. Hence the continuing tensions and controversies on this score.

Importance of the Encyclical

Rerum novarum led to developments within the church that could not be foreseen; some corresponded well to the hoped-for results, others were more or less unwelcome surprises. Here, however, I wish to consider the interpretation of what the pontiff intended and in fact accomplished with this very act of his magisterium, even apart from its unforeseen consequences. I can do no better than to paraphrase a 1984 article by Jean-Marie Mayeur, already cited (in Mayeur 1986, 60–65).

Today it is hard to measure the response accorded to the encyclical outside the world of Catholicism. Jean Jaurès (DBMOF 13:92–105 and HDTFR 494), who, it is true, was still learning about socialism, declared *Rerum novarum* to be "a socialist manifesto in its decisive parts"; the criticism of socialism struck him as a misunderstanding. Several weeks later, he thought that the church "cannot [continue to] be favorable to the social emancipation of workers in the long run, for this would lead to their religious emancipation and to the ruination of Catholicism" (Rebérioux in Droz 1974, 2:161); he predicted that the church "will have to cast its lot with the forces of political and social reaction." All the same, his statement would mean that in his eyes the encyclical, if taken seriously, would place the church outside the reactionary camp.

This was but one of many similar voices. The bulk of the commentators opined that with this step Leo XIII was regaining for the papacy the influence and prestige that he had lost, that it was turning resolutely to the people and to democracy and that this initiative was the harbinger of an important shift of concerns. Up to this point the Vatican had been increasingly isolated and allied only with retrograde institutions and monarchies. Many, Catholics and non-Catholics, used the term "Christian socialists" for those who set about putting *Rerum novarum* into practice. Apparently the church was breaking its old ties and looking to the masses to find a new legitimacy. Thus contemporaries saw a significance in the encyclical going well beyond a "social teaching." The whole stance of the church vis-à-vis modernity was at stake. Such an estimation of Leo's act led to differing interpretations.

On the one hand, as the anticlericals saw it, it was nothing more than a new ruse by which the church was endeavoring to dominate the world and to found a new theocracy by a mobilization of the masses. This view drew support from the interpretation that some integralist or intransigent Catholics gave to the papal document. They underscored the continuity between Pius IX and Leo XIII, not without reason. If the papacy drew near to the "people," it did so mindful of the Middle Ages, as the dependence on Thomist thought attests. Thus "social Christianity is nothing more nor less than an inseparable part of integral Christianity." This is the view of the Christian democratic Georges Goyau (1901, 2:13), a university man and son-in-law of Félix Faure, but at the same time an authoritative exegete of the thought of Leo XIII. At the Ecole française de Rome in 1892, he wrote a much-noted book, *Le pape, les catholiques et la question sociale.*

Progressive Catholics such as Anatole Leroy-Beaulieu could give their assent to these considerations. However, anxious as he was to find a meeting place for the church and what he called "true liberalism," it was not enough for him to celebrate the encounter of the church with the rule of the people, but also with freedom. To him, Leo XIII was linked up, "despite a space of four or five centuries, with the great Guelph popes of medieval times, defenders of the people and allies of the free communes." The return to the Guelph tradition meant that the papacy was asking "of the peoples and of freedom" what it had waited for in vain at the hands of "absolutism and immobility." (Whether this was in keeping with historical Guelphism or not, it was certainly in keeping with the liberal Catholicism of Lamennais and Ozanam.) That is, the rights of the church were to be placed under the protection of the only safeguard that a modern outlook can offer, a free society.

What is notable about this analysis is, first, that it tries to skirt an integralist reading of the encyclical and, second, that it does not separate Leo XIII's social teaching from his political teaching (Murray 1952-54) in the encyclicals *Immortale Dei* (1885), *Libertas* (1888), and the encyclical on the *Ralliement, Au milieu des sollicitudes* (1892). The opening of the church to democracy in the sense of social-justice concerns would not then signify condemnation of modern civilization by a church that, while hostile to liberalism, was friendly to "true liberty," "the freedom of the children of God, who so gloriously upholds the dignity of the human person." From Edouard Lecanuet to Adrien Dansette and Marcel Prélot, liberal Catholic historiography has taken up this interpretation of the main lines of the pontificate of Leo XIII, in the process enhancing his openness to the modern freedoms, so much so that the continuities with his predecessors is downplayed. After all, as bishop of Perugia in Pius IX's time, Pecci was one who proposed a Syllabus of (modern) Errors. Some recent readings, by contrast (Köhler in Jedin 1981, 9:3-25), have gone too far in the other direction. The nuances and change of tone that Leo XIII introduced in comparison with Pius IX also have their importance.

These remarks have not really taken us away from our present purpose, inasmuch as, for Leo XIII, the social teaching of the church and "Christian action in behalf of the people" (his rendering of "Christian democracy" in *Graves de communi* 7, Carlen 1981, 2:480) must indirectly contribute to the formation of institutions favorable to Christian morality. He had in mind nothing less that the re-Christianization of society and the foundation of a new Christendom as thriving as the cities of Italy at the end of the Middle Ages, when the church's influence "penetrated all the parts of the state without let or hindrance" (*Libertas* 46; Carlen 1981, 2:180). In the last analysis, Leo XIII maintained and reformulated Pius IX's condemnations while going beyond them, combining continuity and innovation. His criticism of economic liberalism carried on the line of intransigent Catholics. However, for the first time Rome took up the social question frontally, as the object of an analysis in its own right, and provided a positive teaching with principles of a solution. A step was taken beyond the intellectualistic approach ("Men have departed from true doctrine by reading Rousseau and Voltaire; no wonder society is in such a state of disorder") as well as mere moralism ("Egoism has gained the upper hand; no one is content with the duties of his station any more"). Classism or intergroup relations became the focus of moral analysis, with a glimmer of recognition that the way forward to sounder relations would not consist simply in a return to the ways of the past.

A step like this required and expressed an extension of the role of the magisterium. This rested upon two bases, as Leo XIII stated three years later in the encyclical *Praeclara*, on principles of the gospel as well as on principles of natural reason. Despite recent claims to the contrary, references to gospel teachings are not missing from the encyclical, while claims of natural law and of the common good are also present. These latter ground the right of the pope to speak on a question that concerns the whole of humanity. The Thomist framework is quite influential, of course. But this does not mean by itself that the encyclical is a piece of reactionary and medieval nostalgia. Certainly traditional teaching on natural law, the common good, and property has conspicuously shaped the encyclical. All the same, the absence of any mention of the corporative system or organization of society (a "Christian" social order in the sense that the Fribourg Union used these terms), shows that certain prominent readings of St. Thomas were passed over unutilized. The same comment applies to the old question of usury: Benedict XIV's 1745 encyclical on the subject was consigned to innocuous desuetude by the simple expedient of failing to cite it.

On some important points the encyclical found a receptive consensus in the Catholic world: on the family, the intermediate bodies, the rejection on the one hand of liberal individualism and a secularized society and on the other hand of socialism and a regimentation of industry by the state. Many other questions were left open: to list them is to trace the fracture lines within social Catholicism from 1891 on. The encyclical did not pronounce on matters such as the family wage, the extent of state intervention, or capitalist finance and investment practices (apart from a fleeting reference to "rapacious usury," *usura vorax*, RN 5). As was inevitable with this compromise text, some gave it a narrow construction, others found fertile principles in it, and others still thought it must contain precise instructions. At the time, Anatole Leroy-Beaulieu perspicaciously discerned its bent as well as certain difficulties to which it would give rise (cited from *Les catholiques libéraux, l'église et le libéralisme* in Mayeur 1986, 63–64; see also McManners 1972, 87):

> Rome has spoken; from now on the church has a social doctrine. I hear Catholics assuring us in the ardor of their faith that the question is settled once for all by the infallible magisterium. There is no social problem in their eyes any more; there is only a teaching to be implemented. The most hopeful expect that the application will not take very long.... Have such as these properly comprehended the bearing of the pontifical act and the language of Leo XIII?... Is there really a Catholic political economy, dogmatically fixed, from which no believer may depart without danger of heresy?

The Catholics who "claim to be doing Christian social economics" were divided into several schools. Was there going to be an "economic orthodoxy," with political economy becoming a handmaid of theology? Leroy-Beaulieu left the economics to his famous younger brother, Paul, but was of the opinion that there was a distinction to be observed between the moral and the economic parts of the papal teaching. Moral teaching, whether in social or private ethics, when solemnly declared by the Holy See, would be definitive for the Catholic. Economic doctrines, however, are another matter. After all, the encyclical is surely less an economics lecture than a statement of social ethics.

> The pope enunciates the principles of justice that Christians ought always to have in their hearts in regard to social relationships. At the same time, along with these principles, he indicates, without imposing them, some lines of application that appear to him most appropriate.

For the rest, when he treats economic questions, the pope, far from coming up with ready-made solutions, "refers to the lessons of experience and to the study of facts." Leroy-Beaulieu showed that the encyclical did not claim infallibility; he professed to be content that there was no absolute unity on social questions among Catholics: "Whether it be M. de Mun or Bishop Ireland, the disciples of Le Play or the emulators of Ketteler, it would be regrettable to see eloquent mouths muzzled, even those of our gainsayers."

Two things about this analysis are deserving of notice. One is that it evokes so well the ultramontane climate in which *Rerum novarum* fell. Twenty years after the proclamation of papal infallibility, the encyclical was presented as binding even in its details. Georges Goyau spoke of "the social dogma of the church." The other is the attitude of Leroy-Beaulieu himself, one typical of liberal Catholics: willing to grant the legitimacy of magisterial declarations on issues of social morality, but not looking for any formula or specific solutions that would descend to economic details. It would be premature to say that the question raised here has been altogether laid to rest.

A nuanced conclusion, according to Mayeur, is that *Rerum novarum*, firm in its principles and orientations, was both prudent and open as to the applications and the solutions, none of which are imposed. The encyclical itself did not make social Catholicism, properly speaking, into an ideological system between socialism and liberalism. However, the manner in which the encyclical and the church's social teaching were presented did contribute to make it an ideology (Chenu 1979). Dietrich Bonhoeffer, for instance, would warn German Protestants not "to propound a historical form of social order as based on natural law and therefore final." This would be, he thought, "a relapse into Catholic social teaching" (*Gesammelte Schriften* 2:101)

Christian Democracy

The Christian democracy of the 1890s probably put forth its first shoots in Belgium, followed closely by the Reims area in the north of France (under Harmel's influence) and by the Nord proper, around Lille. Its character was from the first both social (addressing problems of the working class with organizational and educational approaches) and political (doing so through electoral reform and electoral campaigns). In the case of Belgium, the various Catholic groups and programs having to do with the working class (credit unions, friendly societies, confraternities, choruses, even some *patronages*), feeling the need for coordination at the national level, formed a federation called the Ligue démocratique belge in March 1891 with Georges Helleputte of Brussels as president.

Why did one take the adjective "democratic" for this organization? Abbé Pottier certainly used it in a little paper that began publication in the summer of 1889, *Le pays de Liège*. This "first Christian democrat daily" (as it was for a short while in 1892, according to Gérin 508), though shortlived, had successors in Liège and Brussels (Gérin 1959, 191–201) in which the "school of Liège" carried out the dissemination of its ideas (mainly Pottier's) under the banner of Christian democracy. At the beginning, the term was not altogether identified with Pottier's advanced thinking, even in Belgium. The Ligue démocratique could have been called the "Social [Catholic] Federation," perhaps, but the "social Catholics" were still associated too much with paternalistic approaches. "Democracy" seems to have been chosen, in all the Latin countries where it was used, as a term apt to signify something positive for the working class without resorting to the word "socialist" (as in "Christian socialism"). The Flemish or Germanic equivalent was "folk" or "people," as in the "Christian People's party" founded in 1893 by Adolf Daens (Kossmann 1978, 484–86), a parish priest from Flanders. The Ligue démocratique belge was itself called the Belgische Volksbond in Flemish. (The German Catholic Volksverein was thus as "democratic" as any of the other Christian democratic phenomena at its inception in 1890, and shared the main lines of the further development; see chapter 14.) By virtue of the standing enjoyed in Catholic circles by Helleputte and its other founder, Arthur Verhaegen (Kossmann 1978, 481–84), an engineer from Ghent, the leadership of the conservative Catholic party regarded it at first with a benign eye. The Catholic prime minister (who resigned in 1894), August Beernaert, continued to look benevolently upon the movement even as the party leader, Charles Woeste, "turned on [it] with extreme passion" (Kossmann 1978, 484; Rezsohazy 1958, 208).

The original stated purposes of the Ligue démocratique were certainly harmless enough. Any association could join that proclaimed in its statutes that religion, the family, and property were the essential foundations of society. This would weed out the anticlerical and socialist groups, although for a moment friendly relations with some socialists seemed a possibility (Rezsohazy 1958, 201–14, here 202). The real purpose soon became clear: it was to give the lower classes some clout or at least some indirect representation in the ruling Catholic party, dominated since the founding of Belgium by bourgeois. A hot issue immediately thrust the Ligue into political debate, namely the question of extending the franchise (Kossmann 1978, 367–74) — the constitution was being redone. Against the wishes of the Catholic conservative deputies in the chamber, the leaders of the Ligue démocratique backed a scheme that would allow, and indeed oblige, every male over twenty-five years of age to vote. Even in the Ligue, only a minority were for simple one-man, one-vote suffrage. The majority's scheme preserved elements of the prerevolutionary estates, the so-called representation of interests. In the event, the system that was adopted out of sheer fatigue in 1893 for the 1894 elections was a sort of "family-vote" scheme, where a single voter could have from one to three votes.

What this meant electorally was that the Catholic party in some districts had to come to agreement with the Ligue démocratique belge to beat the opposition liberal or socialist candidate (Rezsohazy 1958, 214–26). This occurred in some cases already in 1894, leading to the election of eight deputies, including one priest, Daens (in an extremely bitter campaign that went to a second ballot). There were even two working men from Brussels elected under Catholic auspices. But in other places, as for instance Liège, where, despite Archbishop Doutreloux's best efforts at conciliation, the conservative and the democratic Catholics could not get together and support each others' candidates by sharing the ticket, the radical-socialist coalition made a clean sweep of the elections. On the whole, though, it was a landslide for the clericals: in the new chamber, elected with the extended franchise, there were 108 supporters of the conservative (Catholic) government versus only 48 opposition deputies.

The Vatican line was cautiously progressive until 1898 or so. The pope and his closest collaborators openly favored a new flexibility among established Catholic forces so as to accommodate the legitimate desires of the laboring classes and preserve Catholic unity also in the political realm (Jedin 1981, 9:111–13). A first striking instance of this was the backing received by Pottier and Kurth from Victor Doutreloux (bishop of Liège from 1879 to 1901) in the local Catholic party's preelection skirmishes there in 1893–94, backed up in turn as he was by Cardinal Pierre Lambert Goossens of Mechlin and by the pope himself (Rezsohazy 1958, 218–22, and Gérin 1959, 108–11, 520, 559–64).

The *Osservatore Romano* took notice of Woeste's moral defeat (inasmuch as Fr. Daens got almost as many votes as Woeste in Woeste's home district, Rezsohazy 1958, 226) in an interesting fashion, considering that by this time Daens was in trouble with his bishop. Woeste's well-established local machine could not even get him elected on the first ballot, it opined, because of his false views on the social question, so clearly repudiated by *Rerum novarum*. His electoral base was too narrow for the new franchise. But it remained to be seen how the Christian democratic movement would be able to make common cause with the conservative right. "We would like to see a Christian democracy moderated by the experience of the old Catholic conservatives."

Archbishop Doutreloux found himself besieged during the founding years of Christian democracy by delegations of the conservative Catholic establishment, including Collinet. They endeavored to explain to him the error of his support for Pottier; they made clear that their usual generosity toward the diocesan charities would have to be reconsidered if the archbishop could not rein in his seminary professor. Pottier's focus at the seminary was his course *De jure et justitia;* after *Rerum novarum*, he became activist and effectively encouraged the formation of several trade unions. (Only one survived the cradle, the garment workers' union, but other workers' *cercles*, cooperatives, and societies sprang up, starting a chain that was not to be broken until a solid Christian labor movement was in place.)

Doutreloux got fed up with the conservatives' recalcitrance and decided to write a pastoral letter based on *Rerum novarum*. It appeared in January of 1894 (in time for the old guard to come around to a common minimum platform with the Christian democrats before the October elections), as perhaps the first substantial episcopal commentary on the encyclical. Taking all precautions, Doutreloux had submitted it to Rome for previous approval. Unwitting clerics, however, such as Auguste Castelein, S.J., and Marie-Guillaume Cartuyvels, the pastor of Ste-Foy in Liège who kept Helleputte abreast of local developments in tones of horror, helped the Catholic employers prepare some "respectful observations" for the archbishop to read. All this democracy, they stated, was merely the product of overeducated and underemployed minds, the rotten fruit of too much schooling; these middle-class busybodies roused discontent in "the people," who never before dreamed that they were suffering from injustices.

Taking his cues from Rome as was his wont, Cardinal Goossens then stepped in to reprimand the industrialists for being out of step with *Rerum novarum*. The local president of the Union catholique, the moderate Charles de Ponthière, swung around to come to terms with the "just demands of Christian workers," to use the phrase that had come into vogue since the last congress of Liège. The pope weighed in now with congratulations to Doutreloux for having grasped his meaning so well in its application to the Belgian situation. But Pottier and even more so Kurth, who scored the class bias of the prominent lay leaders with a telling phrase "the strong-boxes in a frenzy," stuck in the conservatives' craw. No agreement was reached, the Catholic vote split, and Liège went to the combined forces of the radicals and the socialists.

Even after Pottier withdrew from the fray (Rezsohazy 1958, 244, 268–71), Christian democratic institutions continued to develop in Belgium. Their place in the Catholic party slowly grew, especially after Helleputte left the leadership of the Ligue démocratique to Verhaegen; this led eventually to a second generation of deputies in parliament. In 1897, Kurth mischievously asked de Ponthière if he would assume the presidency of the Christian democratic committee of Liège. De Ponthière surprised him by resigning from the Union catholique to head the Union démocratique chrétienne until his death in 1913 (Gérin 1959, 140). Along with the Countess Valérie de Stainlein, de Ponthière was an important financial backer of Christian democracy in the Liège region, putting a great deal of his own money into the Christian democratic daily, *La Dépêche* (1901–14).

Chapter 12

THE SECOND CHRISTIAN DEMOCRACY IN FRANCE

Not only the Belgian Christian democrats, but Harmel and Lemire also experienced every encouragement from Rome, as the conservative Catholic forces, unable to warm up to the Republic even under orders, spent a few years in unaccustomed alienation from papal favor (McManners 1972, 94–99). Léon Harmel was of course already highly esteemed by the pope. It was not just that he organized several workers' pilgrimages to papal Rome, starting in 1885; the two Leos were uncannily on the same wavelength, as if preordained, despite their differences of manner. Thus Harmel was a republican without knowing it by 1889, when Leo XIII started laying the groundwork for the *Ralliement.* Harmel, unlike La Tour du Pin, does not seem to have known that a social encyclical was coming; but when it came, it was he who promoted it at the grassroots most effectively.

Harmel and Robert in Reims

Prior to 1889, Harmel was a paternalist who counted on religiously based company structures, patronized by the Christian employer, to alleviate the proletarianization of the working class (following Trimouille 1974, 148–68). After 1893, he was one of the most advanced paternalist social reformers — still "paternalist" only because as an employer he could not shake off his responsibility for "his workers" in "his plant," and at the same time singularly "advanced," because he sincerely advocated autonomous Christian trade unions for workers at large. The missing middle term here was his disappointment with even the elite of Christian employers, the *Patrons du Nord,* on the question of how much freedom workers should enjoy to organize themselves, i.e., the Christian democracy of *Rerum novarum* provenance (Talmy 1962). This disappointment with the Catholic employers, of course, was understandable only within the larger picture of the failure of the whole industrialist class to live up to their responsibilities. Most did not even attempt anything so daring as mixed unions, factory councils and other structures that could have made the life of industrial workers more humane.

In 1889, Harmel saw and welcomed a future in which the working classes would make their voices heard by turning their numerical superiority into effective political majorities; concurrently he dropped the strict tie he had always insisted upon between plant associations (beneficial societies, cooperatives) and religious confraternities. In 1893, he committed himself to workers-only unions. Between those two dates, he still hoped that other employers would see things as he did. Thereafter he realized that he did not have enough in common with his Christian manufacturing colleagues and turned instead to the clergy, the other main component, with the workers, of the Christian democratic movement under Leo XIII.

Rerum novarum confirmed his turn to the people (and away from the obligatory paternalism of his earlier experiments). This had actually taken shape during the election campaign of 1889 in Reims (Trimouille 1974, 155–75; Guitton 1927, 2:1–19). Harmel did not stand for election, but spoke to voters in the cabarets and other meeting places all the same, addressing them man to man with what must have been impressive sincerity. Everyone remarked on Harmel's popular, rough-hewn touch. Now he realized that what set him apart among social Catholics was that he had an innate rapport with common people and an authentic ability to respect their sense of dignity and patiently to elicit their trust (Trimouille 1974, 156).

Reims was perhaps not as totally desolated in terms of working-class Christianity as most other cities in France. It had had a succession of at least moderately alert bishops, and the incumbent from 1874 to 1905 was Cardinal Langénieux, formerly pastor of a large parish populated by workers in Paris and a staunch supporter and admirer of Harmel. If he was no Ketteler, Mermillod, or Manning, he was nevertheless as close to them as the French episcopacy would come in the nineteenth century.

Some spadework had therefore prepared the ground, when an unexpected initiative took place in Reims, from below. Some non-Catholic or nonpracticing workers approached the pastor of Saint-Rémy, having heard of the papal letter on the condition of labor, and declared themselves willing to find out what the church might have to say (Montuclard 1965, 23–38, here 24). Now that a new breeze was blowing in the church, they wanted to study the economic and social questions that affected them; disappointed by anticlericals, they came to see if a priest would help. They were workers, hence democrats, and their circles took the surname of Christian, they later avowed, not because they brought the faith or any particular religious convictions to the task, but because they wanted to see if religion's claim to fulfill their just demands was warranted. One may wonder who had made such a claim on behalf of the church in their hearing, apart from Léon Harmel!

A certain Robert, a locksmith by trade, was the leader of this little group and remained its spokesman at least through the workers' congress at Reims in May 1893 (Montuclard 1965, 265, 267; Trimouille 1974, 163–65). The first result was a "study circle," soon imitated or paralleled by dozens of others in the north of France. Despite the similarity of terminology, these *cercles* [*chrétiens d'études sociales*] had little in common with the *cercles ouvriers* of the OCCO. Nor were they organized by Harmel or the priest, for that matter. They were a direct carryover from the autonomous, one might almost say underground, socialist workers' movements of the time. Only in hindsight can we say that they picked up where Ledreuille and company left off in 1848. Robert and one or two others were on the point of joining or rejoining the church and did so in the course of 1891. Another dozen or so followed in 1894 (and perhaps quite a few more in the sequel, as has been claimed without corroborative detail).

In the next few years, these circles counted several hundred members in Reims and its immediate environs alone. The workers maintained control of them, not allowing any employers to address them except in answer to specific questions. Harmel was invited early on; it is a measure of his stature in the history of social Catholicism that he did not try to refashion this exotic sprout of the labor movement on Catholic soil into an object of direct patronal concern, in accordance with the principles expressed in his *Catéchisme du Patron* (1889). He had the foresight to respect this new development as a highly promising one, even though it was not quite what he had been hoping and praying for. A priest, on the other hand, as opposed to an employer, seemed to be a necessary participant, since the object of interest was what the church could offer in the way of a social tradition.

Leclercq in Lille

Closer to Belgium and its sphere of Christian democratic influence was the Nord (Lille, Roubaix, Tourcoing). Here, as in Pottier's Liège, Christian democracy immediately meant Christian trade unions as well as cooperatives and conferences for the working class (Mayeur 1968:144). The parish clergy, active as they were in the OCCO circles and the company confraternities, were evidently more aware than the industrialists that the rise of socialism, as attested for instance in the 1892 election of Jules Guesde (DBMOF 12:347–58) to the city council of Roubaix, was no transitory phenomenon. They could see that unions were needed. Abbé Jules Bataille (DBMOF 10:221) turned up a couple of willing union organizers in Louis Vienne (DBMOF 15:311) and Florentin Wagnon (DBMOF 15:333), a weaver, then clerical worker and the first president of the "True Workers Union" of the textile industry in Roubaix from the middle of 1893. Unfortunately, Vienne's candidature for the National Assembly against Guesde in the same year was backed by the Catholic industrialists of Roubaix, a particularly hardbitten corner of the industrial Nord. This compromised the union, which nevertheless regrouped. Abbé Bataille, a secondary-school teacher, took a parish in Roubaix a few years later and remained a source of support for the Christian unions which slowly gathered strength after this rocky start.

At the same time, Fernand Leclercq started a metalworkers union in Lille. He had been a laboratory technician at the Catholic University while training himself to become an optician. Beside the union, he started a weekly paper, *Le Peuple* (1893–1908). Modelled after the paper of the Christian democrats of Liège, *Le Bien du Peuple* (1892–95), Leclercq's paper served also as the organ of the Union démocratique du Nord. This was another important borrowing from Belgium, a federation of the Christian trade unions formed in 1895, giving added coherence and strength to the scattered embryonic formations of the Christian labor movement in the Nord. Of course, there was no Catholic party in France as there was in Belgium. The various efforts to form one and to use it for labor rights (or vice versa, use the labor votes for Catholic causes) were unsuccessful and weakened rather than strengthened the development of other regional or national Catholic labor federations (in the view of Trimouille 1974, 175).

It was this same Fernand Leclercq who came to the first (Catholic) Workers' Congress in Reims in May 1893 (Rollet 1947, 1:342–49) and unwittingly became the occasion of Harmel's full conversion to the formula of exclusively workers' unions (as opposed to the "mixed syndicates" he himself had always favored; Trimouille 1974, 165–73). Leclercq was invited to participate as the delegate of two nascent unions in the Nord. Harmel, who had helped organize the conference, even though it was understood that only workers and priests would have any voice or vote at it, felt he had to "direct from the wings" (Trimouille 1974, 168). As one of many other subjects prepared in subsections of the conference, a motion was prepared in favor of *syndicats mixtes*, unions encompassing both employers and employees in a trade. Leclercq, however, proposed a substitute resolution unambiguously in support of "separate," workers-only trade unions. This was heresy to respectable persons, and the participants knew it.

Leclercq took up the basic objection, that such class-based associations only bred further divisions between capitalist and worker, that what was needed was precisely the kind of association that brought the two elements together under one roof. The answer to that, he said, was the formation of parallel groups, employers by themselves and workers by themselves, brought together by a joint council, half of which was appointed by each side. Only thus could the workers express themselves with any freedom at any stage.

The abbé Pottier, who was in attendance, supported this scheme rather than the mixed unions. Another priest and Harmel, who was asked for his views, spoke in favor of the mixed unions, at least as the ideal. When put to a vote, there was a decided hesitation; after the first few hands went up, the rest of the workers present gathered their courage and voted for what, an hour earlier, they had thought was impermissible.

Harmel took the vote very much to heart. From this moment on, he was a partisan of the Christian democratic cause in the form, that of Liège and Lille, that stressed the emancipation of the working class from patronal or bourgeois tutelage. He may have supported it by default, so to speak, only because the humane-educational responsibilities of the upper classes were neglected, but he supported it loyally and publicly (even unfortunately in its anti-Semitic manifestations), right up to the encyclical *Graves de communi* in 1901. Nor did he depart from it in his old age. His participation in meetings in Rome during Holy Week of 1914, when the Christian labor unions had again come under heavy fire from the employers and from integralist circles, was his last contribution to the cause (Trimouille 1974, 195).

The *Abbés Démocrates*

Christian democracy in France came to have three contingents: working-class people, clergy, and "intellectuals." This last was the category for any lay person not of the working class who took an active interest in the movement, especially, of course, by publicizing it in talks or writings or by clarifying theoretical, doctrinal, or historical issues. Employers as a category were not represented here as they were in the OCCO. The clerical contingent, however, formed such a major element in the public image (and also in the grassroots reality) of the movement that they deserve special attention.

The sensational emergence of the *abbés démocrates* in the wake of *Rerum novarum* occurred in two related activities: as elected members of the Chamber of Deputies and as publicists and organizers. Harmel and the half dozen prominent *abbés démocrates* had hundreds of followers in the parish clergy of rural and urban France, many of whom deserve the sobriquet as well, but they will for the most part remain anonymous (HDTFR 861–63). The deputies were Jules Lemire (deputy for Hazebrouck in the Nord from 1893 to 1928) and Hippolyte Gayraud (deputy for the Finistère in the extreme west from 1897 to his death). The principal publicists and organizers were the abbés Paul Naudet, Théodore Garnier, Léon Dehon, Pierre Dabry, and Paul Six (for some others, see Pierrard 1984, 367–70). In 1908, Rome condemned Dabry's and Naudet's periodicals. Lemire and some of the others also came to be suspected of liberalism and were the target of integralist attacks around the same period, but held on to be rehabilitated in the pontificates of Benedict XV or Pius XI.

A colorful cast of characters they were, too colorful and individualistic ever to form a unified movement, much less the clerical component of a Catholic political party. What united them was their alacrity in obeying Leo XIII, when he intimated that priests should get out of the sacristy and go to the people. Jules Lemire, a "dove-eyed" priest in his late thirties, was representative of many in his apostolic zeal, his formation in the intransigence of Louis Veuillot, and in his turn to the social problem. He admired the social stands of Cardinal Manning and, in general, the opportunities for Catholicism in an "Anglo-Saxon" world where the rift between a laicist and a clericalist France did not impose an artificial restraint on Christian initiatives in the form of a concordat and "laic" laws. He was more than ready to "rally" to the Republic as soon as the pope gave the word. The combination of the 1891 encyclical on the labor question and the 1892 encyclical on coming to terms with the republican form of government as a practical matter gave all the *abbés démocrates* what they took to be their marching orders, to the express satisfaction of the pope.

Once Lemire was elected to the Chamber of Deputies (1893), Georges Goyau, the most active of all the lay intellectual publicists of social Catholicism, hailed him in terms that beautifully express what the contemporaries of *Rerum novarum* put into the term "Christian democracy" (Mayeur 1968, 136):

You will represent in our legislative assemblies an element that has been banished for a long time, the democratic clergy.... Every time that you rise to speak, you will find yourself being the interpreter of a large number of young priests spread throughout France, whose voice no one has heard up till now and whose aspirations have remained hidden. Your election marks the entry of this young clergy into public life.... You are the official representative of this new force, a young church shorn of all the ties that bound it to the conservative classes and linking itself to the people, by contrast, with the ties of dedication.

Of course, Goyau knew that there were only a few spots in France — in the extreme north and west, perhaps in the Alsace — where "the people" were still solidly enough Catholic to respond to such a young clergy with enthusiasm. Nor were there many places where Catholics would make common cause with convinced republicans and vice versa, as happened in Lemire's district. Enough Catholics of less-than-bourgeois social status joined with enough republicans and socialists to keep him in his seat. Finally, in 1911, he crossed to the left side of the chamber to take his place there, as anticlericalism waned among the republicans.

The abbé Lemire, with his collaborator, the editor of *La Vie catholique*, Abbé Dabry, organized an unprecedented national conference for priests on the occasion of the fourteenth centenary of the baptism of Clovis in Reims for August 1896 (Rémond 1964). Six hundred priests showed up to discuss pastoral conditions and the professional training of parish priests on the basis of questionnaires previously drawn up, answered and collated after the fashion of Le Play-style monographic sociological studies. It was a grand success for Christian democracy, only possible under cover of the pilgrimages that all other groups of Catholics were also making to Reims that year at the invitation of Cardinal Langénieux and of course under his benevolent protection. This shielded Lemire and Dabry from the charge of organizing priests despite the concordat, apart from their bishops, and possibly in a rebellious spirit. (Bishop Turinaz forbade his clergy to participate in any such free-lance "ecclesiastical congress"; the reactionary bishop of Annecy, Louis Isoard, 1820–1901, wrote an open letter for the columns of *L'Univers* and its die-hard monarchist offshoot, *La Vérité*.)

A second such clerical congress was held under the auspices of the bishop of Bourges in 1900; its stated aim was to study the letter of Pope Leo XIII to the French hierarchy of 8 September 1899 (Carlen 1981, 2:455–64) on the role of the priest in society. In reality, the heyday of the democratic priests was well into its decline by 1900. Although the new field was never abandoned, a hostile attitude would accompany their labors in the church until the era of Pius XI. The case of Abbé Six in Lille illustrates this partial eclipse. In 1894, he founded *La Démocratie chrétienne, revue mensuelle sociale* to serve as the organ of the movement for "separate" (workers-only) unions. Subsequently he was posted to a remote country parish at the other end of the diocese of Cambrai; he even had to let the review die in 1908. Finally, in 1920, in the diocese of Lille that was split off from Cambrai just before World War I, he became diocesan director of social works and was named a monsignor.

Léon Dehon, for his part, collaborated with Léon Harmel in the social training of priests and seminarians at Val-des-Bois since 1892 at week-long summer sessions. To make room for two hundred priests at the same time in 1895, he brought them to his town, Saint-Quentin. Long a chaplain of the OCCO there, he accompanied Harmel into Christian democracy. Originally a secular priest (*abbé*, as distinguished from *père*), then a canon, he founded the Sacred Heart Fathers, which were expelled from France in 1901. In the meantime, he served as the guarantor and defender of the orthodoxy of Christian democracy — his reputation was sealed by an appointment as a consultor to the Congregation of the Index! No wonder then that his *Manuel social chrétien*, published by the Bonne Presse in 1894, functioned as an authoritative defense and exposition of Christian democracy.

The Press; Anti-Semitism

The editor of *Le Peuple français*, Abbé Garnier, was a taurine figure who had founded one of the first people's secretariats in Caen, Normandy, before he went with *La Croix* as a traveling organizer from 1889 to 1894. He represents the all too common alliance of populism with anti-Semitism, which was such a prominent feature of French Catholicism in the 1890s. The Catholic press had imbibed a rough, intolerant, and denunciatory tone from Lamennais and had carried it on through *L'Univers* of Louis Veuillot. When this tradition began to appeal less and less to the new newspaper readers of the fin-de-siècle, a new, more direct and popular but no less harsh language was adopted by the Assumptionist writers of the enormously successful *La Croix*, to be imitated more or less successfully by other Catholic journalists, including many of the *abbés démocrates* such as Garnier. Of course, they were competing with anticlerical and socialist journalism, which was no more fastidious. They were all prone to anti-Semitism (a "scientific" term invented at the time to replace more straightforward terms like Jew-baiting and Jew-hating), which Edouard Drumont (HDTFR 301) had made respectable in France as recently as 1886 with his book *La France juive* (see also Pierrard 1970,

31–54, and on Gayraud, Dehon, and others, 116–31; Mayeur 1986, 155–92; Poliakov 1985, 4:31–51). French republicans and socialists backed away from it in the course of the Dreyfus affair (1894–99, HDTFR 297), as did the abbé Lemire. Naudet was the only emphatic *dreyfusard* among the *abbés démocrates*. But anti-Semitism came to characterize the public stance of the majority of French Catholics, who were thus set on a collision course with the Republic by the mutually reinforcing polemics of the anticlericals in power and the integralists within the church. Leo XIII could only wring his hands over France as he watched the *Ralliement* go down in flames.

Hippolyte Gayraud is perhaps the most bizarre example of a Christian "democrat." The intransigent Catholic opposition to the ills of modern liberal society formed his outlook, as it did that of Lemire and the others as well. But in Gayraud's case, no appreciation at all developed of the advantages of religious freedom in a pluralistic society. He was favorable to the Republic as a form of government, but one to be brought totally under the control of Catholics (through the votes of the masses, whose affections were to be reconquered by Christian democracy). Before entering the Chamber of Deputies, he wrote a book called *The Antisemitism of Saint Thomas Aquinas* (he had been a Dominican, teaching scholastic philosophy, until 1893). When "Americanism" and the "modernist" renewal of theology began to show its head around the turn of the century, he felt duty-bound to pursue all of its manifestations. In other words, he was a complete integralist (Aubert in Jedin 1981, 9:467–80); only instead of being a monarchist like most other French integralists, he was of the republican persuasion.

Another part of France, Bordeaux in the southwest, supplied Paul Naudet to the ranks of the *abbés démocrates*. He founded one of the principal journals of the movement, a weekly, *La Justice sociale* (1893–1908). He also edited *Le Monde* for a while (1894–96), moving himself and *La Justice sociale* to Paris.

Le Monde (not very important at the time), *L'Univers* (weakened by the secession of Elise Veuillot, who took old-style legitimist reaction with her to *La Vérité*), and *La Croix* were all sympathetic to Christian democracy in its early years, reflecting the favor of Leo XIII and Rampolla. *La Croix* put all its rivals in the shade; with its circulation of 150,000 to 180,000 daily, it rivalled all but the handful of metropolitan dailies of mass circulation in France (Albert 1972, 3:333–38; see Mayeur 1968, 648). *La Croix*, run by the Assumptionist Fathers and edited by Father Vincent-de-Paul Bailly, A.A., until his forced exile in 1900, was the mainstay of an exceptionally large publisher of Catholic periodicals, La Maison de la Bonne Presse. Even before it became infamous for its anti-dreyfusard polemics, *La Croix* was important for the spread of Christian democracy in several different regions of France. It did this especially through the project of founding local *La Croix* weeklies to complement its national daily edition, a project taken in hand by the abbés Garnier and Naudet and in the north by friends of Abbé Lemire.

Lyon, in the southeast, also had its Christian democratic weekly edition of *La Croix*. It was to become a breeding ground for an intensely active center of Christian democracy around the long-lived *Chronique sociale* (so called only after 1909, but started in November 1892 as a sort of newsletter for the distributors of *La Croix* in the region; Ponson 1980, 61). The weekly *Croix de Lyon* was edited by Victor Berne. His right-hand man had been an officeworker in one of Lyon's silkworks, Marius Gonin (DHGE 21:605–7). They "networked" with a will for Garnier's half political, half social Union nationale and established contact with Lemire, Harmel, and other Christian democrats. From 1896 to 1898 they hosted three national conferences of Christian democracy (*and* right-wing religious or anti-Semitic nationalism *and* the campaign against the Masons). Gonin, despite these confusions so evident in retrospect, was capable of learning from experience and of accepting correction from Cardinal Couillié on the matter of anti-Semitism (Mayeur 1986, 188–92).

What was the appeal of Drumont's anti-Semitism for the Christian democrats? With the average French Catholic, they shared the various anti-Semitic patriotic and religious motives of the times — except that anti-Semitism based on a theory of racial inferiority is not attested among them. It is clear, however, that some Christian democrats saw in the post-revolutionary emancipated Jewry of the nineteenth century a prime agent in, first, the capitalistic atomization of society (Jewish financiers and industrialists, Panama scandal, etc.) and second, in the plot of the Masonic and socialist "sects" to encompass the ruination of Christian society. Jews were regarded as lined up with Protestants and Freemasons in a plot to gain control first of the bourgeoisie (for example HDTFR 1031 on the fate of the Union générale, a largely Catholic bank in Lyon) and then of the masses (through socialism). In this dangerous world, it was inviting to be able to see a Jewish connection behind the two forces that all Christian democrats opposed, capitalism and socialism. That is why at the national conference of 1896 in Lyon, it was said that anti-Semitism is the "negative" part of the Christian democratic program, while social justice was its positive component.

An Anti-capitalist Strain

At least one further note was sounded in these efforts to sing the songs of Zion in a land becoming alien and secular. Among the most strident anti-capitalistic and hence also anti-Semitic voices were those of some Franciscan friars. Franciscan spirituality was an important element in social Catholicism, as can be seen in the examples of Léon Harmel, Marius Gonin, Nicolò Rezzara, and other activists who belonged to the lay Franciscan Third Order (Mayeur 1986, 193–207, 268). Here too Pope Leo XIII was the first to see the possibilities. In an encyclical of 1882 on St. Francis of Assisi, *Auspicato concessum* (Carlen 1981, 2:69–74), he reminded the friars, sisters, and tertiaries of all the benefits that the Franciscan movement had conferred upon the popular classes in its early history and suggested that it could happen again. Two years later, in *Humanum genus*, he called particularly upon the Third Order to take part in the struggle against Freemasonry. The Third Order, he wrote, "is an authentic school of liberty, fraternity, and equality, not after the absurd fashion in which the Freemasons understand these things, but as Jesus Christ intended them to be and as St. Francis put them into practice."

Léon Harmel had been a fervent member of the Third Order since shortly after his wife died in 1870. Among alert Franciscan friars it was natural to see *Rerum novarum* as a third papal invitation to concentrate on the socio-economic elements in their tradition. One of them, probably the provincial of the Recollects in Marseille, a Father Ferdinand, wrote an article that appeared in February of 1893 with the title, "A Sociological Perspective on the Franciscan Third Order." Two affirmations emerged (Mayeur 1986, 195):

> The Third Order emancipated the peoples of medieval times; it should take up this mission again and work at the deliverance of the people in the modern world.

And:

> The Third Order, without placing itself among the adversaries of capital, should not hesitate to treat capitalism as an enemy.

This use of the term, "capital*ism*," to mean all the faults of a liberal economic system, the abuse rather than the use of capital, actually gave expression to a deep aversion to industrialized society. After all, industrialization was dependent upon great accumulations of capital and was accompanied by market speculations that passed for *usura vorax* among many social Catholics, for example those of the (now dispersed) Fribourg Union. Later in that same year, at Harmel's urging and with the warm approval of the pope and of the minister general of the Friars Minor in Rome, several dozen religious and lay Franciscans gathered at Paray-le-Monial and gave further impetus to the new socially active orientation of the Third Order. They reformulated the issue of capitalism this way: "Whereas, if socialism has become the imminent threat to our society, it is capitalism, to wit, the unjust predominance of capital and the abuses that have resulted therefrom, that is the true cause of the present social disorder." Larger conferences followed in 1895, 1896, 1897, and 1899, after the model of one held by the Italian Franciscan family in Novara in 1893.

It was at the conference at Nîmes in 1897 that the underlying conflict broke out. Father Ferdinand had successfully pushed through a condemnation of capitalism (in his sense) at the national congress of Christian democracy held the previous year in Lyon. It defined capitalism as "the economic system based on the productivity of money as such," a system that ignored the scholastic tradition that money is barren: *pecunia pecuniam parere non potest*. To be sure, the church tolerated the practice of earning interest, within limits; but that only amounted to a "condemnation of the system that makes it unavoidable, namely capitalism." Lyon went on record against capitalism as the modern form of *usura vorax* (RN 5).

A Capuchin, Father Venance, endeavored to distinguish lending at interest from speculation in securities, defending the former as legitimate. On the other side he had to contend not only with the Recollects but also with the *abbés démocrates* (apparently Franciscan tertiaries as well) Dabry, Pastoret, Naudet, and Dehon. But Rome viewed such controversies with mixed feelings: the resolutions coming out of Franciscan assemblies seemed to put the order behind stands that were controversial, ill-considered, and dubious. A papal letter to the general of the Friars Minor in 1898 counselled sweetness, concord and calm in the image of St. Francis' own popular activities. At an international meeting in Rome in 1900, Dehon confidently repeated the condemnation of capitalism; but then the Irish friar, David Fleming, holder of high offices in papal Rome, called the Third Order back to its primarily religious role. Theses in political economy should be advanced and defended by those members who have the calling and the competence, but they should not attempt to turn the Third Order itself into a "a school of sociology nor into an organization meant to promote a political economy," when it should be "a school of Christian perfection." Damaging internal confrontations could be the only result of that course.

The signals were clear. After 1900, there were no more Third Order congresses, priests' congresses, Christian democratic congresses. The workers' meetings (congresses of delegates) had already given way to the celebrities' and speakers' congresses, like those of Lyon. What remained in France was a generation of diocesan and to some extent religious-order priests who were sensitized to and experienced in pastoral work in a workers' milieu, and a few struggling Christian labor unions. These would come together with new forces in new combinations (the Sillon, Action populaire, Semaines sociales), even under the sere winds of Pius X's pontificate. Catholics would not again turn their backs on the working class in total reaction after *Rerum novarum* and the second Christian democracy.

Chapter 13

ITALIAN
CHRISTIAN DEMOCRACY

Perhaps the foremost social Catholic in Italy before *Rerum novarum* was a nobleman from Bergamo, Stanislao Medolago Albani (DSMCI 2:366–71). He was in charge of the "Second Section" (for social and economic concerns) of the national umbrella organization of Catholic associations in Italy, the Opera dei Congressi. As we have seen, he participated fairly assiduously in the work of the Fribourg Union in the 1880s. He was anxious to avoid the worst of the social dislocations and the proletarianization of the lower classes that more advanced industrialized countries like Belgium and France had already experienced. But he had great difficulty in moving the Opera dei Congressi (hereafter OC) to give the social question a prominent position on its list of priorities, dominated as it was by the "papal question," the "Roman Question." To his aid came a professor of economics at the university of Pisa, Giuseppe Toniolo (DSMCI 2:636–44). A young priest from the former papal states, of the new generation born after the unification of Italy, Romolo Murri represents the next stage of a rapidly boiling social-ecclesiastical situation from 1895 on, an Italian *abbé démocrate*. Under the combined influence of Toniolo and Murri, a Sicilian priest, Luigi Sturzo (see De Rosa 1977 and DSMCI 2:615–24), is the third of three truly major figures in the history of Christian democracy in Italy under the popes of the turn of the century, Leo XIII and Pius X. These three figures represent three phases of a segment of social Catholicism in direct local interaction with the papal magisterium.

In the Opera dei Congressi

From 1874 to 1904, when Pius X dissolved it, the OC was the gathering place on the national level for all the various forces and groupings of papalist or "intransigent" Catholicism in Italy. Giambattista Paganuzzi was one of its founders, a lawyer from Venice (DSMCI 2:441–48; De Rosa 1966). In his view, nothing but unyielding opposition to the Italian state that had trampled on the rights of the church was possible for Italian Catholics, until this state would come to terms with the pope, restoring the latter's sovereignty. Such a position was controversial, even in the councils of the OC, until the 1890s, when Paganuzzi himself was named president of the OC and was able to impose his views with unrelenting energy.

He described his approach not long after his installation in 1889 in a letter to a bishop-friend (cited by Tramontin in Malgeri 1980, 1:47–50): "Nothing gets done without dictatorship. With five years of dictatorship, that is, of undivided, serious, efficacious, and all-embracing organization in Italy, we Catholics will arrive at the point where we will have to be taken seriously." In fact, Paganuzzi's OC, by the time it met in its annual congress in Milan in 1897, was an imposing achievement, with most of the dioceses organized and with four thousand parish committees (the basic building blocks of the OC, to which all other confraternities, associations, local election committees, and so forth were affiliated). Although rural credit unions on the Raiffeisen model were a new development, thanks to the OC there were already over five hundred of them. A similar number of mutual-aid societies existed (forerunners of agrarian and industrial unions), besides seventeen student circles at the state universities and a number of regional dailies.

So striking was the size and vigor of these "clerical" organizations, all brought together under one direction, that the government cracked down on them after proletarian civil unrest broke out in May of 1898 in Milan. Seventy diocesan committees were disbanded by police order, along with twenty-six hundred parish committees, six hundred youth groups, and five student circles. Did the government actually believe the OC was fostering subversive activities? From a certain perspective, this could easily be the case. When they led don Davide Albertario away in manacles and condemned him to three years in prison (he served one year), it was clear to all that the fiery priest-journalist was an intransigent opponent of the government. For years, he had been reviling what both intransigents and socialists called "the legal country" for its neglect of "the real country." He was charged with "proclaiming democratic and socialist ideas." But Albertario (DSMCI 2:9–16), editor of the *Osservatore cattolico* in Milan, carried out his opposition only through legally permissible channels. In the face of the undying enmity against the church represented especially by the anticlerical left wing of the ruling establishment, he and the orators of the OC defended Catholic Italy (for them identical with the "real" Italy) by the power of the written and spoken word and through legal organizations. Now, however, he was moving noticeably toward active resistance and even toward Catholic participation in elections. He had begun to interpret the *Non expedit* as enjoining a time of "preparation while abstaining" from politics, a time which was rapidly coming to an end.

There were certainly cracks in the imposing intransigent fortress (Clark 1984, 105–8). Paganuzzi's efforts had paid off, but they could not be sustained: the inner logic of *intransigentismo* could not stand the test of time. On the other hand, neither could the *Kulturkampf* mentality of the left liberals in Italian politics. They had to contend not just with Catholics claiming to represent the "real country," but also with the growing strength of socialism — as did, for their part, the Catholics, whether conservative or progressive.

The great influence of Mikhail Bakunin in Italian socialist history (Guichonnet in Droz 1974, 2:247–52 and 263–75) was giving way to Marxist influences. Filippo Turati would lead the Socialist party of Italy from its formation in 1893 until 1912 with an unorthodox Marxism adapted to a still largely agrarian Italy. Even the northern triangle consisting of Turin, Genoa, and Milan limped along without adequate supplies of coal and iron, until, that is, the second industrial revolution based on electricity could take place. Hence one can say that the real industrialization of Italy did not commence until about 1896. But Italian socialists, under Turati's leadership, did not confine themselves to industrially developing areas. Catholics and socialists both competed to gain the leadership of the rural masses that grew restive under economic deprivation and the influence of Bakunin-style anarchism (Clark 1984, 101–4).

The industrial development that occurred notably between 1896 and 1906 did not provide any relief in the agricultural sector until after the "black years" of unprofitable farming and massive emigration that characterized the 1890s, nor could it begin to absorb the now booming population. When police and troops fired on socialist workers in Milan in early May of 1898, the government took measures to repress both socialists and, as we have seen, organized Catholics. The response of the OC, oddly enough, was to tone down its anti-establishment rhetoric (De Rosa 1966, 174–79). The "papal question" was relegated to second place. Catholic spokespersons, from Paganuzzi on down, insisted as a matter of priority on the vast gulf that separated Catholics, even intransigent ones, from socialists.

Catholics promoted social harmony on principle, staying within the bounds of the law and respecting even usurped authority. Socialists, however, preached revolution, fomented class struggle, and attacked private property. The year 1898 can be seen as a watershed in the development of Christian democracy, as of so much else on the Italian scene, after which nothing was quite the same. First it opened the OC up to Christian democratic activities and propaganda. This would turn out to be but a brief interlude, as the encyclical *Graves de communi* of Leo XIII and the dissolution of the OC by Pius XI put Christian democracy as a movement into eclipse, not only in Italy but in other countries as well. In contrast with 1848–49, however, the reaction of 1902–4 was tempered by efforts to retain the footholds or bridgeheads that Christian democracy had built up in the working classes. The Second Section of the OC was spared dissolution, since its popular bases were of demonstrated value and since Medolago Albani and Toniolo retained the full confidence of the new pope.

Giuseppe Toniolo

In 1889, Toniolo and Medolago Albani founded the "Catholic Union for Social Studies" (Unione cattolica per gli studi sociali; see Aubert 1978, 160, or Jedin 1981, 9:87). Paganuzzi thought it was a useless reduplication of the Second Section of the OC. In reality it was an attempt to focus on the plight of farmers and laborers in new terms, not just as objects of charitable pastoral attention. To maintain this focus, the social Catholics needed to create some distance from the OC's suffocating embrace. They succeeded in this by being loyal and cooperative to a fault, trying not to threaten any break in the OC's line while alerting it to the implications of the social problems that were beginning to wrack Italy.

Toniolo, essentially a professor and theorist, was a wholehearted believer in the corporatist vision of the Christian Middle Ages. There was a difference, however, between his outlook and that of those other intransigent Catholics who would soon take to calling themselves "integral Catholics" or integralists: Toniolo was used to thinking in historical terms, of contemplating the evolution of social institutions.

This historicizing trait in a Neo-Thomist context was also characteristic of Murri and Sturzo. It set them apart from the Thomist philosophers and the theology professors such as Louis Billot, S.J., in Rome. An intriguing special case was the Perugian priest, Umberto Benigni (for whom see Poulat 1977a). He founded the first Christian democratic periodical in Italy in 1893, even before Toniolo's *Rivista internazionale di scienze sociali* got started. Historically minded, but after 1895 a deep-dyed pessimist, Benigni would oppose Murri and Sturzo when they began to claim autonomy from church authority for Christian political activity.

In fact, most intransigents came to take it for granted that what is valid is immutable. When applied to a situation of social unrest such as that of Italy in the grip of industrialization and agricultural crisis, this immutabilism translated into certain sacred "principles." For if the Christian society (Christendom) of yesteryear was a just and humane order of society, and if it was stable and stratified, then this kind of hierarchical order, with its subordination of the lower classes to the higher, is a sine qua non of Catholic social doctrine. Pius X stated this directly as a principle of Catholic social action in his *Motu proprio* of 18 December 1903 (ASS 36:341).

Toniolo did not challenge this thinking. But at the same time, he was unusually sensitive to the fact that *noblesse oblige* did little for the self-esteem of its "beneficiaries"; instead proletarians deeply resented the whole approach. So he sought to overcome the paternalistic defect of the traditional social outlook, just as it was being challenged by Christian democrats in all the theaters of social Catholicism in the 1890s (Spicciani 1984; Pecorari 1981, 1983).

The "Milan Program," which he drew up for the approval of a Social Studies Union meeting in January of 1894, is an excellent illustration (printed in Toniolo 1949, 1:3–14, and Malgeri 1980, 1:497–503). Its title, the "Program of Catholics vis-à-vis Socialism," indicates its approach. The progress of socialism in Italy, both among intellectuals and the working class, even in the countryside, made it imperative for Catholics to propose their alternative. The customary objection, that the workers never had it so good and that the agitation was unjustified, came under withering fire in a tone familiar to intransigents. A whole series of conspicuous social disorders was laid at the feet of atomistic liberal views of society. But then the "Program" outlined four positive points bearing on

- work (a moral duty of all)

- property, especially land (it has a "collective social function," to be enhanced and protected by law for the benefit of the masses)

- industrial wealth or capital and profits (to be opened up to the "participation" of labor!) and

- commerce (where laws should encourage socially responsible finance and banking activities).

Finally, the "Milan Program" posed the question of means toward these programmatic ends. The principal answer was "vocational unions (or corporations)" embracing both employers and employees of a given sector or trade. Neither labor disorganization nor socialist organization were deemed acceptable. But an interesting argument was made, tacitly taking *Rerum novarum*'s lead, for cases where such mixed unions were not likely:

> If the upper classes of property-holders and capitalists decline to enter into mixed groupings with the lower classes (as the organizational ideal promoted by Catholics would suggest), then they should allow the workers to come together in vocational unions for themselves alone and to proceed by the path of legal resistance to claim the rights that are due them. This is not to be understood as closing the door for all time to the classes that at present hold themselves aloof. In other words, while espousing the cause of workers, we shall not lose sight of society as a whole and of its normal order.

That normative order was not to be conceived according to the current bourgeois model nor yet was it to be a socialist dictatorship of the proletariat. Christendom, the "centuries of the people," was the model. In the peroration, the "Program" hailed the dawn of "the Christian democracy of the twentieth century," in which all the ranks of the "social hierarchy" cooperated for "the elevation of the working classes."

Though there was no open hostility, the "Program" met with a muted reception from the episcopate and in the OC. All the same, a public statement had been made and with it a first application of *Rerum novarum* (unmentioned so as not to claim its authority for their own program, no doubt) to Italy in particular. Admittedly, it came from lay Catholic theorists of the social situation, but well-connected ones. They were not disavowed. By insisting on the socialist threat, Toniolo had certainly adopted an astute approach, since the rivalry for the masses' adherence would only become more and more pronounced as the years passed. But the inner tensions between Toniolo's avowedly social program and its unavowed politico-religious premises (bracketing the Roman Question and working within the framework of the existing Italian state), also began to make themselves felt.

After the 1898 *fatti di maggio*, a partial realignment of strains or tendencies within Italian Catholicism took place. The old and bitter opposition between intransigents and transigents faded (e.g., between Paganuzzi and G. B. Scalabrini, 1839–1905, the bishop of the emigrants, who favored conciliation with the Italian state), while that between conservatives and democrats came to the fore (Tramontin in Malgeri 1980, 1:54; see Vecchio 1979, 22). Most of these democratic or populist progressives belonged to the thoroughgoing intransigent tradition: beside Toniolo and Medolago Albani, one can note Filippo Meda, Albertario's right-hand man at the *Osservatore cattolico*, Giacomo Radini Tedeschi, who later as bishop of Bergamo would profoundly influence Pope John XXIII, Nicolò Rezzara, and of course those around Luigi Sturzo in Sicily and Romolo Murri in central Italy. In comparison with Sturzo and especially Murri, all the others took a moderate stance; but none of those named were comfortable with the prevailing Catholic conservatism.

Romolo Murri and Democracy

Murri was a precocious student at the seminary at Fermo and was sent to Rome to study theology (ordained 1893). Thereafter he attended lectures at the state university of Rome, the Sapienza, where he met a handful of young Catholic lay students trying to assert themselves in a hostile environment. They were coopted by the OC, forming a national Catholic student association (FUCI); Murri promptly started to chafe under Paganuzzi's regimentation. But in the meantime he had encountered a new intellectual world, that of socialism as taught at the Sapienza by Antonio Labriola (Droz 1974, 2:262). What socialism meant to Labriola was a liberation from the "scientific" positivism that dominated so much of the culture of the late nineteenth century. He studied under a neo-Hegelian himself, but stood firm against any determinism that would deny that human beings made their own history. About 1890, he came to believe, with Marx, that a revolution would be necessary to inaugurate the socialist order. The effect Labriola's lectures had on Murri was to introduce his keen mind to the realm of time and history, a factor that had been completely neglected in his Neo-Thomist theological studies (Traniello 1977, 19–23; Cecchini 1971, xxxii–xxxiv and 1973, 62–67).

He devoted a considerable part of the years 1894–96 to developing a counterargument, in part using historical materialism as a method, to the effect that Catholicism, not socialism, would provide the key to societal well-being. The historical consideration of conditions of production and exchange became an instrument of analysis for him in the critical task of understanding the new social reality in which and upon which the church was to act. Murri always found the distinction between religious and political spheres or concerns a hard one to draw; basically, he was convinced, as were so many other social Catholics, that the reform of civil society depended upon a religious moralization coming from the church. It was when he insisted that the church itself needed reform (starting with the hierarchy and clergy) so as to carry out that mission, that he got into trouble. In 1907 he was suspended *a divinis*. Upon his election to parliament in 1909 he was excommunicated completely. (He married in 1912; he and the papacy would be reconciled in 1943.) But before all this, he would exercise an enormous influence within Italian social Catholicism, as the undisputed leader of Italian Christian democracy.

In the fateful year of 1898 he turned his intellectual energies to a study of the socialist parties of Europe, with the avowed purpose of creating a Catholic counterforce even more deeply rooted in the just aspirations of the Italian people. In the pages of the noted review he founded, *Cultura sociale*, he displayed the fruits of his voracious reading and took stands on all the relevant issues of political and church life. His leading idea was that the proletariat was indeed to be the bearer and instrument of a historic mission of societal reform. For him, the fairly well-worn phrase about the "alliance of the people and the church" was pregnant with meaning; it dictated a more pronounced siding with the masses than either Leo XIII or Toniolo were ready to endorse (DSMCI 1/1:214). To make that ideal a reality he had plans, the early stages of which went into effect, for propaganda and organizational activities on a large scale. The first stage was a publishing house that would put out a whole range of periodicals and other works.

As the OC slipped into its terminal post-1898 crisis, Toniolo and Meda assumed the role of mediators, urging the old guard around Paganuzzi to turn the OC onto a more popular and democratic course, while urging the young Turks around Murri and Giovanni Battista Valente to maintain harmony with conservative Catholics in the unitary national organization. Valente was a young Genoese layman at the head of the first national Christian democratic newspaper, the *Popolo italiano*. In 1918, after a spell in Germany looking after Italian migrant workers, he would become the founding president of the CIL, the Catholic labor union federation (DSMCI 2:651–56). On 15 May 1899, he published the "Turin Program," also known as the "Christian Democratic Social Program" (Malgeri 1980, 2:353–55; translation in M. P. Fogarty 1982, 319–20). Toniolo could only be pleased. Even apart from mentioning him alongside Leo XIII and Gladstone, the document was frankly corporatist in tone — there is obviously no real Catholic labor movement afoot yet in Genoa or Turin, even less so than in Liège or Lille. (One got started that same year, however, DSMCI 2:410.) Other demands close to the heart of left corporatists were also recited: proportional representation, the referendum, legislation to curb the usual labor abuses, protection of small holdings of land, administrative decentralization. All these essentially political demands only made sense if the authors of the declaration assumed, as they did, that the question of Catholic participation in the political (and thereby more effectively also in the social and economic) life of Italy would soon be resolved.

A protracted struggle ensued in the OC. It came to a head in 1903, just as the younger Christian democratic generation was on the verge of taking charge of the organization, in coalition with the moderates around Meda, Toniolo and Giovanni Grosoli, the head of what was becoming the "Catholic newspaper trust." Pope Pius X dissolved the OC in 1904, leaving its diocesan committees to carry on under the individual control of the local bishops. The reorganization of Catholic Action in Italy in a different framework will concern us later. But even before that, Leo XIII had addressed the problems connected with Christian democracy in the Italian setting and had tried to cut the Gordian knot in his 1901 encyclical, *Graves de communi re* (Carlen 1981, 2:479–85).

This was the encyclical, much noted at the time, that declared "Christian democracy" to be entirely nonpolitical, despite the associations that the term "democracy" naturally called forth. To retain the vigor that the young Christian democrats had brought into the otherwise moribund OC, Leo XIII wished to retain the designation "Christian democracy." After all, he had adopted it himself earlier, especially in encouraging the French protagonists. The pope also wished to endorse and stimulate the popular organizations that the Christian democrats were responsible for (par. 4). But he defined the term "Christian democracy" as *actio benefica in populum* (par. 7: "beneficent Christian action in behalf of the people," not necessarily by or through the people). He contrasted it with "social democracy" that "aimed at putting all government in the hands of the masses" (par. 5). Though this had repercussions in all Catholic countries where Christian democrats were at work, it was intended first and foremost for the Italian situation, where alone political activity in *any* national party was forbidden to Catholics. The Belgian Christian democrats in the Catholic party were assured, for instance, that they need not change their tendencies or aims in the slightest, even though the defense of the stratified hierarchical society dear to the pope (par. 4–6, 9, 16–19) was not uppermost among their concerns. Nor was Abbé Lemire expected to get out of politics in France.

Words aside, Leo XIII was merely remaining consistent with himself and with his earlier encouragement of the Christian democrats. After all, he had long championed the principle that any of several forms of government, including political democracy, may be morally acceptable. What would be erroneous would be to insist that a particular form (monarchy, republic, parliamentary, or social democracy) was alone valid in all circumstances. So Christian democrats like Harmel and Murri, who were convinced that the trend toward democracy was not only ineluctable but also inherently derivative from Christianity, found themselves at odds with the pope. (Harmel piped down, Murri did not.) On the other hand, the pope's understanding of Christian democracy was a severely curtailed one, and it took the wind out of its sails. Until this act of definition, the drive toward the assumption of responsibility *by the people*, including political responsibility, was the main inspiration of the movement and its main contribution to the overcoming of paternalism in social Catholicism. With this declaration, the aged pope cooled the democratic ardor that gave the movement its popular force. It was an attempt at compromise between the Catholics potentially lined up in a conservative party of order and those allying themselves with popular aspirations. The Christian democrats were a product of *Rerum novarum*, but they could not stay entirely within its framework of social assumptions.

Luigi Sturzo

The person who came to terms most effectively with this new situation, underscored by the first acts of Pope Pius X (elected pope in 1903), was a Christian democratic propagandist and organizer in Sicily, Luigi Sturzo. Two formative influences had set him on his career as a Christian democrat and leader of the Italian Populist party (1919–24). One was the series of severe agrarian disturbances in Sicily starting in 1889, known as the Sicilian *fasci* ("bundles," bands), which brought socialist leaders like Giuseppe De Felice to prominence. Another was his year in Rome for graduate studies in theology, during which he came in contact with such figures as Toniolo, Murri, and Radini Tedeschi, who introduced him to the energetic world of Leonine social Catholicism in its Christian democratic phase.

For Sicily, Sturzo found, the centralized structure of the OC was just what was needed to penetrate the clerical clientalistic torpor. With its prestige and official backing, he could and did start a movement of social reform independent of the landowners who dominated Sicilian life through their land-rental agents and other hangers-on. As early as 1895, before he was finished with his doctoral work in Rome, with the determined support of his bishop and his older priest-brother, Sturzo founded parish committees of the OC in and around his hometown of Caltagirone (De Rosa 1977, 58–84). They soon got into the business of organizing farmworkers, artisans, and youth. A forthrightly Christian democratic paper appeared every two weeks starting in 1897. When the first strike of Sicilian peasants under Catholic auspices broke out in 1901, Sturzo supported it in his editorials. In 1903 he himself was called upon to organize the peasant resis-

tance against the big landowners of Caltagirone. Fortunately, it came
to a successful conclusion after two weeks (De Rosa 1977, 58–121 or
1966, 231–52), as the owners agreed to changes in their rental terms.

The decision to resort to strikes was not an easy one for the Catholic peasant associations or their clerical leaders. Until the turn of
the century, it was a tactic in labor disputes that only socialists had
used. Then, in several places almost simultaneously in north and
south, Catholic groups staged strikes. Standing for election to the
town council was another threshold, but it was one that he apparently had considered from the beginning of his activity in Caltagirone
(Bedeschi 1973). In 1902, as part of a concerted effort of Christian
democrats to get elected to "administrative" (municipal or provincial) positions, he won a seat on the town council. (Catholics were
allowed and sometimes encouraged, even under the regimen of the
Non expedit, to vote and be elected in these local contests.) When
his party won the majority in 1905, he became mayor and remained
in this office until 1920, leading an administration distinguished for
honesty if otherwise limited in what it could accomplish.

Given the restrictions placed on Christian democracy by the papal rulings, Sturzo had to rethink the possibilities for the movement.
The informal relaxation of the *Non expedit* that occurred in populous Catholic northern centers (signally Bergamo, but elsewhere as
well) for the 1904 national elections was no solution. He sharply
criticized the tactical coalition of "clericals" and "moderate liberals"
against the socialist threat. Catholics as such did not put forward
any candidates; but the liberals who did and who signed an innocuous formula enjoyed the electoral support of the Catholic bloc.
To supply votes without a political platform on which one could
stand struck Sturzo as an extremely disadvantageous, not to say
irresponsible, political bargain — the "politics of eunuchs" (Clark
1984, 149). And yet, for the present, both Murri's brand of political Christian democracy and Paganuzzi's dream of a compact
centrally directed bloc of Catholics not voting but in opposition were
impossible to realize. If *clerico-moderatismo* was an abdication of
responsibility, were Italian Catholics simply to stay aloof from the political process? That option was becoming increasingly less attractive
or viable.

To these questions Sturzo replied in his important 1905 "Caltagirone Address" (long excerpts in Malgeri 1980, 2:365–76; see also
De Rosa 1966, 275–84, and 1977, 123–44; DSMCI 1/1:215–17). Entitled "Problems of the National Life of Italian Catholics," it set forth
the balance that Sturzo drew from the preceding eight years of Christian democracy ("eight years that seem longer than half a century,"
as he said). What emerged for him was the need for a modern, secu-

lar, national political party of Catholics on the progressive side of the political spectrum: Christian democracy without the name and shorn of its clerical ties to the hierarchy. It would have to be nonclerical to relieve the papacy of responsibility for its moves, but also because a political party worthy of the name could not claim the support of all Catholics on *religious* grounds. As long as such a party failed to materialize in the Italy of the early twentieth century, there was only one realistic alternative. The church, papacy and all, would be yoked as a reluctant political ally to the cart of the liberal-conservatives, whose program was devoid of any attempt to translate Christian social principles into secular political terms. This was in fact already taking place in the Giolitti era (named for the prime minister, Giovanni Giolitti, 1842–1928; see Clark 1984, 146–50), culminating in the so-called Gentiloni pact of 1913 (Clark 1984, 157–58). Swimming against this current while Meda took advantage of it, Sturzo pointed the way forward to an acceptance of religious pluralism in civil society. He would get the chance to launch his "Italian Popular party" after World War I.

In a way more consonant with a modern secular or pluralistic society than Murri had found, Sturzo was able to distinguish and relate the perspectives of the Catholic or clerical reformer of the church and the civic reformer of civil society (De Rosa 1966, 278; see Murri in Malgeri 1980, 2:399–402). He created his own niche in public life strictly in terms of the second category, always treating political or national issues in their own terms. He recommended this approach to his fellow Catholics. His respect for church authority took the form of leaving ecclesiastical or religious issues as such strictly up to the hierarchy — while seeking neither support nor control from the hierarchy in the civil sphere.

As to the Roman Question, he left that up to the pope, whose position he supported. The pope's freedom to operate and communicate with churches in Italy and throughout the world had always been the basic issue. The 1871 "Law of Guarantees" was not much of a guarantee of that freedom: what the Italian state unilaterally "conceded," it could also revoke. In practice, the current situation was satisfactory; the church's freedom of action in Italy was not unduly restricted under Giolitti. But if things went amiss or if there were infringements, there was no legal or constitutional arrangement to which one could appeal. It would be a work of time to create such a structure, one that would do justice to the papacy's unique standing as an independent, international religious authority. In the meantime, it would still be possible and hence needful to create such a party as Sturzo had in mind. The large Catholic population of Italy should play their part in framing national policies on nonecclesiastical matters. Only thus could they be properly integrated into the national political life through their own elites.

Having thus posed the alternative "clerical or lay" and resolved it in favor of a lay or "nonconfessional" party, Sturzo addressed the properly political choice. Should the party situate itself on the right, center, or left of the political spectrum? He rejected the right-wing politics of the liberals of the time as morally and politically anemic. Filippo Meda had recently proposed a center party such as the German Catholics had, but it did not suit don Luigi: "A hybrid stance undercuts all consistency of platform and confuses our political personality with that of the conservative liberals" (in Malgeri 1980, 2:374–75). His conclusion? "What is necessary, I believe, is a democratic [as opposed to conservative] content for the platform of Catholics forming a national party" in the Italy of the early twentieth century.

Sturzo evidently did not have to spell out in what ways his party would be distinct from Italian socialism. Apart from the latter's anti-clericalism (a polite word for the will to repress Christianity in any churchly form), there were clear differences between Catholic and socialist agrarian labor agitation. Catholics bargained collectively for tenants, who then each had their own plots to work; socialists wanted to lease the land *and work it* collectively (De Rosa 1977, 94; DSMCI 1/1:331; more generally, Traniello in Malgeri 1980, 3:287–305). By no means did Sturzo envisage a party of the Catholic proletariat only, or vast programs of nationalization. What he wanted was a decent political representation of those elements that had been excluded from participation up until that time and were assimilable neither to the socialist nor to the liberal blocs — the overwhelming majority of Catholics in Italy, mostly lower-class, still mostly rural, but also workers in factories, small tradesmen, and the Catholic traditional elites insofar as they were sympathetic. The accent must be populist or democratic, with an emphasis on freedom, justice, and decentralization.

The latter point was very important to Sturzo as a southerner. A province like Sicily, in his view, had to be free to set its own priorities, instead of being constantly put at a disadvantage by policies aimed at the further industrial development of the north.

The Centralization of Catholic Action under Pius X

When Pope Pius X (Aubert 1978, 17–23, or Jedin 1981, 9:418–19) was still Cardinal Sarto, patriarch of Venice, he supported Paganuzzi and the Venetian group that dominated the OC. However, he was also appreciative of the younger generation insofar as they were keener to engage the adversary in the public realm, as for example in elections at the level of the municipality. He approved and was pleased with the results of the city council elections of Venice in 1895. At that time the Catholics ("clericals"), in tactical league with moderate liberals (i.e., conservatives), prevailed over the anticlericals and the socialists and started a coalition of long duration in control of local government. Above all, like all intransigents, he desired Catholic cohesiveness ("unity"), and wanted to make sure that the Catholic ranks moved forward together: this was the intransigent, papalist, Paganuzzian ideal, even if Paganuzzi's idea of just how far these closed ranks should move was itself perhaps a bit too restrictive.

It was in this context that he first experienced or heard about Romolo Murri, a young cleric attempting to win the Catholic movement to a conception of Catholic action that was quite daring and advanced. Sarto was not impressed by Murri's protestations of strict obedience to papal directives. The criticisms he made of the lay loyalists in the OC and the more traditional clergy were evidence to Sarto of an agenda that went beyond what the pope had in mind. Some of the boutades in Murri's suspiciously prolific journalistic activity were even aimed at bishops who smiled upon clerical-moderate combinations! In an August 1902 number of *Cultura sociale*, Murri went so far as to publish a sardonic attack on Paganuzzi entitled "The Collapse of Venice" (De Rosa 1966, 211f.). Sarto leapt to Paganuzzi's defense, charging Murri with slander and rank ingratitude.

Leo XIII is often seen as contrasting with Pius IX and Pius X in every respect. If Pius X was conservative and defensive, Pope Leo had been liberal and open. But while there were great and evident differences between the two popes, one cannot assume, for instance, that the rejection of Murri's approaches and the restructuring Catholic Action, which Pius X carried out in his own fashion, changed Leo XIII's policies in any substantial way. These measures ratified the disappointment of the *hopes* that Leo XIII had reposed in Christian democracy, to be sure, but did not represent a retreat from any of his *positions*. The proof of this is in the new statutes that Leo XIII himself gave to the OC in 1902.

With the papal blessings on "Christian democracy" in the limited, nonelectoral, sense of *Graves de communi*, a place for the younger Christian democratic generation had to be found in the OC. Toniolo mediated as well as he could, but the conservative resistance was stubborn. Catholic publications were filled with vigorous attacks and critiques of Murri's wing against the old guard of the OC and vice versa, with the center forces firing away at both (compare Cecchini in Malgeri 1980, 2:81–86, and Poulat 1977a, 282–303). A set of "Instructions" signed by Cardinal Rampolla "on Christian Popular or Christian Democratic Action in Italy" was issued (27 January 1902; ASS 34:401–13), a call to order and harmony. Up to this point, Leo seemed to be calling upon the older generation to share its role in the OC with Christian democratic elements. But it was clear from the new "Instructions" that the relative autonomy that the Christian democrats had fought for (with papal encouragement, they thought), was not to be. Instead there were detailed injunctions, ruling out any independent initiative and inculcating the cohesiveness, through subordination to hierarchical authority, of the whole of Catholic public activity from the press to peasant leagues. "Catholic lay persons are not to go ahead of, but to follow behind their shepherds." Thus, while Leo was still pope and Sarto was still in Venice, Christian democracy as Murri envisaged it received its official coup de grace. Poulat (1977a, 303) describes it as a shift (in the spectrum of options expressed by Italian Catholics at the time) from "center left" to "center right." Leo XIII evidently had wanted an alliance of pope and common people with a balance of forces just left of center, but it had proved to be not viable.

Pius X then watched as the center right under Grosoli, Toniolo, and Medolago Albani tried to establish itself. But the OC was too riven with tensions and inner conflict to sustain that either. Like others, the pope admired, not to say envied, the organizational success of German Catholics. It seems he wished to remodel Italian Catholic Action along the German lines, without as yet acceding to the desire for a Catholic political party (Agócs 1975, 33; see Bendiscioli in Jedin 1981, 9:483–86). Dissolving the OC as a national organization, Pius saw to it that the Second Section remained in place. He renamed it the Unione (cattolica) economico-sociale and confided to its care all the cooperatives and labor organizations and credit unions that continued to grow and spread throughout Italy. He flanked this "Economic-Social Union" with an "Electoral Union" and a "People's Union" for study and the development of a trained body of active Catholic laity. This latter he called the Unione (cattolica) popolare, after the Volksverein in Germany. The pope entrusted its direction to Toniolo. The topmost coordination of these three organizations was retained in papal hands, while local episcopal approval and authorization was required for all of their activities in the individual dioceses of Italy.

Social Catholic Associations and Institutions

After 1898, when Christian democracy was losing its forward movement in France, its greatest expansion was occurring in Italy at ground level. The sturdiest organizational results of Italian social Catholicism, it is true, were the rural credit unions, closely connected with the parishes wherever they were founded. Many of these already existed and many more would be formed during the pontificate of Pius X. But there was a wave also of urban labor foundations from 1899 to 1903; then the brake was applied on the most active forces, those around Murri, as just described. This broke the momentum that had built up and would have to be slowly built again as Murri was pushed out of the church over the intertwined questions of autonomy and reform in church and society. Christian trade unions, which cannot operate simply as organs of the hierarchy if they are to represent labor against capital, had a hard row to hoe under Pius X.

Nevertheless, they and other workingmen's associations connected with the "Economic-Social Union" of the church in Italy did increase and multiply in two phases. From 1899 to 1903 (or perhaps for the most part just in the two years 1901–2; see DSMCI 1/1:337), the first, hectic phase took place in response to spontaneous job actions breaking out all over on the local level. Giolitti's government did not choose to repress them. All of a sudden those young priests or academics who were known as Christian democrats found themselves called upon to help organize workers or advise on negotiations wherever the socialists had not got there first or were not welcome for one reason or another. Hundreds of parishes possessed a labor group of some sort after a spontaneous demonstration of this nature. Christian democracy was thus incorporated in these parish or interparish groups at the grassroots (Cecchini in Malgeri 1980, 2:86–102). Henceforth, the upper echelons of the church hierarchy may have been anxious to exercise a moderating influence over such groups, but they did not want to disband them or chase their members into the arms of the socialists.

The second phase of growth and consolidation, well described by Silvio Tramontin (in Malgeri 1980, 3:205–313; see esp. 288–90 for a Sicilian example), went from about 1906 to 1911. In the latter year, a statistical study with reliable, perhaps even somewhat understated figures was published by the government Ministry of Agriculture, Industry, and Trade. It provides a basis for estimating the extent to which the Catholic labor movement had grown (cited by Zaninelli, DSMCI 1/1:333, and in Malgeri 1980, 3:211–15). Overall, there is no question that socialist organizing efforts had built a larger constituency. But there were certain sectors (agriculture, female textile workers) and geographical areas (especially parts of Lombardy and Venetia, both under Austrian rule until the 1860s) where the Catholics at least held their own.

Both socialists and social Catholics faced formidable challenges in the developing economic situation, even apart from the internal difficulties and differences that afflicted each of them in more or less parallel fashion. The post-boom industrial economy was pursuing greater efficiencies to consolidate its rapid gains of the previous decade; the country as a whole was still predominantly agricultural, did not yet possess a satisfactory system of investment banking or a modern domestic market for its products, and would limp along behind its neighbors to the north for some decades to come. All the same, the Catholic effort had some distinct advantages in comparison with the equally divided and uncertain socialists. For a base of operations, even if it was not uniformly supportive, there was the web of parishes covering Italy, many of them already organized after the pattern propagated by the OC. Around these nodes there was by this time a developing net of parish-based "assistential" organizations, some self-managed: not only sodalities, but mutual-aid or "friendly" societies of various classes of workers, not to mention the rural credit unions promoted by the Second Section of the Opera dei Congressi until 1904 and thereafter by the Economic-Social Union. There were often consumer cooperatives and labor cooperatives in both town and country. For the most part they did not stage walkouts. But even if up until then they had merely presented requests or grievances, they constituted a relatively stable framework for concerted labor action or for founding a more militant union without having to start altogether from scratch. Catholic labor organizers, in other words, could often count upon a fairly well developed base from which to launch their activities, as well as fall-back structures in case they had to regroup after a first effort and try again when the conditions were more favorable.

Thus, when Catholic labor unionism in the urban sectors (not in agriculture!) went into the doldrums again around 1911, it was still possible during and after World War I to pick up the pieces, under pressure from powerful new stimuli, and to form the aforementioned national labor organization, the CIL (Confederazione italiana dei lavoratori). Christian trade unions experienced another, third, period of significant growth in the post-war years until Mussolini's Fascist regime put an end to all such non-Fascist bodies.

In the fifteen years that followed the 1898 repression, despite the stunting of the Christian democratic movement, despite Pius X's conservative leanings and his veiled permission for clerical-moderate electoral coalitions, a real Catholic labor movement took initial shape in Italy. It sank roots especially among the landless farmers but also among urban artisans, employees, and workers. The socialist lead is evident both numerically and in terms of organization. A few figures and dates will give some idea of the proportions of the Catholic movement in context. In Giolitti's Italy, only about 11 percent of workers were organized in union-like associations for the protection of their economic interests. Of these, the "red" Labor *Chambers* counted more than five hundred thousand adherents in 1909, while the "white" or Catholic Labor *Leagues* had about one hundred thousand (compare Guichonnet in Droz 1974, 2:269 with Zaninelli and Tramontin, cited above). Small industry and agriculture were heavily represented in both the red and the white organizations.

These "chambers" and "leagues" were local or at best regional groupings. The socialists also had a head start of a few years in forming national labor federations (metalworkers, 1896; farmworkers, 1901). The first struggling, national Christian trade union was that of textile workers, founded in 1906 by Achille Grandi (DSMCI 2:260) and concentrated around Milan in Lombardy. Perhaps the existence of the Economic-Social Union at the national level offset to some extent the organizational lag of Christian labor, at least in the agricultural sector. But the absence of any Christian labor deputies in parliament certainly held back the white cause. Giolitti could and did officially ignore the existence of Christian unions; the government dealt only with socialists on labor questions, for example, on legislation in support of collectives.

Although unions or "leagues" of farmworkers were still small (only 37,000 of the 100,000 workers organized by the "whites" in 1909–10), they would continue to grow. Even in 1910, they were a force to be reckoned with where they existed. They predominated in the areas of nonirrigated farming in Lombardy (with centers in Milan, Bergamo, Brescia, the latter two veritable Catholic strongholds and the birthplaces respectively of Popes John XXIII, in 1881, and Paul VI, in 1897). They encouraged scientific farming practices suitable for small, entrepreneurial farmers like Roncalli senior (Hebblethwaite 1985, 7, 92). A parish credit union would enable the future pope's father, in 1919, to purchase the farm they lived on (cash crop: silkworm cocoons). Socialist organizers, on the other hand, had more luck in the Po valley with its irrigated fields and large holdings. Venetia presented a similar picture: around Cremona, the redoubtable Guido Miglioli (DSMCI 2:379–84), a son of the soil with degrees in letters and law and, like most other organizers of his generation, inspired by the early Murri, had signal success in organizing the dairy-farm sharecroppers. From 1916 to the Fascist takeover he would be president of the national peasants' union. While areas like those surrounding Bergamo and Cremona really were covered with the much-apostrophized "thick net" of Catholic social institutions, the labor situation of the country as a whole more closely resembled a red and white checkerboard, with the red predominating but not overwhelming the white.

Church-Related Labor Unions

Among the differences between Catholic and socialist unions, which propagandists such as Sturzo, Rezzara, and Miglioli emphasized, was a different approach to the matter of class tensions. Each camp had its internal divisions between reformists and radicals and between their various shadings. The extreme clericals on the one side and the extreme anticlericals and materialists on the other repelled each other mightily, while there were areas of possible overlap between the reformist socialists and social Catholics. One author has spoken of the "love-hate relationship" of the Christian democrats with the socialists. The revolutionary socialists often had the upper hand in grassroots organizing on the socialist side, and even the reformist politicos like Turati aimed ultimately at replacing private property and entrepreneurial initiative with collective state control of land and capital. By contrast, the Catholic unionizers aimed for the most part at redressing the balance between workers and owners by whatever immediate pragmatic agreements could be arrived at. In the longer term, they did not wish to foment class war, but to organize the working classes so that they could soon assume a larger role, aiming ultimately at a future social partnership of the different classes and functions of economic society. We have seen how the early Christian democrats were corporatists. Although the Catholic labor movement had to overcome (or at least bracket out for the time being) a kind of utopian interclass solidarism, so as to get to the stage of labor unions at all, it never forgot that the class struggle was to be provisional and conditional, not final or absolute (Malgeri 1980, 2:88–92).

Thus the attitude of Christian labor unions to strikes was different from that prevailing in much of the socialist labor movement in Italy, with its anarchist and revolutionary as well as reformist tendencies. The Catholics did resort to strikes and work stoppages on occasion, as we have seen. But they regarded them as a last resort, using criteria analogous to those set down for a "just war." In his 1911 report (Malgeri 1980, 3:231; see DSMCI 3:223–25), Mario Chiri knew of 114 local strikes organized by Catholic groups up to 1909, involving over 10,000 workers: 73 of them went in the victory column. In the same period the "strike-happy" socialists staged more than 10,000 walkouts (4,000 under reformist auspices and 6,000 by the anarcho-syndicalists). The cost-benefit ratio of the strikes can probably not be established, but the Catholics, at least, were convinced that theirs was the more effective approach. By defending labor interests aggressively while holding strikes in reserve, the Christian unions were able to settle 175 disputes in the same period, involving almost 80,000 workers, and achieving positive outcomes in 158 of them.

There were some memorable strikes under "white" auspices, both in manufacturing and in agriculture (Malgeri 1980, 3:232f.). Of course, in those areas where the manufacturers or landowners were actually Catholics themselves, a strike action blessed by priests seemed particularly scandalous to some, bringing up the question of labor autonomy. Bergamo, for example, was not only a center of the corporatist but open social Catholicism of Medolago Albani and the thriving economic associationism of Nicolò Rezzara, but also of one of the most prominent clerico-moderate accords in the 1904 and subsequent elections. Radini Tedeschi became its bishop in 1905 and promptly chose the young church history professor at the seminary, don Angelo Roncalli, to be his secretary. In 1907 the bishop could stay out of a prolonged but successful strike in the local textile industry. In 1909, however, a factory at Ranica fired a Catholic union steward. For more than forty days eight hundred workers picketed. Radini Tedeschi saw a principle at stake, the right of labor to organize the better to deal with the powerful organization of capital, and spoke out in support of the workers, even though the discipline of the strikers left something to be desired. Perhaps only one whose intransigent credentials were so well attested could afford to take such a stand in the midst of the clerico-moderate ascendancy. But that he found it an evident duty to defend the right to organize along class lines, while others, including the pope, were still championing "social hierarchy" and "mixed unions," is emblematic of how far the social consciousness of engaged Catholics had evolved, even after *Graves de communi.*

The Italian "Social Weeks" furnish another symptom of the same evolution in outlook among basically or originally intransigent Catholics. Following the example of the French Semaines sociales, themselves an adaptation of the educational work of the German Volksverein, Toniolo's Unione popolare organized a week-long conference each year on a social theme. In 1911 in Assisi, at the sixth Social Week, the "People's Union" discussed presentations on "professional unions." Abbé, now Canon, Pottier, who was transferred from Liège to Rome in 1901, pointed out how it was not necessarily foreordained that unions be Catholic (Malgeri 1980, 3:234). Their aims being economic, unions could be quite independent of the church, just like other economic institutions (cooperatives, banks, insurance companies, manufacturing enterprises, etc.). Catholics could take part in them, so long as their practice and their declared ways, means, and ends were not in conflict with Catholic morality. This latter was unfortunately the case, for historical reasons, where unions idolized the class struggle, rejected private property, or advocated violence as a matter of policy. Thus Pottier, arguing deductively in a Neo-Thomist framework while fully alive to the empirical realities, suggested a perspective in which a unitary labor movement might be envisaged, one quite independent of hierarchical control.

This was, in fact, along with the matter of strikes, the other most troublesome issue for the Christian unions: their *de jure* "confessional character." *De facto* they were of course organizations largely of and for Catholics. There was as yet no practical prospect of making common cause with the socialists. The Socialist party turned down even the symbolic application of Felice Perroni and Guglielmo Quadrotta (DSMCI 2:523–25) of the *Nova et vetera* group in Rome, when they wished to become card-carrying socialists as Christians in 1908. But the practical issue was very close to that of Murri's, the matter of autonomy. In attending to basically secular concerns from a Christian commitment to "natural" justice in the political or economic realm, should Catholics be taking direction from their ordained pastors and bishops? If so, what kind of direction, at what level, with what leeway for the individual's conscientious initiatives in concrete situations?

Should the hierarchy, for example, undertake to adjudicate and compose the differences that arise in a modern capitalistic society between the different economic parties? If not, would the church abdicate all responsibility for the influence of morality on political and economic life? Somewhere between these two extremes Catholics continue to seek a contingently appropriate response, beyond clericalism and doctrinaire liberalism. Around 1910, the discussion focussed on the confessional character of the Christian labor movement, not only in Italy, but, as we shall see, in Germany and France as well. In theological terms, the ecclesiology of the time was insufficiently differentiated to offer much in the way of helpful clarifications. More broadly, the question of the confessional character of Christian labor unions was a practical case study of the longstanding and unsolved theological problem of the relation of the natural and the supernatural. Blondel (1910) commented on it in France, but not in terms that could be immediately helpful or in any way acceptable to integralist Catholics.

One of the reasons for the increasingly dysfunctional relationship between Medolago Albani's Economic-Social Union and the labor unions that formed a small part of its constituency was the official insistence on strict confessionality. The labor leagues were to be oriented to the economic needs and rights of their membership, to be sure, but they were considered first of all to be organs of the church, subordinate to the hierarchy and its judgment as to what were the overriding religious (or ecclesiastical) interests. Even those who would play down the confessionality of workers' associations, like Toniolo, did so only as a tactic, a tactic that was rejected by Pius X in 1910 as base and counterproductive (Malgeri 1980, 3:228–30). And yet, as Tramontin states, this debate contributed to make clear to the union leaders, most of whom subscribed up until then to a mitigated confessional character and control by the hierarchy (after all, they parted with Murri on this point), that this hybrid condition was incompatible with an effective union movement. Some other way or ways of relating Christian values to the secular realities of the workplace would have to be found, other, that is, than subjecting labor organizations to hierarchical control as if it were a matter of the administration of sacraments. As with Sturzo in the political sector, the labor leaders would get their chance during the next pontificate, that of Benedict XV (1914–22).

Chapter 14

THE VOLKSVEREIN AND THE CHRISTIAN LABOR MOVEMENT IN GERMANY

In the early years of the twentieth century, German Catholicism, with its associations, with the Center party strength in the Reichstag and the Landtage, and with the imposing organization of the Volksverein für das katholische Deutschland, was the envy of Catholics elsewhere (E. Ritter 1954, 201; Agócs 1975). In the United States, Fr. Peter E. Dietz emulated its training courses in the social studies institutes he organized under the auspices of the Central Verein (NCE 4:865). Georges Goyau wrote about it in France and Ernesto Vercesi in Italy, among others. Crucial to its origins and character were the legacy of Ketteler and the practical example of Kolping, but especially the wholly uncorporatist influence of Franz Brandts and a last initiative of Ludwig Windthorst. The Volksverein's subsequent responsiveness to a rapidly changing social situation, characterized by the industrial development and labor unionizing of the 1890s (see chapter 6), led it down paths not contemplated at its beginnings.

As in Italy and the other countries with Christian unions, the need for autonomy in the Catholic lay organizations, and especially in the Christian labor movement, forced the issue of hierarchical control. This controversy over the legitimacy of trade unions, the so-called *Gewerkschaftsstreit*, started early in Germany (1900) and involved the Volksverein, the labor movement, and the Center party in a common cause identified with "Cologne" or "Mönchengladbach" in the Rhineland, as opposed to "Berlin" with its episcopal supporters in Breslau and Trier. The stories are so intertwined that they must be told together (for recent brief accounts, beside Aubert 1978, 154ff., see Greschat 1980, 199–208, and Hürten in Rauscher 1982, 2:248–55).

262

Early Years of the Volksverein (1890–1900)

In Central Europe (Boyer 1981, x, 1–4, 113–23), a "Christian" party, especially a "Christian-Social" party, naturally turned to anti-Semitism in its efforts to dislodge the liberals. Windthorst, however, was singularly respectful of the rights of all minorities. He tended to see the Jews as another religious minority, like the Catholics, rather than as privileged or exploitative beneficiaries of economic and political liberalism. (On this see M. Anderson 1981, 251–60; see 391–93 for the following account, based also on E. Ritter 1954, 137–52, Heitzer 1979, 15–57, Brose 1985, 61–81, and ultimately on August Pieper's unpublished memoires.) When representatives of the Central European, aristocratic, corporatist wing of Catholicism inclined to anti-Semitism came up with the idea of a populist organization for Catholics to repel the anti-Catholic propaganda of the newly founded Protestant League in the late 1880s, Windthorst managed to fend them off by pointing to a more serious rival, especially for the Center party: socialism.

The backers of the 1883 Haid theses around Prince Löwenstein had received the support of Bishops Haffner of Mainz and Korum of Trier for their idea of a "confessionalist," anti-Protestant league. Windthorst, for his part, got the backing of influential Rhenish Center party stalwarts. At the Katholikentag in Coblenz in 1890 he had the whole purpose of the proposed organization recast. Now it would be to educate Catholics on a mass basis about their civic duties and outlook, as opposed to the errors of the Social Democratic party program. He also prevailed upon Franz Brandts to be the head of the Volksverein and locate its central offices in Mönchengladbach, where Franz Hitze could take over its day-to-day direction.

The remarkable growth of the Volksverein was due to its timeliness and to a new strategy of direct individual low-cost membership, with local agents, for the most part working closely with parish clergy and lay Catholic leaders of the Center party, and providing the various Catholic men's organizations with a common educational service through its publications and speakers. Its founding coincidentally followed the dismissal of Bismarck by the new emperor, William II, signalling a new approach to social policy on the part of the government. Windthorst died in early 1891, never really having concerned himself much with social legislation; but Franz Hitze, who had been a member of parliament since 1884, took advantage of his well-placed acquaintances (for example, Hans Berlepsch, the social reformer who enjoyed the emperor's confidence until 1896) to propose and modify the social legislation that ensued (Roos in Rauscher 1982, 2:115). With the indirect backing of the new mass organization, as its first expert on social policy, and as the Center party's main spokesperson on labor matters, Hitze became a force to be reckoned with.

Besides Brandts and Hitze among the Volksverein's founders was Karl Trimborn (Schoelen 1982, 534–41, and ZgLb 1:81–102), a lawyer from Cologne active in the Center party. He was vice chairman and succeeded Brandts as chairman in 1914. He was also the regional head of the organization for the Rhineland. The Cologne banker Johann Elkan served as treasurer of the organization until 1912. Other original members of the board, who not only lent prestige to the Volksverein but distinguished themselves through their active commitment, included Adolf Gröber (Schoelen 1982, 231), a lawyer from Württemberg who was a Center deputy in the Reichstag since 1887. He was the chief organizer of the Volksverein for Württemberg. Felix Porsch (Schoelen 1982, 440; ZgLb 1:113–28) represented Breslau (the present Wroclaw in Poland) in the Reichstag from 1881 to 1893, also in the Prussian Landtag from 1884 to 1918 and 1921 to 1930; he was therefore a leading Center politician as well as head of the Silesian region of the Volksverein (this until 1899), while serving on the Church(-State) Council of the huge archdiocese of Breslau under Cardinal Kopp — a delicate combination!

There were other laymen (until 1908, it was an exclusively male organization), including trade unionists, charged with great responsibility in Mönchengladbach, as will be apparent. But the leading clergy had the greater influence, starting with Hitze (Schoelen 1982, 267–300) and his successor as general secretary of the Volksverein, August Pieper (Schoelen 1982, 392–435; ZgLb 4:114–32). Hitze had certainly laid the groundwork for the labor orientation of the organization and exercised great continuing influence; Pieper responded more pro-actively to the rapid social developments of the 1890s. He was in direct charge of the Volksverein's section for "social information" and, together with another priest, of its publishing house, the Volksvereinsverlag.

Hitze and Pieper propagated *Arbeitervereine* ("trade associations" for Catholics only). These trade groups or Catholic workers' clubs pursued the cultural, spiritual, and vocational welfare of the workers under the guidance of priests, more or less in the spirit of Adolph Kolping's *Gesellenvereine* (that is, with an accent on worker self-improvement and without involving any employers). The high level of literacy in Germany, along with the Kolping precedent (presumably significant at least for the priests who were engaged in the work), attenuated the overlay of paternalism that accompanied these efforts. Trade associations were the formula Hitze started out with and saw reinforced by *Rerum novarum* in 1891, but they were not to remain the only form of labor organization among Catholics for long (Aretz in Rauscher 1982, 2:163–69).

The Volksverein idea found an immediate positive response, reflected in the membership figures of 1891, over one hundred thousand. The staff in Mönchengladbach saw themselves as engaged in building up a great popular propaganda and educational apparatus in the interest of Christian social reform. This required first of all a method for broad popular training (*Volksbildung*), by means of what one might call "extension courses" (Heitzer 1979, 25–28). Hitze developed this method quickly.

After launching the work of the Volksverein, Hitze kept close tabs on it, even after he became professor for Catholic pastoral "sociology" (Catholic social teaching) in Münster in 1893. This was the first such chair in Germany, a delayed response to one of Ketteler's proposals to the bishops in 1869. That Hitze, with all his duties, could only be a part-time legislator was not so unusual at the time. Members of parliament were expected to have some other source of income — which was always a sore point with Windthorst and other "democrats." Like many of his colleagues in Berlin, Hitze had to balance his legislative work with other professional occupations.

The first "practical-social course" was held for two weeks in September of 1892 (Heitzer 1979, 233ff.). Having advertised in the Center newspapers and expecting around 50 participants, Hitze was surprised to receive 580 registrations from all over Germany. Designed as an introduction to social questions with practical exercises for organizing at the grassroots, this course was the first of eight similar courses organized by the Volksverein that made the tour of German cities in the next eight years. To encourage continued study after this introduction, Hitze drew up and distributed a list of recommended social-science literature. This was drawn largely from the publications of the so-called academic socialists in the Social Policy Association, which he later joined. One of the more important leaders in the Social Policy Association was Lujo Brentano, of a prominent Catholic family, a champion of trade unions on the English model and professor in Munich. But he was estranged from the church, and there were no other trained Catholic economists or political scientists until some Volksverein personnel went for higher degrees. After 1900 a doctorate in a relevant discipline was a requisite for joining the Mönchengladbach team.

The headquarters staff was also called upon to hold courses or conferences to advance the education of special groups, first the clergy who were heads of Catholic trade associations (1894, Bavaria), then the local agents of the Volksverein and the leadership of trade unions. As August Pieper would later write: "Hundreds of mid- and lower-level popular leaders must be trained, before those for whom social legislation has been passed would learn about it and the opportunities it created" (cited Heitzer 1979, 239; see Heitzer 1979, appendix II, 7, for table of courses given between 1892 and 1914).

Another approach was through publications. In its first numbers, *Der Volksverein*, a sixteen-page periodical that appeared six or eight times a year, only managed to appeal to its readers — the original one hundred thousand members — through its denunciations of social democracy, a popular theme with the clergy and agricultural workers and artisans. In its efforts to find a popular tone, it did not at first propose any alternative social vision beyond moralism and calls for mutual charity. When August Pieper came to Mönchengladbach in 1892, he went for social-political substance at an elementary level, still in rather primitive polemic with socialism (Heitzer 1979, 265). The response was minimal, except for complaints that the magazine was not entertaining enough. Gradually, all the same, the pedagogical efforts of the Volksverein, by dint of persistent organization and courses and other presentations, developed its own audience. By the turn of the century, Pieper and Brandts could look back and take pride in the fact that anti-socialist propaganda had faded somewhat into the background, whereas information and insight into the social problems of industrial Germany were being broadly communicated. A greater attention to social issues and a higher quality of commentary on them could also be found in other Catholic papers, thanks in good part to a press service that the Volksverein started to provide them without charge.

The spread of information and ideas of relevance to the workers' condition was of such high priority that the Volksverein pursued it in several other ways as well. Already in 1893 (an election year), it printed and distributed well over a million two-to-four-page handbills or "flyers" through its membership. This method evidently proved itself effective, since millions of flyers were printed every year thereafter on religious, economic, or social issues.

Objections to the handling of controversial issues were matters to be argued over within the political circles and labor groups close to the Volksverein. Bishops were consulted, if at all, only informally, since the Volksverein was not an ecclesiastical organization in any clerical or canonical sense. The archbishop of Cologne was the most important church official for the Volksverein, given Mönchengladbach's location in his archdiocese. Apart from a few extremely troublesome exceptions, the German episcopate showed understanding and appreciation for the directions the Volksverein took in supporting but also moderating the Catholic labor movement. Two of the archbishops of Cologne, in particular, welcomed the work of Mönchengladbach,

Philip Krementz (archbishop since 1885) and Antonius Fischer (archbishop since 1903; see Hegel 1987, 582–88).

The Rise of Christian Labor Unions

In the years following the great Ruhr coalminers' strike of 1889 and the lifting of the anti-socialist law in 1890, many labor unions (*Gewerkschaften*, as they came to be called) were formed out of earlier guild-like or mutual benefit societies, or as altogether new organizations. Catholic workers were often involved in them. However, anticlericalism in either its "liberal" or its "socialist" form was rife in the labor movement, making it difficult for churchgoing Catholics to feel at home in either the Hirsch-Duncker (liberal) or "free" unions, the latter federated in Carl Legien's "General Commission" and represented in the Reichstag by August Bebel. "When asked late in life why they had" founded or "joined Christian trade unions, many veteran activists responded that insults, practical jokes, and occasional blows from 'enlightened' colleagues had made their lives miserable until they banded together with other Christian workers" (Patch 1985, 7).

Until recently, the free trade unions were the only ones whose history was well known. In the 1980s, however, historians have also produced detailed studies of the Christian unions, those that gathered together in 1899 in the Gesamtverband christlicher Gewerkschaften (henceforth GcG). The works of Hans Dieter Denk, Michael Schneider, and Eric Dorn Brose have cast much light on the struggles of the Christian unions in the period from 1894 into the new century.

The year 1894 is taken as the starting date, because it was in that year that August Brust founded the Union of Christian Miners, which would survive and form the nucleus of the Gesamtverband (Brose 1985, 83–116; Schneider 1982, 55–63). The union he had supported since 1889 had been taken over by the socialists, in the sense that "militant Social Democrats eliminated [Christian miners] from all powerful positions" in the union (Patch 1985, 14). And the Catholic *Arbeiterverein*, to which he also belonged, was not set up to carry out conflicts with employers. Even a writer in the old-line Catholic journal *Historisch-Politische Blätter* had argued in 1892 that trade unions were needed for the improvement of working conditions and pay, alongside the "trade associations" (Aretz in Rauscher 1982, 2:170). So the miner Brust, of Essen, in consultation with local Catholic and Protestant clergy, journalists, and bourgeois party figures, started his rival union.

The original statutes of the new union gave a council of Catholic and Protestant clergyman and other bourgeois notables a decisive influence, as a pledge of willingness to cultivate interclass understanding. Brust was determined to draw Protestant miners as well as Catholic ones, and indeed any miner who would respect the religious sensibilities of their churchgoing brethren. The difference from the free union, now called the "old union," was clear on both scores. The second trait, interconfessionalism, would remain a hallmark of the Christian unions in Germany. The first one, readiness to cooperate across class lines on the basis of the prevailing legal and governmental order, also continued to distinguish the Christian unions from the socialist General Commission, although growing class consciousness and the frustration of not being treated as partners on an equal footing with the bourgeoisie introduced an evolution into the movement that could not be denied expression. Another provision of the statutes would plague the Union of Christian Miners for years: dues were set at half the level of the old union, making it impossible to hire organizers ("agitators") or build up a strike fund. This was to bank too much on the effectiveness of sympathetic bourgeois influence on mine owners and politicians and not enough on labor's own resources.

In due course this became clear to Brust and to a parish priest who edited the union's paper on the side, Heinrich Brauns (ZgLb 1:148–59 and Schoelen 1982, 152–66). When the union finally supported an actual strike (in 1898, precipitated, curiously enough, by some workers taking off work on a holiday recognized only by Catholics), Hitze and Ludwig Weber, the Protestant labor vicar from Mönchengladbach, resigned from this council, or honorary board, of the Christian Miners Union (Brose 1985, 113). Brust and his supporters could now allow this council to fall into innocuous desuetude. The Christian union had overtaken the old union in numbers of members, for the moment; it had retained the support of some Catholic and Protestant clergy; it could afford to let Brust quit the mines and become a full-time union editor, officer, and propagandist (until 1904). Though hard times lay ahead, and despite what the socialists would say, the movement of autonomous Christian trade unions had emerged in Germany.

The manifestation of this was in the congress of Christian unionists held in 1899 in Mainz. Although the miners' union in Essen was the strongest Christian trade union, it was not to remain the only one for long. In Munich, a priest named Lorenz Huber, living modestly on inherited money and devoting himself to the cause of labor, advocated unions in addition to trade groups as early as 1891. When he could not get the support of other leaders of the *Arbeitervereine* to warm up to the idea, he pursued their idea of subsections of the Catholic trade groups to concern themselves with the "material interests" of the workers as well as their mental and spiritual improvement (Denk

1980, 57–58 and 250–55). Although these half-baked structures were of little use, by his untiring efforts Huber was able to form a half-dozen workers from different trades into future union leaders. They had the opportunity to hone their thinking and learn to express themselves in writing in the columns of *Der Arbeiter*, a weekly paper that Huber edited for the trade groups membership. In a way, Huber operated a one-man Volksverein in the heart of Bavaria and, unlike Hitze, he endorsed unionism from the beginning of the 1890s. In his area of influence, for example, the mechanic Carl Schirmer founded a textile workers organization in 1895 that was ripe for incorporation into the national federation of Christian trade unions (GcG) at the turn of the century. Textile workers had also formed Christian unions in other regions (Krefeld, Mönchengladbach, Aachen, etc.; see Schneider for more detailed information, here 1982, 80), as did construction workers, metalworkers, and woodworkers.

But of course Legien's General Commission, with 58 affiliated unions, 269 full-time functionaries, and 21 support funds for union travel and striking workers, was far ahead of the embryonic Christian unions (Brose 1985, 118; see Denk 1980, 256). Just how great the gap had become came home to the German Catholic labor leaders who attended an International Congress for the Defense of Labor in Zurich (August 1897). The list of those who got to know each other at this congress makes for interesting reading. There were two workers from Bavaria encouraged by Fr. Huber: Hans Braun, a stonemason, and the aforementioned Carl Schirmer; the journalist and secretary of the Catholic *Arbeitervereine* of Württemberg, Matthias Erzberger (ZgLb 1:103–12); Johannes Giesberts (Schoelen 1982, 218–30), who was working in the boiler room of the publishing house of J. P. Bachem at the time, but was soon to edit the *Westdeutsche Arbeiterzeitung*; and Paul Weigel of Berlin, a construction worker whose modest interconfessional union would seem so threatening to a concerned integralist in 1900.

They all were determined to promote Christian trade unionism as a result of what they heard in Zurich. On the one hand, they could see the potential of the trade union movement to put workers on the societal map in Germany as in Britain; but on the other, they were unable to make common cause with ideological adversaries unwilling to bury differences in *Weltanschauung* for purposes of economic advancement. But when they got back home, they discovered that the *Arbeiterverein* leaders and the Center party newspaper editorialists really did not mean what they said when they advocated the formation of Christian unions. Schirmer's attempt to open eyes to abuses in the textile industry (a pay system evidently based on some kind of piecework count) by simply collecting and presenting the facts brought down on him the denunciations of the *Augsburger Postzeitung* (Denk 1980, 259). Apart from Lorenz Huber, there was little readiness among trade association chaplains to support even this measured assertiveness on the part of workers' representatives.

But some Christian trade unions (or organizations well on the way to becoming actual unions) had survived birth. August Brust advocated a central organization for all the Christian unions of Germany. Erzberger agreed and helped prepare for it by organizing a conference of South German union leaders and possible supporters of the idea. It was clear to all who seriously contemplated unionization that a national organization, like the free unions' General Commission, was a source of strength and a great stimulus to the expansion of the union movement (Brose 1985, 120–31, who is at pains to put the day-to-day developments in the context of the political life of the empire and of German Catholicism — notably the Volksverein and the Katholikentag at Krefeld in 1898). Meanwhile, August Pieper had come to the conviction that full-orbed Christian unions were a necessity. So he willingly accepted Archbishop Krementz's appointment as head of a new diocesan federation of *Arbeitervereine* in 1898, with his right-hand man in Mönchengladbach, Fr. Otto Müller (ZgLb 3:191–203) as secretary general. At a convention of the *Arbeitervereine* in Essen in October of that year, a resolution was passed in favor of interconfessional trade unionism; the idea was not left to the individual *Arbeitervereine* to bring to realization, since Pieper had Müller, Brauns, Giesberts, and other labor hands commissioned to instigate the founding of new unions.

Thus, when the first National Congress of Christian Trade Unions was convoked in Mainz (for Pentecost 1899), breaches had been made in the Catholic and clerical consciousness of the German church in favor of this further development beyond the trade groups. No howls of indignation greeted the formation of a central committee to promote the formation of more unions. In the "Mainz Guidelines" passed by the forty-eight mostly worker delegates, the basic character of this development was clearly set forth (Patch 1985, 17; Schneider 1982, 123):

> The trade unions shall stand on the foundation of Christianity but will be interconfessional, i.e., embrace members of both Christian confessions. The trade unions shall also be nonpartisan, i.e., affiliated with no particular political party. The discussion of partisan political issues is to be avoided, but the implementation of legal reforms on the basis of the existing social order shall be discussed.

A substantial step toward realizing Brust's plan of a centralized federation of Christian unions was taken by establishing a central committee. As Brose relates (1985, 131):

> Heading the organization was a twelve-member central commission led by Brust, Erzberger, Weigel, Schirmer, and Braun. The commission would gather statistics, edit a new union newspaper, execute the resolutions of future congresses, and promote Christian trade unions of the variety outlined in the Mainz program (*Mainzer Leitsätze*). Fulfillment of this last task had been made easier during the fall and winter of 1898/99 by the establishment of numerous new organizations throughout the West, South, and East, and by the continued growth of the older unions. As a result, there were now 108,000 Christian trade unionists in Germany, 65,000 of whom had joined the national organization at Mainz. And in certain areas of Germany like the Rhineland, Christian unions had managed to regain much of the ground lost to the free unions since the late 1870s.

It must be stressed, with Brose, that neither the interconfessional makeup of the Christian unions nor their party-political independence was a mere theoretical postulate, but a serious practical reality. Unlike the Center party, for instance, which was nonconfessional on principle but in practice Roman Catholic, and unlike the trade groups, which could be Protestant or Catholic but not mixed, the trade unions were *inter*confessional: professing to "stand on the foundation of Christianity" but organizationally independent of any church hierarchy. The emphasis on "positive" if noncanonical Christianity was not necessarily regarded as essential to trade unionism as such, but in the circumstances it was imposed upon Christian workers by the anticlerical attitudes and discriminatory measures of the free unions.

In British or American circumstances, as with the Knights of Labor or the American Federation of Labor, things had not taken such an unhappy turn and hence there was no need to set up a separate Christian labor movement. Thus, at the second congress (Frankfurt, 1900), "Brust and Giesberts declared that ideologically neutral trade unions for all workers were their ideal, that merger between the Christian and free unions could occur if the latter would 'renounce Marxism' and sever their ties with the Social Democratic party" (Patch 1985, 17–18). They were moved to make this point because of signs of movement both within the socialist and the bourgeois camps toward a united labor movement. In 1899 Hans von Berlepsch and Franz Hitze (and Johannes Giesberts) joined to form a new Society for Social Reform uniting progressive bureaucrats, academics, and bourgeois politicians with Christian and Hirsch-Duncker trade unionists. On the socialist side, though, the free unions refused to let down their guard against co-optative moves from the bourgeoisie. The "revisionist" Eduard Bernstein saw some legitimacy and promise in the Christian labor outlook — but he was practically alone in doing so.

The Mainz Guidelines specified unions organized by industry, with local groups of the same industry represented by delegates elected for conventions of the national unions, thus indicating to would-be labor activists the structure they should aim at in the interests of a strong national movement. As tasks of the unions they named funds for insurance against unemployment, sickness, accidents, and disability as well as labor exchanges, as long as government failed to arrange for these needs adequately. Research reports, meetings with speakers, newsletters and newspapers for members, and the presentation of the concerns of workers to their employers were all listed as necessary activities of the unions, once established.

The strike was explicitly deemed an acceptable way of asserting the claims of workers for better treatment, but only "as a last resort and if success seems probable." (Soon it became clear that the constellation of forces demanded rather consistent and frequent resort to strikes — otherwise the membership "resorted" quickly to the free unions.) This was set, however, in a framework sharply distinct from and opposed to the class consciousness characteristic of the prevalent socialist approach. For this reason I cite the fifth Guideline in full (Schneider 1982, 124):

5. UNION TACTICS

It must not be forgotten that workers and entrepreneurs have common interests. Not only are both partners linked inseparably together as labor factors, with a common interest in upholding the right of appropriate compensation for work as distinguished from capital, but they both represent the interests of production of goods as distinguished from consumption.

Both partners legitimately claim the greatest possible return on their stake in the production of goods: the entrepreneur on his capital and the worker on his labor. Without each, capital and labor, there is no production.

It follows that a conciliatory spirit should pervade all the activities of trade unions. Demands must be moderate, but they must be firmly and decisively asserted.

Walkouts may be used only as a last resort and when success seems probable.

The typical Catholic stress on the connectedness of the different groups in society, promoting harmony and averse to any social Darwinism, comes through clearly, in a way comparable to Toniolo's 1894 "Milan Program" (as in chapter 13). Shorn of all specifically corporatist proposals, the heritage of the Volksverein and of Franz Hitze is here integrated into a trade union perspective. An authoritative aura accrued to the Mainz Guidelines over the years. Nevertheless, they were found increasingly unacceptable by the tendency called integralism.

Christian Labor and Volksverein in Synergy

The Gewerkschaftsstreit *(I)*

Adam Stegerwald (ZgLb 1:206–19) was a cabinetmaker in Munich when his comrades in that section of Huber's *Arbeiterschutz* delegated him to go to the 1899 Mainz congress. He had belonged to a Kolping association in 1893; it is an indication of how reluctant most of the Bavarian clergy were to promote trade unionism that, when he joined the Arbeiterschutz, he had to end his Kolping membership. When the new Gesamtverband (GcG; League of Christian Trade Unions) got itself organized and offered him the paid position of general secretary in Cologne, he was of course happy to accept. He started in his new office on 1 January 1903. Thus it was Stegerwald who presided over the development of the GcG, from 84,600 members in 1902 to 188,000 in 1905 and 342,000 in 1913. Although remaining far behind the hopes one could realistically harbor for them, the Christian unions became the second largest body of unionized workers in Germany, at a ratio of 1:6 with the socialist unions. The Hirsch-Duncker unions were left behind in third place (Schneider 1982, 366).

Johannes Giesberts, meanwhile, functioned as liaison between Christian labor and the Volksverein from 1903 to 1914. At first he stayed on as editor of the *Westdeutsche Arbeiterzeitung*, the newspaper of the Catholic trade groups, while also editing the GcG newsletter and later its *Zentralblatt*. In 1905, however, he was elected to the Reichstag (and the following year also into the Prussian legislature), turning the *Westdeutsche* over to the less militant Joseph Joos (ZgLb 1:236–50 and Schoelen 1982, 317–32; Joos was a worker like Giesberts — a pattern-maker; he was also a participant in an intensive Volksverein course; however, he was never a member of a trade union).

After 1900, the Volksverein courses at Mönchengladbach underwent a reorganization in response to the need to train lay workers more intensively; as it was, local bodies, once started, were dying on the vine for lack of local leadership (Heitzer 1979, 239f.). Ten-week-long courses in political economy were the main pillar of this effort, attended each year by dozens of labor leaders. Shorter vacation courses for priests and professional people were also offered, as well as six-day courses for artisans, salespeople, farmers, officeworkers, teachers, civil servants, and technicians. The person in charge of all this was now Heinrich Brauns, the "red priest" who supported August Brust in Essen. Between 1903 and 1905 he also acquired a doctorate in political science.

A third prominent member of the Mönchengladbach labor team, another "red priest" in the eyes of industrialists, was Otto Müller, director of social (labor) organizing. He preceded Brauns by a year in doctoral studies, with a dissertation in economics on "the Christian Trade Unions in Germany" giving special attention to the miners' and textile workers' organizations, the earliest attempt at a comprehensive account of the GcG.

Working with Pieper in the Volksverein since 1899 and studying Hitze's writings, Müller shared the perspective on the labor question that was by now dominant in Volksverein and West German *Arbeiterverein* circles (Aretz in ZgLb 3:192). First of all, given the antisocial attitude of the "liberal" manufacturers and the progress of socialist ideas, it was worse than useless for the clergy to maintain a paternalistic stance toward workers. Although workers as an oppressed "class" might be a threat to social order, the solution was not authoritarianism, but the creation of conditions in which the working class might become an "estate" (*Stand*) on an equal footing with property-owners and others. What he meant by "estate" in contrast to "class" had little to do with corporatist notions. It was simply that "classes," on this understanding, were groupings that fought with each other for survival and predominance in the "class struggle," whereas "estates" would acknowledge other estates' interests and their right to exist and hence would cooperate with each other in the interests of all. The ideal was solidarity not just among proletarians but across all of society. (This ideal of "solidarism" was put into theoretical form above all by Heinrich Pesch, S.J., 1854–1926; see ZgLb 3:136–48, Mueller 1941 and 1980, and Ruhnau 1980.) To talk of the "class struggle" was to designate the problem, not the solution (also Gundlach 1929). To become an estate, what the working class ultimately needed was recognition and integration into the German Empire, which were conspicuously lacking. To gain that recognition, they urgently needed an effective representation of their material interests (through trade unions) as well as knowledge, insight, education (the tasks of the *Arbeitervereine*).

In this "division of labor," Müller pursued the latter tasks, construing them so as to include making propaganda for Christian unionism within his job description. Having been involved with the founding of the *Westdeutsche Arbeiterzeitung* and Pieper's efforts to form an interdiocesan league of *Arbeitervereine*, he became Pieper's right-hand man also in the latter organization, when it was finally established in 1903. Pieper was elected to head the new league and he asked Müller to become its first general secretary. Hardly had it been founded, when the league and Giesberts's *Westdeutsche Arbeiterzeitung* found themselves under fire in an early stage of a protracted controversy over, and at the side of, the interconfessional labor unions.

A frontal attack against the clearly stated interconfessional character of the Christian unions came first in a series of articles in an obscure church paper by Franz von Savigny of Berlin. Then the main Center party paper in Berlin, the *Germania*, picked up his viewpoint, and soon it was widely distributed among the clergy in northeastern Germany. Meanwhile the Frankfurt congress of the Christian trade unions took place (above) and raised the question whether, in principle, a single union movement should not be the goal in view, as a Volksverein publication on the subject suggested. Cardinal Georg Kopp (ZgLb 1:13–28) also addressed the Fulda bishops conference later in 1900 on the subject of labor organizations, opposing interconfessional unions (text in Gatz 1979, 2:408; Brose 1985, 147–57; see also Schneider 1982, 175, Heitzer 1983, 50–60, and Brack 1976, 23–50; also E. Ritter's older narrative, 1954, 313–45, representing the Cologne/Mönchengladbach view of the whole Gewerkschaftsstreit).

The main strength of the opposition rested on the insistence of Leo XIII in *Rerum novarum* (no. 58) that workingmen's associations be placed on religious bases, that "religious instruction have the foremost place" in them (57) so as to maintain the proper moral and religious spirit. In this, Leo simply reflected the common conviction of nineteenth-century social Catholics of all stripes that only the Catholic religion had the moral and spiritual resources that society needed to solve its modern problems. Leo XIII preached this message to political and propertied classes and leaders as well as to labor.

Two issues were generally mixed together in these discussions. Sometimes the issue was the long-term orientation of the Christian unions, whether they should aim at the possibility of cooperation or merger with the free unions when genuine ideological neutrality could be established. Most bishops, it seems, looked askance at this kind of talk, and that is why they approved the Fulda Pastoral of 1900. But sometimes the issue was the interconfessionality of the existing Christian unions. Cardinal Kopp of Breslau and Bishop Michael Felix Korum of Trier definitely disapproved of these confessionally mixed trade unions; so did Pope Pius X, as it turned out. A third issue lay not far behind these two questions in some cases: was it legitimate for a Christian worker to belong to a striking union at all?

Where Cardinal Kopp stood in responding to this nest of questions from time to time was not always clear, except that he was always prone to suspect that the Volksverein line was secularistic, deep down. In the camp of Christian labor, likewise, the fault line of the Mainz propositions began to cause trouble. Giesberts found himself uttering ideas calculated to chill a bishop's ardor for church involvement in unionism ("Let us get rid of the notion that Christian unions are a religious institution") in polarization with Franz Wieber, head of the Christian metalworkers union. The latter pleaded for "positive Christian principles" and an end to any talk about joining up with any socialists (Heitzer 1983, 44–48; see Brose 1985, 154f.).

With an appeal to *Rerum novarum*, the German bishops issued a pastoral letter or instruction in August of 1900, at the instigation of Kopp, the head of the Fulda bishops conference (Gatz 1985, 3:5, 11–20). It was a reminder of the necessity of the religious and moral dimension in the Catholic workers associations. It mentioned their trade groups, but did not say anything about the Christian, interconfessional, trade unions. The bishops of the West and South, for the most part, interpreted their statement as not at all directed against the interconfessional unions, but as warning against any trend to deconfessionalizing the *Arbeitervereine*, which were after all Catholic church organizations. By extension, the bishops could be understood implicitly to discourage the secularization of the Christian trade *unions*. But, as they told their trade union leaders, they had no reservations about the existing interconfessional unions at all. Kopp, supported only by Korum, insisted instead on the address he gave and on the guidelines he attached, which were published along with the pastoral itself (see excerpts from Kopp's speech translated in Brose 1985, 149). The last guideline clearly stated that "the trade-unionist organization of Catholic workers must be Catholic and under the supervision of church authority" (Heitzer 1983, 52). No wonder that Christian trade unionists on strike in 1905 chanted,

> What do I care about *Rerum novorum*,
> I snap my fingers at Kopp and Korum!
> (from Ross 1976, 108, revised)

The bishops being so divided over the question, Pieper and the others at Mönchengladbach had to modulate their public advocacy of unions. The Volksverein was after all not itself a labor organization, but the mass association of all German Catholics of whatever "estate," and wished to become even more so. The *Kölnische Volks-*

zeitung (edited by Julius Bachem and Hermann Cardauns) carried on the fight against the *Germania*, with the *Westdeutsche Arbeiterzeitung*, so closely identified with the Volksverein, seconding its efforts indirectly, to the extent possible.

Meanwhile, on the organizational level, Kopp and Korum encouraged their *Arbeitervereine* to band together in 1903 in what was called "the League of Catholic Trade Associations (Berlin)" under a priest from Luxembourg, Heinrich Fournelle. Franz von Savigny, the retired magistrate, co-founded the League. Workers in the Berlin League were forbidden to join unions, although they could found trade groups for economic and occupational purposes, as long as they stayed within the exclusively Catholic trade association under clerical guidance. This was just the opposite of the practice in Müller's Western Arbeiterverein league, where simultaneous membership in a union was almost required. Immediately people started to speak and write of the antithesis between the Mönchengladbach and the Berlin factions or "tendencies" (*Richtungen:* one more *Richtungskampf* in the history of social Catholicism). If the Rhinelanders were called "democratic," the Berliners gloried in the name of "integral Catholics," as did their allies in Belgium, France, and Italy. By this the integrists simply meant that they were continuing undiminished and unintimidated the nineteenth-century papal campaign for a restoration of church influence over public life in all its dimensions, resisting what one did not yet call pluralism and all its ominous offspring (Poulat 1969a, s.v. "intégrisme" in index; also DSMCI 1/1:48–55).

Those others, who also thought of themselves as carrying on the cause of social Catholicism in an integrally Catholic way, but facing the problems presented by the age in which they lived, could not admit that they were departing in any significant respect from the course indicated by Leo XIII. The publication of *Graves de communi* was apparently not widely noticed in Germany; if it was, German inquirers would be told, as were the Belgians (above, chapter 11), that the pope certainly did not have in mind dismantling any organizations in Germany that the Volksverein supported. Bachem and other journalists pointed out common-sensically that no one ever suggested that Catholic entrepreneurs or bankers not join their trade associations, just because they were not under the control of the hierarchy. And besides, they argued, when Pope Leo wrote *Rerum novarum*, he could not have meant to exclude confessionally mixed trade unions, because none existed then. Others argued from the American case of the Knights of Labor and how Pope Leo had specifically declined to take action against its Catholic members. At various points in the controversy, the Catholic papers in Cologne tried to put an end to it, sure of the support of the ordinaries of Cologne and Paderborn and of the smaller dioceses. In 1904 the bishops "agreed to disagree" about the relative merits of interconfessional unions vs. Catholic trade groups and went their separate ways, encouraging either or both movements (Heitzer 1983, 92). Thus contentiousness flared up again and again.

The Gewerkschaftsstreit *(II)*

Savigny, for one, would not let Kopp accept a compromise that looked like defeat (e.g., Heitzer 1983, 143). And Kopp, with his autocratic leanings, was easily stirred up against the all too autonomous and democratically inclined Volksverein. Was this a Catholic association or not? There were no Protestants in it, to be sure, as there were in the unions. But where was the hierarchical control? Oblivious to the generations of lay initiative that stood behind German Catholicism by this time, the integralist prince-bishop of Breslau could not abide the openness to professedly lay influence and the independence of hierarchical control that the leading priests of the Volksverein displayed. If Kopp suggested in the direction of Fischer in Cologne that he regain control of the Catholic organizations in his province, the latter merely replied that the Christian unions were doing a fine job in preventing the alienation of the entire working class from the church — and let it be understood that anti-union trade associations were not up to the task. Kopp was reduced to proposing that at least a financial accounting of the Volksverein be made to the bishops conference, so as to bring it under a closer supervision than the archbishop of Cologne exercised.

Since there was no agreement in principle as to the legitimacy of mixed trade unions outside the immediate purview of church authority, no common view even, among the German bishops, as to what exactly was at issue, an unseemly contest for signs of favor from the pope began to develop (Brack 1976, 109, 124–41). The reason it kept up right to the end of Pius X's pontificate is easy to see in the light of documentation now available: Pius X sympathized with the Berlin tendency, but was not willing to snub the bulk of the German episcopacy. He respected Cardinal Fischer, which was not always the case with equally engaged princes of the church (e.g., Andrea Ferrari, 1850–1921, archbishop of Milan). So he took the position, most clearly and definitively in the encyclical *Singulari quadam* of 24 September 1912 (in Carlen 1981, 3:135–38), of "tolerating" interconfessional trade unions with certain provisos, while positively blessing and encouraging ecclesiastically organized labor where conditions were favorable. He even went to the trouble of indicating the organizational shape of the labor movement toward which Catholics should work (no. 5). That would consist of Catholic labor organizations under their chaplains on the one side, non-Catholic ones on the other. Representatives of both would form a joint commission or "cartel" for purposes of a united front where cooperation was necessary.

One or two factors emerging prior to *Singulari quadam* deserve mention. One is that the union controversy assumed international dimensions in Catholic circles in the last years of Pius X's pontificate. The year 1908 marked a threshold to a new level of intensity, despite the efforts of most bishops and Volksverein people to lay it to rest. Cardinal Fischer and Cardinal Kopp had a falling-out in that year, due to Kopp's increasing inability to appreciate nuances in the Vatican's diplomatic taking and not taking of positions, thus undermining an external truce that the bishops had agreed to in 1904; Fischer, for his part, did not maintain a scrupulously neutral attitude, but openly favored the Christian trade union movement. Kopp and the leadership of the Berlin League all made visits to the pope (1908 was the fiftieth anniversary of Sarto's ordination to the priesthood); so did Fischer. Subsequently a delegation from the West Germany trade association league — including Giesberts, Müller, and Wieber, the last at one again with his Christian labor comrades — were received by the pope. Once again, in 1910, Heinrich Brauns had to persuade Cardinal Fischer and Peter Spahn (nonlabor Center party politician) to go with August Pieper to Rome to refute integrist distortions (Brack 1976, 182). By this time also, the Berlin *Germania* had come around to seeing that the Christian unions were to be encouraged: by now their membership constituted a significant part of the Center party's constituency, despite Stegerwald's neutrality in respect to bourgeois political parties. This left the journalistic cut-and-slash with the *Kölnische Volkszeitung* to small integrist journals, particularly *Der Arbeiter*, the organ of the Berlin League of Arbeitervereine.

Also in 1908 (2–5 August) an international congress of Christian trade unions took place in Zurich. Despite the best intentions, Carl Mathias Schiffer (head of the large textile workers' union and chair of the GcG from 1904 to 1919; see ZgLb 3:177f.) gave vent to resentment over the constant attacks of the Berlin tendency against interconfessionality. In his irritation, he let slip a phrase of which much would be made in the following months (Brack 1976, 118): "With all respect and reverence for our spiritual guides, especially for our bishops, we have to say, 'Thus far and no farther!'"

Cardinal Fischer adroitly brushed the offending words aside at the Katholikentag in Düsseldorf later in the month, surrounded by thousands of Catholic workers, many of them union members. He also took the occasion to praise the visiting archbishop of Utrecht,

Henricus van de Wetering, who supported the labor movement in Holland, separated by confessions as it was, and who protected it from integrist attacks.

It was also about this time that an international network along the lines of a news service was being spun out of the hands of Umberto Benigni (official in the Vatican curia 1904–11; see Poulat in DSMCI 2:35–37; also Poulat 1969a and 1977a, here 1977a, 358–71). In 1907, he set up a press service, La Correspondance de Rome, and started a society called the Sodalitium Pianum by its handful of fully sworn-in, secret, ultra-pious members. Baron von Savigny helped out with generous contributions for his expenses, as did Pius X himself. Heinrich Fournelle also belonged to the Sodalitium Pianum (Poulat 1969a, 583–88). Through Der Arbeiter, he was able to publish material from La Correspondance de Rome and report affairs in Germany from his perspective, so that Benigni's press service could pick them up and broadcast them internationally. Even in Cologne there were integralists, of course. From Coblenz, one of them operated another integralist press service, the Zentralauskunftsstelle, which kept a sharp eye on the doings of Cologne and Mönchengladbach. This was a priest, Carl-Maria Kaufmann (Poulat 1969a, 310–13; Heitzer 1983, 108, 145), also a member of the Sodalitium Pianum. The Cologne priory of the Dominicans would also become involved as a connection with Thomas Esser, O.P., secretary of the Congregation of the Index in Rome from 1900 to 1917 (Heitzer 1983, 227).

While Benigni et Cie. stirred the waters, his influence in the curia waned earlier than has been commonly stated, as seems clear from the dossier published by Poulat (1969a; see also Poulat 1977a): he quit or was ousted from the Secretariat of State in 1911. He retained the respect of Pius X, however, and in Germany, through Savigny and Fournelle and Paul Fleischer (another Berlin League official), his reports of un-Catholic activities in the labor movement had great influence at key junctures with Cardinal Kopp. Under their influence, Kopp gave credence to the charges of "social modernism" that they conjured up, a modernism in social action that was tolerated if not directly propagated not only by Pieper and Müller, but by Cardinal Fischer himself. Kopp coined the phrase die Verseuchung des Westens (the contamination of the West); although he apologized for it profusely to Fischer, it summed up his recurrent view of Cologne (Brack 1976, 174, and Heitzer 1983, 144–48).

It was not only tendentious reports of the secret Sodalitium Pianum that fueled Kopp's anxiety, however. The pope's aversion to unions not under the strict supervision of the church was suggested by a whole series of curial interventions in regard to developments in other countries (Brack 1976, 106–41). Thus, when the prohibition came out against priests joining Murri's Lega democratica nazionale (28 July 1906), *Der Arbeiter* noticed that it was phrased as a general prohibition against joining *any* association that was not under the bishops' control. And the Berlin paper was of course correct in asserting that the "aconfessional" character (as the Italians called it) of Murri's league was what the Vatican objected to. Nor did one fail to call to Kopp's attention the instructions of the pope to Medolago Albani in 1907 and again in 1909, holding fast against any tendencies to deemphasize the Catholic, religious character of labor unions. The socialist labor press added to the embarrassment of the GcG by reporting on the favor strictly confessional unions received from clerical spokesmen in the Netherlands (see Coleman 1979, 37–48 for the uniquely confessional development of Dutch organizations).

The papal utterance that impressed Kopp the most, however, was *Notre charge apostolique* of 25 August 1910, a letter addressed to the bishops of France ordering that the Sillon be disbanded (see chapter 15). By simply applying the same principles to Germany that the pope laid down as necessary for France, one would have to withdraw all ecclesiastical support for the interconfessional trade unions. Kopp threatened to ask Rome for just such an application to the work of the Volksverein in a letter to Pieper of 9 September 1910; then, as was his way, he denied he had made any such threat (Heitzer 1983, 157, 165). Pieper could after all convincingly refute the crude charges that the Volksverein was deliberately leading German Catholicism into an across-the-board interconfessionalism and withdrawing the laity from the influence of the clergy. But again, after a little while, Kopp could not but become aware again of the great distance that separated Mönchengladbach's democratic spirit, with a respect for pluralism, from the spirit of *Notre charge apostolique*, so akin to Kopp's own outlook. After all, the laborers must know and keep their place in society and not aspire to things that are above their station, nor to equality with their social superiors.

In view of the evident sympathy of the papacy for the Berlin line, Pieper complained that the Volksverein had nobody in Rome who could act as its agent and present its side of the story to curial officials (Heitzer 1983, 168, 174). Or rather, what friends they had were out of favor, suspected of modernism themselves. Pieper and Carl Sonnenschein had both studied in Rome, but Sonnenschein's friend, Murri, could hardly serve as the kind of contact Pieper had in mind.

The Gewerkschaftsstreit *(III):* Singulari quadam *and After*

A series of deaths seems to mark the final phases of the controversy. Cardinal Kopp lost his contact in the Vatican in 1910 (21 November), with the death of Johannes Montel, the dean of the Sacred Roman Rota who also had the ambiguous position of advising the Austrian and German diplomats accredited to the Holy See — he usually kept them very well advised indeed. From this point on, Cardinal Kopp, always easily influenced, came to depend more and more on Fournelle and Savigny for his orientations. Then Cardinal Fischer of Cologne died on 30 July 1912, after having sent his statement on the trade union question to the pope as requested but before *Singulari quadam* was issued (24 September 1912). Both the great episcopal antagonists had been gravely ill, but Kopp hung on until 4 March 1914, preceding Pius X in death by only a few months (20 August 1914). The penultimate phase of the controversy was played out between Kopp and Bishop Karl Joseph Schulte, then of Paderborn, with the new archbishop of Cologne, Felix Hartmann, in the middle.

Schulte mediated an agreed-upon response to *Singulari quadam* with Adam Stegerwald, head of the GcG, whose opinion counted for something by this time. It must be remembered, as Brose has made clear, that the GcG unions really were interconfessional. Not only were there thousands of Protestant workers in the unions, but prominent social Christians like Adolf Stöcker were close to the Christian unions and gave them something of a foothold in the Conservative party as well as the Center. Stegerwald had to think of the effect any stance he might take would have upon the Protestant membership and the social Christians to whom they looked. It did not take him long to come to the prognosis that disaster loomed for the Christian unions unless the bishops could refute the interpretation given to the encyclical by the nonunion press. Schulte and even Kopp saw his point and decided to make it clear that nothing had changed or would change in the relationship of the hierarchy to the interconfessional unions (Brose 1985, 278; see also Brack 1976, 302–17, Heitzer 1983, 211–19, Schneider 1982, 205–8). Stegerwald pointed out passages in the encyclical which social democrats and integralists were already interpreting as meaning "toleration — until further notice," conditional upon good behavior (Schneider 1982, 203). A new ditty went the rounds in Christian labor circles:

> What care we about *Singulari quadam*,
> We stand behind our good old Adam! [Adam Stegerwald, that is]
> (Ross 1976, 109)

Singulari quadam (6), after all, after "lavishing praise upon" the associations of the Berlin League, addressed the question in these terms.

Not a few of you, Venerable Brethren, have asked Us whether it is permissible to tolerate the so-called Christian Trade Unions that now exist in your dioceses, since, on the one hand, they have a considerably larger number of members than the purely Catholic associations and, on the other hand, if permission were denied, serious disadvantages would result. In view of the particular circumstances of Catholic affairs in Germany, We believe that We should grant this petition. Furthermore, We declare that such mixed associations as now exist within your dioceses can be tolerated and Catholics may be permitted to join them, as long as such toleration does not cease to be appropriate by reason of new and changed conditions.

Among the five passages that Stegerwald insisted the bishops explain was the following (*Singulari quadam* 3):

The social question and its associated controversies, such as the nature and duration of labor, the wages to be paid, and workingmen's strikes, are not simply economic in character. Therefore they cannot be numbered among those which can be settled apart from ecclesiastical authority.

In the famous "Essen interpretation" — Stegerwald announced it in a special congress of the GcG in Essen on 26 November 1912, adhering closely to the wording suggested by Schulte and Kopp — this did not mean that "church authorities claimed the right to be involved in any way in the practical settlement of such questions in individual cases," but rather that "the church has the right and duty to voice its position on such controversial matters, insofar as they touch upon the moral law" (Heitzer 1983, 218). Similarly, when the bishops were admonished to "watch diligently that the Catholic members of" the trade unions "do not suffer any harm as a result of their participation" (no. 7), the encyclical was not speaking (according to the Essen interpretation) of "the economic activity of the Christian unions, but of moral or religious harm" that might arise.

These distinctions were certainly reasonable interpretations of the practical intentions of the pope in issuing the encyclical. All the same, they would have been easy enough to make in the text itself, had the pope or his advisers wished to do so. In fact, the integrist mindset resisted just such distinctions, preferring to keep "the thesis" intact while tolerating but not encouraging "the hypothesis" (to cite a famous interpretation of the Syllabus of Errors of 1864 on the part of Bishop Dupanloup; see Jedin 1981, 8:298).

The end result was that the Christian unions were able to avoid deterioration of their position relative to the free unions by retaining the confidence of their core constituency; with outsiders, however, all their attempts to achieve credibility were thwarted. Indeed, the discrediting of the labor movement by the Catholic opponents of

Mönchengladbachism had undermined its potential for growth and influence in the crucial period from 1900 to 1914, all authorities agree. Figures for 1913 (in Schneider 1982, 366) show 2,500,000 workers organized in the free unions; 340,000, or 12 percent of the total of organized labor, were in the GcG. One estimate was that 800,000 Catholic workers were organized in the socialist unions and probably could not be considered practicing Catholics any more. That would mean that 70 percent of the union members in the Catholic population belonged to socialist unions and only 30 percent to Christian ones.

Ten years before there had been less than a million union members all told. Certainly the GcG was poised to organize a greater share of the new members in the following decade than it actually managed to do, most likely a far greater share. Of course, besides the deleterious effects of the *Gewerkschaftsstreit*, other factors reduced their power of penetration. The first among them was the very division of the labor movement between socialists and others, particularly Christians. The moderate doctrine of the Christian unions with its accent on seeking settlements by negotiation and working favorable legislation in coalition with bourgeois forces proved to be a handicap in many cases. Even without the *Gewerkschaftsstreit*, the close ties with the Roman Catholic clergy and with the Center party tended to render the unions' declared religious and party-political neutrality suspect: their opposition to the Social Democratic party suffered very few tactical exceptions. But that they could not narrow the gap between them and the free unions (and that even the Catholic *Arbeitervereine* could only count a quarter of Catholic workers as members, the quarter who were disinclined to sign up with the socialists) must also be laid at the door of the venomous inner-Catholic wrangling.

There were numerous further episodes, including a trial for libel in which Bishop Schulte had to give a deposition; he and the interconfessional unions came out with their honor vindicated. Meanwhile, however, in Rome, Pius X was also reconsidering the whole question with a view to making himself clear at least to clergymen. His outlook was that of an increasingly isolated leader whose orders were constantly being ignored by persons whom he thought he should be able to trust. Poulat (1969a, 455–57; 1971, 104–6) likes to cite a late utterance of the pope, "in a way his testament," in illustration. The pope was addressing the new cardinals he had just created on 20 May 1914 (AAS 6:260–62), at the end of a pontificate. During his term in office he had found it necessary to condemn autonomous Italian Christian democracy, to issue two solemn documents in 1907 against scholarly "modernism" as well as the anti-modernist oath of 1910, and to disband the Sillon, also in 1910. In the same year he reproved Toniolo for suggesting that the religious aspects of labor unions could be downplayed, even for tactical purposes; in 1911 and 1912 he cracked down on the Catholic newspapers of Italy for analogous offenses. As for Germany, he conceded in *Singulari quadam* that interconfessional unions might be tolerated, but never approved and even less encouraged. Had he not made his views clear? How could it be that "so many sailors, so many pilots, even, God forbid, so many captains, trusting in the deceitful science and profane novelties of the time, far from finding safe harbor, had suffered shipwreck!"

> I have not failed to raise my voice to remind the erring, to point out the havoc and show Catholics the way to follow. But not everyone has always understood and properly interpreted what I had to say, clear and precise as it was. Indeed, there were some who persistently came up with arbitrary interpretations, attributing to the pope's words a meaning entirely contrary to his intentions, and taking what was only a prudent silence for consent....
>
> If you ever meet people of the kind that boast of being believers, devoted to the pope and would-be Catholics, but who won't hear of being called "clericals," tell them solemnly that the devoted sons of the pope are those who obey his word and follow it in all things, not those who are always looking for loopholes.... Never cease repeating that, if the pope loves and approves the Catholic associations that aim at material improvements, he has always insisted that moral and spiritual improvement must take first place; when it is a matter of ameliorating the lot of the worker and the peasant, one must always also uphold the love of justice and make use of the legitimate means to maintain harmony and peace between the social classes. Make it clear that the mixed associations, the alliances with non-Catholics for material advantages, are permitted under certain determinate conditions, but that the pope prefers those unions of the faithful where all, having conquered human respect and turned away from any seductive promise or threat, assemble around the embattled flag that is the most glorious of all, for it is the flag of the church....

One would like to know what the new cardinals made of all this, especially Hartmann of Cologne. It is known that the other German, from Munich (Franziskus von Bettinger), and the Viennese (Friedrich Gustav Piffl) could not wait to call off the integralist denunciations; they were happy when another of their number (Giacomo della Chiesa of Bologna, soon to be Pope Benedict XV) did just that.

Pius X had dealt with Murri and excised the cancer of social modernism from the body of Christ. Or had he? In his last years, he came more and more to fear that this kind of modernism, the practical kind, was developing almost wherever priests and even more so wherever lay Catholics were responding to the clamor of the working people. At the center of the problem was nothing other than the question of Christian unionism. It was around this issue that the "last battle" of his pontificate was fought (Poulat 1971, 100–101). What precisely was at issue? It was not any more whether unions of workers were legitimate, to the exclusion of employers; that had long been settled in practice and was simply ignored in theory (as in *Singulari quadam*, 5). Nor, on the other hand, was it whether Catholic workers should simply join and try to influence neutral unions; this was condemned in the case of the Sillon and was an underground issue between Berlin and Mönchengladbach (underground because Pieper never proposed it again between 1902 and 1914 and conceded the point in practice). It was also clear that in some limited circumstances interconfessional trade unions could be condoned (*Singulari quadam*), but that "uniconfessional unions" were the norm. The precise question that had not yet been nailed down and seemed to provide an opening for social modernism to creep in unchallenged was: must Catholic unions be organized like those of the Berlin league and the Unione economico-sociale in Italy? Or may they take on the organizational pattern of their rivals in the field, nationally centralized unions prepared to take coordinated action? This was the way uniconfessional unions in Belgium, the Netherlands, and Austria were set up.

On 21 February 1914, a Jesuit named Giulio Monetti (DSMCI 3/2:570), highly thought of by the pope and by his secretary of state, Cardinal Raphael Merry del Val, published the first of two articles in *La Civiltà cattolica* entitled *"Sindacalismo cristiano?"* (Poulat 1969a, 486–91, or 1971, 93–96). It was an essay in unveiling the presuppositions and systematic underpinnings of unionism, as *Pascendi* (1907; Carlen 1981, 3:71–98) did for scholarly modernism, and it was an equally unfortunate distortion. Turning the clock back to pre–Neo-Thomistic moral theology, Monetti protested against the alleged "social function of property" and the connected new exotic virtue of social justice. Such distributism properly fell, he asserted, under the heading of charity, not justice. In the second installment of 7 March he upheld the complete freedom of workers to choose their line of work and their jobs out of the possibilities open to them. Trade unions constrain that liberty, most notably in the case of strikes, which are also an offense against property (since property confers authority that is defied in strikes). Given this breakdown of authority, the state must step in. Unionism is in the last analysis an open door for "the intervention of the state in private matters, disturbing the legitimate individual liberty that is a good at least as estimable as increases in wages or reductions of working hours." It leads to the state as providence or to social charity, and this is "nothing else than a socialist abuse, by which the state puts its hand in the pocket of some citizens to aid others," violating the right of private property.

This could only be regarded as a trial balloon. Just what form the ultimate anathema would take was not known, but Toniolo set to work to head it off. He knew, from frequent dealings with Pius X, that this could only succeed if the utmost delicacy were observed (Poulat 1969a, 389, and 1971, 96; see Zussini 1965, 154–96). While six more articles questioning the moral legitimacy of Christian unionism were published in the pages of the *Civiltà cattolica*, he mobilized his international contacts in high places, including Cardinal Pietro Maffi of Pisa, Cardinal Désiré Mercier of Mechlin and Franz-Xaver Wernz, the general of the Jesuits since 1906. Wernz did not approve the line that the Jesuit periodical *Civiltà cattolica* was following and was not of the integrist persuasion, much to Pius X's displeasure.

Toniolo imposed a very austere guard on his utterances, but he forged ahead despite the warning from the pope himself that Monetti's views were to be considered authoritative. With the assistance of other veterans of the good fight, whose merits Pius could not contest (notably the greybeard loyalist ultramontane, Léon Harmel), the pope was prevailed upon to go no further and issue no magisterial statement. In April and May of 1914, those with power and influence in the church besieged Pius X. They could not prevent him from making a last futile declaration of principle on Catholic social teaching, at odds with all his best qualified and most experienced advisers, in the nonbinding framework of a fervorino to the new cardinals (above). But they did forestall a formal declaration that would have crippled the Catholic labor movement. *Sic transit gloria ecclesiae!*

The integrists had a straightforward, if oversimplified, notion of papal authority and the obedience that it had a right to command. The others could not well express in public (and to a great extent not make explicit at all) the limits of obedience, the distinctions that Pius X dismissed as loopholes. All were captives of what Bernard Lonergan has called the "classicist notion of culture" (1972, xi); the implication was that there existed one shape of society that could be called Christian, whereas any other structure was a deviation from the norm. All the same, the prelates who would choose Pius X's successor could feel the societal ground shift beneath their feet — and they could tell the difference between the faith in which they were raised and the version that the integrists were carrying to sectarian and unChristian extremes.

Chapter 15

PATERNALISM AND DEMOCRACY IN FRANCE, 1900–1914

In the Catholic France of the turn of the century all was not a wasteland, even though church-state relations were at their lowest point since the Commune and getting worse. They were heading irresistibly, in fact, toward the hostile revocation of the concordat at the end of 1905: the Separation (as it is so often written, with a capital S) of church and state. The radical bourgeois masters of France were bent on a *Kulturkampf*, a dangerous game of stoking the fires of anti-clericalism. It conjured up a nationalistic reaction not only in the ranks of anti-Semites and monarchists but of democratically minded kinds of youthful enthusiasts as well (P. Cohen 1988). If the heyday of Dehon, Harmel, Lemire, and other Christian democrats was over, they still remained on the scene or not far from it, while new forces gathered.

De Mun's Association Catholique de la Jeunesse Française (ACJF) went into a new phase, stimulated both by the threats to the church proposed by the government following the Dreyfus affair and by increased awareness of the social problem (Molette 1968). In Lyon, the group around Marius Gonin and the monthly *La Chronique sociale* (Ponson 1980) would partly mirror and partly stimulate the changes in social Catholicism that helped make the reign of Pius X so contentious also in France. From the circle around La Tour du Pin, Henri Lorin struck out in a new direction with a liaison organization called the Union d'études des catholiques sociaux. Together with the Lyon activists, this gave rise to the Semaine sociale held in Lyon in 1904, the first of the annual summer study conferences or workshops of that name that would be held for many years to come (Rollet 1958,

288

2:39–52). In the north of France, from an unlikely quarter, some Jesuits would make a new departure in Volksverein-like activity under the name of *Action populaire* (abbreviated AP, see Droulers 1969). In Paris, Marc Sangnier's youth movement, the Sillon, was about to experience its brightest hours (J. Caron 1966). The Sillon and the ACJF would give new vitality to the study circles inaugurated by the old OCCO or the movement of Démocratie chrétienne.

These developments took place in three main phases. From the resolution of the Dreyfus affair to the Separation (ca. 1899–1905), social Catholics in general developed a greater differentiation between an electoral-political orientation and a concern with the social as such. While Albert de Mun and Jacques Piou tried to pick up the pieces from the political catastrophe of Catholic France with a new party, the Action libérale populaire (HDTFR 4–5; also Martin 1978, 145–78), study groups of youth and others sprang up in numbers substantial enough for Marc Sangnier to organize national congresses (not just for the Sillon-related groups) in 1902, 1903, and 1904. The Semaine sociale responded to the need for a more intensive and advanced level of theoretical social reflection, while seeking also to bring together the centrifugal tendencies of social Catholicism (paternalistic vs. democratic) into some sort of practical entente. The Action populaire, founded well after *Graves de communi*, was also resolved to be politically neutral, that is, open to the whole political spectrum from conservative to democratic. Two current political forces, however, remained outside the AP's pale. One was the anticlericalism so prevalent among radicals and socialists. The other was the reactionary wing represented by the Action française, which attacked the republic itself and hence the *Ralliement*. The hope was that progress could be made on the social front, and in what concerned church-state relations, even if no political-party unity of French Catholics could be achieved.

Then came the trauma of the separation (second phase). In the disorganization that attended the unilateral abrogation of the concordat, all the conditions of Catholic action changed; everything officially having to do with the church — the hierarchy and its chanceries, the clergy and their parishes, the religious orders and all their oeuvres — had to be re-established with nothing or next to nothing in the way of structures and sources of support. In the very period when the Catholicisms of neighboring countries were adjusting to modern conditions with some degree of success, at least in comparison with previous decades, French Catholicism was shaken by organizational cataclysm.

Just at this time (1905–6), Marc Sangnier was bringing the Sillon to a clearer consciousness of its own democratic charism (to use a term not current at the time). It needed elbowroom and achieved it by cutting its ties with all the movements with which it had affinities. Recognizing that other Catholics legitimately honored other political tendencies, the Sillon respectfully declared its autonomy from the hierarchy in its political options, while declaring an undiminished discipleship in matters of faith and morals. Realizing further that there were non-Catholic elements in French society with convergent political outlooks, and feeling that it was a matter of civic responsibility to give real democrats a viable political platform, it put out feelers to freethinkers, socialists, and humanists of various kinds through the formation of the "greater Sillon" (1907-8). This was the very time, however, when the organizational imperative for the French church seemed to be to close ranks in view of the new church-state problems caused by the Separation (McManners 1972, 169).

The third phase was marked, on the extreme right, by decreasing willingness to tolerate a spectrum of views: in the aftermath and confusion of the Vatican condemnation of scholarly modernism (1907), integrist journalists made bold to assimilate advanced social and political views to the condemned modernism. Pius X tended to see his authority as being seconded only by such hyperorthodox elements. He virtually abandoned the *Ralliement* by 1909, giving reactionary Catholics free rein for their attacks on the Third Republic. Divergences among Catholics as to applications of Leo XIII's social teaching in the new situation were upgraded to the level of heresies. Some integrists, like Msgr. Delassus, the nemesis of Abbé Lemire in the Nord, and the jurist Joseph Rambaud in Lyon, were in direct contact with Umberto Benigni in the Sodalitium Pianum. Others, like Charles Maignen or Emmanuel Barbier, were not. But all were unanimous in interpreting the ills of the French and Roman Church as a product of (the) Revolution and, what was new, of seeing social Catholics in particular in the ranks of the revolutionaries as having gone over to the side of the enemy.

In France as elsewhere, therefore, the period ca. 1907-14 was characterized by the attacks of the integrists and the manifest displeasure of the Vatican for anything that smacked of autonomous action. Social Catholics with the same ultramontane loyalties as the integrists found it hard to comprehend that this backward-looking, purely defensive attitude found favor with the pope, or that this was the kind of unity that Pius X actually wanted. The Sillon was condemned in 1910 after censures against individual *abbés démocrates;* the Semaine sociale and the Action populaire were gravely threatened with sanctions. At this point, the French developments meld into the international or Roman trade union controversy (above, chapter 14). In the event, no official condemnation of trade unionism as incompatible with Catholic social teaching came forth in 1914 nor, of course, at any later point.

New and Old Social Catholics 1900–1905

Politics and Social Action

"Association" became once more the watchword of the times in a highly determinate context, that of the Law of Associations of 1901. René Waldeck-Rousseau, the prime minister from 1899 to 1902, had an interest in widening the area of autonomy of labor organizations so that they could play a responsible role in society, and conversely in strictly limiting and regulating the field of action of religious congregations, so as to reduce their anti-republican influence (as in the schools and in the anti-Semitic press campaigns of the Assumptionists' *La Croix* during the Dreyfus affair). The Ferry decrees of 1880 had not seriously stunted the growth of Catholic schools, but that was to change. Whatever may be said about the inner consistency of this project, the Law of Associations, once introduced by the government, was changed in the legislature into an instrument by which religious orders could be suppressed in France. The way a liberal republican regime could frame this was to require permission by way of legislative action for any association "with headquarters outside France whose rules implied a renunciation of the Declaration of the Rights of Man" (HDTFR 63). Great latitude was thereby given to the Chamber of Deputies to refuse or revoke authorization of orders and congregations that were deemed more troublesome than helpful to republican France.

Thomas Kselman (HDTFR 63) sums up the outcome:

> Confusions about the provisions of the law led to a delay in its application until after the elections of May 1902. The Radicals won a clear majority and, led by the new government of the anticlerical Emile Combes, rigorously enforced the Law of Associations. Thousands of schools were closed, the property of the orders was confiscated and sold by the state, and those members of orders who wished to continue as religious had to leave France. Protests by the secular clergy against the measure led to the suspension of salaries and to administrative action designed to curtail contacts between Rome and the French church. The conflict over the Law of Associations formed the background for the separation of church and state that took place in 1905.

One may merely note that in contrast with the German *Kulturkampf* the end result was a church really independent of the state in all respects and with its freedom of action largely restored. However, the church in France was shorn of its accustomed sources of income and even of title to its church buildings and reduced, in law, to the private sphere. The process of regrouping on this new basis took decades.

In regard to noncanonical Catholicism, organizations such as the Association Catholique de la Jeunesse Française continued to be legally unaffected and operated without harassment from the government. The Action populaire was run by Jesuits, who were not allowed to exist as such in France after the Law of Associations went into effect, but who, as private persons and allegedly diocesan priests, could set up a perfectly legal society with purposes in keeping with republican loyalties. The leaderships of both the French Jesuits (Droulers 1969, 65–66) and the ACJF (Molette 1968, 195, 216) were anxious not to be forced into an exclusively defensive and negative posture by the measures of a hostile government and electorate. An engagement in nonpolitical *actio benefica in populum* (as *Graves de communi* suggested) was something positive, in keeping with the mission of the church, and a crying need all at the same time. For similar reasons the party of Catholic ralliés, the Action libérale, added the term *populaire* to their party's name (though not consistently), in honor of Albert de Mun's long service in the cause of social understanding and because it implied a positive social policy that the party could stand for, beyond defending the secular connection of church and state in France. In fact, however, the party was dominated by social conservatives, not unlike the *clerico-moderatismo* of Italy.

After all, democratic leanings tended to polarize social Catholics, lining up paternalists against democrats (see, e.g., Mayeur 1968, 229). In view of the gathering storm in France, great efforts were made not to allow this tension to drive another wedge into the already fragmented Catholic elite on top of all the other issues that divided French Catholics (legitimists vs. ralliés, liberals vs. socials, bourgeois vs. proletariat, patriots vs. dreyfusards, and now generational tensions as well). Many of the developments we are about to present may be seen in this light as attempts to move beyond the misplaced and ineffective formulas of paternalism without offending social conservatives and without running afoul of papal directives for Italy, in the wake of *Graves de communi*. Thus the ACJF actuated a definite shift toward the concerns of the working class, while also serving in some sort as the youth auxiliary of Albert de Mun's and Jacques Piou's new political party, the Action libérale populaire. The Action populaire of Gustave Desbuquois, S.J. (Droulers 1969, 66–69, 99, and DMR 1:91), supported all tendencies in social Catholicism, particularly the wing dedicated to worker participation ("democracy"), unlike the earlier generation of Jesuits in the patronal unions of the Nord; it avoided political party affiliation not only to comply with *Graves de communi*, but also to devote itself to its social purposes and clientele without raising political animosities. The *Chronique sociale* group also kept the Action libérale populaire at arm's length for the same reasons: it did not want its "democratic" action and propaganda submerged in a basically conservative party. Earlier it had been part of Abbé Garnier's Union nationale, but now it removed itself from the arena of party politics altogether, not associating itself with any new party.

The Sillon was a special case. Like Gonin, Sangnier eschewed party ties, but engaged in a political education of a decidedly democratic cast. Shying away also from amalgamation with the other Catholic youth movement (the ACJF), the Sillon developed as close a set of informal relationships as possible with the hierarchy and the papacy. As Sangnier tried to make clear, the Sillon was dedicated to the socio-political ideal of a certain variety of democracy. It was not the "Christian democracy" defined by Leo XIII in *Graves de communi* (which he acknowledged was an obligation of Christian love of neighbor in all eras, including the present), but a way of life never before realized. Far from presenting it as obligatory on all Catholics, the Sillon merely asked for the elbowroom to develop and propagate it on its own, without claiming the church's authority for it at all. There was a strong suggestion, all the same, that for the *future* good of the faith and of humanity, it would be needful to move toward an alliance of Catholicism and democracy updating Lamennais's vision. Meanwhile, the Sillon expected its members, as a group of Catholics, to depend on the clergy for their religious formation and guidance. Was this a coherent stance?

The Association Catholique de la Jeunesse Française

The ACJF, being a creation of de Mun's, had always had a strong political tinge, as was self-evident in the Third Republic down to the Dreyfus affair: young Catholics grew up supposing that the remedy for the church's unsatisfactory position in French society would be political, just as the causes of the malaise were commonly supposed to be. But since there was never a Catholic party in France representing the majority of concerned Catholics — de Mun being no "French Windthorst" (Jedin 1981, 9:104) — their political guides and aspirations lacked a party framework. De Mun was not inclined toward democracy, nor was the first president of the ACJF. It was only when two younger men, born in 1873, moved up into leadership positions that the ACJF began to take a more effective interest in the lot of the lower classes.

Henri Bazire became vice president of the ACJF in 1897 and was its president from 1899 to 1904, while carrying on some practice of law and preparing for a political career in the footsteps of Albert de Mun. Having reached thirty years of age, he stepped down to be succeeded by Jean Lerolle. At the turn of the century, the ACJF counted a membership of perhaps three thousand to five thousand, all young Catholic men who enjoyed the benefits of good schools and a higher education. Bazire turned their energies decisively in the direction of the working people. In a ringing declaration in 1900, he portrayed this development as anything but a distraction from the religious ends of the association. Indeed, to take up social as well as religious questions in their study circles was a natural part of their "integral Catholicism": they would be engaged in matters of concern to working people *because* they were Catholics (*"Sociaux parce que catholiques"*; see Molette 1968, 341). He laid plans for the next three annual May conferences of the ACJF to take up burning social issues of the hour, starting with the question of unionism in 1903 and going on to treat of credit unions and similar institutions in 1904 and the conditions under which children and youth worked in 1905.

Since all the local branches of the ACJF were expected to study the same questions and carry out Le Play-type surveys of local conditions, the effect in sensitizing these young men of mostly bourgeois background to the social implications of an industrial economy was considerable. It also seems to have galvanized their efforts at organizing study groups of young people who were not in a lycée or university, who were, in other words, not destined for one of the liberal professions but for office work or manual labor on the land, in a shop, or in a factory. Whereas up to 1903 the majority of these nonstudent associates seem to have been farmers, groups of urban workers became more common thereafter. At the beginning of Bazire's term of office, there were about a hundred such groups; when he left there were more than eleven hundred (Molette 1968, 446).

Another result of the 1903 social conference of the ACJF was to form ties with a Christian union in Paris. Bazire's successor, Jean Lerolle, embodied the most direct connection (Molette 1968, 352, 433; Talmy 1966, 81). In the background here is the question of the "yellow unions," company unions which exercised a powerful attraction for some French Catholics. The social-policy signals sent out by the presence of the reformist socialist Alexandre Millerand in Waldeck-Rousseau's cabinet were such that industrialists saw they might have to deal with unions after all. Some of them then secretly started to finance tame unions among workers who were reluctant to strike when their socialist comrades did. Such "yellow" unions were at first looked upon as a promising development by the younger generation of social Catholics, but soon (by 1902), both the *Chronique sociale* group in the southeast and the ACJF pulled back from them (Molette 1968,

345f; Ponson 1980, 75; Talmy 1966, 80). The few small Christian democratic unions in the north, center, and west of France could not make much headway, even by the relatively modest standards of the struggling French socialist labor movement (HDTFR 1024), given the opposition of the employers and the emergence of company unions; with the appearance of the encyclical, *Graves de communi*, ecclesiastics found it even more difficult to support them than before (Pierrard 1984, 397–400).

But besides the Christian democratic unions and the *jaunes*, there was a third type of worker organization for Catholics, represented by the Syndicat des employés du commerce et de l'industrie (SECI; *employés*, that is, clerical workers). It went back to a foundation of the Christian Brothers in 1887 and was largely confined to the Paris region (Caldwell 1966; Coornaert in Scholl 1966, 241–50), where it had 2,258 members in 1901. Actually it was not yet a trade union, being organized more for mutual assistance such as a job exchange and a self-financed sick pay plan than for collective bargaining. But it was to be the mainstay of the future French Catholic labor movement.

In its early years it was encouraged by leaders of social Catholicism such as Harmel and La Tour du Pin. It represented an element in their social vision of a people organized by professions rather than by classes. La Tour du Pin even had a formula to describe its niche in the social order: it was a "free union in the organized profession." That is, it was a voluntary association within the profession(s) that remained to be organized. It had its own study commission to examine concrete problems faced by its membership; this was headed by Jean Lerolle since before 1900. Years later, the labor leader Jules Zirnheld (DBMOF 15:353) described this modest but unprecedented relationship in the following terms (cited in Molette 1968, 352).

> You were a young student then, Lerolle, I a young employee [bank clerk, in fact]; you were the teacher, I the disciple. We put together a fine example of true collaboration of classes and our team did good work. You brought us the learning that you got in the morning at the Institut catholique; we brought you the experience that we got every day at work.

At the ACJF conference at Chalon-sur-Saône in 1903, Lerolle's report led to a resolution affirming the necessity of union organization and recognizing the union movement as worthy of support. That so many workers were unorganized thus appeared for the first time to many upper-class youth as an undesirable and remediable situation. The earlier Christian democratic formula of parallel *syndicats* for workers and employers seems to be what they had in mind. They went on to discuss the question just then much in the public arena, whether unions could engage in profit-making endeavors, such as cooperative bakeries, and whether they should have enhanced legal status, which might require employers to deal with them. There was much hesitation on these points among the young people as among their older and in some cases more expert consultants. When Joseph Zamanski proposed, after a report on collective bargaining, that the labor law of 1884 be changed to permit unions to bargain for all the employees of a plant in such wise that noncompliance would be actionable in the courts, it took the persuasion of Henri Lorin to garner a bare majority (Talmy 1966, 86–87).

After Chalon, the Bazire-Lerolle line was characteristic of the ACJF. Support for the practically nonexistent Christian labor movement in France from the ACJF was a small but important breakthrough. On it others could build. In the long term, it was (according to McManners 1972, 92), "infinitely more effective than the pamphlets of socially minded priests or the much misunderstood devotion of *'la classe dirigeante'* to the workers."

Semaines sociales

Another nucleus of advanced social consciousness among young Catholics formed around Gonin's periodical (*La Chronique sociale*) and social secretariat in Lyon (Ponson 1980, 69, 77–84). In 1902, Joseph Vialatoux, a lawyer and the son of a lawyer, met Gonin, who, as he later put it, "showed me what Christianity *does* and revealed to me a Christian Catholicism *in action*." Vialatoux was able to live frugally on his inheritance, when, shortly thereafter, he abandoned the law and went into popular education for the *Chronique*'s groups across the countryside around Lyon. He thus joined the small group of independently wealthy gentlemen (Victor Berne, Auguste Crétinon, and others) from the Catholic bourgeoisie of Lyon who departed from the prevailing orthodoxy of a hierarchically stable class society.

In this they would seem to be very like the Sillon; and indeed there were close resemblances and contacts. But Gonin and his friends, although they came down on the same side of the social question as did the Sillon, saw themselves as practicing Catholicism first and foremost, "integral" Catholicism. For them this meant pursuing social justice as well as cultivating the life of prayer and the sacraments. But in a foundational reappraisal of the relation between the church and the people of France that took place in stages as the Separation neared and was consummated, they realized that the majority of the nation really was anticlerical — and that the desperate clinging to positions of power and influence in the nation's recent history on the part of churchmen in league with anti-social reactionaries was largely responsible! From that insight, it followed that a continuation of the strategy of "religious defense" would only serve to discredit Catholicism all the more. It would be necessary to "labor differently" (Ponson 1980, 127), not — unlike the "plus grand Sillon" — in the political arena, but within the continuing framework of Catholicism as constituted in parishes, "oeuvres," and dioceses. This option meant that it was in the church for the long haul, even if that meant, as it did after 1907, some shrinkage in its field of action and numbers of adherents.

In a way, this reduced role on the local level was balanced by a specific national role, that of being the permanent office and publishing arm of the Semaines sociales. As an institution, the Semaines had no other permanent address; there were other centers of gravity, one in the Nord (with the professors of the Institut Catholique of Lille, Adéodat Boissard and Eugène Duthoit) and of course one in Paris. As the Semaines sociales grew in importance, the Secrétariat social of Lyon, a social action arm of *La Chronique sociale*, served a national audience as well as a local one (Ponson 1980, 139–41).

The pathbreaking Semaines sociales were the joint project of Henri Lorin in Paris and Marius Gonin in Lyon, the latter "of the people," as the saying went, the former a cosmopolitan figure of the *grande bourgeoisie parisienne* (*Catholicisme* 7:1082–84). Lorin dedicated himself at an early age, not exactly as an *homme charitable* (like de Melun) or an *homme des oeuvres* (Maignen 1927), but precisely as a *catholique social* without other profession, even though he was a graduate of the prestigious Ecole polytechnique (HDTFR 898). He belonged to the school of La Tour du Pin from early on (Talmy 1963, 21) and was a member of the Fribourg Union. He immersed himself in the debates of the Neo-Thomist moralists and also in the *Summa theologiae* itself.

In 1902, Lorin became head of the new Union d'études des catholiques sociaux; he formed it as a center where the adherents of the various social Catholic periodicals could come together and perhaps coordinate their research, instead of remaining in their isolation and duplicating each other's efforts (Rollet 1958, 2:37). La Tour du Pin's Conseil des Etudes no longer could pretend to fill this niche, representing as it did only one of the tendencies into which the OCCO had fragmented: the political de Mun did not see eye-to-eye with either the theoretical La Tour du Pin, who was now tending in the direction of the Action française because of its monarchism, or with Harmel, the Christian democrat. *L'Association catholique*, no longer affiliated with the OCCO, was still the most respected organ of social Catholicism; its editor, Henri Savatier (Pierrard 1984, 402) took the initiative of establishing contacts with some other social Catholic reviews. From this arose the conviction that a kind of lobbying think-tank in close touch with social policy legislation was needed if Catholic social ideals were to have any influence. With Albert de Mun as its principal channel into the workings of the assembly, the Union d'études des catholiques sociaux performed a modest but valuable service.

Lorin's vision — and his personal fortune — were capable of more than this, however. When Gonin suggested an annual study conference to replace the Christian democratic congresses of earlier years, the two men's paths converged into the high-level annual week-long conferences that the Semaines sociales were to become (Talmy 1966, 91–105, Rollet 58, 2:39–52, Pierrard 1984, 375–377, and Ponson 1980, 81–84). Among other things, they would become the main platform on which Lorin would introduce and sum up the chosen social theme each year. With his relentless deductive reasoning in the manner of Neo-Thomism, his summations sometimes shocked the uninitiated and provoked the objections of the disputatious in the years of the integrist onslaught.

Clericalism, Anticlericalism, and the Sillon

The Sillon: Origins, Rise, and Fall

The Sillon (see HDTFR 938 and the 1966 work of Jeanne Caron) started among senior secondary students in a meeting place called the "Crypt," and was named after a magazine, Le Sillon (the Furrow), that was founded by two former members of "the Crypt" in 1894. Behind that is the particular non-Jesuit genius loci of the elite school they had attended in Paris, the Collège Stanislas, run by an approved congregation, the Marianists. After the youthful enthusiasms of their years together in school, it was a fateful moment when Marc Sangnier decided to resign from the army officers' corps and devote himself full-time to "the Cause" in 1900 (J. Caron 1966, 120–28).

He and his friends had some experience of popular sentiment and were intuitively convinced that democracy was the wave of the future. They became acutely aware of the obstacles placed in its path by their own kind, especially their elders of the ruling liberal bourgeoisie, intent as they were on preserving their privileged position in society; it was with this element that the clericalist leadership, the public persona of Catholicism, identified. The Sillonists responded to an ideal of democracy more or less obscured by its most prominent proponents. Their own intensely assimilated Catholic Christianity made them deplore the anticlericalism of the forces at the head of the democratic movement, mostly socialists, freethinkers, and radical laicist republicans. Marc Sangnier was the charismatic and inspirational spokesman for the Sillon, which is inseparable from his person. He discoursed with ease and assurance from an original intuition of authentic democracy and authentic modern Christianity that appealed to his generation even while it struggled to achieve an appropriate organizational form. Its main lines, features, and requirements gradually emerged in the years 1900–1905 and were codified to a certain extent, with the assistance of the philosophically trained Léonard Constant, at assemblies in October 1905 and February 1906 (J. Caron 1966, 305–512).

The Sillon was a "friendship" more than an organization, Sangnier was fond of repeating: it was not a "federation" but a "union" of the likeminded. Its relationships with the hierarchical church were important to it, but could not be conventional. Democracy and the church? Sangnier was well aware that this was a theme on which stands had already been taken, most notably Leo XIII's definition of "Christian democracy" in *Graves de communi*. Were not the limits of action already fixed? Over a period of years, Sangnier and his friends on the one side and Pope Pius X with his secretary of state on the other engaged as it were in an intricate ballet to find the forms in which they could interact to the benefit of the church in the modern world. It started with a movement in which Sangnier led first one pilgrimage to Rome in 1903, in the early months of Pius X's pontificate, and then another, *da capo*, in 1904. By this time, some of the initial fruits of the Sillon's approach were ready to be introduced to high church dignitaries.

There were the study circles, in which sons of the bourgeoisie and the occasional aristocrat mingled with rural and urban working people (not the industrial proletariat as yet) on a basis of easy familiarity; the groups in view were the same as those reached by the ACJF, but the democratic atmosphere was different. Whereas the ACJF "gathered" Catholic youth together under the patronage of their betters in the perspective of *Graves de communi*, the Sillon "penetrated" lay environments and worked there as a Christian ferment, planting the seeds of future structures, and did so democratically, as "friends," not patrons (J. Caron 1966, 258–68). There were also the *Jeunes Gardes*, formed to keep order as marshals at public events. They attained a certain notoriety when they quelled anticlerical disturbances and even more when they obstructed the inventory of some congregational property that was to be confiscated by the government. In Rome their perfect discipline and smart uniform appearance were sure to attract notice; upon inquiry, one would be told that their leader was a man of the people, whom even notables' sons obeyed in strict paramilitary subordination; the democratic element was maintained by the selection of officers from any rank of society and by *tutoiement,* the familiar form of address that all *Jeunes Gardes* used with each other, no matter what their rank in the guard or station in society.

After 1905, their principal public activity was hawking the Sillonist paper, *Eveil démocratique,* two Sundays a month, while talking up the cause on the streets. (The Action française paid the Sillon the ultimate compliment of forming their own units of "newsboys of the king.") In their own circle, the *Jeunes Gardes* practiced an intense prayer life, marked among other things by all-night vigils. One member of the Parisian group was to be influential later on in the American Catholic Worker movement: Peter Maurin (Ellis 1981, and A. Sheehan 1959).

Merry del Val and Pius X, for their part, responded with signs of favor, so much so that there was talk of Marc Sangnier as the pope's fair-haired boy. A meeting of minds, however, did not eventuate (J. Caron 1966, 292f.). As to papal and hierarchical authority, the Sillonists were anxious to accept its central role in their religious life, but wanted it understood as not determinative of Catholics' political or constitutional options. After all, the opposition of opinion between monarchists and republican Catholics was tolerated, despite the *Ralliement;* the Sillon acknowledged that it would be inappropriate to ask the bishops or the Vatican to approve their own developing views and political choices; they claimed the freedom to pursue their own political line on their own responsibility. That implied then a loose but loyal relationship of the Sillon to the hierarchy, that of a band of brothers free-lancing out in front of the main body, reconnoitering new social and political territory for its possibilities, exploring alternatives to the bankrupt strategy of "religious defense."

When the Separation came, however, Pius X sided with those few who still thought that it might be possible and would certainly be desirable to re-establish the union of church and state in France. In the encyclical *Gravissimo officii munere* (10 August 1906), issued with some delay after the law of Separation was passed, the rejection of the Sillon's self-understanding was already suggested in the *ostinato* passages. But there were still some intervening measures before the dance wound up to its dramatic finale. The pope's letter to the French hierarchy, *Notre charge apostolique* of 25 August 1910 (AAS 2:607–33), sounded a reprise of the theme of an unchanging social order set forth at the beginning of Pius X's reign. As to the Sillon, he regretfully invited it to dissolve itself and place its groups under the authority of the bishops in each diocese. It complied immediately and without protest.

For at the beginning of his pontificate, as was noticed in connection with Toniolo (see chapter 13), between the first and the second of the Sillon's pilgrimages to Rome, Pius X had issued a *Motu proprio* establishing the basic norms of "Christian popular action" or Christian democracy (ASS 36:339–45). In retrospect, one can see that Pius X thought that the essentially static character, the unchangeableness of the good social order, was a matter of faith (or at least of sound philosophy, *proxima fidei*). This was evident in a much-cited address that he gave at Padua in 1896 as Cardinal Sarto (Ponson 1980, 281f.): "it will never be possible to unite...the rich and the poor..., except by placing between them the cross" of Christ. By contrast, the young men of the Sillon, and before them the Christian democrats, including Sturzo, Murri, and even Toniolo, assumed that the good order of society, being set in history, would change from time to time; indeed, to adapt a phrase of John Henry Newman's, that it would have to change in order to preserve its identity and moral validity. The Sillon brought this divergence to the fore in an especially insistent way, simply because the democracy it sought to foreshadow was "utopian," that is, never before realized. And while societal mutability was not a stated theme of either Sillon manifestoes or *Notre charge apostolique*, it was as firmly rejected by the latter, immobilist, as it was sustained by the former, evolutionary in its outlook. Sangnier found it entirely natural and appropriate that after an age of feudalism would come an age of monarchy, to be succeeded now by an age of democracy (J. Caron 1966, 345–50).

The Sillon's Brand of Democracy

Marc Sangnier declared in one of his 1905 statements (J. Caron 1966, 323) that the democracy with which he was concerned was not Christian democracy in the meaning of *Graves de communi re*, but had to do with the civil organization of the body politic, of the nation, and hence belonged to that vast area of free opinion and persuasion in which the Catholic Church had no binding doctrines to impose. Hence the members of the Sillon looked to the hierarchy for instruction in the faith, which they drew on for inspiration and to maintain the dedication and motivation they needed for their educational campaigns; whereas their particular political persuasions, though consonant with the faith, were not fixed in their religious heritage and did not fall to the magisterium to determine.

"As he fought for his rights to formulate a political and social philosophy free from ecclesiastical control," McManners writes (1972, 102–3; see J. Caron 1966, 305ff.),

Marc Sangnier brought his highly original theories to a sharper definition. Democracy, he argued, was the best of governments, because it
demanded the exercise of the greatest virtues; it was "the social organization which tends to maximize the conscience and civic responsibility
of each individual." Christianity had made democracy conceivable, for
Christianity alone treats men as truly equal, and inspires true fraternity.
But parliamentary democracy was a second best; the ideal State was not
a multitude ruled by "sterile parliamentarianism," but the "harmonious
and organic expression of free social groupings," especially trades unions
and co-operatives. In the reformed society there would be complete economic equality (the new Sillonist journal, *L'Eveil démocratique*, created
in October 1905, was run by a co-operative, in which each worker received payment solely according to his needs). On the other hand, society
needs leadership, so the authentic superiority of an *élite* would have to be
recognized. The affairs of the Sillon were managed, not by "election," but
by "selection," and its chief operated the selective process to bring picked
members of the working class from the Circles into the central organization of the movement. Albert de Mun's Oeuvre des Cercles had relied on
the *classes dirigeantes*, described by Sangnier in 1906 as "fallen now from
their elder brother status and for long in the position of directing nothing
at all"; the Sillon was to rely on an aristocracy of intelligence and character, drawn chiefly from the workers. So it would be in the democratic
State of the future. A dedicated, unrewarded leadership would operate
through "the organic expression of free social groupings"; it would be
a combination of Plato's Republic with anarcho-syndicalism. But the
way to the goal was not through violence; change would come from the
moral education of the working class, chiefly through the inspiration of
Christianity.

In practice was this Romantic vision a doctrine of the Right or of
the Left? Through the complex and broken terrain of the confused debate on social issues, a clearly posted frontier line twisted its way, and
in a controversy with Guesde and the socialists in a public meeting at
Roubaix in March 1905 Sangnier crossed it.

> We are convinced that the different systems of property holding are
> called to succeed one another [like the different systems of polit-
> ical authority], and in our view only narrow and limited minds
> see contemporary capitalism as endowed with a strange and evil
> immortality.... The wage-earning system will last only for a time,
> and one day humanity will see a worthier, freer, more human social
> organization, one corresponding better to the needs of a regenerated
> society. (J. Caron 1966, 319)

What Charles Maurras (HDTFR 625–27) had to say about all this
is interesting and important: his Action française (HDTFR 3–4) and
Sangnier's Sillon grew up as equal and opposite attractions for the
public-spirited youth of "the generation of 1905–1914" (P. Cohen
1988). When Sangnier pointed out the dilemma of an agnostic pos-

itivist (Maurras) appealing to Catholics in terms of their Catholic tradition, Maurras retorted (as cited in Arnal 1985, 27):

> A sole dilemma exists, but it is between those who wish to build society on the virtue of citizens and those who place the frailty of men within a social organization. Social Christians, historically and rationally, are ranked in this latter group with the Action française. Sillon is unhappily on the other side in bad company.

This attempt to consign Sillonist democracy simply to the camp of liberal individualism points to an affinity that the Sillon bore to the nineteenth-century liberal Catholic tradition, to be sure. But it overlooked the element of associationism that linked it equally to the social Catholic tradition — not to mention the universalism (catholicity) of human solidarity that that tradition had always upheld.

The author of *Notre charge apostolique* was closer to the mark when he acknowledged that the Sillon's concern for human dignity was "noble" (AAS 2:613). The human emancipation summed up in the terms "liberty," "equality," and "fraternity," he went on to note, was only the negative side of democracy in Sangnier's outlook; what the movement was after positively was "the greatest possible participation of each person in the government of society. And this includes a threefold element, political, economic and moral." But this seductive doctrine was, after all, a doctrine, and one unfortunately opposed at every point to "Catholic truth" (AAS 2:615), for the latter had a different conception of the authority intrinsically necessary for human society: obedience to external authority was capital, as were relations of subordination between unequal members of the human family. The Sillon, although filled with the best of intentions, was pursuing the "chimera" of social equality (AAS 2:628). In the unkindest cut of all, it was accused of "enfeoffing its religion to a political party" (AAS 2:623).

Modernism and Anti-Modernism

Once the Sillon had differentiated itself from all the other social Catholic groupings in France (and before it was condemned by Rome), it started to seek out allies for "the vast collective movements" of which Sangnier had long dreamed (J. Caron 1966, 132). Since clerical avidity for control had engendered a deep-rooted anticlericalism, it was clear that France was not a Catholic country and not going to become one again in the foreseeable future. But that did not mean that the desire for a more perfect democracy was not widespread even among those who could not see its roots in Christianity. So the Sillon sought out alliances with non-Catholic groups and movements, such as co-operativism (see HDTFR 421 for Charles Gide) and trade unionism, in fact with any democratic element that was willing to respect the sincerity of the Sillonists' Catholic convictions.

Although Marc Sangnier had decided against standing for elections at the beginning of his public career, he now spoke more and more of forming a political party, one which would rescue the democratic cause from the priest-eating politicians who had been exploiting it for so long. In a way, the times were propitious. The Sillonist declaration of acceptance of a regime of separation of church and state was henceforth completely credible; anticlerical opponents would be hard put to discredit Sangnier as paving the way for a return of clerical domination as in the early years of the Third Republic. Now one could debate more substantive political issues. But of course this abdication of the strategy of "religious defense" was held against him in many a bishop's office and seminary, as well as in Rome. The Sillon's exploration of nonconfessional or interconfessional unionism also went against the grain.

For a time starting in 1907, the talk was of a *plus grand Sillon*, associating Protestants and nonbelievers with the political program implicit in Sangnier's vision of democracy (J. Caron 1966, 550). A daily newspaper would be necessary to support any worthwhile electoral efforts, so one was planned, *La Démocratie*. It started the same month the Sillon came to an end, but was allowed to continue as Marc Sangnier's purely political organ.

Meanwhile, the bible scholar Alfred Loisy had been condemned as a "modernist"; in the summer of 1907, two solemn declarations were issued on papal authority describing and condemning "modernism" (*Lamentabili sane exitu* [DS 3401–66] and *Pascendi dominici gregis* [DS 3475–3500]; see G. Daly 1980, esp. 165–219). Sangnier had already been accused of modernism once in 1904 (J. Caron 1966, 287f.), in the company not only of Loisy and Abbé Félix Klein (the "Americanist," 1862–1953), but of Abbé Naudet, the author Georges Fonsegrive, and Léon Harmel! These "Christian democrats" were represented as "modernists" in a different field of endeavor. The main common element seems to have been a willingness to countenance any change at all: in dogmatic teaching, for the modernists, or in societal structures, for the social Catholics. The irony is that the modern social and economic innovations against which nineteenth-century social Catholics had inveighed were now tacitly accepted by Pius X as traditional elements of the Catholic social outlook (AAS 2:612):

One will not build the city otherwise than God has built it...; no, civilization need not be invented, nor the new city built in the clouds. It

has been, it exists — it is the Christian civilization, the Catholic city.
One need only restore and repair it unceasingly on its natural and divine
foundations, against unwholesome utopias, revolt and lack of respect:
omnia instaurare in Christo.

When the attacks started again after the Separation and *Pascendi*,
this tactic of lining up modernist liberals and social Catholics side
by side as merely two variants of the same disease became standard.
Whereas the German, Belgian, and Dutch episcopates paid little heed
to this tactic, on the grounds that modernism as described in *Pascendi* had few if any adherents among their clergy, there were quite
a few bishops in Italy and France who saw modernism in every new
departure from the most reformable conventions of church life. Conspicuous Christian democrats were highly suspect. Alarm bells were
set ringing by writers with growing influence in conservative ecclesiastical circles: Julien Fontaine, S.J., the priest-journalists Emmanuel
Barbier, Bernard Gaudeau, Henri Delassus, Charles Maignen, the Assumptionist père Salvien (Charles Miglietti), Paul Boulin, and their
lay counterparts Joseph Rambaud, Jacques Rocafort, and others.

But even bishops free of integrist leanings would see the Sillon's
evolution as troublesome, for it was out of line with papal policy for
the French church after the Separation. Thus, in 1907, François Delamaire, who had been named coadjutor and effective archbishop of
Cambrai in the Nord just after *Gravissimo officii*, ordered the seminary rector to keep the Sillon and its publications at bay (J. Caron
1966, 605-10). His concern was obedience and unity behind the
pope's marching orders. When Sangnier asked the bishop to delin-
eate what political stands were to be considered as mandatory for
all Catholics — was it solely the repeal of the law of Separation? —
Delamaire declined. It was asking too much of the hierarchy to spec-
ify beforehand what political decisions would be secular and hence
not of concern to the pastor as such and which ones would require
hierarchical direction (J. Caron 1966, 612-21). For his part, Sangnier thought it was asking too much to expect Catholics to sign their
political preferences over to the hierarchy with a blank check.

Given the presence in the archdiocese of Cambrai of the most
notable political *abbé démocrate*, Jules Lemire, recently re-elected to
the Chamber of Deputies with the approval of Rome, it is easy to
understand that a problem could arise. One did, despite the long acquaintance of Lemire and Delamaire and the favor the new bishop
showed to Abbé Six. Following controversial remarks Lemire made
in parliament apropos of the Separation (for which see Mayeur 1968,
343-51), Merry del Val took the occasion, in a letter to Delamaire destined for publication, to make the connection with the anti-modernist

encyclical *Pascendi*. Its section on the "modernist errors concerning church and state" (*Pascendi* 23) should clear up "the fundamental misconception on which certain priests and lay Catholics base their line of conduct" (Mayeur 1968, 348).

In a year there followed the Roman condemnation of two Christian democratic newspapers, *La Justice sociale* and *La Vie catholique;* their respective editors, the abbés Naudet and Dabry, were forbidden to take up any other journalistic endeavors (ASS 41:141). It would be tedious to reproduce all the further cases in which Pius X's increasingly integrist policies manifested themselves (see, e.g., Poulat 1969a and Arnal 1985, 49–62). Before examining the critical labor union question in the French context, then, one more instance must suffice. When the doctrinal condemnation of the Action française could no longer be avoided, in 1914, Pius X withheld its promulgation; even though it was clear that Charles Maurras preached an immoral nationalism (Aubert 1978, 550) that "enfeoffed" a mutilated Catholicism to its political line, it would not be until 1927 that a pope would say so publicly.

The Labor Union Controversy under Pius X: France

Internal Relationships in French Catholic Social Catholicism

During the years of the Separation, the desire to coordinate the different wings of French social Catholicism was reinforced by the sense of the church being almost literally under siege (McManners 1972, 166–69). Or, to put it another way, the differences of orientation were masked by the external threat of the anticlericals. However, once separation of church and state in France actually took effect and the Conseil d'état manifested a willingness to let the French church live in comparative freedom (and penury), it almost seems that the alternative visions of French Catholicism felt free to assert themselves once more. Now that French Catholics were no longer bound to the state by concordat, they could shape their church according to their own ideas of what it should be. And without state support of bishops and clergy, those in a position to contribute large sums to church organizations might also expect to see their wishes heeded even more than in the past.

Within the minority constituted by social Catholics, by 1909, the alignment of tendencies was the following. The Semaines sociales constituted an intellectually adventurous wing. This direction, spurred on by Henri Lorin's deductive Neo-Thomistic thinking and by Marius Gonin's practicality and rootedness in Franciscan spirituality, supported by *La Chronique sociale* and its Secrétariat social in Lyon, was avowedly democratic and alert to the backslidings of paternalists. More moderate was the eclectic Action populaire, the Jesuit center at Reims. On principle, the AP, like the Semaines sociales, was open to all varieties of social Catholicism. Its leading figure, Gustave Desbuquois, like his Jesuit superiors in France and in Rome, was less interested in pushing premises to new conclusions than in disseminating solid received doctrine. He was regarded as part of the democratic wing inasmuch as he included support for Christian trade unionism in the category of received or at least permissible doctrine. Relations were close between these two focusses, since each respected the other's independence and did not attempt any kind of a takeover. An older Jesuit social Catholic institution of the region, the center at Mouvaux for the *Patrons du Nord*, felt slighted; it was out of step with the democratic trend of most of the rest of social Catholicism and was regarded as retrograde by the Jesuit authorities in Rome.

Of course, the Action populaire also maintained close ties particularly with the Jeunesse catholique (ACJF), which had long been entrusted to the spiritual guidance of Jesuit chaplains. The AP was also the main place where Catholic France could turn at any time for information and assistance about setting up study circles, credit unions or labor organizations. Organizations as disparate as diocesan social bureaus and the struggling union of employees (SECI) looked upon the AP as a source of support, printed materials and expertise. The AP was undoubtedly the next best thing to a permanent central institution for French social Catholicism, while the Semaines sociales continued as an "itinerant university"; the latter at the cutting edge, the former a continuing resource and enabler.

The Sillon represented the most advanced or utopian thinking in French social Catholicism. Its indirect influence would be great over the next forty years, but in 1910 it was abolished as an organized movement. The ACJF received some reinforcements from the dissolution of the Sillon, on its way to becoming 150,000 strong by 1914 (McManners 1972, 174). Concurrently, however, the *Ralliement* practically expired, for the Action libérale party no longer enjoyed the favor of the recently appointed bishops and the Vatican. A hint of the pope's preferences came, for example, when an unrepentant royalist such as the bishop of Montpellier, François de Cabrières, was named cardinal in 1911.

Albert de Mun soldiered on; although sickness had reduced his public appearances, he was active in parliament and wrote often in right-wing Parisian papers, publishing his memoires of 1870–75, *Ma vocation sociale*, in 1908. Gradually he was affected by the labor sympathies of the ACJF; in 1912 he finally accepted the labor union idea: Zirnheld had demonstrated the actuality of what he had always thought impossible, that ordinary workers could organize themselves effectively for common action (Droulers 1969, 261).

One bright spot for democracy was Brittany, where ordinary workers were still practicing Catholics in large numbers. With the aid and encouragement of a Christian democratic daily in Rennes, the *Ouest-Eclair*, this constituency shook off the control of upper-class monarchists in their voting habits and gave the paper its leading circulation in the region. Although Abbé Félix Trochu was removed from the staff by his archbishop in 1910, the lay aristocrat who co-founded the paper, Emmanuel Desgrées du Lou, was not to be budged (Arnal 1985, 55–57; see also Arnal 1980 and 1982). The lot of the reactionary politician in the arch-Catholic extreme west of France was not a happy one.

The Integrist Campaign

In the Nord, meanwhile, the dominance of the Catholic monied class made itself felt not only in the Lille conurbation, where the *Patrons du Nord* held forth from their retreat house at Mouvaux, but also in Reims, where Christian democracy had taken its rise in France in 1893 (Droulers 1969, 243). The hectic publishing activity there of the Action populaire was a thorn in the flesh of integrist circles because of the support it provided to the idea of unionization. A first attack was launched at the Semaines sociales, however, rather than at the AP. In 1909 Père Fontaine, who had seen his earlier attacks on Alfred Loisy corroborated by supreme authority with the issuance of the encyclical *Pascendi*, turned his attention to social Catholic deviations (in his *Modernisme sociologique*, Paris, 1909; see Talmy 1966, 107). No doubt his definition of social modernism went right to the heart of what was modern about the social Catholicism of the Semaines sociales, but it did so in an exaggerated fashion, drawing consequences that did not necessarily follow:

> [Social modernism] professes an egalitarianism incompatible with any hierarchy and any idea of authority and subordination. It advocates the autonomy of the human person, the equal worth of human agents, the equation of rights..., an equation that necessarily involves equality in the possession and enjoyment of the goods of this world. Private property, diverse and unequal like the sources that produce it, should henceforth disappear.

Henri Lorin was directly targeted, for he based his social thought on two principles here garbled and rejected, the ontologically equal dignity of human beings and the "equivalence of human agents," as both he and Fontaine phrased it. Instead of arguing for the abolition of private property, however, Lorin used the related equality principles as a basis for his view of the need for labor unions and for collective bargaining. Eugène Duthoit took issue with Fontaine on this basic misinterpretation immediately, in the preface of his own Semaine sociale lectures that were ready for the presses. The main effect of this response was to associate the Action populaire, which published the book in question, Duthoit's *Vers l'organisation professionelle*, with the suspicions of heterodoxy that were spreading out from the Semaines sociales (Droulers 1969, 245–47). This despite the heroic effort on the part of Père Desbuquois to keep the AP above polemics. His policy was not to dignify charges of unorthodoxy, especially by fellow Jesuits, with a public response.

Fontaine received the approbation of Cardinal Merry del Val and proceeded to publish a sequel (*Le Modernisme social*, 1911) in which Duthoit was now the main target, alongside of Lorin, Adéodat Boissard (another professor from Lille and co-founder of the Semaines sociales), Abbé Charles Calippe (Poulat 1961) and some innocuous bystanders. The objections can be summed up briefly; tendentious and overstated as they were, they became even less precise as they were repeated by imitators and popularizers of Fontaine. The main charge was that they were democrats, i.e., that they opposed paternalism — this was thought to suffice all by itself. The explanation, if one was needed, was that these democrats were ignoring natural law. They were said to teach unnuanced equality, subverting the social hierarchies; they were also playing into the hands of the atheist state that was destroying the freedom to be religious (Talmy 1966, 109).

The development of labor unions, which Lorin, Duthoit, and Boissard, among others, had taken upon themselves to encourage and defend, became *the* divisive issue above all others; as we have seen, this was also the case in Germany and Italy. Faced with this question, a churchman was forced to opt one way or the other — either to move forward to upholding the rights of workers to form unions, confessional or other — or backward to insisting so rigorously on the confessionality of unions as to render them ineffective as labor organizations.

The so-called discourse of Sarlat was indicative of this (Talmy 1966, 115, Ponson 1980, 265, Droulers 1969, 267–71). The founder of a federation of Catholic credit unions, Louis Durand of Lyon, an early friend of *La Chronique sociale*, delivered an address at the federation's congress on 12 May 1912 at Sarlat. It insisted at great length on the Catholic character of all social oeuvres for Catholics. In a version modified slightly to gain Roman approval, it was the object of an unusual encomium from Merry del Val as representing the doctrine of the pope himself. As Droulers (1969, 268) asks: "Was this not to come down on one side of the discussions that had been going on in France for more than twenty years, since the corporative program of La Tour du Pin was put forth?" Was the religious character of unions to be insisted upon in a sense that rendered nugatory their role as representing labor? Was collective bargaining in itself to be branded as an abuse? Should further theoretical developments of a corporatist regime of the future all be rejected a priori? By hindsight, of course, it is easy to recognize that this and similar moves in the subsequent months belonged to the skirmishing preparatory to *Singulari quadam*, skirmishing that picked up again thereafter and culminated in the trial balloon of the *Civiltà cattolica* articles in the spring of 1914. In this form, the polemic was aimed at preparing the way for a condemnation of the union idea itself, and not just its anticlerical embodiments.

Père Desbuquois of the AP, however, could not know this at the time. Even when indications of the pope's hostility to unions as such could not be overlooked, he found them impossible to credit. Occasional encouragements and signs of favor from on high for the AP's efforts could only increase his perplexity and that of his superiors. Like the Volksverein, the Action populaire felt that it was simply an unknown in Rome and hence made special efforts to make itself known (Droulers 1969, 321–30). In fact, it was well represented in Rome, not only by the Jesuit general, Franz Xaver Wernz, but by clerical friends such as the monsignori Gaston Vanneufville, Jules Tiberghien, and Louis Glorieux. Antoine Pottier was still in Rome as well; he had put in a good word for unionism at the Italian Social Week of Assisi in 1911. The need for unions to be Catholic, he said (Malgeri 1980, 3:234), was "neither absolute nor immutable," but contingent upon the prevalence of unacceptable ideas in the red unions of the time: ideas on class struggle, the use of violence, the abolition of private property. The trouble was not that the AP's backers in Rome were not well-connected or did not spread the word — it was just that they could not defend "social modernism" without being regarded as tainted with it themselves.

For example, the pope thought Wernz was dragging his feet (Poulat 1969a, 391): why did he continue to defend lines of thought and action opposed to those of the *Civiltà?* Now, *those* Jesuits had the pope's confidence; why was not the entire society following their lead?

Merry del Val multiplied his efforts to achieve the effect of a condemnation of specific points in the case put forward on behalf of trade unionism, without actually having to issue another solemn declaration involving the public humiliation of men who had served the church loyally. In December 1912, the rector of the Catholic Institute of Lille received a "confidential memoire" from Merry del Val containing a message for Duthoit and the other leading lights of the Semaines sociales (Talmy 1966, 122–24). He followed up in early January 1913 with a letter to Albert de Mun (Talmy 1966, 124f.; Droulers 1969, 286f.). In the same month, he asked Joseph Lemius (Poulat 1969a, 390f.; see also G. Daly 1980, 232–34), procurator of the Oblates of Mary Immaculate, to prepare an analysis of the teaching of the AP. He thus had in view for censure all the main national representative institutions of French social Catholicism of the period.

The letter to de Mun was personally laudatory, but repeated the points found objectionable in the memoire for Duthoit. Some social Catholics were emphasizing justice at the cost of charity. They would reduce property to its social function and consider its equitable distribution to be a matter of justice rather than charity; as a practical matter, did they not write charity off altogether? On the other hand, they create new obligations, such as that of belonging to "certain social organizations" (read: unions), whereas natural law preserves liberty. "And what is worse," what they call "natural law" is not based "on the eternal principles engraved on the conscience, but on the contingencies with which experience and history are concerned." "Experience" and "history" having already been condemned as sources of doctrine in *Pascendi* (G. Daly, index s.v.), this was a chilling indication of what awaited such tendencies in social Catholicism, unless speedily corrected. Integrist publications expatiated freely on Merry del Val's admonitions.

Duthoit and Lorin hastened to comply with Merry del Val's request for a retraction (publicly professed in due course at the Semaine sociale of Versailles later in 1913) in the following terms (Talmy 1966, 124):

We profess: 1. That the right of property is inviolable and that the bad use made of it does not suppress this right. 2. That there are only two natural societies: the family and political society; that the various modes of professional organization, aiming, within political society, to uphold order, justice, peace and respect for the family among persons of the same profession, depend on circumstances; hence, the constitution of the professions in determinate societies is only of the historical order. 3. That justice and charity are clearly distinct in themselves from the outset and hence also in regard to the sanctions that they carry.

Against the background of many further tell-tale indications, Father General Wernz thought it was incumbent upon him to ask Cardinal Merry del Val if the AP of Reims was (also) on the wrong track (February 1913). Merry del Val would not say that; after running through a repertory of diplomatic phrases, however, he pulled out Lemius's critical report and handed it to the Jesuit general; he did not approve everything in it, he said, but it showed what accusations were being made (Droulers 1969, 290).

A revealing document it is, not only of Merry del Val's inclinations, but of the settled view of a valued counselor, one regarded as a judicious and insightful ecclesiastic; after all, Lemius had been the principal drafter of the encyclical *Pascendi*. His conclusion was: "The Action populaire does not understand the necessity of keeping the worker in his place as worker; nor the grave consequences that can follow from damage done to the social order, which is, after all, the essential interest of human societies" (Poulat 1969a, 390f.). "Any one can see the danger of such an institution," placed, as the AP was, so as to penetrate the church with "a new social thought, opposed to the traditional social thought that it qualifies as liberal" (Poulat 1969a, 390f.; Droulers 1969, 293). In fact, this refusal to teach the worker to "stay in his place, which is that of a subordinate," this tendency to favor "egalitarianism," means that, "at bottom," the AP shares "the socialist idea."

This indictment came at the end of a twenty-two-page typed analysis. What was the bill of particulars? It was based on a (quick) reading of some of the AP's publications; cited in particular was its *Année sociale internationale 1912*, a thousand-page "monster" (Droulers 1969, 110) that was the third of a series. Besides insinuating that "the AP is persuaded of the possibility of resolving the social question without reference to religion and the supernatural" (Droulers 1969, 293), which was not the case, Lemius noted less inaccurately that in the purely economic and social domain, "what it seeks to promote first and foremost is the creation of unions." Since labor unions of a formally religious nature were not permitted under French law, the AP had recourse to the distinction between "the thesis and the hypothesis" and had to "content itself with the supernatural spirit" that would animate otherwise "purely professional trade-union groupings." That was Reims's position and that was where it went wrong. The kind of social action that can be actuated through labor unions, Lemius went on, reflects "a stubborn hostility to employers" and to "paternalism." According to "the Christian principles of social economy," however, consumer goods depend on the prudent management of production (on the part of the industrialist, whose authority must therefore not be challenged); their cost is affected by wage rates; it would follow that, rather than encouraging unionization, church spokesmen should be teaching workers to be content with their wages.

The Jesuit Counterattack

Before this bombshell landed on Desbuquois's desk, he had already responded firmly but cautiously to the letter to de Mun in a February 1913 issue of the Jesuit review *Etudes* (Droulers 1969 298f.). The most daring move was to compare the authority and weight of Merry del Val's two letters with that of *Rerum novarum* (or other encyclicals): *Rerum novarum*, as the only encyclical devoted to the condition of labor, continued to provide the basic authoritative synthesis, while lesser documents "put a fragmentary, precise and determinate aspect in relief." The latter, then, must be interpreted in the context of the former and not the other way around. The integrists, of course, took the opposite tack: the more recent elucidations showed which interpretations of the earlier document were acceptable.

A confidential response of the AP to the Lemius document was worked up and sent off to Rome on 19 April 1913 (Droulers 1969, 303–10). Only one point in it needs comment; that is the matter of distinguishing between "the thesis and the hypothesis." Thus, where the critical report objected that the AP wished to see labor unions founded, even in circumstances where a primarily religious union was not possible, its author was indulging in doctrinaire purism, in Desbuquois's view. "He [Lemius] does not seem to understand that one can distinguish between the thesis and the hypothesis; he has evidently never made contact with the reality" of the world of labor (Droulers 1969, 304). This usage of "thesis" and "hypothesis" went back at least to 1864 and the reception of Pius IX's Syllabus of Errors (Aubert 1978, 41). What it conveyed was that in a desirable set of circumstances (the "thesis"), the Roman Catholic Church's guidance would be universally accepted and embodied in the laws and institutions of Catholic countries. In that case, labor unions could be economic organizations of a religious character like the idealized guilds of the Middle Ages, without difficulty. Indeed, there might not be any need for labor unions as such, since the relation of capital and labor would be humanely arranged from the outset within each profession. However, this "thesis" unfortunately no longer existed, and the liberal "hypothesis" prevailed in the world in which one had to lead one's Christian life. The class struggle was part of this reality. Capital, including the *Patrons du Nord* and other Catholic employers, clearly had the upper hand in this struggle, for which there is no place in "the thesis." Redressing the balance would obviously have to cost the factory owners something, which accounts for their opposition to the labor movement. Taking refuge in a nonexistent "thesis" was not a responsible alternative.

Père Desbuquois, here representative of social Catholics in general, was as ultramontane as his critics. His idea of the obedience owed to the pope was unnuanced, unconditional. And yet he and those like him did not abandon their insights under pressure from the pope. How did they bring this off? They were prepared at any time to render obedience to a clear and formal command, of course. Short of this, they had to read signals that perplexed them. The distinction between the "thesis" and the "hypothesis" was one of the few expedients available to them to justify a course of conduct at variance with papal pronouncements, when they thought the course was the right one. The pope was expected to speak in terms of the "thesis" (Christian civilization and the Christian state), whereas the pastoral expert was expected to apply these ideals to "life such as it is," which varied from country to country (Droulers 1969, 211, 193).

The stubborn efforts of Desbuquois to defend the social movement did have an effect. It was an important part of the resistance (other parts of which have already been mentioned, chapter 14) that delayed and finally blocked the condemnation of trade unionism that was in prospect all through 1913 and until Pius X died. Seconded by the Jesuit general, Wernz, this resistance at least made the pope hesitate. The integrist attacks did not let up either, however. Up until this time, the integrist attacks and the Vatican warnings were publicized broadly (in *La Croix* etc.), while the replies of those criticized took place confidentially or in the form of cautious statements that could be interpreted as grudging retractions. But just after the New Year of 1914, under the leadership of Léonce de Grandmaison, the Jesuits of the *Etudes* in Paris launched a public counterattack in the form of a long editorial entitled "Critiques négatives et tâches nécessaires." It was an impassioned call for an end to the denunciations of Catholic pastors and activists engaged in difficult and "necessary tasks" on the part of those who seemed to spend their whole lives in nothing but "negative" and irresponsible "criticism."

Some of this criticism, as its victims in various countries were beginning to realize, was orchestrated by Msgr. Benigni of the news service A.I.R. in Rome. In fact, Fr. Rutten's priest secretary, Floris Prims (Poulat 1969a, 54; Droulers 1969, 365f.; Colsen 1955, 530–34), had "penetrated the cover" of one particularly naive conspirator in Ghent, Alphonse Jonkx (Poulat 1969a, 70 et passim). Prims kept Desbuquois informed in France, Poels in the Netherlands, and especially Hubertus Höner (Poulat 1969a, 12) in Germany. It was there that the first revelations about Benigni's Sodalitium Pianum were made, in the pages of the *Düsseldorfer Tageblatt* of 3 February 1914 (Poulat 1969a, 422). In April, Benigni's receptionist at the Roman office of the A.I.R. almost fell over backward when Prims walked in and introduced himself. Simultaneously, early in 1914, as noted in the last chapter, the Jesuits of the *Civiltá cattolica*, exempt from the authority of Wernz and in direct consultation with the pope, returned to the charge in a most ominous way with Fr. Monetti's articles questioning unionism across the board.

It could not escape Père Desbuquois's notice that all the authors cited explicitly for massive criticism in the Monetti articles were prominent French social Catholics. La Tour du Pin was the first to be mentioned by name; a phrase of his from the Association catholique of 15 March 1887 about corporatist estates forming "perfect societal organisms, little states within the state," was dragged in to bolster the assertion that labor unions aimed by nature at being independent of state authority, a law unto themselves (*Civiltá cattolica* 65, 1:389). Nor was this merely a single maladroit move; on the next page "the declarations of the Fribourg Union" and the proceedings of the Semaine social of Rouen were held up for censure. The whole school of La Tour du Pin was to be discredited, even though it only formed a preparatory stage toward the union idea itself. In the next installment (*Civiltá cattolica* 65, 1:551f.), the *Civiltá* articles went on to cite two democratically inclined union supporters, both French: Henri Bazire in a programmatic discourse of 1905 and Adéodat Boissard at the Marseilles Semaine social (Jarlot 1964, 349–51). The attack was not against the exaggerations of careless minor propagandists, but against the movement's leading authorities. Hence, even though Père Desbuquois was suffering from one of his periodic bouts of fatigue, brought on by overwork, the AP responded on many levels to the new threat, while also establishing or reactivating contacts in Italy, Belgium, and elsewhere (Droulers 1969, 346–75). The need to protect the work of the AP was a major factor in the determination of the Jesuit generalate in Rome to wage a campaign to prevent an anti-union *Syllabus* from being issued (Droulers 1969, 360; see the end of chapter 14 above).

The Settled Views of Père Desbuquois

How can one explain the firmness with which Desbuquois, here standing in for many another social Catholic of Pius X's time, proposed an alternative vision of the church's social message? The difference from their conservative adversaries is perhaps best described as one of orientation. Both sides strove to orient themselves with the aid of the common Catholic tradition as shaped in ultramontane Catholicism. Both sides felt they were carrying on Leo XIII's legacy. But whereas Louis Fichaux, Rambaud, and Billot (and Pius X as well) stuck to old charts, tested for centuries, in steering the church's course, the

AP crew and others like them noticed that the world was advancing into uncharted waters — and the church was in the same boat, willy-nilly.

In Desbuquois's first recorded utterance on the church's social action (in 1907; see Droulers 1969, 192, and for the following section, 191–229), he stated that the broad masses of the populace in twentieth-century France "insist that one deal with their life *such as it is*." Moreover, they were right to insist on it, that being the church's mission. The labor question, as Ketteler had said forty years previously, was still largely a question of existence, of precariously earning a living, and only secondarily one of raising the worker's social status. With this population, in these conditions, the church could only connect religiously if it paid attention to the improvement of working conditions.

Work, after all, was not something of marginal importance to human beings in any age, but something intimately connected with the person's life before God. Most people had to work with their hands; to earn one's living by work was a central fact of the human condition, willed as such by the creator, who also wills the salvation of the human race. "This twofold law, the law of work and the law of sanctification, does it not lead back to one? Human beings are to become holy in and by their work" (Droulers 1969, 196). Labor was also the central problem of the modern liberal world; or, to put it in other words, the role of the industrial working class was the critical issue capable of plunging the advanced societies into a most intractable crisis. What were the means by which Christianity could bring its valid and necessary perspectives on the dignity of labor to bear on the social crisis?

The answer was to promote association, of course, against individualism, the root of so much social havoc. In the light of the realities of modern industrialism and commerce, this meant trade unionism (Droulers 1969, 194, 200, 217–27). Already in 1909 and then more elaborately in 1912, Desbuquois and his Jesuit colleague at the AP, Maurice Rigaux, spelled out what Christian trade unions had to offer to modern societies under strain.

Père Desbuquois accepted as irreversible certain major developments of the French and industrial revolutions: equality of rights before the law, the expansion of personal choice (accompanied by personal responsibility), the division of labor, and industrialization that made increased productivity possible — and hence also the world of credit, finance, and accumulation of capital that was part of these modern developments. He did not accept it all uncritically or without reservation; basically, however, he was a reformist, not a counter-revolutionary. He could envisage good coming of these modern developments — if they were tempered with associational counterforces and the spirit of Christian brotherhood (Droulers 1969, 201).

> May [coming generations] arouse trade unionism to the Christian spirit! [The Christian labor movement] faces a splendid mission: to organize work; to make it the artisan of social harmony and peace; to equip religion, by the formation of an elite, with the greatest capability for penetration among the working class.

His reformism could be fairly radical at times, all the same. In 1910, commenting on the papal letter in regard to the Sillon, Desbuquois noted the "contemporary fact" of the "rise of the popular classes" (cited in Droulers 1969, 208). He accounted for the "enhanced role of the masses in human life" with "a very simple reason: labor occupies a preponderant place," indeed,

> the popular masses are the great agent of this new life. Consequently, their share of influence grows, their dependence lessens. They are aware of this, they say it, they quite rightly wish to see it acknowledged. On one particular point, they have a more precise desire: they intend to have a role in the study and disposition of their working conditions, a claim in the economic realm which is perfectly legitimate.... Equally legitimate is the tendency to gain for labor a priority over capital.... Why not encourage everything that enhances labor, that gives it its primary place in the economic order?

Wage-earning, he went on to say, is not necessarily wage-slavery. Without closing the door on alternate ways to rectify prevailing conditions, it would be better (Droulers 1969, 209) to avoid the "chimera of a radical transformation of the contemporary economic situation; let us leave that to the socialists and the utopians, while working to improve the existing regime; the ordinary worker can find the realization of his rights and of his essential desiderata in the refinement of the wage system." This would necessarily come about through associations of workers resembling trade unions in that they would assert and protect the interests of working people.

Conclusion

Almost in spite of their declared eclecticism, the Jesuits of the Action populaire in Reims developed a coherent social teaching distinct from that of the social conservatives and also from La Tour du Pin's corporatism. Behind the anti-labor attitudes of social conservatives lurked economic liberalism — this was the "social modernism" (Droulers

1969, 206, 218) that deserved to be shunned by all Catholics. Behind references to self-denial as the gospel virtue that would heal the tensions between capital and labor (à la Périn), they detected the Malthusian assumption of an irremediable scarcity of resources (Droulers 1969, 194). On the other hand, their modern approach resulted in a dilution of the corporative-regime idea (Droulers 1969, 222) to the point where it became a simple working hypothesis, a mere exemplification of the ideal. This ideal visualized a society organized for productive purposes, not according to materialistic principles but in keeping with the dignity and destiny of human beings.

In a time of ecclesiastical reaction, the cause of social justice showed that it had sunk roots so deep in some bastions of Catholicism that it could not be eradicated even by the concerted opposition of free-lance critics and hierarchical authorities. Leading social Catholics mounted stubborn and reasoned resistance against massive residual and recrudescent paternalism in the church. To be sure, they could not protect the Catholic labor movement from being stunted in its growth. But they did keep the possibility of trade unions for Catholic workers alive for future developments. Unlike 1848, the door was not altogether closed on democracy this time.

EPILOGUE

Social Catholicism in Europe arose in defense of working people in traditional ways of life — farming and trades — when they were threatened by what Joseph Schumpeter (1942, 83) has called the "creative destruction" of modern industrial capitalism. The responses of "social Catholics" (even though they were a small minority, a *pusillus grex*) defy simple characterization.

Attempting a bird's-eye view at the end of a study of the first century of industrialization on the continent, one can distinguish national variants, of course — the Belgian, French, German, and Italian cases are those that have loomed largest in our presentation. In spite (or because) of the recent origins of the nation-state experience on the part of Belgians, Germans, and Italians, it was the national experience and its connection with the Holy See, as a sort of international spiritual capital for Catholics, that occupied the center of interest. Hence lateral influences mediated internationally from one country's social Catholics to another's were weak in comparison with those that flowed to and from the center of Catholicism (Droulers 1983b). Nevertheless, in the case of the Christian labor movement, an international secretariat was formed as early as 1908 (Schneider 1986, 495).

Within each national movement one can again find a plurality of perspectives, reflecting positions influenced by liberalism, conservatism, reaction, radicalism, communitarianism, cooperativism, socialism. All the same, without pretending to draw a sociogram of nineteenth-century social Catholicism (Komonchak 1985, Gabriel 1981), one may note a general sequence of stages that took place in most of the countries studied. The focus of this book has been on the economic sector in its relationship to Catholicism. Hence the emphasis here will be on the labor movement's prehistory and history, to the relative neglect of much else that could rightly be placed under the heading of Catholic social teaching and practice.

In terms of social Catholic outlook or thought, the beginnings, under the auspices of Lamennais (founder of "liberal Catholicism")

319

or the "conservatives" Adam Müller in Germany and Villeneuve-Bargemont in France, gave way to predominantly "intransigent" inner-Catholic trends as the century moved into its second half and final third. This "intransigence" is characterized by the rejection of the prevailing secular ideology, economic liberalism, as well as its younger rival, socialism, in the name of Catholicism or tradition. Paternalistic approaches are necessarily dominant in these early decades before *Rerum novarum*, with compassionate clergy, industrialists, and professionals providing the most effective assistance to suffering members of the working class. One recalls Abbé Ledreuille's warning to the well-to-do Parisians in 1845, however, and Mermillod's in 1868, that these efforts were still only half-hearted.

It might seem that the time had come to move toward enabling workers to take more responsibility for their own professional and organizational development. In Germany the Kolping movement made a start in that direction, as did Fr. Cronenberg's association in Aachen and Bishop Ketteler's endorsement of the trade union idea. But throughout the 1870s and into the 1880s in Germany, Bismarck repressed clerical activities and workers' associations with equal zeal. The center of gravity of social Catholic developments moved back to France.

After a redoubling of paternalistic efforts (e.g., by Maignen and de Mun), the corporatist ideal of the social Catholic theorists in Austria and France (La Tour du Pin) made quite a dent in the widespread Catholic opposition to government intervention in labor questions. In the years just before *Rerum novarum*, there was a small but lively campaign to resurrect corporatist institutions as the embryo of a properly organized future society.

Rerum novarum (1891) justified governmental intervention. More importantly, perhaps, it sparked the movement called Christian democracy. This marks a new phase of social Catholicism, picking up threads that had been dropped since 1848. "Christian democrats" were still militantly anti-liberal (in the sense of opposing bourgeois economic values such as individual labor contracts and freedom from state regulation in commerce or industry). The *abbés démocrates* aimed at enhancing the church's moral influence in society; they and their sympathizers in social Catholicism tended to present the church and the Catholic tradition as defenders of the masses. Their goal was not a workers' state; but Christian democrats did promote something approaching universal manhood suffrage, which was of course an anti-paternalist stance.

Léon Harmel (1829–1915) illustrates almost too neatly this progression of phases characteristic of nineteenth-century social Catholicism. As partner and manager of a family firm, he started out with the social conscience inherited from his father, *le bon père*, and continued the paternalistic in-house clubs, confraternities, and social insurance plans already in place in the middle of the century. He honored Charles Périn of Louvain as the Christian economist par excellence. In the 1870s and 1880s, when confronted by La Tour du Pin's theories with their corporatist horizons, his Christian zeal led him to test various associationist initiatives, to see if they were promising building-blocks of a future "corporatist regime." At the same time he was induced by his Franciscan spirituality and by contact with his workers to downplay rather than magnify class differences and to entrust to workers all the responsibilities that they were capable of meeting. When *Rerum novarum* appeared, followed in France by the call to rally to the republic, he found himself already a "Christian democrat," although one still comfortable with his responsibilities as employer, businessman, and leader of a Christian workers' movement.

If the Christian democracy of Abbé Pottier in Liège or Abbé Lemire across the border in northernmost France marks a threshold, it does not signal the end of paternalistic practice or theory in social Catholicism. Only since the 1944 Christmas Message of Pope Pius XII and definitively since Vatican II's *Gaudium et Spes* (no. 73 on participation of all in the life of society and in the government of the state), has it been officially stated that the paternalism of the *classes dirigeantes* should yield to a more democratic ideal (see also *Dictionnaire de théologie catholique*, Tables générales 3:3457–58). It would be a mistake to see that theoretical advance as having taken place under Leo XIII, despite the signs of favor he gave to the two *abbés démocrates* just mentioned as well as to Léon Harmel and others. Here there is a striking parallel with Leo's teaching on church and state and its limits, as interpreted by John Courtney Murray.

In 1901, with the encyclical *Graves de communi re* (Carlen 1981, 2:479–85), Leo XIII unmistakably signaled that he was not comfortable with a generalized call for autonomy for workers' organizations. In his opinion, they might in certain cases very well be autonomous from employer control (*Rerum novarum* 49, in Carlen 1981, 2:254). But autonomy from ecclesiastical guidance or clerical leading-strings was not what he had in mind (*Rerum novarum* 54, 57; Carlen 1981, 2:255–56). For how then could the church play its role as arbiter of economic morality, part of its mission to the world? How would such autonomous labor unions be any more beneficial to society than manufacturers' or bankers' associations, whose social consciousness and conscience left much to be desired? Was such autonomy a step forward? Not in Leo's eyes and still less so in those of his successor, Pope Pius X (1903–14)!

This was nevertheless the path Christian labor was forced to take in competition with the much stronger socialist unions. In general, one can say that the Christian unions were the second strongest branch of unionism in each country, far behind the socialists but ahead of the "liberal" or bourgeois-allied unions. In Germany, the socialists outnumbered the Christians by roughly six to one, although in the Rhineland and Westphalia in 1903 some 40 percent of all organized workers belonged to a Christian union (Schneider 1986, 495). In Austria the proportion was fifteen to one, narrowing to five to one by 1930. In Belgium, however, Christian and socialist union movements were roughly equal in strength.

The idea of condemning labor unionism in the name of Catholic social teaching was dropped with the death of Pius X and the accession of Benedict XV. When the soldiers came back from World War I, management and labor often found themselves at loggerheads, as before. Robert Talmy (1966, 133–235) has narrated the further history of the *Patrons du Nord* down to 1930, exposing most of the inside story behind a key pronouncement of the Holy See of 1928/1929, a letter of the Sacred Congregation of the Council to Achille Liénart, recently appointed bishop of Lille. With this letter of 5 June 1928 to the administrator of the diocese *sede vacante* (when re-dated 5 June 1929 and published in the *Acta Apostolicae Sedis*), the magisterium took a firm and explicit position endorsing the legitimacy of labor unions not under management control (Droulers 1981, 138–61). The moral obligation of employers to act paternalistically was thus replaced by their obligation to respect their workers' rights, in particular their right to organize on their own. This development was subsequently confirmed in Pius XI's major social encyclical, *Quadragesimo anno* (1931; see Nell-Breuning in Curran and McCormick 1986, 60–68).

In the light of their revival after World War I, it is safe to say that the formation of Christian labor unions with varying degrees of autonomy was the most striking development in social Catholicism throughout Europe in the period before 1914. By the time World War I broke out, lay leaders had accrued enough confidence and status to challenge the characteristic paternalism that had prevailed earlier and continued to have the upper hand in the church. Such were Adam Stegerwald and Heinrich Imbusch in Germany, Leopold Kunschak in Austria, Achille Grandi in Italy, P. J. S. Serrarens and René Debruyne in the Netherlands and Belgium, Jules Zirnheld and Gaston Tessier in France (Schneider 1986, 495). Equally indispensable were the clergy who made labor questions their special cause: from Franz Hitze and August Pieper to Heinrich Brauns and Otto Müller in Germany, Alois Scheiwiler in Switzerland, Luigi Sturzo in Italy, Ceslaus Rutten and Henry Poels in the Low Countries, and in France, the Christian Brothers, the abbé Bataille, and (less directly but no less effectively) Père Desbuquois.

The newer Christian trade-union movement drew strength and inspiration from the previous types of nineteenth-century social Catholicism that had been contending for dominance: the *patronage* movement, industrial paternalism, and the corporatist ideal. Even though unionism could not replace them, its rise represented a challenge to them that set off the controversies we have retold. It limited the *patronages* to youth work; it battled industrial paternalism and company unions; it largely supplanted corporatist efforts at organization. The divisiveness and hostility of Catholics and socialists within the labor movement has often been noted and deplored. It was not this, however, but the tension with paternalism that made sparks fly within the Catholic household, for while the Catholic union leadership basically accepted the system of industrial capitalism, it could not do so on the terms of the *Herr im Haus* mentality of the barons of industry. Hence it also wakened or aggravated tensions over authority and clerical patriarchalism in modern Catholicism itself. The bitter attacks of integrist Catholic writers upon it were the immediate consequence.

Workers, after all, were considered to be part of that *imperitum vulgus* (Leo XIII) that, like women and children, were permanently in the care of the educated and the propertied class, since they were incapable of looking after their own affairs properly. This question of fact about the capabilities of members of the working class seemed to be based on the irrefragable testimony of empirical observation — until anomalies accumulated densely enough to raise doubts at least in the more perceptive. In an age when feminism was still embryonic, it was unionism that forced the issue in the Catholic Church as in society at large.

Union sympathizers could, however, appeal to a central tenet of philosophical anthropology especially emphasized by the Neo-Thomists among the social Catholics, the dignity of the human person. This theme was at the core of Liberatore's and Ketteler's remonstrances against economic liberalism from early on; Leo XIII anchored the official papal teaching to it, especially in *Rerum novarum*. No less surely than John Stuart Mill's brand of liberalism, the Thomistic notion of the intrinsic dignity of the human person ultimately had to resist a pertinacious paternalism that denied practical responsibility to adult human persons of a whole very large and increasingly important class.

"Pertinacious" paternalism — for it is not in doubt that social Catholicism, like other approaches to social reform in the nineteenth century, like any number of instances in the history of labor movement in general and of course also in the history of socialism, had to begin with paternalist assistance. When decisions were taken and control was exercised over irresponsible, incapable, or simply uneducated workers "for their own good," it *was* often necessary and helpful. One may see paternalism as the cradle of the modern Catholic labor movement and even, in a mitigated form, as its school. To the extent that the educative and emancipatory element wanes or becomes merely pro forma, however, paternalistic "benevolence" serves as nothing more than a transparent mask for control, one-sided economies, efficiency, convenience, or other ends that do not necessarily conduce to greater respect for human dignity.

How does one draw the line between properly parental and unduly paternalistic relationships? Paul Bureau (a friend of Abbé Lemire), a Catholic social thinker who was also highly appreciative of Anglo-Saxon institutions, made the most pointed observation that I have found from the period. In a family, he wrote, the father seeks to rear his children to become independent and self-sufficient, not to remain as children. An employer may allow other interests the upper hand, overlook the fact that his interests and those of his workers are not identical, and turn a blind eye to the fact that the workers can rightfully claim to be treated as adults. In this case, the boss reacts like a father who "cannot imagine that his children will join together to look after their interests against him" (cited by Reid 1985, 585–86).

Paternalism was thus a major issue throughout the period, though neither at that time nor since has it been isolated for thematic theological (social-ethical) treatment. It would appear from the utterances of clerical leaders like August Pieper of the German Volksverein and Gustave Desbuquois, S.J., of the French Action populaire that the time was not ripe for a thorough sorting out of the issue. They both wished to steer clear of theoretical discussions that had the potential of creating difficulties for their practical efforts. Perhaps that caution helped stave off the Roman condemnation that hung over their organizations like a Damoclean sword.

If paternalism (vs. autonomy) was the apple of discord, the Neo-Thomistic anthropology championed by Pope Leo XIII provided all those who could still be considered social Catholics at the end of the period with some commonly shared and characteristic elements. One has already been mentioned as highlighted in *Rerum novarum* and received with joy in the ranks, namely the central importance accorded to the dignity of the human person as immediate to God.

Another such element had hardly made its thematic appearance yet, although one can find it hidden almost wherever one looks, often under the term "Catholicism" or "social Catholicism" itself. That is the notion of human solidarity (Pesch 1905, 1:408–55). It emerged out of the struggle for a humane outlook on the political economy waged on two fronts against both liberalism and socialism, as has been repeatedly pointed out (see above, chapter 10). In an early phase, it was mainly liberal individualism that had to be repelled, and many a social Catholic did not shrink from calling for "Christian socialism." Later, when the potential benefits of modern capitalism could be discerned and distinguished from individualistic abuses, and when socialism as a term had become attached to the anti-religious labor movement and its theorists, the essential mutuality of human beings in their life and labor came to be called "solidarity" and its theoretical underpinnings "solidarism" (Cort 1988, 288–90, and Mulcahy 1952).

Heinrich Pesch, S.J., the most noted theorist of Catholic solidarism, studied economics in Berlin in the tradition of the *Kathedersozialisten*. Although he published his basic works before World War I, they received little notice as the battle over unionism raged in Catholicism in Pius X's reign. In their reception and interaction with the rest of social Catholicism, they belong to the period after World War I. And that is another chapter, an apt starting point for another volume on the history of social Catholicism.

REFERENCE LIST

Abel, Wilhelm. 1974. *Massenarmut und Hungerkrisen im vorindustriellen Europa: Versuch einer Synopsis.* Hamburg: Parey.

———. 1978. *Agrarkreisen und Agrarkonjunktur: Eine Geschichte der Land- und Ernährungswirtschaft Mitteleuropas seit dem hohen Mittelalter.* 3d rev. and enl. ed. Hamburg: Parey.

Agócs, Sándor. 1975. "'Germania doceat!' The Volksverein, the Model for Italian Catholic Action, 1905-1914." *Catholic Historical Review* 61:31-47.

Albert, Pierre. 1972. "La presse française de 1871 à 1940." Bellanger, Godechot, et al., 3:133-688.

Alexander, Edgar. 1953. "Social and Political Movements and Ideas in German and Austrian Catholicism (1789-1950)." Moody 1953, 325-583.

Amann, Peter. 1970. "A *Journée* in the Making: May 15, 1848." *Journal of Modern History* 42:42-69.

Anderson, Margaret Lavinia. 1981. *Windthorst: A Political Biography.* New York: Clarendon Press.

Anderson, Robert D. 1984. *France, 1870-1914: Politics and Society.* Boston: Routledge & Kegan Paul.

Antonazzi, Giovanni. 1957. *L'enciclica Rerum novarum, testo autentico e redazioni preparatorie dai documenti originali.* Rome: Edizioni di storia e letteratura.

Arbeiter und Arbeiterbewegung im Vergleich: Berichte zur internationalen historischen Forschung. 1986. Edited by Klaus Tenfelde. Historische Zeitschrift, Sonderheft 15. Munich: Oldenbourg.

Aretin, Karl Otmar von. 1970. *The Papacy and the Modern World.* Translated by Roland Hill. New York: McGraw-Hill.

Aretz, Jürgen. 1982. "Katholische Arbeiterbewegung und christliche Gewerkschaften — Zur Geschichte der christlichsozialen Bewegung." Rauscher 1982, 2:159-214.

Arnal, Oscar. 1980. "Why the French Christian Democrats Were Condemned." *Church History* 49:188-202.

———. 1982. "The Nature and Success of Breton Christian Democracy: The Example of *L'Ouest-Eclair.*" *Catholic Historical Review* 68:226-48.

———. 1985. *Ambivalent Alliance: The Catholic Church and the Action Française, 1899-1939.* Pittsburgh: University of Pittsburgh Press.

Aubert, Roger. 1952. *Le pontificat de Pie IX (1846-1878).* 2d ed., 1964. Paris: Bloud et Gay.

————. 1970. *Il pontificato di Pio IX (1846–1878)*. Edited by Giacomo Martina. 2 vols. Turin: S.A.I.E.

————. 1978. *The Church in Secularised Society*. The Christian Centuries 5. New York: Paulist Press.

————. 1981a. "The Catholic Movement in France and Italy." Jedin 1981, 7:227–39.

————. 1981b. "The First Phase of Catholic Liberalism." Jedin 1981, 7:269–92.

L'Avenir 1830–1831: Antologia degli articoli di F. R. Lamennais e degli altri collaboratori. 1967. Edited by Guido Verucci. Rome: Edizioni di Storia e Letteratura.

Bachem, Karl. 1927–32. *Vorgeschichte, Geschichte, und Politik der deutschen Zentrumspartei*. 9 vols. Cologne: Bachem. Reprint, Aalen: Scientia, 1968.

Baechler, Christian. 1982. *Le parti catholique alsacien, 1890–1939: Du Reichsland a la république jacobine*. Paris: Ophrys.

Barbier, Emmanuel. 1923–24. *Histoire du catholicisme libéral et du catholicisme social en France, 1879–1914*. 5 vols. Bordeaux: Y. Cadoret.

Barthélemy-Madaule, Madeline. 1973. *Marc Sangnier 1873–1950*. Paris: Seuil.

Bauer, Clemens. 1931. "Wandlungen der sozialpolitischen Ideenwelt im deutsche Katholizismus des 19. Jahrhunderts." *Die soziale Frage und der Katholizismus. Festschrift zum vierzigjährigen Jubiläum der Enzyklika Rerum novarum*, 11–46. Paderborn: Schöningh.

————. 1964. *Deutscher Katholizismus: Entwicklungslinien und Profile*. Frankfurt: Josef Knecht.

Becker, Winfried. 1981a. *Georg von Hertling, 1843–1919*. Vol. 1: *Jugend und Selbstfindung zwischen Romantik und Kulturkampf*. Mainz: Grünewald.

————. 1981b. "Der Kulturkampf als europäisches und als deutsches Phänomen." *Historisches Jahrbuch* 101:422–46.

————. 1982. "Peter Reichensperger (1810–1892)." ZgLb 5:41–54.

————. editor. 1986. *Die Minderheit als Mitte: Die Deutsche Zentrumspartei in der Innenpolitik des Reiches 1871–1930*. Paderborn: Schöningh.

Bédarida, François, and Jean Maitron, editors. 1975. *Christianisme et monde ouvrier*. Paris: les Editions Ouvrières.

Bedeschi, Lorenzo. 1973. *La terza pagina de "Il Popolo."* Rome: Ed. Cinque Lune.

Bellanger, Claude, Jacques Godechot, et al. 1969–76. *Histoire générale de la presse française*. 5 vols. Paris: Presses universitaires de France.

Berenson, Edward. 1984. *Populist Religion and Left-Wing Politics in France, 1830–1852*. Princeton, NJ: Princeton University Press.

Beutter, Friedrich. 1971. *Die Eigentumsbegründung in der Moraltheologie des 19. Jahrhunderts*. Paderborn: Schöningh.

Biéler, André. 1982. *Chrétiens et socialistes avant Marx*. Geneva: Ed. Labor et fides.

Bigler, Robert M. 1972. *The Politics of German Protestantism: The Rise of the Protestant Church Elite in Prussia, 1815–1848*. Berkeley: University of California Press.

Birke, Adolf M. 1971. *Bischof Ketteler und der deutsche Liberalismus: eine Untersuchung über das Verhältnis des liberalen Katholizismus zum bürgerlichen Liberalismus in der Reichsgründungszeit.* Mainz: Grünewald.

Blackbourn, David. 1980. *Class, Religion and Local Politics in Wilhelmine Germany: The Centre Party in Württemberg before 1914.* New Haven, CT: Yale University Press.

Blasina, Paolo. 1987. "'Allez ou peuple': Una lettera dell'abbé Lemire a Leone XIII." *Cristianesimo nella storia* 8:219–26.

Blondel, Maurice. 1910. "La 'Semaine Social' de Bordeaux." *Annales de Philosophie chrétienne* (in eight installments, 1909–1910).

Bock, Edward C. 1977. *Wilhelm von Ketteler, Bishop of Mainz: His Life, Times, and Ideas.* Lanham, MD: University Press of America.

Böhme, Helmut. 1978. *An Introduction to the Social and Economic History of Germany: Politics and Economic Change in the 19th and 20th Centuries.* New York: St. Martin's Press.

Bonhoeffer, Dietrich. 1958–61. *Gesammelte Schriften.* Edited by Eberhard Bethge. 4 vols. Munich: C. Kaiser.

Bowen, Howard R. 1968. "Müller, Adam Heinrich." IESS 10:522–23.

Bowman, Frank P. 1973. *Le Christ romantique, 1789: Le sans-culotte de Nazareth.* Geneva: Droz.

Boyer, John W. 1981. *Political Radicalism in Late Imperial Vienna: The Origins of the Christian Social Movement, 1848–1897.* Chicago: University of Chicago Press.

Brack, Rudolf. 1976. *Deutscher Episkopat und Gewerkschaftsstreit 1900–1914.* Cologne: Böhlau.

Brakelmann, Günter. 1962. *Die soziale Frage des 19. Jahrhunderts.* Bielefeld: Luther-Verlag.

Brandl, Manfred. 1975. "Deutsche katholische Stimmen zu Sozialismus und Kommunismus, zur sozialen Lage und Industrialisierung bis 1850." Langner 1975, 165–93 and 225–37.

Bressolette, Claude. 1977. *L'abbé Maret: Le combat d'un théologien pour une démocratie chrétienne 1830–1851.* Paris: Beauchesne.

Brose, Eric Dorn. 1985. *Christian Labor and the Politics of Frustration in Imperial Germany.* Washington, DC: Catholic University of America Press.

Brown, Marvin L. 1977. *Louis Veuillot: French Ultramontane Catholic Journalist and Layman, 1813–1883.* Durham, NC: Moore.

Brugerette, Joseph. 1933–38. *Le prêtre français et la société contemporaine.* 3 vols. Paris: P. Lethielleux.

Bruhat, Jean. 1972. "Le socialisme français de 1815 à 1848." Droz 1972, 1:331–406 and 501–34.

Buchheim, Karl. 1963. *Ultramontanismus und Demokratie: Der Weg der deutschen Katholiken im 19. Jahrhundert.* Munich: Kösel.

Bünter, Adelhelm. 1985. *Theodosius Florentini: Wegbereiter aus christlicher Leidenschaft.* Fribourg: Imba.

Bureau, Paul. 1902. *Montceau-les-Mines et le paternalisme.* La Chapelle-Montligeon: Imprimerie-Librairie de Notre-Dame de Montligeon.

Bussmann, Walter. 1981. "Europa von der Französischen Revolution zu den nationalstaatlichen Bewegungen des 19. Jahrhunderts." T. Schieder, HEG 5:404–615.

Caldwell, T. B. 1966. "The Syndicat des employés du commerce et de l'industrie (1888–1919)." *International Review of Social History* 11:228–66.

Calvez, Jean Yves, and Jacques Perrin, editors. 1961. *The Church and Social Justice: The Social Teaching of the Popes from Leo XIII to Pius XII, 1878–1958.* Translated by J. R. Kirnan. Chicago: H. Regnery.

The Cambridge Economic History of Europe. 1966– . Edited by H. J. Habakkuk, Peter Mathias, and M. M. Postan. 7 vols. Cambridge University Press.

Carlen, Claudia, editor. 1981. *The Papal Encyclicals.* 5 vols. Wilmington, NC: McGrath.

Caron, François. 1979. *An Economic History of Modern France.* New York: Columbia University Press.

Caron, Jeanne. 1966. *Le Sillon et la démocratie chrétienne, 1894–1910.* Paris: Plon.

Cathrein, Victor. 1890. *Moralphilosophie: Eine wissenschaftliche Darlegung der sittlichen, einschliesslich der rechtlichen Ordnung.* 2 vols. 5th ed. Freiburg: Herder.

―――. 1904. *Socialism: Its Theoretical Basis and Practical Application.* New York: Benzinger.

Cecchini, Francesco Maria, editor. 1971. Romolo Murri, *La Vita Nova, 1895–1896.* Rome: Storia e letteratura.

―――. 1973. *Murri e il murrismo: Studi storici.* Urbino: Argalìa.

Chadwick, Owen. 1981a. *The Popes and European Revolution.* Oxford History of the Christian Church. Oxford: Clarendon Press.

―――. 1981b. "Christianity and Industrial Society." *The Christian World: A Social and Cultural History.* Edited by G. Barraclough. New York: H. N. Abrams.

Chenu, Marie-Dominique. 1979. *La "doctrine sociale" de l'église comme idéologie.* Paris: Cerf.

Cholvy, Gérard. 1985. "La restauration catholique en France au xixᵉ siecle (1801–1860)." *Migne et le renouveau des études patristiques* 1985, 61–89.

―――, and Yves-Marie Hilaire. 1985–88. *Histoire religieuse de la France contemporaine.* 3 vols. Toulouse: Privat.

Die christlichen Gewerkschaften in Österreich. 1975. Edited by Franz Grössl. Vienna: Europaverlag.

Christliche Philosophie im katholischen Denken des 19. und 20. Jahrhunderts. 1987– . Edited by Emerich Coreth, Walter M. Neidl, and Georg Pfligersdorfer. Graz: Styria.

Christensen, Torben. 1962. *Origin and History of Christian Socialism, 1848–54.* Acta Theologica Danica 3. Aarhus: Universitetsforlaget.

Cipolla, Carlo M. 1976. *The Economic History of World Population.* 7th ed. Harmondsworth: Penguin.

———, general editor. 1976–77. *The Fontana Economic History of Europe.* Vol. 3, *The Industrial Revolution 1700–1914*; vol. 4, *The Emergence of Industrial Societies.* New York: Barnes & Noble.

Clark, Martin. 1984. *Modern Italy, 1871–1982.* Longman History of Italy, 7. New York: Longman.

Cohen, D. K. 1969. "The Vicomte de Bonald's Critique of Industrialism." *Journal of Modern History* 41:475–84.

Cohen, Paul. 1988. "Heroes and Dilettantes: Action française, Le Sillon, and the Generation of 1905–1914." *French Historical Studies* 15:673–87.

Coleman, John A. 1979. *The Evolution of Dutch Catholicism 1958–1974.* Berkeley: University of California Press.

Colsen, Jozef Petrus. 1955. *Poels.* Roermond-Maaseik: J. J. Romen.

Conzemius, Victor. 1968. "Adolf Kolping (1813–1865)." *Rheinische Lebensbilder* 3:221–33. Düsseldorf: Rheinland Verlag.

———. 1972. *Propheten und Vorläufer: Wegbereiter des neuzeitlichen Katholizismus.* Zürich: Benziger.

Cort, John C. 1988. *Christian Socialism: An Informal History.* Maryknoll, NY: Orbis.

Curran, Charles E., and Richard A. McCormick, editors. 1986. *Readings in Moral Theology, No. 5: Official Catholic Social Teaching.* New York: Paulist.

Cuvillier, Armand. 1948. *P.-J.-B. Buchez et les origines du socialisme chrétien.* Paris: Presses universitaires de France.

———. 1954. *Un journal d'ouvriers: l'Atelier 1840–1850.* Paris: Editions ouvrières.

Daly, Gabriel. 1980. *Transcendence and Immanence: A Study in Catholic Modernism and Integralism.* Oxford: Clarendon Press.

Dansette, Adrien. 1961. *Religious History of Modern France.* 2 vols. New York: Herder and Herder.

Davis, Charles. 1982. " 'Fluent Benthamites and Muddled Coleridgians:' The Liberal and Conservative Traditions in Discourse." Papers of the Nineteenth-Century Theology Working Group, VII: AAR 1982 Meeting, 45–53. Edited by Garrett Green and Marilyn C. Massey. Berkeley: Graduate Theological Union.

De Gasperi, Alcide. 1931. *I tempi e gli uomini che prepararono la "Rerum novarum."* New edition with foreword by G. Andreotti. Milan: Vita e Pensiero, 1984.

Dehon, Léon. 1894. *Manuel social chrétien.* Paris: Bonne Presse.

———. 1976– . *Oeuvres sociales.* Naples: Edizioni Dehoniane.

Denk, Dieter. 1980. *Die Christliche Arbeiterbewegung in Bayern bis zum Ersten Weltkrieg.* Mainz: Grünewald.

De Rosa, Gabriele. 1966. *Il movimento cattolico in Italia dalla Restaurazione all'età giolittiana.* 4th ed. Bari: Laterza, 1976.

———. 1977. *Luigi Sturzo.* La Vita sociale della Nuova Italia, 27. Turin: Unione Tipografico-Editrice Torinese.

Derré, Jean-René. 1962. *Lamennais, ses amis et le mouvement des idées à l'époque romantique, 1824–1834.* Paris: C. Klincksieck.

———. 1963. *Metternich et Lamennais, d'après les documents conservés aux Archives de Vienne.* Paris: Presses universitaires de France.

Deufel, Konrad. 1976. *Kirche und Tradition: Ein Beitrag zur Geschichte der theologischen Wende in 19. Jahrhundert am Beispiel des kirchlich-theologischen Kampfprogramms P. Joseph Kleutgens S.J., Darstellung und neue Quellen.* Munich: Schöningh.

Dietrich, Donald J. 1985. "Priests and Political Thought: Theology and Reform in Central Europe, 1845–1855." *Catholic Historical Review* 71:519–46.

Dokumente: Etappen der katholisch-sozialen Bewegung in Österreich seit 1850. 1980. Sankt Pölten: Katholische Arbeitnehmerbewegung Österreichs.

Dorr, Donal. 1983. *Option for the Poor: A Hundred Years of Vatican Social Teaching.* Maryknoll, NY: Orbis.

Dorneich, Julius. 1979. *Franz Josef Buss und die katholische Bewegung in Baden.* Freiburg: Herder.

Droulers, Paul. 1954. *Action pastorale et problèmes sociaux sous la Monarchie de Juillet chez Mgr d'Astros.* Paris: Vrin.

———. 1957. "Le cardinal de Bonald et la question ouvrière á Lyon avant 1848." *Revue d'histoire moderne et contemporaine* 4:281–301. Reprint, Droulers 1982, 191–213.

———. 1961. "Des évêques parlent de la question ouvrière en France avant 1848." *Revue de l'Action Populaire*, no. 147: 442–60.

———. 1969. *Politique sociale et christianisme. Le père Desbuquois et l'Action Populaire: Débuts, syndicalisme et intégristes (1903–1918).* Paris: Editions Ouvrières.

———. 1975. "Catholicisme et mouvement ouvrier en France au xixᵉ siècle: L'attitude de l'épiscopat." Bédarida and Maitron 1975, 37–65.

———. 1981. *Politique sociale et christianisme. Le père Desbuquois et L'Action populaire: Dans la gestation d'un monde nouveau (1919–1946).* Paris: Editions Ouvrières; Rome: Gregorian University Press.

———. 1982. *Cattolicesimo sociale nei secoli xix e xx: Saggi di storia e sociologia.* Politica e Storia 49. Rome: Edizioni di Storia e Letteratura.

———. 1983a. "Christianisme et innovation technologique: Les premiers chemins de fer." *Histoire, économie et société* 2:119–32.

———. 1983b. "Relazioni europee fra i cattolici sociali nel'800." *Genesi della coscienza internationalista nei cattolici fra '800 e '900*, 17–34. Padua: Gregoriana.

Droz, Jacques. 1966. "Religious Aspects of the Revolutions of 1848 in Europe." *French Society and Culture since the Old Regime*, 133–49. Edited by E.M. Acomb and M.L. Brown. New York: Holt, Rinehart and Winston.

———, general editor. 1972–78. *Histoire générale du socialisme.* 4 vols. Paris: Presses universitaires de France.

———. 1972a. "Le Socialisme allemand du *Vormärz.*" Droz 1972, 1:407–54.

———. 1972b. "Les débuts du socialisme." Droz 1972, 1:535–43.

Dru, Alec. 1963. *The Contribution of German Catholicism.* New York: Hawthorn.

Duchrow, Ulrich. 1987. *Global Economy: A Confessional Issue for the Churches?* Translated by David Lewis. Geneva: WCC Publications.

Duroselle, Jean Baptiste. 1951. *Les débuts du catholicisme social en France (1822–1870).* Paris: Presses universitaires de France.

———. 1955. "Les 'filiales' de la Congrégation." RHE 50: 867–91.

———. 1958. "Un project de 'mission ouvrière' à Paris au milieu du xixe siècle." *Archives de sociologie religieuse* 6:36–46.

Ebert, Kurt. 1975. *Anfänge der modernen Sozialpolitik in Österreich.* Vienna: Verlag der Österreichischen Akademie der Wissenschaften.

Ederer, Rupert J., translator. 1981. *The Social Teachings of Wilhelm Emmanuel von Ketteler, Bishop of Mainz (1811–1877).* Washington, DC: University Press of America.

Elbow, Matthew H. 1953. *French Corporative Theory, 1789–1948.* New York: Columbia University Press.

Ellis, Marc H. 1981. *Peter Maurin: Prophet in the Twentieth Century.* New York: Paulist.

Engels, Friedrich. 1975. "Progress of Social Reform on the Continent." *Karl Marx Friedrich Engels Collected Works* 3:392–408. New York: International Publishers.

Epstein, Klaus. 1959. *Matthias Erzberger and the Dilemma of German Democracy.* Princeton, NJ: Princeton University Press. Reprint, New York: Howard Fertig, 1971.

———. 1966. *The Genesis of German Conservatism (1770–1806).* Princeton, NJ: Princeton University Press.

Evangelisches Staatslexikon. 1987. 3d rev. ed. 2 vols. Stuttgart: Kreuz.

Evans, David Owen. 1951. *Social Romanticism in France 1830–1848.* Oxford: Clarendon.

Filthaut, Ephrem. 1960. *Deutsche Katholikentage 1848–1958 und die soziale Frage.* Essen: Driewer.

Fischer, Wolfram. 1972. *Wirtschaft und Gesellschaft im Zeitalter der Industrialisierung.* Göttingen: Vandenhoeck & Ruprecht.

———. 1982. *Armut in der Geschichte: Erscheinungsformen und Lösungsversuche der "Sozialen Frage" in Europa seit dem Mittelalter.* Göttingen: Vandenhoeck & Ruprecht.

———. 1984. *Germany in the World Economy during the Nineteenth Century.* London: German Historical Institute.

Focke, Franz. 1978. *Sozialismus aus christlicher Verantwortung. Die Idee eines christlicher Sozialismus in der katholischsozialen Bewegung und in der CDU.* Wuppertal: Hammer.

Fogarty, Gerald P. 1982. *The Vatican and the American Hierarchy from 1870–1965.* Stuttgart: A. Hiersemann. Reprint, Wilmington, DE: Michael Glazier, 1985.

Fogarty, Michael P. 1957. *Christian Democracy in Western Europe, 1820–1953.* Reprint, Westport, CT: Greenwood Press, 1974.

Fortescue, William. 1987. *Revolution and Counter-Revolution in France 1815–1852*. Historical Association Studies. Oxford: B. Blackwell.

Foucher, Louis. 1955. *La philosophie catholique en France au xixᵉ siècle, avant la renaissance thomiste et dans son rapport avec elle (1800–1880)*. Paris: J. Vrin.

Franz, Albert. 1914. *Der soziale Katholizismus in Deutschland bis zum Tode Kettelers*. Mönchengladbach: Volksverein.

Friedberger, Walter. 1978. *Die Geschichte der Sozialismuskritik im katholischen Deutschland zwischen 1830 und 1914*. Frankfurt am Main: Lang.

Fries, Heinrich, and Georg Schwaiger, editors. 1975. *Katholische Theologen Deutschlands im 19. Jahrhundert*. 3 vols. Munich: Kösel.

Fry, Karl. 1949–52. *Kaspar Decurtins: Der Löwe von Truns 1855–1916*. 2 vols. Zurich: Thomas.

Fulvi Cittadini, Maria. 1980. *Christianesimo sociale nell'ottocento: Ideologie e movimenti intorno a J. Léon Le Prévost*. Vatican City: Libreria Editrice Vaticana.

Gabriel, Karl, and F.-X. Kaufmann, editors. 1981. *Zur Soziologie des Katholizismus*. Mainz: Grünewald.

Gadient, Veit. 1944. *Der Caritasapostel Theodosius Florentini*. Lucerne: Rex.

Gadille, Jacques. 1973. "France, VI: période contemporaine." DHGE 18:132–57.

———. 1974. *Les catholiques libéraux au xixᵉ siècle*. Grenoble: Presses universitaires. U. de Grenoble.

———. 1975. *Civilisation chrétienne: Approche historique d'une idéologie (xviiiᵉ-xxᵉ siècle)*. Paris: Beauchesne.

Gall, Lothar. 1980. *Bismarck: der weisse Revolutionär*. Frankfurt: Propyläen.

Gatz, Erwin. 1971. "Das erste Vatikanische Konzil und die soziale Frage." *Annuarium Historiae Conciliorum* 3:156–73.

———. 1977–85. *Akten der Fuldaer Bischofskonferenz*. 3 vols. Mainz: Grünewald.

———. 1982. "Caritas und soziale Dienste." Rauscher 1982, 2:312–51.

———. 1983. *Die Bischöfe der deutschsprachigen Länder, 1785/1803 bis 1945: Ein biographisches Lexikon*. Berlin: Duncker and Humblot.

Geehr, Richard S. 1990. *Karl Lueger: Mayor of Fin de siècle Vienna*. Detroit: Wayne State University Press.

Gérin, Paul. 1959. *Catholiques liégeois et la question sociale (1833–1914)*. Brussels: Etudes Sociales.

Good, David F. 1984. *The Economic Rise of the Hapsburg Empire, 1750–1914*. Berkeley: University of California Press.

Görres, Joseph. 1926– . *Gesammelte Schriften*. Edited for the Görres-Gesellschaft by W. Schellberg et al., Cologne, 1926–58; continued by Heribert Raab, 1985– . Paderborn: Schöningh.

Gottfried, Paul. 1979. *Conservative Millenarians: The Romantic Experience in Bavaria*. New York: Fordham University Press.

Goyau, Georges. 1897–1912. *Autour du catholicisme social*. 5 vols. Paris: Perrin.

——. 1905–9. *L'Allemagne religieuse: Le Catholicisme (1800–1870)*. 3 vols. Paris: Perrin.

Graham, John T. 1974. *Donoso Cortés: Utopian Romanticist and Political Realist*. Columbia: University of Missouri Press.

Grassl, Hans, editor. 1957. *Franz Xaver Baader, Gesellschaftslehre*. Munich.

——. 1968. *Aufbruch zur Romantik, Bayerns Beitrag zur deutschen Geistesgeschichte 1765–1785*. Munich.

——. 1975. "Franz von Baader (1765–1841)." Fries and Schwaiger 1975, 1:274–302.

Grebing, Helga. 1985a. *Arbeiterbewegung: Sozialer Protest und kollektive Interessenvertretung bis 1914*. Munich: DTV.

——. 1985b. *History of the German Labour Movement*. Dover, NH: Berg.

Greipl, Egon Johannes. 1984. "Römische Kurie und katholische Partei: Die Auseinandersetzungen um die Christlichsozialen in Österreich im Jahre 1895." *Quellen und Forschungen aus Italienischen Archiven und Bibliotheken* 64:284–344.

Grenner, Karl Heinz. 1967. *Wirtschaftsliberalismus und katholisches Denken: Ihre Begegnung und Auseinandersetzung im Deutschland des 19. Jahrhunderts*. Cologne: Bachem.

Greschat, Martin. 1980. *Das Zeitalter der Industriellen Revolution: das Christentum vor der Moderne*. Stuttgart: Kohlhammer.

Griffiths, Richard M. 1965. *The Reactionary Revolution: The Catholic Revival in French Literature, 1870–1914*. New York: F. Ungar.

Groethuysen, Bernhard. 1927–30. *Die Entstehung der bürgerlichen Welt- und Lebensanschauung in Frankreich*. 2 vols. Halle: Niemeyer. Reprint, Frankfurt: Suhrkamp, 1978.

——. 1968. *The Bourgeois: Catholicism vs. Capitalism in Eighteenth-century France*. Introduction by Benjamin Nelson. New York: Holt, Rinehart & Winston.

Groh, John E. 1982. *Nineteenth Century German Protestantism: The Church as Social Model*. Lanham, MD: University Press of America.

Guichonnet, Paul. 1974. "Le socialisme italien des origines à 1914." Droz 1974, 2:237–78.

Guitton, Georges. 1927. *Léon Harmel, 1829–1915*. 2 vols. Paris: Spes.

Gundlach, Gustav. 1929. "Zur Geistesgeschichte der Begriffe Stand-Klasse." Now in Gundlach, *Die Ordnung der menschlichen Gesellschaft*, 2:191–204. Cologne: J. P. Bachem, 1964.

Gurian, Waldemar. 1929. *Die politischen und sozialen Ideen des französischen Katholizismus 1789–1914*. Mönchengladbach: Volksverein.

Haller, Karl Ludwig von. 1816–1826. *Die Restauration der Staatswissenschaften*. 6 vols. Winterthur.

Hamerow, Theodore S. 1958. *Restoration, Revolution, Reaction: Economics and Politics in Germany, 1815–1871*. Princeton, NJ: Princeton University Press.

——. 1983. *The Birth of a New Europe. State and Society in the 19th Century*. Chapel Hill, NC: University of North Carolina Press.

Hanisch, Ernst. 1975. *Konservatives und revolutionäres Denken: Deutsche Sozialkatholiken und Sozialisten im 19. Jahrhundert.* Vienna: Geyer.

Hartl, Friedrich. 1971. *Franz von Baader.* Wegbereiter heutiger Theologie 5. Graz: Styria.

Hebblethwaite, Peter. 1985. *Pope John XXIII: Shepherd of the Modern World.* Garden City, NY: Doubleday.

Hegel, Eduard. 1987. *Das Erzbistum Köln zwischen der Restauration des 19. Jahrhunderts und der Restauration des 20. Jahrhunderts 1815–1962.* Geschichte des Erzbistums Köln, vol. 5. Cologne: J. P. Bachem.

Heilbroner, Robert L. 1953. *The Worldly Philosophers: The Lives, Times and Ideas of the Great Economic Thinkers.* New York: Simon and Schuster.

Heitzer, Horstwalter. 1979. *Der Volksverein für des katholische Deutschland im Kaiserreich 1890–1918.* Mainz: Grünewald.

————. 1983. *Georg Kardinal Kopp und der Gewerkschaftsstreit 1900 bis 1914.* Cologne: Böhlau.

Henderson, William Otto. 1975. *The Rise of German Industrial Power, 1834–1914.* Berkeley: University of California Press.

Heyer, Friedrich. 1969. *The Catholic Church from 1648–1870.* London: Black.

Hickey, S. H. F. 1985. *Workers in Imperial Germany: The Miners of the Ruhr.* Oxford: Clarendon Press.

Histoire économique et sociale de la France. 1976–82. Fernand Braudel and Ernest Labrousse, general editors. 4 vols. Paris: Presses universitaires de France.

Hollenbach, David. 1979. *Claims in Conflict: Retrieving and Renewing the Catholic Human Rights Tradition.* New York: Paulist.

Hollerbach, Alexander. 1974. "Das Verhältnis der katholizischen Naturrechtslehre des 19. Jahrhunderts zur Geschichte der Rechtswissenschaft und Rechtsphilosophie." Langner 1975, 113–33.

Huber, Ernst-Rudolf. 1957–84. *Deutsche Verfassungsgeschichte seit 1789.* 7 vols. Stuttgart: Kohlhammer. Vols. 1–3, 2d rev. ed. 1967–70.

————, and Wolfgang Huber, editors. 1973–83. *Staat und Kirche im 19. und 20. Jahrhundert: Dokumente zur Geschichte des deutschen Staatskirchenrechts.* 3 vols. Berlin: Duncker and Humblot.

Hürten, Heinz. 1982. "Katholische Verbände." Rauscher 1982, 2:215–77.

————. 1986. *Kurze Geschichte des deutschen Katholizismus 1800–1960.* Mainz: Grünewald.

Isambert, François-André. 1967. *Buchez ou l'âge théologique de la sociologie.* Paris: Cujas.

Iserloh, Erwin. 1975. *Die soziale Aktivität der Katholiken im Übergang von caritativer Fürsorge zu Sozialreform und Sozialpolitik, dargestellt an der Schriften W. E. v. Kettelers.* Mainz: Akademie der Wissenschaften und der Literatur.

————. 1988. "Ketteler, Wilhelm Emmanuel von (1811–1877)." *TRE: Theologische Realenzyklopädie* 18:109–13.

Jarlot, Georges. 1938. *Le régime corporatif et les catholiques sociaux.* Paris: Flammarion.

————. 1964, 1973. *Doctrine pontificale et histoire.* 2 vols. Rome: Gregorian University Press.

Jedin, Hubert, general editor. 1980–81. *History of the Church.* American edition co-editor, John Dolan. 10 vols. New York: Crossroad.

Kaelble, Hartmut. 1986. *Industrialization and Social Inequality in 19th Century Europe.* Leamington Spa/Heidelberg: Berg.

Kall, Alfred. 1983. *Katholische Frauenbewegung in Deutschland: eine Untersuchung zur Gründung katholischer Frauenvereine im 19. Jahrhundert.* Munich: Ferdinand Schöningh.

Kaufmann, Franz-Xaver. 1979. *Kirche begreifen: Analysen und Thesen zur gesellschaftlichen Verfassung des Christentums.* Freiburg: Herder.

Keller, Emile. 1865. *L'Encyclique du 8 décembre 1864 et les principes de 1789, ou l'Eglise, l'état et la liberté.* Paris: Poussielgue.

Kemp, Tom. 1985. *Industrialization in Nineteenth-Century Europe.* New York: Longmans.

Klinkenberg, Norbert. 1981. *Sozialer Katholizismus in Mönchengladbach: Beitrag zum Thema Katholische Kirche und Soziale Frage im 19. Jahrhundert.* Mönchengladbach: B. Kühlen.

Knoll, August Maria. 1932. *Der soziale Gedanke im modern Katholizismus: Von der Romantik bis Rerum novarum.* Vienna: Reinhold.

Knoll, Reinhold. 1973. *Zur Tradition der Christlich-Sozialen Partei: Ihre Früh- und Entwicklungsgeschichte bis zu den Reichsratswahlen 1907.* Vienna: H. Böhlau.

Koehler, Benedict. 1980. *Ästhetik der Politik: Adam Müller und die politische Romantik.* Stuttgart: Klett-Cotta.

Köhler, Oskar. 1981. "The Development of Catholicism in Modern Society." Jedin 1981, 9:190–256.

Kolping, Adolph. 1975–87. *Adolph-Kolping-Schriften.* 5 vols. Edited by Hans Joachim Kracht. Cologne: Kolping-Verlag.

Komonchak, Joseph A. 1985. "The Enlightenment and the Construction of Roman Catholicism." *CCICA Annual,* 31–59.

Kossmann, Ernst Heinrich. 1978. *The Low Countries 1780–1940.* Oxford: Clarendon.

Kselman, Thomas A. 1983. *Miracles and Prophecies in 19th Century France.* New Brunswick, NJ: Rutgers University Press.

La Tour du Pin, René de. 1907. *Vers un ordre social chrétien: Jalons de route (1882–1907).* Paris: Librairie National. 5th ed. Paris: Beauchesne, 1929.

Lambert, Willi. 1987. "Franz von Baader (1765–1840)." *Christliche Philosophie* 1:150–73.

Lamennais, Félicité de. 1971–81. *Correspondance générale de Lamennais.* 9 vols. Edited by Louis Le Guillou. Paris: A. Colin.

Landes, David S. 1969. *The Unbound Prometheus: Technological Change and Industrial Development in Western Europe from 1750 to the Present.* Cambridge University Press.

Lange, Rudolf. 1955. *Franz Joseph Ritter von Buss und die soziale Frage seiner Zeit.* Freiburg: Herder.

Langlois, Claude. 1985. *Le Catholicisme au féminin: les congrégations françaises à supérieure générale au xixe siècle.* Paris: Cerf.

Langner, Albrecht. 1974. "Grundlagen des sozialethischen Denkens bei Wilhelm Emmanuel von Ketteler." *Theologie und Sozialethik im Spannungsfeld der Gesellschaft,* 61–112. Edited by A. Langner. Paderborn: Schöningh.

———, editor. 1975. *Katholizismus, konservative Kapitalismuskritik und Frühsozialismus bis 1850.* Paderborn: Schöningh. See 11–73 for Langner's "Zur konservativen Position in der politisch-ökonomischen Entwicklung Deutschlands vor 1848."

———, editor. 1978. *Säkularisation und Säkularisierung im 19. Jahrhundert.* Paderborn: Schöningh.

Lannon, Frances. 1987. *Privilege, Persecution, and Prophecy: The Catholic Church in Spain 1875–1975.* Oxford: Clarendon Press.

Latreille, André, et al. 1957–62. *Histoire du catholicisme en France.* 3 vols. Paris: Spes.

Le Goff, Jacques. 1988. *Your Money or Your Life: Economy and Religion in the Middle Ages.* Cambridge, MA: Zone Books.

Le Guillou, Louis. 1966. *L'évolution de la pensée religieuse de Félicité Lamennais.* Paris: A. Colin.

———. 1987a. "Die philosophische Gegenrevolution in Frankreich: Louis de Bonald (1753–1840), Joseph de Maistre (1753–1821) and François-René de Chateaubriand (1768–1848)." *Christliche Philosophie* 1:445–58.

———. 1987b. "Félicité-Robert de Lamennais (1782–1854)." *Christliche Philosophie* 1:459–76.

———. 1987c. "Im Schatten von Lamennais: Henri Lacordaire (1802–1861) und Charles de Montalembert (1810–1870)." *Christliche Philosophie* 1:477–85.

Le Guillou, M. J., and Louis Le Guillou. 1982. *La Condamnation de Lamennais.* Textes Dossiers Documents 5. Paris: Beauchesne.

Lenhart, Ludwig. 1966–68. *Bischof Ketteler: Staatspolitiker, Sozialpolitiker, Kirchenpolitiker.* 3 vols. Mainz: v. Hase und Koehler.

Lepper, Herbert, editor. 1977. *Sozialer Katholizismus in Aachen.* Mönchengladbach: Kühlen.

Levillain, Philippe. 1983. *Albert de Mun: Catholicisme français et catholicisme romain du Syllabus au Ralliement.* Rome: Ecole Française de Rome.

Lill, Rudolf. 1964. *Die ersten deutschen Bischofskonferenzen.* Freiburg: Herder. Also in *Römische Quartalschrift* 59 (1964): 127–85 and 60 (1965): 1–75.

———. 1978. "Kirche und Revolution. Zu den Anfängen der katholischen Bewegung im Jahrzehnt vor 1848." *Archiv für Sozialgeschichte* 18:565–75.

———. 1981. "The Beginnings of the Catholic Movement in Germany and Switzerland." Jedin 1981, 7:216–27.

Lonergan, Bernard. 1972. *Method in Theology.* New York: Herder & Herder.

Lönne, Karl-Egon. 1986. *Politischer Katholizismus in 19. und 20. Jahrhundert.* Frankfurt: Suhrkamp.

McLeod, Hugh. 1981. *Religion and the People of Western Europe, 1789–1970.* Oxford: Oxford University Press.

McManners, John. 1969. *The French Revolution and the Church.* New York: Harper & Row.

———. 1972. *Church and State in France, 1870–1914.* New York: Harper & Row.

Maier, Hans. 1969. *Revolution and Church: The Early History of Christian Democracy 1789–1901.* Notre Dame, IN: University of Notre Dame Press.

———. 1983. *Katholizismus und Demokratie.* Freiburg: Herder.

Maignen, Charles. 1927. *Maurice Maignen, Directeur du Cercle Montparnasse, et les origines du mouvement social catholique en France (1822–1890).* 2 vols. Luçon: S. Pacteau.

Malgeri, Francesco, general editor. 1979–81. *Storia del movimento cattolico in Italia.* 6 vols. Rome: Il Poligono.

Maritain, Jacques. 1936. *Integral Humanism: Temporal and Spiritual Problems of a New Christendom.* Translated by Joseph W. Evans. New York: Scribner, 1968.

Martin, Benjamin F. 1978. *Count Albert de Mun, Paladin of the Third Republic.* Chapel Hill, NC: University of North Carolina Press.

Martin, Oliver. 1984. *Les Catholiques sociaux dans le Loir-et-Cher: De l'Oeuvre des cercles ouvriers au parti démocratique, 1875–1926.* Blois: Association éditrice le clairmirouère du temps.

Martina, Giacomo. 1974. *Pio IX (1846–1850).* Rome: Gregorian University Press.

———. 1986. *Pio IX (1851–1866).* Miscellanea Historiae Pontificiae 51. Rome: Gregorian University Press.

Marty, Martin. 1969. *The Modern Schism. Three Paths to the Secular.* New York: Harper & Row.

Marx, Karl. 1975–. *Karl Marx, Frederick Engels Collected Works.* New York: International Publications.

Massey, Marilyn Chapin. 1983. *Christ Unmasked: The Meaning of the Life of Jesus in German Politics.* Chapel Hill, NC: University of North Carolina Press.

Mayeur, Jean Marie. 1968. *Un prête démocrate, l'abbé Lemire (1853–1928).* Paris: Casterman.

———, editor. 1975. *L'Histoire religieuse de la France, xixᵉ-xxᵉ siècle: problèmes et méthodes.* Paris: Beauchesne.

———. 1980. *Des parties catholiques à la démocratie chrétienne: xixᵉ-xxᵉ siècles.* Paris: A. Colin.

———. 1986a. *Catholicisme social et démocratie chrétienne: Principes romains, expériences françaises.* Paris: Cerf.

———. 1986b. "Un nouveau modèle des prêtres: les 'abbés démocrates.'" *Eglises sociétés et ministères: essai d'hermeneutique historique des origines du christianisme à nos jours,* 131–44. Paris: Centre Sèvres.

Meerts, Kristin. 1982. "De Leuvense hoogleraar Victor Brants: een brugfiguur in het sociaal-katholicisme (1856–1891)." *Bijdragen tot de geschiedenis* 65:197–233.

———. 1983. "De Leuvense hoogleraar Victor Brants: Sociale ideeën tussen katholieke romantiek en realisme (1856–1891)." *Bijdragen tot de geschiedenis* 66:101–30.

Migne et le renouveau des études patristiques: Actes du colloque de Saint-Flour 7–8 juillet 1975. 1985. Edited by André Mandouze and Joël Fouilheron. Théologie Historique 66. Paris: Beauchesne.

Milward, Alan S., and S. B. Saul. 1973. *The Economic Development of Continental Europe: 1780–1870.* Totowa, NJ: Rowman and Littlefield.

———. 1977. *The Development of the Economies of Continental Europe, 1850–1914.* Cambridge: Harvard University Press.

Misner, Paul. 1989. "Letteratura recente sul cattolicesimo sociale tedesco nel diciannovesimo secolo." *Bollettino dell'Archivio per la storia del movimento sociale cattolico in Italia* 24:266–86.

———. 1990. "Adam Müller and Adam Smith: A Romantic-Catholic Response to Modern Economic Thought." *Religion and Economic Ethics,* pp. 175–98. Edited by Joseph F. Gower. Annual Publication of the College Theology Society, 1985, vol. 31. Lanham, MD: University Press of America.

Mokyr, Joel. 1976. *Industrialization in the Low Countries, 1795–1850.* New Haven, CT: Yale University Press.

Molette, Charles. 1968. *L'Association catholique de la jeunesse française, 1886–1907.* Paris: Colin.

———. 1970. *Albert de Mun, 1872–1890: Exigence doctrinale et préoccupations sociales chez un laic catholique.* Paris: Beauchesne.

Montalembert, Charles de. 1852. *Catholic Interests in the Nineteenth Century.* London: Dolman.

Montuclard, Maurice. 1965. *Conscience religieuse et démocratie: La deuxième Démocratie chrétienne en France, 1891–1902.* Paris: Editions du Seuil.

Moody, Joseph N., editor. 1953. *Church and Society: Catholic Social and Political Thought and Movements, 1789–1950.* New York: Arts, Inc.

———. 1969. *The Church as Enemy: Anticlericalism in Nineteenth Century French Literature.* Washington, DC: Corpus Books.

———. 1983. "The Condemnation of Lamennais: A New Dossier." *Theological Studies* 44:123–30.

Morsey, Rudolf. 1979. "Joseph Görres (1776–1848)." ZgLb 3:26–35.

———. 1985. "Streiflichter zur Geschichte der deutschen Katholikentage 1848–1932." JCSW 26:9–24.

Moss, Bernard H. 1976. *The Origins of the French Labor Movement, 1830–1914: The Socialism of Skilled Workers.* Berkeley: University of California Press.

Mueller, Franz H. 1941. *Heinrich Pesch and His Theory of Solidarism.* St. Paul, MN: College of St. Thomas.

———. 1971. *Kirche und Industrialisierung: Sozialer Katholizismus in den Vereinigten Staaten und in Deutschland bis Pius XII*. Osnabrück: A. Fromm.

——. 1980. *Heinrich Pesch: Sein Leben und seine Lehre*. Cologne: J. P. Bachem.

——. 1984. *The Church and the Social Question*. Washington, DC: American Enterprise Institute.

Mulcahy, Richard E. 1952. *The Economics of Heinrich Pesch*. New York: Henry Holt.

Müller, Adam Heinrich. 1809. *Die Elemente der Staatskunst*. 3 vols. Berlin: G. D. Sander. Reprint, Jena: G. Fischer, 1922, 2 vols.

Mun, Albert de. 1908. *Ma vocation sociale: Souvenirs de la fondation de l'Oeuvre des cercles catholiques d'ouvriers (1871–1875)*. Paris: Lethielleux.

Murray, John Courtney. 1952. "The Church and Totalitarian Democracy." *Theological Studies* 13:525–63.

——. 1953a. "Leo XIII on Church and State: The General Structure of the Controversy." *Theological Studies* 14:1–30.

——. 1953b. "Leo XIII: Separation of Church and State." *Theological Studies* 14:145–214.

——. 1953c. "Leo XIII: Two Concepts of Government." *Theological Studies* 14:551–67.

——. 1954. "Leo XIII: Two Concepts of Government. II. Government and the Order of Culture." *Theological Studies* 15:1–33.

Neitzel, Sarah C. 1987. *Priests and Journeymen: The German Catholic "Gesellenverein" and the Christian Social Movement in the 19th Century*. Bonn: Röhrscheid.

Nelson, Benjamin. 1949. *The Idea of Usury: From Tribal Brotherhood to Universal Otherhood*. 2d ed. University of Chicago Press, 1969.

Neumann, Peter, editor. 1985. *Soziale Frage und Kirche im Saarrevier: Beiträge zu Sozialpolitik und Katholizismus im späten 19. und frühen 20. Jahrhundert*. Saarbrücken: Saarbrücker Druckerei und Verlag.

Nipperdey, Thomas. 1983. *Deutsche Geschichte 1800–1866: Bürgerwelt und starker Staat*. Munich: Beck.

Noonan, John Thomas. 1957. *The Scholastic Analysis of Usury*. Cambridge: Harvard University Press.

Nord, Philip G. 1984. "Three Views of Christian Democracy in 'Fin de siècle' France." *Journal of Contemporary History* 19:713–27.

Novak, Michael. 1989. *Catholic Social Thought and Liberal Institutions: Freedom with Justice*. New Brunswick, NJ: Transaction.

O'Brien, Patrick, editor. 1983. *Railways and the Economic Development of Western Europe 1830–1914*. New York: St. Martin's Press.

Oelinger, Josef. 1982. "Franz Joseph Ritter von Buss (1803–1878)." ZgLb 5:9–24.

Palmade, Guy P. 1972. *French Capitalism in the Nineteenth Century*. New York: Barnes & Noble.

Palmer, Robert R. 1961. *Catholics and Unbelievers in 18th Century France*. Princeton, NJ: Princeton University Press.

Patch, William L., Jr. 1985. *Christian Trade Unions in the Weimar Republic, 1918–1933: The Failure of "Corporate Pluralism."* New Haven: Yale University Press.

Paulhus, Normand J. 1983. "The Theological and Political Ideals of the Fribourg Union." Ph.D. dissertation, Boston College.

Pecorari, Paolo, editor. 1977. *Ketteler e Toniolo: Tipologie sociali del movimento cattolico in Europa.* Rome: Città Nuova.

———. 1981. *Giuseppe Toniolo e il socialismo: Saggio sulla cultura cattolica tra 1800 e 1900.* Bologna: Pàtron.

———. 1983. *Luigi Luzzatti e le origini dello "statalismo" economico nell'età della Destra storica.* Padua: Signum.

Périn, Charles. 1861. *De la richesse dans les sociétés chrétiennes.* 2 vols. Paris: Jacques Lecoffre.

Pesch, Heinrich. 1901. *Liberalismus, Socialismus und christliche Gesellschaftsordrung.* 2d ed. 3 vols. in 2. Freiburg: Herder.

———. 1905–23. *Lehrbuch der Nationalökonomie.* 5 vols. Freiburg: Herder.

Phayer, Michael. 1970. *Religion und das gewöhnliche Volk in Bayern in der Zeit von 1750–1850.* Munich: Wölfle.

———. 1977. *Sexual Liberation and Religion in Nineteenth-Century Europe.* Totowa, NJ: Rowman & Littlefield.

Pierrard, Pierre. 1977. *1848 . . . les Pauvres, l'Evangile et la Révolution.* Paris: Desclée de Brouwer.

———. 1984. *L'Eglise et les ouvriers en France 1840–1940.* Paris: Hachette.

———. 1985. "L'Abbé Migne journaliste." *Migne et le renouveau des études patristiques* 1985, 93–118.

Poliakov, Léon. 1985. *The History of Anti-Semitism.* Vol. 4: *Suicidal Europe 1870–1933.* Translated by George Klin. Oxford: Oxford University Press.

Ponson, Christian. 1980. *Les Catholiques lyonnais et la Chronique Sociale, 1892–1914.* Lyon: Presses Universitaires de Lyon.

Poulat, Emile, editor. 1961. *Le "Journal d'un prêtre d'après-demain" 1902–1903.* Tournai: Casterman.

———. 1969a. *Intégrisme et catholicisme intégral: Un réseau secret international antimoderniste: La "Sapinière," 1909–1921.* Tournai: Casterman.

———. 1969b. "Le catholicisme devant l'ébranlement de son système d'emprise: Etude critique (à propos de l'ouvrage du P. Droulers)." *Archives de sociologie des religions,* no. 28: 131–47.

———. 1971. "La dernière bataille du pontificat de Pie X." *Rivista di storia della chiesa in Italia* 25:83–107.

———. 1975. "Pour une nouvelle compréhension de la démocratie chrétienne." RHE 70:5–38.

———. 1977a. *Catholicisme, démocratie et socialisme: Le mouvement catholique et Mgr Benigni.* Tournai: Casterman.

———. 1977b. *Eglise contre bourgeoisie: Introduction au devenir du catholicisme actuel.* Tournai: Casterman.

Pounds, Norman J. G. 1985. *A Historical Geography of Europe, 1800–1914.* New York: Cambridge University Press.

Pulzer, Peter G. 1989. *The Rise of Political Anti-Semitism in Germany and Austria.* 2d ed. Cambridge, MA: Harvard University Press.

Quellen zur Geschichte der sozialen Frage in Deutschland. 1955–57. 2 vols. Edited by Ernst Schraepler. Göttingen: Musterschmidt.

Raab, Heribert. 1978. *Joseph Görres: Ein Leben für Freiheit und Recht.* Paderborn: Schöningh.

Rauscher, Anton, editor. 1975. *Deutscher Katholizismus und Revolution im frühen 19. Jahrhundert.* Paderborn: Schöningh.

———, editor. 1981–82. *Der soziale und politische Katholizismus: Entwicklungslinien in Deutschland 1803–1963.* 2 vols. Munich: Olzog.

———. 1985. "Christlich-soziale Bewegung." StL 1:1138–43.

———. 1987. "Katholische Sozialphilosophie im 19. Jahrhundert." *Christliche Philosophie* 1:752–67.

Reardon, Bernard M. G. 1985. *Religion in the Age of Romanticism: Studies in Early Nineteenth-Century Thought.* Cambridge: Cambridge University Press.

Reichensperger, Peter. 1847. *Die Agrarfrage aus dem Gesichtspunkt der Nationalökonomie, der Politik und des Rechtes.* Trier: Lintz.

Reid, Donald. 1985. "Industrial Paternalism: Discourse and Practice in Nineteenth Century French Mining and Metallurgy." *Comparative Studies in Society and History* 27:579–607.

Reiss, Hans Siegbert, editor. 1955. *The Political Thought of the German Romantics, 1793–1815.* New York: Macmillan.

Rémond, René. 1964. *Les deux Congrès ecclésiastiques de Reims et de Bourges, 1896–1900.* Paris: Sirey.

———. 1976. *L'Anticlericalisme en France: De 1815 à nos jours.* Paris: Fayard. New edition, Brussels: Editions Complexe, 1985.

Renault, François. 1971. *Lavigerie, l'esclavage africain, et l'Europe, 1868–1892.* 2 vols. Paris: E. de Boccard.

Rezsohazy, Rudolf. 1958. *Origines et formation du catholicisme social en Belgique, 1842–1909.* Louvain: Publications universitaires.

Riha, Tomas. 1985. "German Political Economy: The History of an Alternative Economics." *International Journal of Social Economics* 12, nos. 3/4/5: 1–252.

Ring, Mary. 1935. *Villeneuve-Bargemont: Precursor of Modern Social Catholicism, 1784–1850.* Milwaukee: Bruce.

Ritter, Emil. 1954. *Die katholisch-soziale Bewegung Deutschlands im 19. Jahrhundert und der Volksverein.* Cologne: Bachem.

Ritter, Gerhard A., editor. 1976. *Arbeiterbewegung, Parteien und Parlamentarismus: Aufsätze zur deutschen Sozial- und Verfassungsgeschichte des 19. und 20. Jahrhundert.* Göttingen: Vandenhoeck & Ruprecht.

Rivières, Madeleine des. 1984. *Ozanam: Un savant chez les pauvres.* Montreal: Bellarmin.

Rivinius, Karl Josef. 1982. "Der Weg des deutschen Katholizismus in der ersten Hälfte des 19. Jahrhunderts." *Theologie und Glaube* 72:216–25.

———. 1983. "Die Indizierung Theodor Wackers: Streit um den Charakter der Zentrumspartei im Kontakt der Auseinandersetzungen um die christlichen Gewerkschaften." JCSW 24:211–35.

———. 1985. "Kaplan Georg Friedrich Dasbach und der Rechtsschutzverein für die Bergleute im Saarrevier." JCSW 26:221–50.

Roegele, Otto B. 1982. "Presse und Publizistik des deutschen Katholizismus 1803–1963." Rauscher 1982, 2:395–434.

Rollet, Henri. 1947–58. *L'action sociale des catholiques en France (1871–1914)*. 2 vols. Paris: Desclée de Brouwers.

Roos, Lothar. 1980. "Wilhelm Emmanuel Frhr. von Ketteler (1811–1877)." ZgLb 4:22–36.

———. 1982. "Kapitalismus, Sozialreform, Sozialpolitik." Rauscher 1982, 2:52–158.

Ross, Ronald J. 1976. *Beleaguered Tower: The Dilemma of Political Catholicism in Wilhelmine Germany*. Notre Dame, IN: Notre Dame University Press.

Ruhnau, Clemens. 1980. *Der Katholizismus in der sozialen Bewährung: Die Einheit theologischen und sozialethischen Denkens im Werk Heinrich Peschs*. Paderborn: F. Schöningh.

Rürup, Reinhold. 1985. "Deutschland im 19. Jahrhundert, 1815–1871." *Deutsche Geschichte* 3:7–20. Göttingen: Vandenhoeck & Ruprecht.

Santa Ana, Julio de, editor. 1980. *Separation without Hope?* Maryknoll, NY: Orbis Books.

Savart, Claude. 1985a. *Les catholiques en France au xixe siècle: le temoignage du livre religieux*. Theologie historique 73. Paris: Beauchesne.

———. 1985b. "Un éditeur révolutionnaire au service de la tradition." *Migne et le renouveau des études patristiques* 1985, 145–58.

Schatz, Klaus. 1986. *Zwischen Säkularisation und zweitem Vatikanum: Der Weg des deutschen Katholizismus im 19. und 20. Jahrhundert*. Frankfurt: Knecht.

Schenk, Hans Georg. 1966. *The Mind of the European Romantics*. London: Constable.

Schieder, Theodor, editor. 1968– . *Handbuch der europäischen Geschichte* (HEG). 7 vols. Stuttgart: Klett.

———. 1975. *Staatensystem als Vormacht der Welt 1848–1918*. Propyläen Geschichte Europas 5. Frankfurt: Ullstein.

Schieder, Wolfgang. 1963. *Anfänge der deutschen Arbeiterbewegung: Die Auslandsvereine im Jahrzehnt nach der Julirevolution von 1830*. Stuttgart: Klett.

Schnabel, Franz. 1929–37. *Deutsche Geschichte im neunzehnten Jahrhundert*. Freiburg: Herder. Reprint, Freiburg: Herder, 1964–65 in 8 vols.

Schneider, Michael. 1981. "Kirche und soziale Frage im 19. und 20. Jahrhundert, unter besonderer Berücksichtigung des Katholizismus." *Archiv für Sozialgeschichte* 21:533–53.

———. 1982. *Die Christlichen Gewerkschaften, 1894–1933*. Bonn: Neue Gesellschaft.

———. 1986. "Christliche Arbeiterbewegung in Europa: Ein vergleichender Literaturbericht." *Arbeiter und Arbeiterbewegung im Vergleich*, 477–505.

Schoelen, Georg. 1982. *Bibliographisch-historisches Handbuch des Volksvereins für das Katholische Deutschland.* Mainz: Grünewald.

Scholl, S. Hermann, editor. 1966. *150 ans de mouvement ouvrier chrétien en Europe de l'Ouest 1789–1939.* Louvain: Nauwelaerts.

Schumpeter, Joseph A. 1942. *Capitalism, Socialism, and Democracy.* New York: Harper.

Shanahan, William O. 1954. *German Protestants Face the Social Question.* Notre Dame, IN: University of Notre Dame Press.

Sheehan, Arthur. 1959. *Peter Maurin: Gay Believer.* New York: Hanover House.

Smith, Adam. 1776. *The Wealth of Nations: An Inquiry into the Nature and Causes of the Wealth of Nations.* Edited by R. H. Campbell and A. S. Skinner. 2 vols. Oxford: Clarendon, 1976.

Soboul, Albert. 1976. "Le choc révolutionnaire, 1789–1791." *Histoire économique et sociale de la France,* 3/1:5–64.

Sperber, Jonathan. 1984. *Popular Catholicism in Nineteenth-Century Germany.* Princeton, NJ: Princeton University Press.

———, Marjorie Lamberti, Margaret Lavinia Anderson, and Vernon L. Lidtke. 1986. "Catholics and Politics in Nineteenth-Century Germany" (symposium). *Central European History* 19:45–122.

Spicciani, Amleto. 1984. *Agli inizi della storiografia economica e medioevistica in Italia: La corrispondenza di Giuseppe Toniolo con Victor Brants e Godefroid Kurth.* Rome: Jouvence.

Stearns, Peter N. 1960. "The Nature of the *Avenir* Movement." *American Historical Review* 65:837–47.

———. 1966. "Individualism and Association in French Industry." *Business History Review* 40:297–320.

———. 1967. *Priest and Revolutionary: Lamennais and the Dilemma of French Catholicism.* New York: Harper and Row.

———. 1978. *Paths to Authority: The Middle Class and the Industrial Labor Force in France, 1820–48.* Urbana: University of Illinois Press.

Stegmann, Franz Josef. 1965. *Von der ständischen Sozialreform zur staatlichen Sozialpolitik: Der Beitrag der Historisch-politischen Blätter zur Lösung der sozialen Frage.* Munich/Vienna: Olzog.

———. 1969. "Geschichte der sozialen Ideen im deutschen Katholizismus." *Geschichte der sozialen Ideen in Deutschland,* 325–560. Edited by Helga Grebing. Munich: Olzog.

———. 1974. *Der soziale Katholizismus und die Mitbestimmung in Deutschland: vom Beginn der Industrialisierung bis zum Jahre 1933.* Paderborn: Schöningh.

———. 1975. "Der Frühsozialismus in katholischen Periodica." Langner 1975, 145–64.

———. 1979. "Franz von Baader (1765–1841)." ZgLb 3:11–25.

———. 1985. "Baader." StL 1:503–6.

Strunk, Reiner. 1971. *Politische Ekklesiologie im Zeitalter der Revolution.* Munich: Kaiser.

Sutton, Michael. 1982. *Nationalism, Positivism and Catholicism: The Politics of Charles Maurras and French Catholics, 1890–1914.* Cambridge: Cambridge University Press.

Tal, Uriel. 1975. *Christians and Jews in Germany: Religion, Politics and Ideology in the Second Reich 1870–1914.* Ithaca, NY: Cornell University Press.

Talmon, Jacob L. 1952. *The Rise of Totalitarian Democracy.* Boston: Beacon.

Talmy, Robert. 1962. *Une forme hybride du catholicisme social en France: l'Association catholique des patrons du Nord, 1884–1895.* Lille: Facultés catholiques.

———. 1963. *Aux sources du catholicisme social: L'école de La Tour du Pin.* Paris: Desclée.

———, editor. 1964a. *René de La Tour du Pin.* Paris: Bloud et Gay.

———, editor. 1964b. *Albert de Mun.* Paris: Bloud and Gay.

———. 1966. *Le Syndicalisme chrétien en France (1871–1930): Difficultés et controverses.* Paris: Bloud et Gay.

Tenfelde, Klaus. 1977. *Sozialgeschichte der Bergarbeiterschaft an der Ruhr im 19. Jahrhundert (1815–1889).* Bonn-Bad Godesberg: Neue Gesellschaft.

Tilly, Richard. 1966. *Financial Institutions and Industrialization in the Rhineland 1815–1870.* Madison, WI: University of Wisconsin Press.

Toniolo, Giuseppe. 1948–53. *Opera omnia.* 20 vols. Rome: Studium.

Touchard, Jean. 1968. *Aux origines du catholicisme social: Louis Rousseau (1787–1856).* Paris: Colin.

Tramontin, Silvio. 1980. *Un secolo di storia della chiesa: Da Leone XIII al Concilio Vaticano II.* 2 vols. Rome: Studium.

Traniello, Francesco, and Sandro Fontana. 1977. "Aspetti politici-sociali." *Romolo Murri nella storia politica e religiosa del suo tempo,* pp. 15–68. Rome: Cinque Lune.

Traniello, Francesco, editor. 1983. *Dalla prima democrazia cristiana al sindacalismo bianco.* Rome: Cinque Lune.

Treue, Wilhelm. 1970. *Gesellschaft, Wirtschaft und Technik Deutschlands im 19. Jahrhundert.* Stuttgart: Klett. Reprint, Munich: DTV, 1975.

Trimouille, Pierre. 1974. *Léon Harmel et l'usine chrétienne du Val-des-Bois (1840–1914).* Lyon: Presses Universitaires de Lyon.

Valerius, Gerhard. 1983. *Deutscher Katholizismus und Lamennais: Die Auseinandersetzung in der katholischen Publizistik 1817–1854.* Mainz: Grünewald.

Vecchio, Giorgio. 1979. *La democrazia cristiana in Europa (1891–1963).* Milan: Mursia.

Vidler, Alec R. 1954. *Prophecy and Papacy: A Study of Lamennais, the Church and the Revolution.* New York: Scribner.

———. 1964. *A Century of Social Catholicism 1820–1920.* London: SPCK.

Vierhaus, Rudolf. 1988. *Germany in the Age of Absolutism.* New York: Cambridge University Press.

Vigener, Fritz. 1924. *Ketteler: ein deutsches Bischofsleben des 19. Jahrhunderts.* Munich: R. Oldenbourg.

Wallace, Lillian Parker. 1966. *Leo XIII and the Rise of Socialism*. Durham, NC: Duke University Press.

Wandruszka, Adam, and Peter Urbanitsch. 1973–1985. *Die Habsburger Monarchie 1848–1918*. 5 vols. Vienna: Verlag der österreichischen Akademie der Wissenschaften.

Wangler, Thomas E. 1982. "American Catholic Expansionism 1886–1894." *Harvard Theological Review* 75:369–93.

Waterman, A. M. C. 1983. "The Ideological Alliance of Political Economy and Christian Theology, 1798–1833." *Journal of Ecclesiastical History* 34:231–44.

Weber, Wilhelm. 1981. "Wirksamkeit und Unwirksamkeit der katholischen Soziallehre." *Internationale katholische Zeitschrift "Communio"* 10:122–29.

Weill, Georges. 1904. *Histoire de mouvement social en France (1852–1902)*. Paris: F. Alcan.

———. 1979. *Histoire de catholicisme libéral en France (1828–1908)*. Geneva: Slatkine.

Weinzierl, Erika. 1961. "Aus den Anfängen der christlichsozialen Bewegung in Österreich: Nach der Korrespondenz des Grafen Anton Pergen." Rpt. in Weinzierl, *Ecclesia Semper Reformanda: Beiträge zur österreichischen Kirchengeschichte im 19. und 20. Jahrhundert*, pp. 107–28. Vienna: Geyer, 1985.

Weiss, Otto. 1971. "Klemens M. Hofbauer, Repräsentant des konservativen Katholizismus und Begründer des katholischen Restauration in Österreich." *Zeitschrift für bayerische Landesgeschichte* 34:211–37.

Yzermans, Vincent A., editor. 1954. *All Things in Christ: Encyclicals and Selected Documents of Saint Pius X*. Westminster, MD: Newman.

Ziebura, Gilbert. 1985. "Frankreich von der Grossen Revolution bis zum Sturz Napoleons III, 1789–1870." T. Schieder, HEG 5:187–318.

Zucker, Stanley. 1984. "Philipp Wasserburg and Political Catholicism in Nineteenth Century Germany." *Catholic Historical Review* 70:14–27.

Zussini, Alessandro. 1965. *Luigi Caissotti di Chiusano e il movimento cattolico dal 1862 al 1915*. Turin: Giappichelli.

INDEX OF SUBJECTS

349

INDEX OF PERSONS